W9-BXH-288

You have the book — now keep it <u>current</u> with a new, reliable update service...

HAZARDOUS WASTE REGULATION UPDATE

Because you know that compliance with hazardous waste laws can be vital to the very survival of your business, you won't want to miss this opportunity to subscribe to HAZARDOUS WASTE REGULATION UPDATE, a quarterly service that gives you definitive interpretations and analysis on the full scope of the hazardous waste program.

Prepared and edited by David J. Lennett, co-author of this book, these updates provide you with authoritative guidance on such vital issues as present requirements, waste listings and delistings, land disposal restrictions, generator regulations, transportation standards... and <u>much more!</u>

Sign up now for our FREE TRIAL OFFER and we'll send you the latest update for a 15-day FREE examination. See details of this Special Offer on the order card below.

MAIL CARD TODAY!

If order card below has been removed, write to:
Professional and Reference Division,
McGraw-Hill Book Co., 26th Floor
1221 Avenue of the Americas
New York, NY 10020

FREE TRIAL OFFER CARD

☐ YES! Reserve my Charter Subscription to HAZARDOUS WASTE REGULATION UPDATE. I understand I'll receive my first Update and an invoice for $195.00, the annual price for four quarterly Updates. After 15 days' examination, I'll either send you my remittance or simply write "cancel" across the invoice, return it, and the matter will be closed.

Check the appropriate box below if you wish to have your order charged to your credit card or billed to your company.

☐ Charge my account: ☐ VISA ☐ MASTERCARD

ACCOUNT # _____

Date Card Expires _____ Signature _____

☐ Bill my company: Purchase Order # _____

Name _____
(please print)

Company _____

Address _____

City _____ State _____ Zip _____

Offer valid only in the U.S. and all orders are subject to acceptance by McGraw-Hill.

NO POSTAGE
NECESSARY
IF MAILED
IN THE
UNITED STATES

BUSINESS REPLY MAIL

FIRST CLASS MAIL   PERMIT NO. 26   NEW YORK, NY

POSTAGE WILL BE PAID BY ADDRESSEE

McGraw-Hill Book Company
E. T. Matthews — 26th Floor
1221 Avenue of the Americas
New York, NY 10124-0025

Hazardous Waste Regulation: The New Era

KF
3946
F67
1987

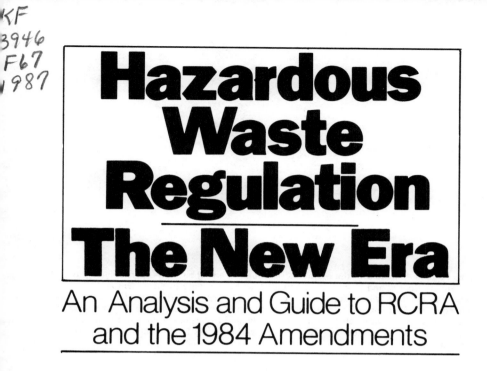

Hazardous Waste Regulation
The New Era

An Analysis and Guide to RCRA
and the 1984 Amendments

Richard C. Fortuna
and
David J. Lennett

McGraw-Hill Book Company

New York St. Louis San Francisco Auckland Bogotá Hamburg
Johannesburg London Madrid Milan Mexico Montreal New Delhi
Panama Paris São Paulo Singapore Sydney Tokyo Toronto

Tennessee Tech Library
Cookeville, TN
WITHDRAWN

Dedication

This book is dedicated to the Members of Congress and their staffs, particularly those of the House Energy and Commerce Committee and the Senate Environment and Public Works Committee, who labored for three years to achieve the fundamental reforms embodied in HSWA, and to the men and women in the public and private sector whose task it is to implement those reforms. It is also dedicated to Susan Fortuna and Francine Rudoff, without whose understanding, patience, and love this book would not have been written.

Library of Congress Cataloging-in-Publication Data

Fortuna, Richard C.
  Hazardous waste regulation—the new era.

  1. Hazardous wastes—Law and legislation—United States.   I. Lennett, David J.
  I. United States. Laws, statutes, etc. Resource conservation and recovery act of 1976.
  II. Title.
KF3946.F67   1986   344.73'0462   86-11392
                       347.304462
ISBN 0-07-021634-7

Copyright © 1987 by McGraw-Hill, Inc. All rights reserved. Printed in the United States of America. Except as permitted under the United States Copyright Act of 1976, no part of this publication may be reproduced or distributed in any form or by any means, or stored in a data base or retrieval system, without the prior written permission of the publisher.

1 2 3 4 5 6 7 8 9 0   8 9 8 7 6 5

ISBN 0-07-021634-7

The editors for this book were Betty Sun and Nancy Amy, the designer was A Good Thing, Inc., and the production supervisor was Thomas G. Kowalczyk. It was set in Times Roman by David E. Seham and Associates.

Printed and bound by Arcata Graphics/Halliday

Foreword

Managing the *billions* of gallons of hazardous waste produced in the United States each year in a manner that protects both human health and the environment is an extraordinarily difficult task. It is also an extremely important task.

It is a sad fact that such protection was not adequately considered in many waste management decisions of the past. The thousands of contaminated sites that need to be cleaned up under the federal Superfund program are a constant reminder of the severity of the problem. The complexity and expense of correcting these mistakes of the past prove that the old adage "an ounce of prevention is worth a pound of cure" is applicable to hazardous waste management. That adage summarizes the philosophy underlying the 1984 amendments to the Resource Conservation and Recovery Act (RCRA), the law that established this Nation's basic hazardous waste management system in 1976.

The RCRA program is closely related to the Superfund clean-up program. What RCRA is meant to do is to assure the public that, although we may be *discovering* new Superfund sites on a daily basis, at the very least we are taking steps to prevent the *creation* of new Superfund sites. Hazardous waste can and must be handled in a manner that is safer than it was in the past. That is what RCRA is supposed to be about.

When RCRA was first enacted in 1976, very little was known about the nature and extent of the problem. However, since 1976, literally hundreds of in-depth studies and analyses have been performed by a broad range of interests regarding many aspects of the issue. In the Congress, dozens of hearings have been held before House and Senate Committees, and numerous reports have been presented by research offices such as the General Accounting Office, the Congressional Research Service, and the Office of Technology Assessment. State and federal agencies have compiled new data and, in the course of establishing and implementing regulatory programs, have developed "track records" that can be evaluated.

In early 1982, a three-year process began to amend and extend RCRA. This process presented the Congress with an opportunity to review the wealth of information that was not available in 1976, and to consider whether the existing RCRA program was developing and operating in a satisfactory manner. In a bipartisan, bicameral, and virtually unanimous manner, we concluded that the program was seriously deficient in several important respects. First, progress in developing and implementing the program was too slow and unfocused. Second, regulations that had been issued were weak and contained too many loopholes. Third, enforcement of the regulations needed substantial improvement. And last, but certainly not least, much of the hazardous waste was still not being managed in an environmentally acceptable manner. In short, the program was not encouraging the fundamental shifts in waste management practices ("the ounce of prevention") necessary to protect human health and the environment ("the pound of cure"). Our "preventive" laws and regulations, unless changed, would continue to contribute to the creation of additional Superfund sites.

The passage of the Hazardous and Solid Waste Amendments of 1984 (HSWA) marked the culmination of the legislative process that began in 1982 and an important milestone in federal hazardous waste regulation. HSWA "rewrote the book" on hazardous waste management and redirects the RCRA program by closing numerous regulatory loopholes, encouraging waste management practices that prevent or minimize environmental releases, and ensuring stringent regulation and cleanup of releases when they do occur. Some observers were surprised by the scope of the legislation and attributed it to Congressional frustration over the management style and direction at the Environmental Protection Agency (EPA) during the early part of the 1980s. These observers missed the point. The 1976 law required significant modifications to accomplish the detailed, substantive agenda we had before us. The frustration we may have felt toward EPA management emphasized the importance of the task before us; it did not form the basis of the substantive agenda.

The future of hazardous waste management lies in waste reduction and minimization as well as in advance forms of recycling and treatment. We stand at the threshold of the most significiant changes to date that this nation or any nation has undertaken to control and regulate the generation, handling, storage, treatment, transportation, and disposal of hazardous waste. This transition will not occur overnight. With the cooperation of the regulated community, federal and state regulatory agencies, and the public, the task of modernization can be accomplished much sooner than it could be without such cooperation. HSWA was designed to encourage this cooperation.

Books like this one make an important contribution to bringing the future closer to reality. The authors offer unique insights and provide the reader with a better understanding of the changes in waste management that are expected to follow the enactment of HSWA. Greater awareness of what is expected will help to facilitate the process of change that must occur if we are to protect human health and the environment from the risks associated with hazardous waste. People who are in the business of managing hazardous waste must understand that they are also in the business of environmental protection.

John H. Chafee
U.S. Senate

Contents

Hazardous Waste Regulation: The New Era

Guide to the Guide

This book is a detailed analysis and description of the federal hazardous waste regulatory program established by Congress with the passage of the Resource Conservation and Recovery Act (RCRA) in 1976. Particular emphasis will be placed on recent amendments to RCRA enacted by Congress, embodied in the Hazardous and Solid Waste Amendments of 1984 (HSWA).

Readers are forewarned that the regulatory program is complex. There are sets of regulations that identify hazardous wastes and distinguish waste management practices from product manufacturing operations. There are also regulations specifically directed toward the firms or persons that make the waste (generators), transport the waste (transporters), and manage the waste at treatment, storage, or disposal facilities (TSDFs). For the TSDFs, there are two sets of regulations, one applicable when the facility receives a RCRA permit (permitting standards) and the other applicable until that permit has been obtained (interim status standards). The permitting process is governed by application, issuance, and modification procedures, as well as public participation requirements. Finally, there are regulations governing the role of the states in the regulatory program.

Overlaying these regulations are federal and state enforcement authorities, changes to the regulations mandated by HSWA which will be phased in over time, and a large number of guidance documents and policy statements which further shape the regulatory program.

RCRA itself is divided into Subtitles, and each Subtitle is divided into sections. Subtitle C of RCRA is the portion of RCRA which authorizes the U.S. Environmental Protection Agency (EPA) to issue and enforce regulations regarding hazardous waste. Subtitle C of RCRA contains Sections 3001–3019 of RCRA, which govern the following subjects:

RCRA Section	Content of Section
3001	Designating Wastes as Hazardous
3002	Generator Requirements
3003	Transporter Requirements
3004, 3005	TSDF Standards, Permit Application Procedures
3006	State Regulatory Programs
3007	Inspections
3008	Federal Enforcement and Penalties for Non-Compliance
3009	State Regulatory Programs
3010	Notification Requirements
3011	Grants to States
3012	Inventory of Pre-RCRA Waste Sites
3013	Authority to Require TSDF Monitoring, Analysis and Testing
3014	Used Oil Recycling Regulations
3015	Expansions During Interim Status
3016	Inventory of RCRA and Pre-RCRA Federal TSDFs
3017	Hazardous Waste Export
3018	Hazardous Waste Discharges into Sewers
3019	Exposure Information and Health Assessments

Other Sections of RCRA also relate to the hazardous waste regulatory program:

RCRA Section	Content of Section
1002	Congressional Findings Regarding Hazardous Waste
1003	Objectives of RCRA and National Policy Regarding Hazardous Waste
1004	Definitions
1006	Integration of RCRA with Other Laws
2008	Creation of Office of Ombudsman in EPA
6001	Application of RCRA to Federal Facilities
7002	Citizen Suits
7003	Suits to Address Sites Posing an "Imminent and Substantial Endangerment" to Public Health or Environment
7004	Public Participation
7006	Judicial Review of EPA Regulations and Other Actions
7010	Prohibition on Injection of Hazardous Waste into or above Underground Sources of Drinking Water
8002	Studies to Determine Whether Certain Wastes Should be Designated Hazardous

Finally, Congress established in HSWA a new Subtitle I of RCRA, exclusively devoted to the regulation of underground tanks storing petroleum and a large number of toxic chemicals. Subtitle I contains Sections 9001–9010 of RCRA covering the following areas:

RCRA Section	Content of Section
9001	Definitions and Scope of Regulatory Program
9002	Notification Requirements
9003	Tank Standards
9004	State Programs
9005	Inspections, Monitoring, and Testing
9006	Federal Enforcement Authorities
9007	Application of Subtitle I to Federal Facilities
9008	State Programs
9009	Studies of Certain Underground Tanks
9010	Money for Program

To implement many of these statutory provisions, EPA has issued and will be issuing regulations. When these regulations are issued, they appear in the *Federal Register,* a daily compilation of all regulations issued by all federal agencies. The regulations are generally accompanied by preambles which explain the regulations and discuss why they were issued. In most cases, before an agency issues a regulation, a draft is proposed for public comment, and that proposal is also placed in the *Federal Register.* The proposal, however, has no legal force or effect until it is finalized.

The various federal regulations are compiled annually into the Code of Federal Regulations (CFR). EPA regulations are in volume 40 of the CFR. The hazardous waste regulations are Parts 124, 260–268, 270, and 271 of the 40 CFR. The Subtitle I underground tank regulations can be found in Part 280. The breakdown of these Parts by subject area is as follows:

40 CFR	Content
Part 260	Definitions and Petition Procedures
Part 261	Designating Hazardous Wastes Subject to Regulation
Part 262	Generator and Export Requirements

Part 263	Transporter Standards
Part 264	TSDF Permitting Standards
Part 265	TSDF Interim Status Standards
Part 266	Standards for Certain Recycling Practices
Part 267	Temporary Standards for Permitting New Land Disposal Facilities (In general—no longer applicable)
Part 268	Land Disposal Restrictions
Part 124, 270	Permitting and Public Participation Procedures
Part 271	State Program Requirements
Part 280	Subtitle I Program

The transportation of hazardous waste is also governed by regulations issued by the U.S. Department of Transportation (DOT) under the Hazardous Materials Transportation Act (HMTA). DOT regulations can be found in volume 49 of the CFR at Parts 171–179.

This book generally follows the structure of the EPA regulations. Several additional chapters are included to discuss areas of particular complexity and importance, including significant concepts in the 1984 Amendments.

For example, Chapter 1 is a brief historical overview of the federal regulatory program and an introduction to the scope and nature of the 1984 amendments. Chapters 2 and 3 collectively describe and identify: the hazardous waste designation process; the current universe of hazardous wastes and the Congressional mandate under HSWA to expand the scope of current coverage; the complex regulations governing hazardous waste recycling; and the nuances of distinguishing between waste management and product manufacturing operations. Chapter 4 describes the generator standards, including the new requirements applicable to small quantity generators and hazardous waste exports mandated by the 1984 Amendments. Standards applicable to transporters are discussed in Chapter 5.

Chapter 6 examines the permit application and review process, and the procedures for a TSDF to qualify for interim status or obtain a final permit. Chapter 7 describes general requirements applicable to many TSDFs. Chapter 8 discusses the technical requirements applicable to individual TSDFs during interim status and at permitting.

Chapters 9 through 11 highlight many of HSWA's substantial and detailed changes to the TSDF standards, particularly in the area of land disposal. Chapter 9 focuses on the Congressionally mandated scheme to restrict and prohibit the future land disposal of many hazardous wastes. Chapter 10 discusses the detailed design changes for both new and existing land disposal facilities. Chapter 11 analyzes the monitoring and cleanup responsibilites imposed on TSDF owners/operators during interim status and at permitting.

TSDF standards for tanks storing hazardous waste, and the Subtitle I regulatory program under development for underground tanks storing petroleum and toxic chemicals are described in Chapter 12. Chapter 13 reviews federal enforcement authorities. Chapter 14 focuses on the role of the states in the regulatory program.

An implementation schedule for the 1984 Amendments is included in Appendix H.

As a final note, readers should recognize that the regulatory program will be rapidly evolving in the next several years, partly as a result of the 1984 Amendments. Consequently, new or modified regulations, policies, and guidance documents will be issued which may not be included in this book. To the extent that the authors have been able to anticipate such activity, we have provided an indication at the appropriate location in the book. However, readers are strongly encouraged as a matter of course to seek the most up-to-date information from state and federal regulatory officials.

Despite the authors' efforts to ensure comprehensive factual coverage, all questions and situations are not addressed. Wherever questions of interpretation arise, the assistance of private counsel, EPA, or authorized states should be sought. EPA has also established a hotline in order to assist in understanding RCRA requirements (800-424-9346). Readers should also note that while the work has been widely reviewed by individuals within EPA, the views and policy statements represent only those of the authors and should not be interpreted as those of EPA or other groups except where explicitly identified.

ACKNOWLEDGMENTS   The authors are extremely grateful for the valuable assistance provided by the many people who kindly agreed to review drafts of this work. At the risk of not identifying everyone, we wish to express our thanks to Karen Alexander, Robert Axelrad, Michael Barclay, Joanne Bassi, Jane Bloom, Susan Bromm, David Case, Eileen Claussen, Alan Corson, Gary Dietrich, Susan Egan, Bill Fisher, Lisa Friedman, George Garland, Mark Greenwood, Linda Greer, Terry Grogan, Lloyd Guerci, Ridgway Hall, John King, Douglas MacMillan, Nelson Mossholder, Bill Philipbar, Eldon Rucker, Suzie Ruhl, Debbie Rutherford, Arline Sheehan, Steve Silverman, John Skinner, Sandy Stengel, Matt Strauss, Michael Steinberg, Bruce Weddle, Peter Weiner, and Marcia Williams. We would also like to thank Carol Larivee, Beth and Jim Lawler, Connie Mahan, Robin Oegerle, Jackie Scott, and Ken Walsh for their assistance in manuscript preparation.

CHAPTER ONE

Major Mid-Course Corrections

For generations, miraculous achievements have been made in the nature and quality of many of the goods and services we enjoy everyday. However, the same resources and energies necessary for these achievements were not directed toward the back end of the production cycle, toward controlling the myriad wastes generated in the course of producing the desired goods and services. Consequently, many of our past and current waste management methods present substantial risks to present and future generations, thereby posing a host of difficult policy choices regarding the cleanup of past mistakes and the nature and pace of a transition to an improved waste management norm for American industry.

An intrinsic part of this policy debate has been the federal regulatory program for hazardous waste management, and its inability to obtain substantial improvements over past practices. A 1976 law entitled the Resource Conservation and Recovery Act (RCRA) established the federal regulatory program, providing the U.S. Environmental Proctection Agency (EPA) with authority to issue and enforce rules governing hazardous waste management.[1] Eight years later, in response to an EPA record of failed attempts to protect the public from the improper management of hazardous waste, and a substantial number of studies recommending new policy directions for the regulatory program, Congress enacted what many consider the most significant rewrite of any environmental law, the Hazardous and Solid Waste Amendments of 1984 (HSWA).[2] This book is an integrated analysis of the current and future federal hazardous waste regulatory program, with special emphasis on the reforms instituted by HSWA.

To understand the nature and origin of the recent changes, HSWA must be placed in an historical perspective. After all, RCRA remained essentially the same for eight years. Yet in 1984 Congress legislated fundamental changes in the regulatory program, in an overwhelmingly bipartisan manner, without Reagan Administration support, and at a time when other environmental laws were languishing in the Congress. This chapter will briefly describe the history of the RCRA program prior to the passage of HSWA, and introduce the reader to some of the important concepts contained in HSWA.

Although it is difficult to discern the motives of 535 legislators, an overriding theme does emerge in Congressional debate on the 1984 amendments. There was extreme and widespread dissatisfaction with the regulatory program as it existed and it was clear that EPA had no coherent vision of a waste management strategy which would minimize current or future risk to human health and the environment. Furthermore, even if EPA had developed such a strategy, it was not likely to be capable of implementing it without suitable encouragement from Congress, because the EPA RCRA program was a product of alternating stages of benign neglect, crisis management, and misguided ideologies. As Senator George Mitchell (D-ME), one of the principal sponsors of the Senate HSWA bill (S. 757), stated on the Senate floor before it passed by a vote of 93-0:

> It has become evident that a strong congressional expression of disapproval of EPA's slow and timid implementation of the existing law is necessary, as well as a clear congressional directive mandating certain bold, preventive actions by EPA which will not be taken otherwise, despite the existing, broad authorities contained in RCRA.
>
> EPA has not implemented the Resource Conservation and Recovery Act aggressively. The Agency has missed deadlines, proposed inadequate regulations, and even exacerbated the hazardous waste problem by suspending certain regulations. It has become evident that this slow, plodding course will be continued in the absence of a clear congressional directive. This is not acceptable. Accordingly, S. 757 provides more specific guidance to EPA as to how the broad grants of authority of the existing RCRA law should be used.[3]

However, dissatisfaction with the performance and motivation of EPA appointees, is only a small part of the story behind HSWA. It was equally well recognized through numerous studies and investigations that the hazardous waste laws required revision irrespective of political leadership. These bold, preventive actions of which Senator Mitchell spoke necessitated fundamental changes in the law and in national hazardous waste management policy. In place of the RCRA program as it existed in the early 1980s, Congress substituted its vision of a new era of hazardous waste regulation. This vision placed greater emphasis on reducing drastically the use of those management practices which were proven environmental risks, and encouraging more benign forms of waste management. This vision was manifested in a series of RCRA amendments intended to shift the program toward long-term risk prevention. For example, one aspect of this policy shift was to restrict the types and quantities of hazardous wastes which could be land disposed. In expressing his support for a new initiative in this area, Congressman Norman Lent (R-NY), a principal sponsor of the HSWA bill (H.R. 2867, P.L. 98-616) in the House of Representatives, stated:

> For too many years we have permitted the practice of dumping hazardous wastes in the land to go virtually unchecked. Even now that the EPA is requiring landfills to be lined, I do not feel confident that these liners will remain secure in the long term.

Therefore I believe it is appropriate for the Congress to intervene at this time and to establish a new policy which calls for a review of known hazardous wastes and a determination whether these wastes are appropriate for land disposal.[4]

Other Congressional initiatives focused on loopholes in the regulatory program and their environmental consequences, based on a series of public and private sector reports. In short, HSWA is a blueprint for the future, containing a detailed substantive Congressional agenda for policy directions and program initiatives.

THE "CRADLE-TO-GRAVE" LEGISLATIVE SCHEME

In 1976, Congress granted EPA broad authority to develop a comprehensive hazardous waste management regulatory program through the enactment of Subtitle C of RCRA.[5] Sections 3001–3010 represented the core of the authority, empowering EPA to issue regulations: identifying which wastes would be subject to controls; regulating the generators, transporters, treaters, storers, and disposers of that waste; and establishing minimum standards for states to run approved RCRA regulatory programs in lieu of EPA.

Section 3001 of RCRA authorized EPA to identify characteristics of hazardous waste and list particular wastes as hazardous after developing criteria for such identification and listing. The criteria would take into account the "toxicity, persistence, degradability in nature, potential for accumulation in tissue, and other related factors such as flammability, corrosiveness and other hazardous characteristics."

Section 3002 of RCRA empowered EPA to issue standards for generators of waste determined hazardous under Section 3001: including recordkeeping, reporting, labeling, containerization, and waste tracking requirements. Regulations issued pursuant to Section 3003 would impose recordkeeping and waste tracking requirements on hazardous waste transporters.

Sections 3004 and 3005 established a permitting scheme for hazardous waste treatment, storage, and disposal facilities (TSDFs) based on standards issued by EPA which would "protect human health and the environment." The standards were to include recordkeeping, reporting, monitoring, inspection, maintenance, and waste tracking requirements, as well as location, design, construction, and operating standards to minimize the risk from such facilities. Congress also specified the need for financial responsibility assurances "consistent with the degree and duration of the risk" associated with the TSDF. Permit application, issuance, and revocation procedures would be developed, and existing facilities were conferred "interim status," allowing them to operate until a decision on their permit application was made.

Sections 3006 and 3009 established a state/federal relationship whereby states could operate the RCRA program in lieu of EPA if their regulations were "equivalent" to and "consistent with" the federal regulations, and the states provided for adequate enforcement. On an interim basis, states could operate the RCRA program if their program was "substantially equivalent" to the federal program. Significantly, states could impose more stringent requirements than the federal regulations.

Section 3010 of RCRA required generators, transporters, and facility owners/operators to notify EPA of their activity within 90 days after the Section 3001 regulations were issued.

The language in Subtitle C of RCRA granted EPA enabling authority in very general terms, to issue regulations "as may be necessary to protect human health and the environment," thereby providing EPA with wide latitude in designing the particulars of the regulatory program. Since very little information was available regarding hazardous waste management nationally at the time of RCRA's passage, and hazardous waste is generated by many sectors of our economy, the general delegation authority was an approach which provided EPA with maximum discretion to respond administratively to the variety of industry practices as it deemed appropriate. On the other hand, Subtitle C did not provide specific guidance in many areas that would later prove controversial, such as the regulation of waste to be recycled, whether and to what extent generators producing small amounts of waste should be regulated differently than larger generators, and whether particular waste management practices should be preferred over others. This lack of guidance would eventually contribute to regulatory inertia at EPA because of challenges to EPA authority by the regulated community, and a realization at EPA that for many of these issues the resolutions were as political as they were technical, since the supporting scientific data could not be precise enough to rely upon alone to make a decision.

THE CARTER YEARS: WAITING FOR THE PROGRAM

Congress set a statutory deadline of April 1978 for the promulgation of the Subtitle C regulations. However, by April 1978, EPA had not even proposed for comment the regulations Congress requested, and EPA would provide no indication when it would do so. Whether or not Congress was overambitious in providing only eighteen months to issue the regulations could be interminably debated, but of greater importance was the low priority accorded the program at the outset and the unnecessary delays which resulted. The Carter Administration consistently underfunded the program by requesting less than Congress authorized, and then not spending the money Congress appropriated.[6]

In September 1978, the Environmental Defense Fund (EDF) and several other organizations sued EPA to force the promulgation of the Subtitle C regulations. In this kind of litigation, known as "deadlines litigation," the Court often places the recalcitrant agency on a schedule for complying with the mandate of Congress. This was the procedure followed in the EDF case, in which EPA submitted to the Court its estimation of when the necessary regulations could be issued, and the Court ultimately incorporated EPA's suggested deadline of December 1979 for the Subtitle C regulations into a Court order.[7]

Unfortunately, EPA could not meet its own schedule, and in the fall of 1979 submitted to the Court a second schedule for the promulgation of Subtitle C regulations. This second schedule, again adopted by the Court, required promulgation of the Section 3002, 3003, and 3010 regulations by February 1980; the Section 3001 and 3006 regulations, and portions of the TSDF standards under Sections 3004 and 3005 by April 1980; and the remainder of the TSDF standards by the fall of 1980.[8]

The Carter Administration substantially met the second schedule, but there were notable exceptions. By February 1981, there were still no permitting standards for land disposal facilities (i.e., landfills and seepage lagoons), the facilities which were receiving large amounts of waste and causing the greatest environmental harm. Consequently, these facilities could continue to operate without substantial environmental controls indefinitely. EPA also failed to issue permitting standards for underground tanks storing hazardous waste, despite a growing body of information indicating a strong likelihood of leakage from many of these tanks. Moreover, in areas where EPA had issued regulations, the regulations were largely incomplete. For example, EPA had not yet identified or listed many waste streams that should be managed as hazardous waste (see Chapter 2). It also exempted the burning of hazardous waste for energy recovery from regulation despite potential environmental impacts resulting from the widespread practice (see Chapter 3), and it generally exempted from regulation generators who produced less than 1000 kg/mo (2200 lbs/mo) (see Chapter 4). Hazardous wastes discharged into sewers also were exempt from regulation regardless of whether the discharges were adequately regulated under RCRA or other environmental laws (see Chapter 3). When it promulgated the first set of regulations, EPA pledged to address these shortcomings and others in the near future when additional information was obtained and as agency resources would allow. Nevertheless, four years after RCRA's passage, the program had barely begun, very significant regulations had not been issued, and there were glaring problems with the regulations that had been issued.

FROM DELAYS TO DESTRUCTION: THE REAGAN TEAM TAKES OVER

Although the RCRA program left by the Carter Administration was barely underway and still incomplete, it was targeted at the outset by the Reagan Administration for a substantial overhaul. Even before President Reagan was inaugurated, his designated Director of the Office of Management and Budget (OMB) David Stockman, outlined a plan for rescinding, revising, or deferring health and safety regulations he deemed too costly, including the RCRA regulations.[9] And almost immediately after taking office, President Reagan signed Executive Order 12291 which empowered OMB to review and withhold proposed or final regulations developed by EPA and other agencies until those agencies responded to OMB cost concerns about the regulations.[10] A newly created President's Task Force on Regulatory Relief, headed by Vice President Bush, announced on March 25, 1981, that the RCRA regulations were among a list of regulations which would be reviewed by the Task Force because of the additional burden they would place on the private sector.[11]

Newly appointed EPA Administrator Anne Gorsuch was soon joined by the Reagan Administration choice for Assistant Administrator in charge of the RCRA program, Rita Lavelle, and together they began implementing the Stockman/Bush deregulatory agenda. However, as the deregulation proponents soon discovered, there was precious little in the program to deregulate, no matter how hard they tried.

On June 26, 1981, Administrator Gorsuch notified David Stockman that EPA was not going to request permit applications from owners/operators of existing incinerators and storage surface impoundments, thereby unilaterally suspending the permitting standards for those facilities issued earlier that year.[12] The decision to suspend these standards, EPA later admitted, was largely based on unsubstantiated cost-of-compliance data submitted by a major trade association and other members of the regulated community.[13]

On October 1, 1981, EPA announced a deferral of financial responsibility regulations issued earlier that year, thus postponing their effective date. In addition, EPA announced an intention to eliminate a portion of those requirements for reasons unmentioned.[14]

In February of 1982, EPA deferred three reporting and recordkeeping requirements, including the submission of groundwater monitoring data and the preparation of groundwater quality assessments if contamination is detected. EPA announced it intended to eliminate the latter requirement entirely.[15]

Also in February 1982, EPA temporarily lifted the prohibition on the landfilling of liquid containerized wastes and simultaneously proposed to eliminate the prohibition altogether.[16] This EPA action precipitated a major backlash including lawsuits by the Hazardous Waste Treatment Council and the Environmental Defense Fund, resulting in the reinstatement of the ban only 25 days after it was lifted.

In fact, in almost every instance where EPA had delayed, suspended, or suggested the elimination of RCRA regulations, EPA could not subsequently find factual support for its actions and the regulations later became effective. The incinerator regulations were reinstated after EPA admitted that the regulated community never presented sufficient justification to suspend the rules, and the U.S. Court of Appeals held the suspension was illegal.[17] The financial responsibility rules were reinstated because

EPA could find no public opposition to the requirements.[18] The ground-water monitoring recordkeeping and reporting requirements became effective in August 1982; the proposal to modify or eliminate these requirements never materialized.[19]

While it could be argued that these deregulatory initiatives ultimately did no harm since they never amounted to anything, the valuable time lost, the waste of resources expended, and the chaos resulting from the constant suspension and reinstatement of regulations severely wounded the program in its formative years. Furthermore, little or no progress was made where it was needed, such as closing the loopholes and listing additional wastes.

EPA was in no hurry to promulgate the most important regulations not yet issued—the permitting standards for land disposal facilities—even though it had already missed two Court deadlines for promulgation. In October 1981, Administrator Gorsuch requested two more years from the Court to issue the regulations, but the Court refused and ordered the regulations promulgated by February 1, 1982.[20] EPA appealed the ruling, but the Court of Appeals ordered EPA to issue the regulations by July 15, 1982, and the Agency did so.[21]

Once EPA had issued the required permitting standards, EPA was then in no hurry to issue permits for individual TSDFs under those standards. By September 30, 1984, only 5 land disposal facilities and 17 incinerators had received RCRA permits. The estimated remaining population of approximately 1500 land disposal facilities and 200 incinerators could continue operating as interim status facilities under minimum controls. For example, regulations governing interim status landfills require groundwater monitoring but no cleanup of contamination once detected. Interim status incinerator standards do not include minimum performance standards for the incinerator. EPA chose not to require substantial improvements in the design and performance of TSDFs while they were in interim status, because the Agency believed it was more efficient to do so in the permitting process.[22] Consequently, the limited nature of the interim status standards and the small number of facilities actually permitted combined to produce a lack of significant improvements in waste management practices by HSWA's passage.

EPA'S ENFORCEMENT RECORD

At the same time that the regulatory program was suffering from palpitations, EPA's enforcement program was anemic. Internal memoranda written by a chief EPA enforcement official in early 1983 revealed an enforcement resource shortfall of "crisis" proportions. These memoranda described an enforcement program which could not meet half of the already minimal enforcement goals for fiscal year 1983; where available resources were decreasing rather than increasing; and a program which appeared to be in such disarray that papers could not be filed or typed because of an acute shortage of support staff.[23] In testimony before the Congress in 1985, EPA officials distributed a chart which showed that as of September 1982, there were only 2 full-time technical staff assigned to RCRA's enforcement program in Headquarters *and* the Regional offices, as compared to 250 positions in March of 1985 and 344 positions requested in the FY86 budget.[24]

EPA has found it very difficult to recover from this early dereliction of duty. For example, an April 1985 Congressional study on EPA and state enforcement of groundwater monitoring regulations revealed:

1. EPA's RCRA data base was still inaccurate.
2. Fifteen percent of the nation's land disposal facilities had *no* groundwater monitoring wells and enforcement action had been *taken against only* 40 percent of them.
3. Twenty-five percent of the land disposal facilities had inadequate well systems, and only 48 percent of these had been the subject of formal enforcement action.
4. Only 41 percent of the land disposal facilities were in complete compliance with the groundwater monitoring regulations.[25]

These findings were especially startling because the regulations had been in effect since November 19, 1981, TSDF owners/operators had been given 18 months time before this date to install the appropriate systems, and the regulations are universally regarded as some of the most important regulations issued by EPA thus far.

EPA's lackadaisical enforcement program brought criticism from a variety of sources. As an industry trade journal poignantly observed:

> Normally the site of a regulatory agency in turmoil is not calculated to bring tears to anyone's eyes. . . . What it (the chemical industry) needs and what it expects from the Reagan Administration is an agency that will discharge intelligently its responsibility to the American people. That means cleaning up and protecting the environment. . . . In a highly competitive industry, companies cannot afford to spend their resources on environmental protection, however well conceived the rules, unless they perceive those rules are backed up by a credible enforcement policy.[26]

A CONFLUENCE OF VOICES FOR REFORM

Perhaps as significant as the substantive agenda before the Congress was the wide array of interests identifying deficiencies in national policy and the need for fundamental changes. State agencies, environmental groups, academic bodies and a growing number of hazardous waste management firms in the private sector issued a variety of reports and proposals for reform. All argued that if waste management practices were to improve, the regulatory program had to encourage the improvement for several reasons. First, hazardous wastes often were disposed along the path of least regulatory control and least cost. Second, the use of more expensive but preferred methods of management were dependent upon regulations and restrictions that brought about their use. If the choice of management options for a particular waste stream remained the sole discretion of the waste generator, the generator was likely to choose the least-cost option rather than the environmentally preferable option.

Supporting these conclusions was an EPA survey of waste management practices in 1981 which revealed that most waste was managed in surface impoundments, landfills, and underground injection wells, while very small quantities were recycled or incinerated.[27] The survey found that of the approximately 71 billion gallons of hazardous waste managed during 1981, almost half were managed in surface impoundments, 8.6 billion gallons were disposed via underground injection wells, and 800 million gallons were landfilled. These numbers dwarfed the approximately 450 million gallons estimated to have been incinerated, and the approximately 4 percent of the waste estimated to have been recycled in 1981. The survey determined that while many generators recycle, they recycle only small portions of their hazardous waste streams.

Complementing the EPA survey were a substantial number of studies documenting both the shortcomings of land disposal and the existence of alternatives. Some studies documented the failure of particular land disposal facilities (including state-of-the-art facilities), while others described national trends concerning the poor design and/or location of these facilities. The studies of alternatives to land disposal found that waste reduction and treatment are environmentally preferable alternatives—the technologies exist to address the various types of hazardous waste—but loopholes or weak regulatory programs provide a disincentive to the regulated community to employ these alternatives.

These studies were performed by such diverse organizations as the State of California's Office of Appropriate Technology, the National Academy of Sciences, and the Office of Technology Assessment, a research arm of the Congress. Chapter 9 contains a more detailed description of these and other efforts.

Segments of private industry also argued that the use of improved management techniques would not expand as long as they had to compete against weak regulations, and the generator was free to manage its waste using the least-cost option. This blending of public and private interests was a unique addition to the debate and provided direction and support in structuring the 1984 amendments.

THE CONGRESSIONAL RESPONSE—HSWA

The RCRA Reauthorization process, which began in 1982,[28] presented Congress with an opportunity to address a wide assortment of problems plaguing the RCRA program: delays in regulatory development, loopholes in existing regulations, poor enforcement, and a lack of overall policy direction. These different problems required a variety of solutions, and in some cases unique approaches toward addressing environmental problems.

Since HSWA contains a large number of regulatory initiatives and modifications, these approaches are often overlooked when examining the specifics of particular provisions. Therefore, as an introduction to the more detailed discussion of particular provisions in subsequent chapters, the following section will discuss briefly the broader public policy implications of HSWA.

Addressing Delays in Regulatory Development

Congress was faced with major gaps in the regulatory and permitting program which EPA was approaching with varying degrees of enthusiasm. For example, new waste listings were not forthcoming; regulations governing such activities as the burning and blending of hazardous waste and the permitting of underground tanks had not yet been promulgated; and very few permits for other TSDFs had been issued.

The regulatory gaps were no longer subject to Congressional or court-ordered deadlines because the general Congressional mandate of the 1976 law to promulgate regulations had been met even though those regulations contained significant loopholes. Based on EPA's past performance in the RCRA program, Congress had little confidence that the still-needed regulations would be issued without new deadlines for promulgation. The necessity for deadlines was accentuated by OMB pressure to reduce EPA's budget, and increasing OMB influence over EPA regulatory development.[29] A schedule for permitting facilities had not previously been included in RCRA.

Thus, Congress established new deadlines for many aspects of the next phase of RCRA program development, including reports to support this development. These deadlines were negotiated with EPA, and modified at EPA's behest.[30] A chronology of these deadlines can be found at Appendix H to this book.

Perhaps even more significant than the deadlines themselves is the way Congress enforced some of these deadlines. Rather than require EPA to develop regulations to implement a particular policy, in some cases Congress banned certain activities in the law itself. The advantages to this approach were twofold. One was the conservation of EPA resources; these provisions might necessitate the development of EPA guidance to facilitate implementation, but they would not require more resource-intensive data gathering and rulemaking to justify their underlying policy. Second, these provisions could be implemented quickly since rulemaking was not required, a process that often takes several years to complete. This approach was particularly useful where yes-or-no decisions were called for, and EPA seemed incapable of making a decision. Examples included restrictions on the landfilling of bulk liquids, prohibiting the injection of hazardous waste above underground sources of drinking water, and prohibiting the installation of bare steel underground product storage tanks.

Minimum Regulatory Controls

Perhaps even more innovative than the statutory directives was the use, in several instances, of minimum regulatory controls (MRCs) that would be triggered in the event EPA failed to issue regulations by a date certain. The purpose of the MRCs (sometimes referred to as "hammers") was to substitute for the status quo of no regulation, statutory controls that would address the most obvious deficiencies in the status quo. Thus, Congress would be assured of achieving a limited measure of environmental protection by a specified date.

A prime example of this approach concerns the development of small quantity generator regulations where, if regulations lowering the exemption to 220 lbs/mo were not issued by March 31, 1986, certain requirements are imposed by statute for such previously exempted waste. The triggering of the MRCs, however, does not relieve EPA of the obligation to issue more comprehensive regulations. This provision is described in Chapter 4.

Another example concerns the land disposal restrictions of HSWA. In this case, if EPA fails to decide by a certain date whether certain untreated wastes should continue to be land disposed, impoundments and landfills receiving those wastes must then meet certain design standards, and the generator must certify to EPA that disposal of those wastes is the only practicable management alternative available to the generator. Again, EPA is not relieved of the responsibility to make a decision on prohibiting the land disposal of these wastes when the MRCs become effective. This provision is described in Chapter 9.

Performing Surgery with Specificity

In response to a variety of the loopholes described above, Congress developed statutory approaches that are noteworthy for their level of detail; thus they resemble regulations. Incorporating such a level of detail into federal law is unusual for Congress, because of concerns that a rigid statutory scheme would prevent EPA from resolving administratively unanticipated issues that would inevitably arise in the future. However, in several instances, Congress overrode those concerns because a provision required more rapid implementation than would be possible if EPA had to issue regulations implementing the provision. In addition, EPA was able to provide the technical basis for the statutory provision.

One example of this approach is a HSWA provision that sets minimum design standards for new, replacement, and expansion landfills and surface impoundments; and for many existing impoundments. Two or more liners are required by this provision, and a prototype acceptable dual-liner system of a top synthetic liner and a bottom clay liner is described in the law. This liner system is deemed an acceptable design until EPA issues regulations or guidance documents implementing the dual-liner requirement. A limited opportunity is also provided for an owner/operator to demonstrate that another design, coupled with facility location characteristics and operating practices, are equivalent to the protection afforded by the dual-liner requirement. This provision is further described in Chapter 10.

Another example concerns the waste tracking requirements as they apply to previously unregulated small quantity generators. These generators are required to ensure waste shipments are accompanied by a form called a manifest beginning August 5, 1985, and the statute specifies which parts of the manifest form they must fill out. Chapter 4 includes additional information on this provision.

Reversing the Course of Past Mistakes

Recognizing that the number of problem waste sites requiring cleanup was continuing to grow, and that some of these sites were interim status facilities allowed to operate under RCRA, Congess enacted several landmark provisions in an attempt to halt this trend.

First, Congress required that many existing unlined surface impoundments be retrofitted or closed by November 8, 1988. This provision reversed a prior EPA exemption from liner requirements for existing impoundments in its land disposal regulations, as described in Chapter 10.

Second, Congress created an additional responsibility for owners/operators of TSDFs receiving a RCRA permit. Under a HSWA provision, these owners/operators must clean up releases that threaten human health and the environment from all waste management units, solid or hazardous, at the facility regardless of when the waste was placed in the units. Consequently, environmental contamination previously ignored within the regulatory program because it was caused by an old hazardous waste unit, or a non-hazardous waste unit, will now be addressed during the permitting process. In this manner, Congress established a "good neighbor policy" for TSDFs, whereby permits would only be awarded to TSDFs that were not contributing to further environmental degradation from past or present solid or hazardous waste management practices. This provision is described further in Chapter 11.

Finally, Congress provided EPA with additional authority to require cleanup from an owner/operator of a TSDF while the facility is in interim status. As stated above, EPA's interim status regulations do not impose cleanup requirements on facilities contaminating groundwater, and in some cases, the contamination is already quite extensive because the TSDF has been leaking for years. Under a provision in HSWA, however, EPA may issue an interim status cleanup order as necessary to protect human health and the environment, thus filling a gap left by EPA regulations. Additional information on this provision can also be found in Chapter 11.

Developing a National Waste Management Strategy

There is an emerging national consensus that land disposal is the least preferred management option.[31] Prior to HSWA, EPA had developed regulations which were, ostensibly, technology neutral. On their face, these regulations neither encouraged or discouraged the use of alternative management practices, leaving the management decision to the generator of the waste. However, weaknesses in the land disposal regulations indirectly biased the regulatory regime toward land disposal because they resulted in cheap disposal costs. EPA's policy on land disposal remained at best uncertain at a time when a significant number of states were moving away from land disposal under their own state laws and regulations.[32]

Congress established in HSWA a framework for encouraging waste reduction, recycling, and treatment strategies; and discouraging continued reliance on land disposal. This was accomplished in many ways. First, Congress explicity stated it is national policy that the generation of hazardous waste should be reduced or eliminated as soon as possible. Second, Congress established as RCRA objectives the need for "proper management in the first instance," and the "minimization of the land disposal of hazardous waste." Third, Congress required generators and TSDF owners/operators to certify periodically that they have waste reduction programs in place. Fourth, Congress provided a regulatory agenda for EPA to implement a land disposal minimization policy over a six-and-a-half-year period. Fifth, the standard by which EPA would make management decisions was designed to highlight the generic problems associated with land disposal, such as the long-term containment uncertainties compared with the period of time the wastes remain hazardous. Finally, Congress established presumptions against the land disposal of several categories of wastes, thereby declaring the continued land disposal of those wastes inappropriate by a specified date unless EPA could prove otherwise, and Congress prohibited other disposal practices as described above. Chapter 9 will describe these provisions in greater detail.

Strengthening Enforcement Tools

Concerned about an ineffective and overburdened enforcement program, Congress provided additional enforcement authorities to EPA and to third parties.

To achieve better compliance with interim status regulations, Congress required owners/operators to certify compliance with certain requirements by November 8, 1985, or lose interim status and thus their legal right to continue operating. This provision is described in Chapter 13. In addition, to ensure compliance with the retrofit requirements for surface impoundments, a statutory ban was placed on the continued use of unlined impoundments by November 8, 1988, with certain variances, and those variances must be applied for by the owner/operator by November 8, 1986, or else the retrofit requirement is imposed. This provision is described in Chapter 10.

Perhaps of greater importance were the variety of informational access and citizen suit authorities provided to third parties when EPA and the states are not taking appropriate action. For the first time in environmental statutes, citizens and states were given the authority to seek the cleanup of sites posing an imminent and substantial endangerment, authority normally reserved for EPA. In addition, citizens were authorized to seek fines payable to the U.S. Treasury for regulatory and permit violations, to be used in concert with already granted authority to sue recalcitrant companies for non-compliance.

Supporting these authorities were a variety of requirements designed to make more information available to third parties. These requirements include mandatory inspections of TSDFs operated by federal and state governments, and mandating states to incorporate public access to information provisions similar to the federal government as a condition for receiving authorization to run the RCRA program. These provisions and many others will be more closely examined in Chapters 13 and 14.

Addressing Cross-Media Environmental Concerns

Although groundwater contamination is typically associated with hazardous waste management, Congress expressed concern about gaps in the regulatory program addressing air, soil, and surface water contamination. Thus, the scope of interim status cleanup orders and HSWA requirements for permittees to clean up continuing releases from solid waste units is not limited to groundwater contamination. In addition, HSWA requires owners/operators seeking a permit for surface impoundments and landfills to provide information on all potential pathways of human exposure to hazardous waste releases (see Chapter 11). The 1984 amendments also require EPA to examine the domestic sewage exemption and promulgate regulations under RCRA or the Clean Water Act to ensure hazardous wastes deposited into a sewer system are adequately controlled. Finally, HSWA requires EPA to issue regulations controlling air emissions from uncovered tanks and land disposal facilities by May 8, 1987.

Summary

Discussions about the content, impact, and philosophy behind the 1984 amendments is frequently dominated by the discussion of loopholes and land disposal restrictions. While this focus is correct, at the same time there is an even broader unifying theme to the provisions and actions of the 1984 amendments: certainty that waste would be properly managed in the first instance and certainty that the waste would not continue to pose hazards for generations to come. Of course, the majority of this intention has focused on all forms of land disposal, but no method of hazardous waste management is exempt from the search for certainty instituted by the 1984 amendments. It was also clear to the Congress that this desire for certainty could not occur by simply delegating large blocks of regulatory responsibility to the Agency as it had done in the past, irrespective of who inhabits the White House. During the 3-year reauthorization process, the Congress and the public in general had come to recognize that Agency discretion in many ways had become its own worst enemy: too much of it *was* just as bad as too little. In the case of the hazardous waste program there had been *too much discretion* for far too long a period of time. In a program that sorely needed leadership and appeared unable to choose among potential policy options, the Congress substituted its judgment on a wide range of hazardous waste issues.

In conclusion, Congress and the public had recognized that 8 years after the original enactment of RCRA, EPA had developed only the broad outlines of a national hazardous waste program. The 1984 amendments, therefore, mark the transition from the program's infancy to adulthood.

NOTES

1. P.L. 94-580, 90 Stat. 2795 (1976), 42 U.S.C. 6901 *et seq*. RCRA represented a major overhaul of the Solid Waste Disposal Act of 1965, P.L. 89-272, 79 Stat. 992.

2. P.L. 98-616, 98 Stat. 3221 (1984) from HR 2867, 98th Cong., 2nd Sess.

3. 130 *Congressional Record* S9151 (daily ed. July 25, 1984) (statement of Senator Mitchell).

4. 129 *Cong. Rec.* H6501 (daily ed. Aug. 4, 1983) (statement of Representative Lent).

5. One of the most commonly asked questions about RCRA is why is a law regulating hazardous waste called "RCRA." The answer is RCRA is a law containing a series of subtitles, only some of which address hazardous waste management directly. Other sections address solid waste management (Subtitle D) and the recovery and recycling of solid waste materials (Subtitles B, E, F). The recycling provisions were considered very important at the time of RCRA's passage because of the energy crisis of the 1970s. In fact, Subtitle C of RCRA, the principal portion of the law devoted to hazardous waste regulation, did not receive nearly the attention it receives today when RCRA was enacted in 1976.

6. *Hazardous Waste Disposal,* Subcommittee on Oversight and Investigations, Committee on Energy and Commerce, U.S. House of Representatives, 96th Congress, 1st Session, 1979, at 35-38.

7. *State of Illinois v. Costle,* 12 ERC 1597 (D.D.C. 1979).

8. *State of Illinois v. Costle,* Civ. Act. No. 78-1689 and consolidated cases (D.D.C.) (order of Dec. 18, 1979).

9. "The Stockman Manifesto," *Washington Post,* Dec. 14, 1980, pp. Cl, 5.

10. 46 *Fed. Reg.* 13193 (Feb. 19, 1981).

11. Press Release of Vice President Bush, March 25, 1981.

12. 46 *Fed. Reg.* 38318 (July 24, 1981).

13. 47 *Fed. Reg.* 27518 (June 24, 1982).

14. 46 *Fed. Reg.* 48197,8 (Oct. 1, 1981).

15. 47 *Fed. Reg.* 7841 (Feb. 23, 1982).

16. 47 *Fed. Reg.* 8304 (Feb. 25, 1982), reversed 25 days later, 47 *Fed. Reg.* 12316 (March 22, 1982).

17. *EDF v. Gorsuch,* 713 F. 2d 802 (D.C. Cir. 1983).

18. 47 *Fed. Reg.* 16544,5 (April 16, 1982).

19. 47 *Fed. Reg.* 44938,9 (Oct. 12, 1982).

20. *State of Illinois v. Gorsuch,* 530 F. Supp. 340 (D.D.C. 1981).

21. *Citizens for a Better Environment v. Gorsuch,* 12 ELR 20755 (D.C. Cir. 1982).

22. 45 *Fed. Reg.* 33159 (May 19, 1980).

23. Memorandum from Edward Kurent, Associate Enforcement Counsel for Waste to Robert Perry, Associate Administrator and General Counsel, dated Feb. 23, 1983, and Memorandum from Edward Kurent, Associate Enforcement Counsel for Waste to Michael Brown, Enforcement Counsel, dated Jan. 12, 1983, both reprinted in *Hazardous Waste Control and Enforcement Act of 1983,* Hearings before the Subcommittee on Commerce, Transportation and Tourism of the Committee on Energy and Commerce, U.S. House of Representatives, 98th Cong., 1st Sess., Ser. No. 98-32 at 416-428.

24. Statement of Jack McGraw, Acting Assistant Administrator for Solid Waste and Emergency Response, U.S. Environmental Protection Agency, before the Subcommittee on Oversight and Investigations, Committee on Energy and Commerce, U.S. House of Representatives, April 29, 1985, and supporting materials.

25. *Groundwater Monitoring Survey,* Subcommittee on Oversight and Investigations, Committee on Energy and Commerce, U.S. House of Representatives, 99th Cong., 1st Sess., April 1985, at 1-6.

26. "We Need a Credible EPA," *Chemical Week,* Oct. 21, 1981, at 3.

27. National Survey of Hazardous Waste Generators and Treatment, Storage and Disposal Facilities Regulated Under RCRA in 1981, Prepared for EPA by Westat, Inc., April 1984.

28. The U.S. House of Representatives had passed a RCRA Reauthorization bill in 1982 (H.R. 6307). See 128 *Cong. Rec.* H6745-6777 (daily ed. Sept. 8, 1982). Although the bill contained only thirteen provisions, those provisions would have lowered the small quantity generator exemption, required corrective action for continuing releases, and mandated controls on the burning of hazardous waste in industrial boilers. The Senate, however, did not pass a companion bill.

29. See, for example, Olsen, The Quiet Shift of Power: Office of Management and Budget Supervision of Environmental Protection Agency Rulemaking Under Executive Order 12291, 4 *VA. J. Nat. Res. L.* 1 (1984).

30. 130 *Congressional Record* S9174 (July 25, 1984).

31. *Siting Hazardous Waste Management Facilities: A Handbook,* published by the Conservation Foundation, the Chemical Manufacturers Association and the National Audubon Society, 1983, at 21.

32. Testimony of Rita Lavelle, Assistant Administrator for Solid Waste and Emergency Response, U.S. Environmental Protection Agency, before the Subcommittee on Natural Resources, Agriculture, Research, and Environment, Committee on Science and Technology, U.S. House of Representatives, Dec. 16, 1982.

CHAPTER TWO

What Wastes Are Hazardous?

"I hate definitions," was the familiar refrain of one of England's most eloquent and distinguished prime ministers.[1] Perhaps he had an early draft of our hazardous waste regulations. The wise reader should be prepared for the byzantine paths that our current hazardous and solid waste definitions follow.

For better or worse, however, definitions are an essential if sometimes frustrating component of hazardous waste regulation, and their complexity must be put into context, for they touch virtually all sectors of American industry and commerce. Any definition of hazardous waste is inescapably imprecise and complex. The danger is that many materials and wastes that are generally regarded as harmful and dangerous are not listed or identified as hazardous under the current system and therefore may not be properly managed. HSWA mandated a variety of significant changes to the federal regulations to minimize this danger. In order to appreciate the changes that will be introduced by the 1984 RCRA Amendments, it is first necessary to examine the problems that led to the changes and the system of definitions that apply today for identifying hazardous wastes.

Chapters 2 and 3 of this book describe and discuss the process of determining whether a material in question is a hazardous waste, solid waste, or neither. Chapter 2 will examine the materials that are and will be *hazardous* on the basis of either manufacturing process (listed waste) or intrinsic chemical/physical properties (identified wastes). Chapter 3 will examine whether these materials are *wastes* rather than products, and therefore hazardous wastes.

As a legal matter, the chapters should probably be reversed. A substance must first be a "solid" waste before it can be a "hazardous" waste.[2] However, as a practical matter, the determination regarding whether a substance is first a solid waste, or whether it is more like a product, is very complex. This is particularly true when determining how and if the myriad potential "recycling" practices affect how a material is regulated. Therefore, our readers are urged to read Chapter 2 first, because no matter how dangerous a substance may be, if it has not been either listed or identified as hazardous under federal regulations, it is *not* regulated as a hazardous waste under RCRA. However, states are not limited to the Federal universe of hazardous wastes and may designate additional wastes as hazardous under state law.[3]

BACKGROUND

When the process of reauthorizing or renewing RCRA began in early 1982, one of the most glaring inadequacies in the federal regulations was the small number of wastes that were either listed or identified as hazardous as compared to the relatively large number of exclusions, exemptions, and opportunities for delisting a waste. Several studies and state programs verified the view that more wastes, generators, and facilities were exempt from RCRA control than were subject to it.[4] Table 2-1 summarizes the scope of wastes designated as hazardous under individual state programs.

For example, the residue from the production of many pesticides such as the carbamates, most dioxin wastes, many chlorinated aliphatic and aromatic solvents, dyes and pigments, and paint production wastes were not designated as hazardous.[5] Wastes that were discharged into a publicly owned sewage treatment facility were statutorily exempt from RCRA control.[6] Hundreds of millions of gallons of waste oil escaped control annually due to the Agency's failure to act on a congressional mandate to regulate used oil recycling. Much of the waste is believed to be hazardous and has been so regulated by various states.[7]

Over 90 percent of all hazardous waste generators were exempt from regulation on the basis that they generated less than one ton of hazardous waste per month and hence were deemed "small generators," who could dispose of their wastes into sanitary landfills.[8]

In addition, thousands of facilities that managed hazardous wastes were exempted until the Administrator promulgated regulations to the contrary because they were "beneficially" using or reusing, or "legitimately" accumulating, storing, or recycling hazardous wastes. While these designations were intended to be interim safeguards against sham or bogus "recycling" practices, such recyclers were not required to receive prior Agency approval of the practice. As a consequence, determination of what constituted "beneficial" or "legitimate" recycling were essentially left to the sole judgment and discretion of the generators and facility operators, pending Agency inspections or enforcement actions of which there were previous few. In fact, it was not until January 1983 that EPA issued its first enforcement policy to identify and curtail sham recycling situations.[9]

As a result, some very creative and potentially dangerous on-going practices were legally sanctioned under the operative federal regulations including: road oiling with dioxin-containing wastes that created the Times Beach, Missouri, sites; the burning of hazardous wastes as fuels in both industrial and residential boilers; the use of metal-containing wastes for fertilizers and fill material; and numerous other uses that constituted little more than disposal of hazardous wastes without environmental control.

In fact, approximately 15 of the first 115 "Superfund" sites were recycling facilities.[10] A summary of over 82 damage cases that have resulted from so-called hazardous waste "recycling" facilities was provided as Appendices A and B to the Agency's redefinition of solid and hazardous waste, which will be discussed and analyzed in Chapter 3.[11]

Lastly, even if a waste was listed by EPA as hazardous, the Agency's process for delisting a waste from hazardous waste control was so inviting

Table 2-1

Hazardous Waste Generation Estimates by EPA and the States

State[a b]	Quantity (tonnes) EPA estimate	State estimate	Universe Same as EPA	State additions[c]
Alabama[b]	730,000	265,680		PCBs.
Alaska[b]	130,000	360		PCBs.
Arizona[b]	160,000	4,280,000		PCBs, waste oil.
Arkansas	370,000	No data[d]		PCBs, waste oil.
California[e]	2,630,000	15,000,000		Approximately 4 mmt is oilfield waste; also includes mining waste, small generators, PCBs.
Colorado[b]	180,000	775,490		PCBs.
Connecticut[b]	610,000	102,000	x	Extrapolated from 3 months manifest data.
Delaware[a]	300,000	272,000	x	—
Florida	960,000	No data	x	—
Georgia[b]	700,000	38,500,800		Some delisted waste; 99.7% is high volume, aqueous solutions, neutralized on site and discharged to sewers and receiving waters.
Hawaii	30,000	No response		—
Illinois[a]	2,530,000	1,810,000		Manifest data only.
Indiana	1,280,000	94,900,000		Includes 92.3 mmt of steel industry wastes, pending delisting and currently regulated under NPDES permit.
Idaho	80,000	No response		—
Iowa	300,000	No response		—
Kansas[a]	350,000	45,300		Refinery waste, small volume generators.
Kentucky[a]	700,000	415,000	x	
Louisiana[a]	1,250,000	38,800,000		Fly and bottom ash, small volume generators, substances with LD$_{50}$.
Maine[b]	130,000	5,290		Mineral spirits, tanning industry waste, small volume generators, infectious waste.
Maryland[a]	590,000	272,100		Waste oil, PCBs, fly ash, and other unspecified waste.
Massachusetts[b]	820,000	172,000		Waste oil.
Michigan[b]	1,990,000	408,000		Extrapolated from manifest data; 280 compounds (including waste oil) not on EPA list.
Minnesota[b]	360,000	181,000		PCBs, crank case oil.
Mississippi[a]	340,000	1,810,000	x	
Missouri[a]	910,000	658,930		Waste oil.
Montana[a]	50,000	91,200	x	
Nebraska[b]	120,000	0.5% of national total)		Special waste including infectious waste.
Nevada	50,000	No response		—
New Hampshire[a]	100,000	9,980		Imported PCBs, waste oil.
New Jersey[a]	3,120,000	855,000		Manifest data only; waste oil, PCBs, some delisted waste, and other unspecified compounds.
New Mexico	60,000	No data		Small volume generators, PCBs, waste oil.
New York[b]	2,320,000	1,270,000		PCBs.
North Carolina	1,330,000	No response		—
North Dakota[a]	30,000	125,000	x	
Ohio[a]	2,570,000	3,260,000		Solid waste on a case-by-case basis.
Oklahoma[b]	230,000	3,570,000		PCBs.
Oregon[b]	200,000	19,100		PCBs and other unspecified compounds.
Pennsylvania[b]	2,550,000	3,628,000		Other unspecified compounds.
Rhode Island[a]	190,000	1,600		A generally broader definition which includes waste oil, low-level radioactive.
South Carolina[b]	1,140,000	1,587,000		Waste oil, paint waste, unstabilized sewerage sludge.
South Dakota[b]	10,000	1,590		Waste oil.
Tennessee[a]	1,820,000	4,300,000	x	
Texas[a]	3,010,000	29,146,960		Generally different definition which includes sludge, fly and bottom ash, water soluble oils, boiler sludges, PCBs, and other solid waste.
Utah[a]	110,000	558,000	x	
Vermont[b]	30,000	9,070		Waste oils, infectious waste, PCBs, industrial laundries, some waste delisted by EPA, and other unspecified compounds.
Virginia[b]	1,220,000	181,000		PCBs.
Washington[b]	380,000	616,000		Additional unspecified waste.
West Virginia	790,000	No response		—
Wisconsin[a]	630,000	81,600		—
Wyoming	40,000	No response		—
Guam[b]	n/a	1,450	x	—
Puerto Rico[b]	560,000	417,000	x	—
North Mariana Island	n/a	No response		—
American Samoa	n/a	0		—
District of Columbia	140,000	No data	x	—
Virgin Islands	n/a	No response		—
Total	41,200,000 (excl. 2 terr.)	250,000,000 (excl. 10 states, 3 terr.)		

[a] State data based on inventory.
[b] State data based on consultant and/or State agency estimates.
[c] PCBs are currently regulated under TSCA. EPA is considering transferring regulation of this substance to RCRA jurisdiction.
[d] A few States did not supply information to this survey.
[e] The State figure of 15 million tonnes is from the testimony of S. Kent Stoddard, Office of Appropriate Technology, House Subcommittee on Natural Resources, Agriculture Research and the Environment, Dec. 8, 1982; it is based on a recent State study.

Conversions:
gallons × 0.00378 = metric tons
tons × 0.907 = metric tons
cubic feet × 0.02828 = metric tons
cubic yards × 0.76441 = metric tons

SOURCE: State estimates and associated information by ASTSWMO unless noted otherwise; EPA estimates by Office of Solid Waste for 1980.

that over 142 temporary delistings had been granted, while not one new waste had been listed. In one case, untreated waste piles (that also contained PCBs) were about to be delisted when runoff from the pile was discovered to be contaminating surface waters.[12]

Collectively, these findings provided the impetus for major revisions—more proscriptive revisions—to the nation's hazardous waste management system. The balance of this chapter is devoted to a description and analysis of the current universe of hazardous wastes, the procedures for delistings, recent new listings of hazardous wastes, and an examination of the impact of the 1984 RCRA Amendments on the future scope of waste listings and delistings. Chapter 3 will build on this process of identifying hazardous wastes by examining its relationship to hazardous waste recycling practices and various types of production processes.

DEFINITIONS OF HAZARDOUS WASTE

Statutory Definition

The term "hazardous waste" is defined in the RCRA law itself as a solid waste, or combination of solid wastes that, because of its quantity, concentration, or physical, chemical, or infectious characteristics, may:

1. cause, or significantly contribute to, an increase in mortality or an increase in serious irreversible, or incapacitating reversible, illness; or

2. pose a substantial present or potential hazard to human health or the environment when improperly treated, stored, transported, or disposed of, or otherwise managed.[13]

It is clear from an examination of this statutory standard that it is structured to be both preventive and anticipatory. A waste material or solid waste need not necessarily present an imminent or irreversible harm to be classified as a hazardous waste. Moreover, exposure to the waste need not clearly "cause" harm in order to be hazardous. The material can either "cause or signficantly *contribute* to an illness" when it is improperly managed. The wastes may also "pose a substantial present or *potential* hazard" (emphasis added).

As such, the statute provides the Agency with very broad authority to identify and regulate hazardous wastes. This standard also means that hazardous waste management activities may be regulated even if they are operating and have operated without incident in order to prevent the occurrence of reasonable mismanagement scenarios.

In addition, unlike some other environmental statutes, the basic standard of protection under RCRA does not consider cost as a basis for failing to institute regulatory controls.[14] The genesis of this approach can be traced to the original legislation and has been reinforced by the 1984 RCRA Amendments.[15]

Despite the cost of the many new remedial and preventive measures required by these Amendments, there was a conspicuous and conscious effort to maintain RCRA's previous policy of regulating "as may be necessary to protect human health and the environment." Decisions to undertake or withhold action are to be based solely on this standard.

Regulatory Definition—Four Categories of Hazardous Wastes

Based upon the statutory definition,[16] a material qualifies as a hazardous waste if it falls within any one of the four categories discussed below *and* it does not qualify for any of the exemptions or exclusions discussed in Chapter 3.

1. EPA may list a waste, usually from a specific production process, as hazardous, based principally upon the presence of specific hazardous *constituents* in the waste *or* because the waste consistently exhibits one or more characteristics of a hazardous waste (40 CFR Part 261 Subpart D). In addition, EPA may list a product as a hazardous waste if it is discarded in a pure or off-specification form and contains specific hazardous constituents.

2. Those solid wastes and waste generation processes that have not been specifically listed by EPA may nevertheless be identified as hazardous solely on the basis that they exhibit one or more of the four *characteristics* of hazardous waste irrespective of the manufacturing process from which it is generated. The four characteristics are: ignitability (I), corrosivity (C), reactivity (R), or toxicity (EP). In this case, "toxicity" means the ability or tendency to leach certain constituents via a specific extraction procedure (40 CFR Part 261 (Subpart C).

3. It is a *mixture* of a listed hazardous waste and any other material, or is a mixture of a characteristic waste and any other material, provided the mixtue still exhibits characteristic (40 CFR 261.3(a) (iii), (iv)).

4. It is a residue that is "derived from" the treatment, storage, or disposal of a listed waste (40 CFR 261.3(c)), such as incinerator ash.

In general, a waste material becomes a hazardous waste when it first satisfies any of the specific criteria upon which its classification as hazardous waste is based. That is, the first time it exhibits a characteristic, or meets the description of a listed waste, a listed waste mixture, or is derived from the management of a listed waste, it is then considered hazardous.[17] The following sections will examine each of these four hazardous waste categories. Figure 2-1 summarizes the categories of RCRA listed and characteristic hazardous wastes, including the subgroups of these four broad categories that are discussed in further detail in the balance of this chapter. Chapter 3 will examine the even broader category of residual materials that are solid wastes, and how we distinguish between regulated waste management practices, and actual manufacturing operations.

Figure 2-1

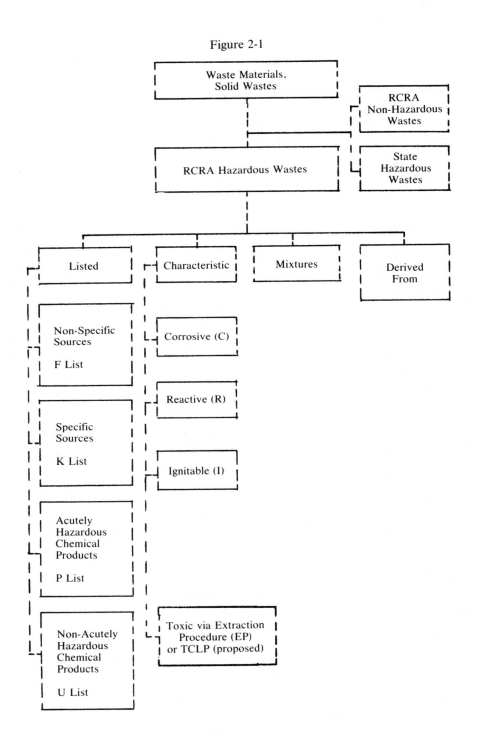

LISTED HAZARDOUS WASTES

Appendices VII and VIII to 40 CFR Part 261

Appendix VIII to 40 CFR Part 261 contains the hazardous constituents EPA looks for when determining whether to list a hazardous waste under RCRA. However, a typical misconception is that all wastes containing one or more of approximately 375 constituents listed in this Appendix are themselves hazardous wastes, and that is not true. The presence of an Appendix VIII chemical in a waste merely raises the possibility that the waste could be designated as hazardous.

Indeed, a separate regulatory action is required for each and every hazardous waste listing by EPA. In this rulemaking, EPA identifies the Appendix VIII constituents in the waste and explains why they are present at sufficient concentrations to justify regulating the waste's management. EPA's decision as to whether a waste should be listed as hazardous will depend upon the Agency's determination of the significance of that constituent and that constituent's effect on human health and the environment if the waste is improperly managed. In some cases, even if a waste contains any of the toxic constituent(s) listed in Appendix VIII, EPA may conclude that the waste is not capable of posing a substantial present or potential hazard to human health or the environment when improperly managed upon consideration of eleven factors such as the concentration, persistence, and degradation of the constituent in the waste; action taken by other governmental agencies; and such other factors as may be appropriate.[18]

Thus, having an Appendix VIII constituent in your waste merely means that your waste stream or categories of wastes are suitable for inclusion but a regulatory action for it may not have been drafted yet.

Appendix VIII also plays an important role in the groundwater monitoring and cleanup program for permitted land disposal facilities, and in defining the extent of the cleanup requirements for those facilities, which will be discussed in detail in Chapter 11. Moreover, Appendix VIII constituents are used in evaluating petitions to delist a hazardous waste to determine the presence of additional hazardous constituents (see discussion below), and in establishing the principal organic hazardous constituents (POHC's) upon which incineration destruction efficiency and land treatment demonstrations are based (Chapter 8).

Appendix VII to the 40 CFR Part 261 regulations is in effect a catalogue of those constitutents which have caused certain wastes to be listed. Grouped by waste stream, Appendix VII names the specific Appendix VIII constitutent(s) that caused the waste to be listed. It is important to realize, however, that this list is not a complete list of constituents of concern. Once EPA identifies several constituents, demonstrating the need for regulation of the waste, the Agency frequently will not identify the remaining constituents of concern. This lack of knowledge about the composition of many listed wastes resulted in deficiencies in EPA's delisting procedure (discussed below). Readers interested in examining Appendices VII and VIII are directed to the CFR.

Other Listing Criteria

In addition to the presence of an Appendix VIII constituent, the regulations[19] specify several other criteria or bases by which wastes are listed as hazardous:

1. It exhibits 1 of the 4 characteristics of a hazardous waste: toxicity, ignitability, reactivity, and corrosivity.

2. It has been found to be fatal to humans in low doses, shown to be acutely toxic to animals, or is otherwise capable of causing or significantly contributing to an increase in serious irreversible, or incapacitating reversible, illness. (Wastes listed in accordance with these criteria will be designated acutely hazardous wastes.)

3. The Administrator may also list classes or types of hazardous wastes if he or she has reason to believe that individual wastes, within the class or type of waste, typically or frequently are hazardous under the definition of hazardous waste found in Section 1004(5) of the Act. The Agency recently invoked this authority to bring certain groups of chlorinated wastes under RCRA control.[20]

4. A new statutory basis for either listing or identifying (through development of a new characteristic) a waste as hazardous is contained in Section 3001(b) (1) of RCRA, as amended.[21] It differs from the class listing authority discussed above by requiring that the Administrator (in cooperation with the Agency for Toxic Substances and Disease Registry and the National Toxicology Program) also identify or list those hazardous wastes which shall be subject to the provisions of Subtitle C, the hazardous waste regulations, *solely because of the presence* in such wastes of certain constituents (such as identified carcinogens, mutagens, or teratogens) at levels in excess of levels which endanger human health. The great potential of this provision, which has not yet been utilized by the Agency, will be discussed below in the section dealing with the impact of the 1984 Amendments on the waste listing and identification process.

Hazardous Waste Lists

Based upon these criteria, the waste is placed on one of four hazardous waste lists:

1. Hazardous wastes from non-specific sources (largely spent solvents). Wastes are found in 40 CFR 261.31 and are referred to as the "F" List (Table 2-2).

Table 2-2

Hazardous wastes from non-specific sources.

Industry and EPA hazardous waste No.	Hazardous waste	Hazard code
Generic:		
F001	The following spent halogenated solvents used in degreasing: tetrachloroethylene, trichloroethylene, methylene chloride, 1,1,1-trichloroethane, carbon tetrachloride, and chlorinated fluorocarbons; and sludges from the recovery of these solvents in degreasing operations.	(T)
F002	The following spent halogenated solvents: tetrachloroethylene, methylene chloride, trichloroethylene, 1,1,1-trichloroethane, chlorobenzene, 1,1,2-trichloro-1,2,2-trifluoroethane, ortho-dichlorobenzene, and trichlorofluoromethane; and the still bottoms from the recovery of these solvents.	(T)
F003	The following spent non-halogenated solvents: xylene, acetone, ethyl acetate, ethyl benzene, ethyl ether, methyl isobutyl ketone, n-butyl alcohol, cyclohexanone, and methanol; and the still bottoms from the recovery of these solvents.	(I)
F004	The following spent non-halogenated solvents: cresols and cresylic acid, and nitrobenzene; and the still bottoms from the recovery of these solvents.	(T)
F005	The following spent non-halogenated solvents: toluene, methyl ethyl ketone, carbon disulfide, isobutanol, and pyridine; and the still bottoms from the recovery of these solvents.	(I, T)
F006	Wastewater treatment sludges from electroplating operations except from the following processes: (1) sulfuric acid anodizing of aluminum; (2) tin plating on carbon steel; (3) zinc plating (segregated basis) on carbon steel; (4) aluminum or zinc-aluminum plating on carbon steel; (5) cleaning/stripping associated with tin, zinc and aluminum plating on carbon steel; and (6) chemical etching and milling of aluminum.	(T)
F019	Wastewater treatment sludges from the chemical conversion coating of aluminum.	(T)
F007	Spent cyanide plating bath solutions from electroplating operations (except for precious metals electroplating spent cyanide plating bath solutions).	(R, T)
F008	Plating bath sludges from the bottom of plating baths from electroplating operations where cyanides are used in the process (except for precious metals electroplating plating bath sludges).	(R, T)
F009	Spent stripping and cleaning bath solutions from electroplating operations where cyanides are used in the process (except for precious metals electroplating spent stripping and cleaning bath solutions).	(R, T)
F010	Quenching bath sludge from oil baths from metal heat treating operations where cyanides are used in the process (except for precious metals heat-treating quenching bath sludges).	(R, T)
F011	Spent cyanide solutions from salt bath pot cleaning from metal heat treating operations (except for precious metals heat treating spent cyanide solutions from salt bath pot cleaning).	(R, T)
F012	Quenching wastewater treatment sludges from metal heat treating operations where cyanides are used in the process (except for precious metals heat treating quenching wastewater treatment sludges).	(T)
F024	Wastes, including but not limited to, distillation residues, heavy ends, tars, and reactor clean-out wastes from the production of chlorinated aliphatic hydrocarbons, having carbon content from one to five, utilizing free radical catalyzed processes. [This listing does not include light ends, spent filters and filter aids, spent dessicants, wastewater, wastewater treatment sludges, spent catalysts, and wastes listed in § 261.32.].	(T)
FO20	Wastes (except wastewater and spent carbon from hydrogen chloride purification) from the production or manufacturing use (as a reactant, chemical intermediate, or component in a formulating process) of tri- or tetrachlorophenol, or of intermediates used to produce their pesticide derivatives. (This listing does not include wastes from the production of Hexachlorophene from highly purified 2,4,5-trichlorophenol.).	(H)
FO21	Wastes (except wastewater and spent carbon from hydrogen chloride purification) from the production or manufacturing use (as a reactant, chemical intermediate, or component in a formulating process) of pentachlorophenol, or of intermediates used to produce its derivatives.	(H)
FO22	Wastes (except wastewater and spent carbon from hydrogen chloride purification) from the manufacturing use (as a reactant, chemical intermediate, or component in a formulating process) of tetra-, penta-, or hexachlorobenzenes under alkaline conditions.	(H)
FO23	Wastes (except wastewater and spent carbon from hydrogen chloride purification) from the production of materials on equipment previously used for the production or manufacturing use (as a reactant, chemical intermediate, or component in a formulating process) of tri- and tetrachlorophenols. (This listing does not include wastes from equipment used only for the production or use of Hexachlorophene from highly purified 2,4,5-trichlorophenol.).	(H)
FO26	Wastes (except wastewater and spent carbon from hydrogen chloride purification) from the production of materials on equipment previously used for the manufacturing use (as a reactant, chemical intermediate, or component in a formulating process) of tetra-, penta-, or hexachlorobenzene under alkaline conditions.	(H)
FO27	Discarded unused formulations containing tri-, tetra-, or pentachlorophenol or discarded unused formulations containing compounds derived from these chlorophenols. (This listing does not include formulations containing Hexachlorophene synthesized from prepurified 2,4,5-trichlorophenol as the sole component.).	(H)
FO28	Residues resulting from the incineration or thermal treatment of soil contaminated with EPA Hazardous Waste Nos. FO20, FO21, FO22, FO23, FO26, and FO27.	(T)

2. Hazardous wastes from specific sources (such as distillation ends from aniline production). Wastes are found in 40 CFR 261.32 and are referred to as the "K" list (Table 2-3).

3. Discarded commercial chemical products and all off-specification species, containers, and spill residues thereof that exhibit acute toxicity. These wastes are found at 40 CFR 261.33(e) and are designated the "P" wastes (see Tables 9-1, 9-2, 9-3).

4. Discarded commercial chemical products that are listed for reasons other than acute toxicity. These wastes are found at 40 CFR 261.33(f) and are designated the "U" wastes. See Tables 9-1, 9-2, 9-3 and additional discussion below.

As one can see from an examination of the four lists of hazardous wastes (F, K, P, and U), each waste on the list is given a separate and distinct EPA Hazardous Waste Number (e.g., F005, K001). In addition, each listed waste is given a hazard code. The hazard codes indicate the Administrator's basis for listing the classes or types of wastes that have been placed on these lists. Table 2-4 explains the codes for listing of wastes as hazardous.

An examination of the tables and hazard codes reveals that some wastes are listed for more than one reason. For example, wastes may exhibit a characteristic (I, R. C, EP), and be toxic (T) due to the presence of high concentrations of Appendix VIII constituent, or be acutely hazardous (H). See EPA hazardous waste numbers F005, F007, F020, K013, P065, and U169 as representative examples of variety of reasons for listing a waste as hazardous.

Commercial Chemical Products

A separate discussion of the commercial chemical products [(261.33(e) and (f)] P and U list wastes is provided because the conditions and activities that govern the listing and control of these materials as hazardous wastes are substantially different from those that are applied to other materials that are more commonly viewed as wastes.

The critical point to remember about these lists is the limitations to their use. In particular, only certain formulations[22] of the products listed in 261.33(e) and (f) are considered hazardous waste:

1. any commercial chemical product (CCP) or manufacturing chemical intermediate (MCI) having the generic name listed in 261.33(e) or (f);

2. any off-specification CCP or manufacturing chemical intermediate;

3. any container or inner liner removed from a container that has been used to hold any CCP or MCI including off-specification CCP unless the empty container meets certain conditions;[23]

4. any residue or contaminated soil, water, or other debris resulting from the cleanup of a spill into or on any land or water or a CCP of MCI including any off-specification CCP or MCI.[24]

Table 2-3

Industry and EPA hazardous waste No.	Hazardous waste	Hazard code
Wood preservation: K001	Bottom sediment sludge from the treatment of wastewaters from wood preserving processes that use creosote and/or pentachlorophenol.	(T)
Inorganic pigments:		
K002	Wastewater treatment sludge from the production of chrome yellow and orange pigments.	(T)
K003	Wastewater treatment sludge from the production of molybdate orange pigments	(T)
K004	Wastewater treatment sludge from the production of zinc yellow pigments	(T)
K005	Wastewater treatment sludge from the production of chrome green pigments	(T)
K006	Wastewater treatment sludge from the production of chrome oxide green pigments (anhydrous and hydrated).	(T)
K007	Wastewater treatment sludge from the production of iron blue pigments	(T)
K008	Oven residue from the production of chrome oxide green pigments...........................	(T)
Organic chemicals:		
K009	Distillation bottoms from the production of acetaldehyde from ethylene	(T)
K010	Distillation side cuts from the production of acetaldehyde from ethylene	(T)
K011	Bottom stream from the wastewater stripper in the production of acrylonitrile...........	(R, T)
K013	Bottom stream from the acetonitrile column in the production of acrylonitrile	(R, T)
K014	Bottoms from the acetonitrile purification column in the production of acrylonitrile	(T)
K015	Still bottoms from the distillation of benzyl chloride	(T)
K016	Heavy ends or distillation residues from the production of carbon tetrachloride	(T)
K017	Heavy ends (still bottoms) from the purification column in the production of epichlorohydrin.	(T)
K018	Heavy ends from the fractionation column in ethyl chloride production...................	(T)
K019	Heavy ends from the distillation of ethylene dichloride in ethylene dichloride production.	(T)
K020	Heavy ends from the distillation of vinyl chloride in vinyl chloride monomer production.	(T)
K021	Aqueous spent antimony catalyst waste from fluoromethanes production	(T)
K022	Distillation bottom tars from the production of phenol/acetone from cumene	(T)
K023	Distillation light ends from the production of phthalic anhydride from naphthalene ...	(T)
K024	Distillation bottoms from the production of phthalic anhydride from naphthalene	(T)
K093	Distillation light ends from the production of phthalic anhydride from ortho-xylene ...	(T)
K094	Distillation bottoms from the production of phthalic anhydride from ortho-xylene	(T)
K025	Distillation bottoms from the production of nitrobenzene by the nitration of benzene...	(T)
K026	Stripping still tails from the production of methy ethyl pyridines	(T)
K027	Centrifuge and distillation residues from toluene diisocyanate production	(R, T)
K028	Spent catalyst from the hydrochlorinator reactor in the production of 1,1,1-trichloroethane.	(T)
K029	Waste from the product steam stripper in the production of 1,1,1-trichloroethane ...	(T)
K095	Distillation bottoms from the production of 1,1,1-trichloroethane	(T)
K096	Heavy ends from the heavy ends column from the production of 1,1,1-trichloroethane.	(T)
K030	Column bottoms or heavy ends from the combined production of trichloroethylene and perchloroethylene.	(T)
K083	Distillation bottoms from aniline production	(T)
K103	Process residues from aniline extraction from the production of aniline..................	(T)
K104	Combined wastewater streams generated from nitrobenzene/aniline production	(T)
K085	Distillation or fractionation column bottoms from the production of chlorobenzenes......	(T)
K105	Separated aqueous stream from the reactor product washing step in the production of chlorobenzenes.	(T)
Inorganic chemicals:		
K071	Brine purification muds from the mercury cell process in chlorine production, where separately prepurified brine is not used.	(T)
K073	Chlorinated hydrocarbon waste from the purification step of the diaphragm cell process using graphite anodes in chlorine production.	(T)
K106	Wastewater treatment sludge from the mercury cell process in chlorine production......	(T)
Pesticides:		
K031	By-product salts generated in the production of MSMA and cacodylic acid	(T)
K032	Wastewater treatment sludge from the production of chlordane............................	(T)
K033	Wastewater and scrub water from the chlorination of cyclopentadiene in the production of chlordane.	(T)
K034	Filter solids from the filtration of hexachlorocyclopentadiene in the production of chlordane.	(T)
K097	Vacuum stripper discharge from the chlordane chlorinator in the production of chlordane.	(T)
K035	Wastewater treatment sludges generated in the production of creosote..................	(T)
K036	Still bottoms from toluene reclamation distillation in the production of disulfoton...........	(T)
K037	Wastewater treatment sludges from the production of disulfoton..........................	(T)
K038	Wastewater from the washing and stripping of phorate production........................	(T)

Continued

33

Table 2-3   Continued

Industry and EPA hazardous waste No.	Hazardous waste	Hazard code
K039	Filter cake from the filtration of diethylphosphorodithioic acid in the production of phorate.	(T)
K040	Wastewater treatment sludge from the production of phorate	(T)
K041	Wastewater treatment sludge from the production of toxaphene	(T)
K098	Untreated process wastewater from the production of toxaphene	(T)

Table 2-4   Codes For Listed Hazardous Wastes

Code	Explanation
I	Exhibits ignitability characteristics.
C	Exhibits corrosivity characteristics.
R	Exhibits reactivity characteristics.
EP	Exhibits EP toxicity characteristics. This indicates that the wastes leach certain metals and/or pesticides above a given concentration when subjected to a standard extraction procedure (EP) protocol. Frequently, these wastes are referred to as "toxic" hazardous wastes. However, these wastes are properly termed EP toxic wastes to indicate that they fail the extraction procedure characteristic text.
T	Denotes toxic wastes; namely those that contain one or more of the constituents on the Appendix VIII list and are present in such form and/or concentration that EPA listed it on that basis. Primarily F, K, and U wastes.
H	Denotes that the waste is listed due to the fact that the listed material itself possesses such acute toxicity that it is a hazardous waste. Primarily P wastes.

These limitations pose numerous problems. First, the terms "commercial chemical products" or "manufacturing chemical intermediate" refer only to a chemical substance that is manufactured or formulated for commercial or manufacturing use and which consists of the commercially pure grades of the chemical, all technical grades of the chemical, and all formulations of the chemical in which the listed P or U chemical is the *sole active ingredient*. As such, formulations and products that contain one listed pesticide when discarded or managed in any manner that constitutes hazardous waste management would be subject to regulation as a hazardous waste. Ironically, however, should that same formulation contain a second active ingredient it would *not* be considered a hazardous waste. (Technical-grade materials frequently consist of several active ingredients.) The Agency has recently proposed to redress this deficiency for commercial chemical products containing acutely hazardous constituents (261.33(e)). The Agency has also stated an intention to propose similar revisions for mixtures of non-acutely hazardous commercial chemical products (261.33(f)).[25]

Second, this provision and these lists usually take effect only when a company is discarding old inventory or an off-spec species, when they are burned or used to produce fuels in lieu of their intended use, or when they are applied to land or contained in products applied to land in lieu of their intended use. As such, these lists do not apply to materials such as a manufacturing process waste that contains any of the substances on the P or U lists, nor to a sludge produced from the use of a product on the P or U lists (such as byproduct produced from the use of pentachlorophenol "U 242").[26] Where a manufacturing process waste is deemed to be a hazardous waste because it contains a substance on P and U lists, such waste will be listed in either the 261.31 or 261.32 lists.

However, readers should note that EPA has begun regulatory action to make substantial additions to these lists. Based on a petition from the State of Michigan, EPA recently proposed to add 109 other commercial chemical products to these lists.[27]

An additional consideration must be kept in mind when dealing with chemicals on the 261.33(e) and (f) lists. Spills of these chemicals, or leaks from a product storage tank, may constitute illegal disposal under RCRA because the spillage and leakage of these products in pure or off-specification form is considered "discarding," unless the spill material is "recycled" in accordance with applicable regulations (e.g., where spilled solvent is re-inserted into a solvent reclamation tank, such activity is not considered disposal). When such spills or leaks occur, the volume-discard will usually determine whether the activity constitutes illegal disposal (the volume or quality of waste necessary to trigger such a finding may be very small, particularly when the waste is highly toxic). Spills or products of the 261.33(e) list are regulated to very small levels (2.2 lbs.) because the waste is designated acutely hazardous. Spills of the 261.33(f) products will be regulated as "other wastes" subject to the small quantity generator exemption[28] (see Chapter 4).

Similarly, those firms that are not ordinarily covered by RCRA due to their management of products rather than wastes, must nevertheless comply with RCRA requirements in the event of a leak of the materials. Such firms must then obtain an EPA ID number and comply with generator standards.

Recent and Future Waste Listings

There were very few new wastes listed by the Agency from 1981 to 1984. However, during 1985 and 1986, several new listings have been finalized including:[29] chloro-dioxins, -dibenzofurans, -phenols (1-14-85); Cl-C6 chlorinated aliphatics (2-10-84); EDB (2-13-86); small generator wastes (3-24-86); certain solvent mixtures and still bottoms (12-31-85); TDI, DNT, TDA wastes (10-23-85); 1,1,2-trichloroethane, benzene, 2-ethoxyethanol, 2-nitro propane (2-15-86). New *proposed* listings include: 174 commercial chemical products (5-15-84); acutely hazardous product mixtures (2-13-86); UDMH (12-20-84); dimethoate (10-30-83); diphenylamine (2-25-86); carbamate pesticide wastes (12-20-84); hexavalent chrome (10-30-80); lead alkyl production wastes (3-4-86); methylbromide (4-25-85); organobromides (11-8-84); certain mining wastes (10-2-85); waste oil (11-29-85).

For the following wastes and waste categories, the Agency had until February 1986 to decide whether or not to list them as hazardous per Section 222 of HSWA: chlorinated aliphatics, dioxin, dimethyl hydrazine, toluene diisocyanate (TDI), carbamates, bromacil, linuron, organo-bromines, solvents, refining wastes, chlorinated aromatics, dyes and pigments, inorganic chemical industry wastes, lithium batteries, coke byproducts, paint production wastes, and coal slurry pipeline effluent.

In addition to this process-specific listing activity, which lists wastes from one production process at at time, the Agency is currently examining ways in which to utilize the new generic listing authority established under HSWA RCRA 3001(b)(l): listing wastes as hazardous based upon the concentration of specific constituents irrespective of the process from which the wastes are generated. Many pesticides remain outside RCRA control due to the absence of a process-specific listing and the inapplicability of the current waste characteristics to most organics. A similar level of activity to revise the delisting process and to develop additional characteristic tests to identify, rather than list, new groups of hazardous wastes is also underway. The advantage of a constituent concentration-based listing or a characteristic test is that it simultaneously controls numerous wastes under RCRA without imposing the burden of separately listing new wastes or processes one at a time.

Waste Oils

The 1984 Amendments add a new section 3014(b) to RCRA that requires the Administrator to propose whether to list or identify used automobile and truck crankcase oil as hazardous under 3001 by November 1985, and to finalize a determination whether to list all used oils by November 1986. In addition to the listing decision, the Agency must issue standards governing the reuse and recycling of used oils that are either listed or identified as hazardous waste in a manner which "assures that facilities which recycle used oil will need to comply fully with the standards applicable to owners and operators of any hazardous waste TSDF."[30] The Agency recently *proposed* to list used oil as a hazardous waste and simultaneously proposed management standards for facilities that recycle, treat, store, or dispose of used oil.[31] The proposed management standards for facilities that recycle used oil are discussed in Chapter 3. The proposed listing of used oil as a hazardous waste applies to used oil when disposed of, recycled in any manner, or when accumulated, stored, or treated prior to being disposed or recycled. The proposed definition of used oil includes, but is not limited to, all of the following petroleum-derived or synthetic oils which are contaminated through use or subsequent management: lubricants (engine, turbine, or gear); hydraulic fluids (including cutting, grinding, machining, rolling, stamping, quenching, and coating oils); or insulating fluid or coolants. In addition, used oil derived from the pyrolysis of scrap tires would also be covered by the used oil listing after use and contamination. Used oils containing any concentration of PCBs and the disposal of used oils containing 50 ppm or greater of PCBs are subject to control under the Toxic Substances Control Act (TSCA) (40 CFR 761). Waste oils would have the hazardous waste number of F030.

Petroleum wastes that *would not* be RCRA listed "used oils" include: crude oil or virgin fuel oil spilled on the land or water; oily sludge in the bottom of crude or fuel oil storage tanks; and wastes from petroleum refining operations such as API separator sludge. The Agency has also proposed to conditionally exclude from the used oil listing, used oil that has been re-refined into lubricant. "De minimus" quantities of used oil mixed with wastewater, and rags that are incidentally contaminated with used oil would also be exempt. The delisting procedures for used oil would be the same as those that apply to any other hazardous waste. The Agency recently solicited additional comment on the proposed used oil listing to examine alternatives to listing.[32]

The Agency has also issued a final rule that establishes a specification, or hazardous constituent limit, for waste materials or mixtures that are burned as fuels. The limits are used to distinguish between those blends or shipments that are used oil fuels (UOF), which can be burned in all types of combustion devices, and those that are off-spec used oil fuel (OUOF) or are hazardous waste fuels (HWF) by virtue of exceeding the limits or due to the fact that used oils were mixed with hazardous wastes, which may be burned only in industrial boilers, furnaces, and incinerators. The scope of proposed regulatory controls on used oils recycling; and the final controls on used oils and hazardous wastes that are burned for energy recovery are discussed in Chapter 3.[33] Due to the complexity of determining which used oil and/or hazardous waste mixtures are RCRA hazardous wastes, a separate discusssion is provided below.

Hazardous Waste in Containers

Under circumstances where specified amounts of waste remain in a container, the container itself may become a hazardous waste.[34] See Chapter 8 for detailed discussion.

"Special" Wastes, Mining Wastes

A number of other wastes are in a state of regulatory limbo, due to interim statutory exclusions. Their regulatory status awaits the outcome of statutorily directed studies to determine whether wastes from the "extraction and beneficiation" of certain ores should be listed as hazardous. These wastes are frequently termed "special wastes." The results of the recently concluded and long overdue special studies of wastes governed by the interim statutory mining waste exclusion are discussed in Chapter 3.

Aside from the special studies, which re-examine interim statutory exclusions for certain "extraction and benefication" mining wastes, the Agency recently proposed to restore the listings of several wastes (Table 2-5) from the processing and smelting of certain ores.

This proposed listing amounts to a re-interpretation or limiting of the scope of the interim statutory exclusion for mining wastes generally. The proposed re-interpretation removes "ore processing and smelting wastes" from the category of "extraction and beneficiation" mining wastes that remain exempt until the special waste studies are completed and a separate determination made whether to list them as hazardous.[35]

Table 2-5   Smelter Wastes Proposed for Relisting

Industry	EPA hazardous waste No.	Hazardous waste	Hazard code
Primary copper	K064	Acid plant blowdown slurry/sludge resulting from the thickening of blowdown slurry from primary copper production.	(T)
Primary lead	K065	Surface impoundment solids contained in and dredged from surface impoundments at primary lead smelting facilities.	(T)
Primary zinc	K066	Sludge from treatment of process wastewater and/or acid plant blowdown from primary zinc production.	(T)
Primary aluminum	K088	Spent potliners from primary aluminum reduction.	(T)
Ferroalloys	K090	Emission control dust or sludge from ferro-chromium-silicon production.	(T)
	K091	Emission control dust or sludge from ferro-chromium production.	(T)

CHARACTERISTIC HAZARDOUS WASTES

Criteria for Identifying the Characteristics of a Hazardous Waste

Once it is determined that a waste is not a listed hazardous waste, the generator must then determine if the waste exhibits a *characteristic* that makes it hazardous. This broad class of hazardous waste, called "characteristic" or "identified" wastes, is based on the same statutory criteria discussed above and are distinguished from listed hazardous wastes by two additional criteria, such that the characteristic can be:[36]

1. measured by an available standardized test method that is reasonably within the capability of generators of solid waste or private sector laboratories that are available to serve generators of solid waste; or

2. reasonably determined by generators of solid waste through their knowledge of their waste.

EPA has developed four characteristics of hazardous waste: ignitability, corrosivity, reactivity, and toxicity. Exceeding the limits of one of these tests for a hazardous waste characteristic means the waste is hazardous, or in the case of a petition for delisting, means the waste would remain hazardous.

The generator should be aware of several practical differences between waste listings and waste characteristics. The listing of a waste is directed at specific types of wastes and/or waste generation or production processes. Characteristic tests, however, are applied to each individual batch of generated waste material. Thus, several wastes generated by a given industrial process may be "listed" as a group (e.g., see F005 listed wastes). If such solid wastes are not listed, however, then each waste from that process must be tested, or otherwise evaluated, to determine if any waste(s) exhibit one of the four hazardous characteristics (discussed below).

In addition, a listed waste is hazardous regardless of the concentration of hazardous constituents in each batch. (The concentration of constituents in each batch may be relevant, however, in determining whether a waste continues to exhibit a characteristic.) Listed wastes are designated as hazardous through a general evaluation conducted by the generator or TSDF to determine whether the waste or production process meets the description contained in 40 CFR Parts 261.31, 261.32, and 261.33 (e), (f). Listed wastes remain hazardous until they are "delisted" through a separate administrative proceeding. In contrast, characteristic wastes are identified as hazardous on the basis of performance tests to uniformly detect the presence of specific characteristic among representative samples of a waste material, and remain hazardous as long as the waste continues to exhibit the hazardous characteristic(s).

Moreover, as discussed below, a characteristic waste can be rendered non-hazardous through removal of the characteristic, which may entail mixing with non-hazardous wastes to render the mixture as a whole non-hazardous. Mixing or dilution, however, cannot automatically eliminate or "dilute out" a listing.

As a practical matter, the Agency believes that the criteria for developing characteristic tests, or standardized testing protocols reasonably within the capabilities of the regulated community, have made it difficult to develop characteristics for wastes that may be infectious, carcinogenic, teratogenic, mutagenic, or the like. At the time of the 1980 regulations, EPA did not believe that reliable testing protocols for these characteristics were generally available. However, many states have gone beyond this limited program and developed their own characteristic test.

Characteristics of Hazardous Wastes

A waste that is not listed may nevertheless be a hazardous waste if it exhibits any one of the following four characteristics of a hazardous waste:

1. *Ignitability.* This characteristic identifies solid wastes that are capable of causing a fire or exacerbating a fire once it has started during routine handling of material.[37] For *liquids,* it is defined as an aqueous solution containing less than 24% alcohol by volume, with a flash point of less than 60°C (140°F). Ignitable *nonliquids* are those which under normal conditions can cause fire through friction, absorption of moisture, or spontaneous chemical changes, and can burn so vigorously when ignited that it creates a hazard. Ignitable *compressed gas* and *oxidizing compounds* are defined by the Department of Transportation (DOT) regulations.[38]

2. *Corrosivity.* This characteristic reflects concerns about wastes with either high or low pH that could corrode metal containers and in turn cause acute injury through burns or dangerous reactions with other wastes. A solid waste exhibits corrosivity if a representative sample of the waste has *either* of the following properties: it is aqueous and has a pH less than or equal to 2, or greater than or equal to 12.5; *or* it is a liquid and corrodes steel at a rate greater than 6.35 mm (0.250 inches) per year at a test temperature of 55°C (130°F). As with ignitability, the regulations specify the test methods to be used and allow demonstrations for equivalent methods.[39]

3. *Reactivity.* Tests for reactivity are aimed at identifying wastes that are unstable and may react violently or explode during stages of its management. Since no uniform test for all states of reactivity currently exists, the Agency has developed a list of reactions and waste conditions that are deemed to exhibit reactivity. A solid waste exhibits reactivity if a representative sample of the waste has any of the following properties:[40] normally unstable and readily undergoes violent change without detonation; reacts violently with water; forms potentially explosive mixtures with water; generates toxic gases or vapors in a sufficient quantity to pose a danger when mixed with water; is a

cyanide- or sulfide-bearing waste which, when exposed to pH conditions between 2 and 12.5, can generate toxic gases, vapors, or fumes in a quantity sufficient to present a danger to human health or environment; is capable of detonation or explosive reaction if it is subjected to a strong initiating source or if heated under confinement; is a forbidden explosive as defined by DOT regulations, or is a Class A explosive, or a Class B explosive as defined in DOT regulations.[41]

The Agency has also issued an interim guidance to test wastes for toxic gas generation reactivity, particularly those wastes that release hydrogen cyanide (HCN) or hydrogen sulfide (H₂S) when reacted with other wastes. The guidance states that wastes containing more than 250 milligrams total available HCN or 500 milligrams of total available H₂S per killogram of waste shoudl be regulated as a hazardous waste.[42]

4. *Toxicity (EP Toxic).* While the term toxicity connotes a general sense of danger or potential harm, in this context it has a very specific meaning. This characteristic measures the potential of a waste to leach toxic constituents into groundwater when land disposed, assuming specified mismanagement of co-disposal in a municipal landfill.[43] A chemical procedure designed to measure the leaching potential is part of the regulation and is called the extraction procedure (EP Toxicity Test).

The current EP test involves exposing and agitating a sample of waste material under acid conditions (to simulate potential co-disposal in a municipal landfill), and analyzing the extract to determine whether it contains (has leached) significant concentrations of substance for which EPA has issued primary drinking water standards[44] under the Safe Drinking Water Act at levels at least 100 times greater than the concentration allowed under the drinking water standards. The EP toxicity testing protocol is contained in 40 CFR Part 261, Appendix II.[45]

Table 2-6 lists the 3 waste characteristics (ignitability, corrosivity, and reactivity), 14 compounds that are detected by the current EP test (8 metals and 6 pesticides), and the maximum acceptable concentration of constituents in the leachate if the material is to pass the EP test (and not considered to be a hazardous waste). Any concentrations in excess of those specified in Table 2-6 means that the waste is EP toxic, and therefore a hazardous waste. These are termed the D wastes, as are those wastes that exhibit the characteristics of ignitability, corrosivity, and reactivity. These wastes carry EPA Hazardous Waste Numbers as identified in Table 2-6.

Problems with Existing Characteristic Tests

The characteristic tests serve a critical function in the hazardous waste designation process. They supplement a listing process which is cumbersome and slow, requiring EPA to first gather data on a multitude of man-

Table 2-6

EPA hazardous waste number	Characteristic/Contaminant	Maximum concentration (milligrams per liter)
D001	Ignitability	
D002	Corrosivity	
D003	Reactivity	
D004	Arsenic	5.0
D005	Barium..	100.0
D006	Cadmium.......................................	1.0
D007	Chromium......................................	5.0
D008	Lead..	5.0
D009	Mercury	0.2
D010	Selenium......................................	1.0
D011	Silver..	5.0
D012	Endrin (1,2,3,4,10,10-hexachloro-1,7-epoxy-1,4,4a,5,6,7,8,8a-octahydro-1,4-endo, endo-5,8-dimethanonaphthalene.	0.02
D013	Lindane (1,2,3,4,5,6-hexa chlorocyclohexane, gamma isomer.	0.4
D014	Methoxychlor (1,1,1-Trichloro-2,2-bis [p-methoxyphenyl]ethane).	10.0
D015	Toxaphene ($C_{10}H_{10}Cl_6$ Technical chlorinated camphene, 67–69 percent chlorine).	0.5
D016	2,4-D, (2,4-Dichlorophenoxyacetic acid).	10.0
D017	2,4,5-TP Silvex (2,4,5-Trichlorophenoxypropionic acid).	1.0

ufacturing processes and then complete a separate rulemaking to justify each new waste listing. Considering the complexity of our industrial economy and the continuing development of new industrial processes, EPA's task of listing hazardous wastes is an uphill climb at best. To the extent that characteristics are developed for a wide range of toxicity concerns, inevitable inadequacies in the lists would be ameliorated by this alternative designation method.

The principal shortcoming in the current characteristics is that the EP toxicity characteristic is the only toxicity characteristic, and its use is extremely limited. The EP is concerned with the leaching potential of only 14 constituents, as compared to the approximately 375 constituents in Appendix VIII that can cause a waste to be listed. At one point, EPA had planned additional characteristics for organic toxicity, carcinogenicity, mutagenicity, teratogenicity, bioaccumlation potential, and phytotoxicity, but they were never developed because EPA claimed it could not develop adequate testing protocols. A number of states, however, have characteristics based on concentration of certain constituents in the waste, carcinogenicity, acute toxicity, and persistence and bioaccumulation.

In addition, even for the 14 chemicals within the scope of the EP, the test has technical problems which grossly impair its effectiveness for some wastes (e.g., oily wastes), and have drawn criticism for an overall weakness in measuring leaching potential.

For these reasons, HSWA includes several provisions aimed at strengthening the characteristic side of the designation. First, by March 8, 1987, EPA is required to improve the EP characteristic so that it more accurately reflects the leaching potential of wastes. Second, EPA is directed to develop new characteristics, particularly for toxicity, by November 8, 1986. Finally, the Agency is required to identify or list wastes which would be considered hazardous solely because the wastes contain constituents at levels in excess of levels which endanger human health. In effect, this latter approach (sometimes referred to as generic listing) combines positive features from both the listing and identification process; particularly, the designation of hazardous due to the presence of certain constituents without the need to ascertain each industrial process or subprocess generating the waste. The statute does not establish a deadline for completion of the generic listing task.

At first it may appear that this new authority to develop an additional waste characteristic (3001(g),(h)) duplicates the other new authority under 3001(b), which directs the EPA to generically list or identify new wastes based solely on the presence in such wastes of certain constituents such as carcinogens, at levels in excess of levels that endanger human health (discussed above). Both reflect concerns regarding different inadequacies of the EP toxicity characteristic.

In the case of the new concentration-based listing authority (3001(b)), the concern is that the existing extraction procedure, which determines whether a waste exhibits the characteristic of toxicity, is primarily designed to determine the leaching potential of metals from a given waste material and in turn fails to detect the presence of any organic compounds other than a relatively few pesticides. In addition, the new authority of 3001(g) and (h) reflects concerns that even for the metal-bearing wastes, the current extraction procedure is inadequate to detect the presence of metals in a manner that is consistent with protection of human health and the environment, particularly when the metals are contained in an oily waste.[46]

In response to HSWA's mandate under RCRA 3001(g) and (h), EPA has proposed to replace the EP toxicity characteristic with a characteristic test known as the organic toxicity characteristic (OTC). The OTC will be used to identify those wastes with a potential to leach organic constituents into groundwater. The characteristic entails the use of a new extraction procedure (the toxic constituent leach procedure—TCLP), and the establishment of protective levels of constituents in the extraction leachate for 38 additional organic constituents.[47] The levels have been established based upon: a variety of chronic and acute health, environmental, and subsurface transport factors; and the potential of solvents to mobilize other constituents. [48]

Due to the inability of the TCLP to detect metals, the current extraction procedure (EP) and levels for the 8 EP toxicity characteristic metals are maintained until further refinements are made to the TCLP used in the OTC. With minor modifications, the Agency has also proposed to use the OTC modeling process and the TCLP extraction procedure for purposes of making determinations on the prohibition of wastes from land disposal. This latter process and its related problems for this purpose are discussed in Chapter 9.

In addition to the new OTC, the Agency will soon propose to revise the existing EP toxicity characteristic for metals that will likely result in uniform reductions of the regulatory levels of the 8 EP toxicity characteristic metals (currently 100 times drinking water standards, Table 2-6) and the addition of nickel and thallium to the EP. Revisions to other characteristic tests include improvements to detect: the presence of metals in oily waste samples, the ignitability of solid hazardous wastes, and tests for certain properties of reactivity.

WASTE MIXTURES AND WASTES "DERIVED FROM" OTHER WASTES

At many manufacturing locations, hazardous waste is often mixed with non-hazardous waste before it is managed. The question then arises as to the regulatory status of the treatment, storage, or disposal units receiving such mixtures and the status of mixtures themselves. The answer lies in EPA's mixture rule.

The "mixture rule" states that the entire volume of mixed waste that includes any listed hazardous waste (including a waste derived from listed hazardous waste) is regulated as a hazardous waste, regardless of the concentration of the listed waste in the mixture, *unless* the mixture falls within the following exemptions:[49]

1. The listed hazardous waste in the mixture was listed *solely* because it exhibits a hazardous waste characteristic (e.g., ignitability, corrosivity; also see hazard codes in Tables 2-2, 2-3, and 2-4) *and* the mixture no longer exhibits that characteristic; or
2. If the generator can demonstrate that the mixture consists of wastewater, the discharge of which is subject to regulation under either Section 402 or Section 307(b) of the Clean Water Act (including wastewater at facilities which have eliminated the discharge of wastewater), *and* the hazardous waste mixed with the wastewater is one of the following:

   • carcinogenic spent solvents listed in 40 CFR 261.31, provided that the concentration of the solvents in the flow to the waste-

water treatment system (as calculated by the specified equation) does not exceed 1 ppm;
- non-carcinogenic spent solvents listed in 40 CFR 261.31, provided that concentration of the solvents in the flow to the wastewater treatment system (as calcuated by the specified equation) does not exceed 25 ppm;
- discarded commercial chemical products listed in 40 CFR 261.33 arising from de minimis losses in manufacturing operations;
- wastewater resulting from laboratory operations involving listed toxic wastes in small amounts. Specific concentration limits on such discharges are placed on this exemption in accordance with a specific equation.[50]

These exemptions from the mixture rule have been provided for minor spills, leaks, and cleanup residues that result from *manufacturing* processes without which a firm's entire wastewater treatment system would be subject to RCRA control.

One of the most important features of this rule is that mixtures of a characteristic hazardous waste and a non-hazardous waste are regulated differently than a mixture of a listed waste and a non-hazardous waste. Aside from these narrow exemptions, the mixture rule is structured to prevent "dilution from being the solution to pollution." While this principle holds for most listed waste mixtures, wastes that are hazardous solely by virtue of exhibiting one of the four characteristics (or listed wastes that were listed solely because they exhibited a characteristic), may be removed from hazardous waste regulation by mixing the wastes with other wastes or materials or by treatment. In other words, a characteristic waste mixture remains hazardous until it no longer exhibits any of the four hazardous waste characteristics. Therefore, characteristic waste may be diluted to avoid a hazardous designation. A number of states and the OTC proposal, however, prohibit dilution for the purpose of altering a waste's designation.

A listed waste first becomes a hazardous waste when the waste meets the listing description. A mixture of listed waste and solid waste becomes hazardous when one or more listed wastes are *first* added to the solid waste. Characteristic waste (including a waste mixture) becomes hazardous when the waste exhibits any of the characteristics.

The general principle of "once a listed waste always a hazardous waste" also extends to treatment and processing residues "derived from" listed wastes, unless it has been specifically exempted or delisted.[51] Delisting and "derived from" rules are discussed below.

There are two conspicuous and indeed questionable anomalies to the general policy and requirements of the mixture rule. Mixtures of two or more commercial chemical products as well as mixtures of two or more listed solvents are also currently exempt from hazardous waste control, even though commercial chemical products with a sole active ingredient or single solvent formulations are covered. These exemptions have been recognized as being ill-advised. The Agency has redressed the solvent mixture loophole, and has proposed modifications to the policy and content of the commercial chemical products list. The Agency has also proposed to designate acute hazardous discarded commercial chemical products with multiple active ingredients as hazardous waste by establishing low acceptable concentration levels of hazardous ingredients.[52] (See discussion below under "derived from" rule.)

Mixtures of Hazardous and Radioactive Wastes

Due to the statutory exclusion of these wastes from the definition of solid waste, these waste mixtures will be discussed in Chapter 3.

Mixtures of Hazardous Waste and Used Oils

The final waste fuel specification establishes a rebuttable presumption that used oil containing more than *1000 ppm* total halogen is deemed to have been mixed with hazardous wastes and as such the mixture is a hazardous waste via the mixture rule. Once such mixtures are burned for energy recovery, they are deemed a hazardous waste fuel (HWF) and subject to the full spectrum of RCRA controls 262 through 265. The Agency states that the rebuttal process places the burden on the used oil burner or blender to show that the halogens present are a result of incidental contamination through use of the oil rather than from mixing with hazardous constituents. The Agency will not presume the mixing has occurred unless "significant concentrations" of Appendix VIII constituents are found in the used oil, generally defined as those above 1000 ppm.[53]

One of the most frequently asked questions regarding this presumptive indicator of adulteration is its relationship to the used oil fuel spec, which established a *4000 ppm total* halogen level (Chapter 3), and the policy governing mixtures of used oils and characteristic wastes (policy explained below). The 4000 ppm level is established to guard against the hazards of burning chlorinated wastes, while the 1000 ppm presumption is used as a presumptive indicator of mixing. It is clear that the 1000 ppm rebuttable presumption takes precedence over the 4000 ppm fuel spec. That is, even a mixture of used oil and hazardous waste that is within a 1000/4000 ppm range of halogen is deemed to be a hazardous waste unless the presumption is rebutted. In the event that the mixture contained in excess of 4000 ppm total halogen and a generator was successful in rebutting the presumption, then the material could only be burned in industrial boilers and furnaces if it was diluted or treated to meet the spec level of 4000 ppm. Also note that dilution of used oils containing various metals and organics listed in the spec can be achieved through dilution, *except for* those situations where the mixture exceeds 1000 ppm total halogen and the generator was unsuccessful or did not attempt to rebut the presumption. Thus, the first and foremost rule is that any mixture of used oil and hazardous waste or any solid waste that is burned for energy recovery and which exceeds the 1000 ppm total halogen level is regulated as a hazardous waste fuel *unless and until* the presumption is affirmatively rebutted.

Under the proposed used oil listing (see note 31) mixtures of characteristic wastes and used oil (which would now be a listed hazardous waste rather than merely a solid waste) are deemed to be hazardous wastes even if the resulting mixture does not exhibit a waste characteristic. However, if the characteristic wastes and used oil are blended or combined through a production process rather than through blending or mixing, the mixture is *not* a hazardous waste, even if the resulting mixture does exhibit a hazardous waste characteristic. Unlike the use of the 1000 ppm total halogen level as a presumptive indicator of adulteration, there is no analogous presumptive indicator or criteria to distinguish between inadvertment and deliberate blending for characteristic wastes. Nevertheless, the 1000 ppm total halogen level would override this rather perverse characteristic waste mixture policy.

The Agency has proposed to amend the mixture rule to provide that a mixture of non-hazardous wastewaters and used oil caused by a "de minimus" loss of lubricating oil, hydraulic oil, or metal-working fluid due to spills or dripping would not be subject to regulation as a used oil.[54] Under the proposed rule all other mixtures of hazardous waste and used oil, irrespective of generator size, would be regulated as hazardous wastes. Household used oil is not a hazardous waste until it is aggregated at collection centers. The Agency has proposed to exempt all "industrial wipers" that are contaminated with used oil provided that the oily rag does not exhibit the characteristic of hazardous waste.

The used oil listing proposes to regulate under RCRA mixtures of used oil that contain PCBs. The Agency states that in situations where both RCRA and TSCA regulations would apply, the Agency would use the more stringent set of requirements. It is not clear whether this proposal, if finalized, would require the permitting of existing PCB storage facilities under RCRA. However, the Agency expresses some skepticism regarding the need for this level of control given existing regulations under TSCA.

Since used oil would be a listed hazardous waste, any mixtures of used oil and virgin material would generally be hazardous wastes. However, where the used oil did not exceed the 1000 ppm total halogen and was intended to be burned for energy recovery, virgin oil could be added to bring the mixture within the other parameters of the used oil fuel spec. Such mixtures must still be regulated as a solid waste, but not a hazardous waste. It could be burned in non-industrial boilers. The policy governing the addition of virgin oil to used oil that contains characteristic wastes would depend largely on whether the characteristic wastes occur via manufacturer or via blending. It does not appear that the addition of virgin oil can change the status of characteristic waste mixtures.

Wastes Derived From Other Wastes

Related to the mixture rule, the Agency's "derived from" rule states·that any solid waste generated from the treatment, storage, or disposal of a hazardous waste, including any sludge, spill residue, ash, emission control dust, or leachate (not including precipitation run-off) is a hazardous waste *unless:*[55]

1. It is specifically excluded by a separate regulatory action (certain pickle liquors sludge is the only waste so excluded at present) and does not exhibit a hazardous waste characteristic;[56]
2. The solid waste is not a listed waste nor derived from a listed waste and does not exhibit any of the four characteristics;[57] or
3. It is a listed waste, contains a listed waste, or is derived from a listed waste, *and* it has been specifically excluded through a separate regulatory action[58] (i.e., delisted).

Thus, in the case of treatment residues generated from the treatment of a listed waste, all of the residues remain hazardous unless specifically delisted. In effect, the burden of proof is on the manager of the waste to prove that his waste is no longer hazardous through the delisting mechanism, or the treatment residues must be managed as hazardous waste.

While the burden is appropriately placed, the "derived from" rule poses significant impediments to the treatment of listed hazardous wastes. For example, proper incineration of acutely hazardous waste results in the destruction and removal of more than 99.9999% of the original waste material. However, due to the fact that small amounts of uncombusted waste material remain after incineration (1/1,000,000 of original waste volume); and due to the operation of the "derived from" rule (*any* residuals remain acutely hazardous as do any subsequent mixtures of these residues and other wastes or materials), *all* the residues containing these exceedingly minute amounts of uncombusted waste from such treatment are classified as acutely hazardous wastes. This may involve a larger volume of ash and scrubber residue than wastes which were originally incinerated. The rule was originally constructed in this mannter due to the lack of an organic toxicity characteristic. The Agency so acknowledged these deficiencies in the original regulations,[59] and recently proposed[60] a revision to this rule. It would require that the residues of certain treatment processes, which resulted in virtually complete destruction of such wastes, be managed as regular hazardous wastes, rather than acutely hazardous wastes, by establishing acceptable concentration levels of acute constituents. A separate delisting would be required in order to establish that treatment had rendered the waste non-hazardous. This rulemaking is significant because it would prevent "over regulation" of wastes that had been properly treated, and allow the residuals to be managed. Currently, there are appropriate prohibitions on the land disposal of certain acutely hazardous wastes (e.g., dioxins). In addition, most landfills will not accept acutely hazardous wastes for disposal. Thus, current regulations fail to distinguish between properly treated residues of acutely hazardous wastes and the acutely hazardous wastes themselves.

GENERAL RULEMAKING AND DELISTING PETITIONS

General Rulemaking Petitions

Generic authority is provided to all members of the regulated community and the public to seek modifications of the regulations to loosen or tighten regulatory controls. The mechanism provided is termed a rulemaking petition, which falls into one of three categories:

1. Any person may petition the Administrator to add, modify, or revoke any provision of the hazardous waste regulations (40 CFR 260.20).
2. Any person may seek to add a testing or analytical method to Part 261 (Identification and Listing of Hazardous Waste). To be successful the person must demonstrate that the proposed method is equal or superior to the corresponding method prescribed in Parts 261, 264, and 265 in terms of its sensitivity, accuracy, and precision (40 CFR 260.21).
3. Any person may seek to exclude a waste at a particular generating facility from the lists of hazardous wastes in Part 261. In general, to be successful the (delisting) petitioner must demonstrate that the waste produced by a particular facility does not meet any of the criteria under which the waste was listed as a hazardous waste. In addition, the 1984 Amendments require that the petitioner demonstrate that the waste would not be hazardous for other reasons and adds several procedural requirements to the delisting process. The delisting process will be discussed in detail below.

This petitioning authority is the most basic and frequently used vehicle for prompting action to either correct or address regulatory deficiencies of all kinds. Such petitions, however, are generally limited to regulatory provision and cannot be used to seek or limit enforcement actions, inspections, or monitoring.

Delisting Petitions

Prior to the enactment of HSWA, the delisting process was replete with procedural and substantive shortcomings. One of the principal shortcomings was that the petitioner's burden in a delisting process was merely to demonstrate that the waste did not meet any of the criteria for which it was listed. In the case of listed wastes, this consisted of demonstrating the waste did not contain the constituents listed in Appendix VII of 40 CFR Part 261, or the waste did not leach the constituents at concentrations of regulatory concern. Since Appendix VII represented an incomplete list of constituents of concern, EPA was delisting wastes which may be toxic because of the presence of other Appendix VIII constituents. In addition, petitioners and EPA were relying heavily on the EP to demonstrate the waste's leaching potential. For many wastes (e.g., oily wastes), the EP was inadequate; in other cases, results were suspect because of technical flaws in the procedure. Moreover, the EP was designed to mimic leaching from co-disposal in a municipal landfill; the results did not necessarily reflect the consequences of other disposal situations proposed by the petitioner (i.e., disposal in an impoundment or on-site monofill), or impacts on air and surface water resulting from any type of mismanagement.

Finally, the delisting process was not subject to public review. Although the delisting petitions were theoretically considered petitions for rulemaking and thus subject to notice in the *Federal Register* and public comment, EPA extensively granted "temporary exclusions" without an opportunity for public review. These temporary exclusions generally could remain in effect indefinitely. As of January 1985, 142 temporary exclusions had been granted, but only 3 final delistings had been issued after public notice and an opportunity for comment. From the standpoint of the regulated community, keeping pace with delisting procedures and sampling protocols and frequencies proved to be a formidable task.

New Procedures and Standards for Evaluating Delisting Petitions

Previous deficiencies notwithstanding, delistings for any type of waste are usually granted only on a facility-specific basis; in fact, only one industry-wide delisting application (tanneries) has been submitted to date. In addition, a successful delisting technically is not an EPA determination that the waste is not hazardous. Rather, to be granted a delisting means that certain conditions must be maintained. The disposer of delisted material must ensure that: the quality and integrity of delisted material is maintained through the continued application of the specified management method that renders the waste non-hazardous; the integrity of the treated material (treatment quality) is maintained even when it is mismanaged (such as placed into a sanitary landfill), and the waste is tested to ensure that it does not exhibit a characteristic.

HSWA mandates several significant changes to the delisting process. First, when evaluating a petition to delist a waste generated at a particular facility, the Administrator must now consider factors (including additional constituents) *other than those for which the waste was originally listed* if he or she has a reasonable basis to believe that such additional factors could cause the waste to be a hazardous waste. In addition, the Agency must provide notice and an opportunity for comment before ruling on a petition on the basis of these additional factors.

The establishment of this new substantive standard for delistings in conjunction with previous requirements for such petitions in effect establishes a two-pronged test for all current and future delisting petitions:

1. Consideration of the factors for which the waste was listed (in all cases), and

2. Consideration of the factors and Appendix VIII constituents other than those for which the waste was listed in cases where the Administrator has a reasonable basis to believe that these additional factors could cause the waste to be hazardous.[61]

It should also be noted that it is EPA, not the petitioner, who must determine whether the waste is hazardous for reasons *other than those* for which it was originally listed. The burden is on the petitioner to demonstrate that the waste is non-hazardous for the constituents listed in Appendix VII (those for which the waste was *originally listed*). The Agency must meet a threshold standard, a "reasonable basis to believe that such additional factors could cause the waste to be a hazardous waste" before it can request additional information and before it can in turn deny the delisting on the basis of additional factors and/or constituents. In addition, the Agency must provide opportunity for notice and public comment before granting or denying a petition on the basis of these additional factors and/or constituents.[62]

The second important change mandated by HSWA is the prohibition against the continued use of temporary exclusions without an opportunity for public notice and comment, and the forced expiration of those already granted. All temporary exclusions already granted expire on November 8, 1986; thus, if EPA has not granted a final delisting by that date after an opportunity for public comment, the waste is again subject to regulation. EPA may discontinue temporary exclusions earlier if petitioners are not providing the new information now needed to process the petition under the HSWA standard.[63]

Procedures for Complying with HSWA and Revised Delisting Regulations

HSWA and the existing RCRA regulations impose specific procedures and requirements governing the submission and evaluation of delisting petitions for hazardous wastes.[64] Guidance has also been provided on the specific type of analytical data required for a petition to be considered complete, and the proper sampling protocols.[65]

For petroleum refinery wastes, the standard extraction procedure (EP) is designed to detect the presence of metals and certain pesticides in an aqueous extraction medium. For oily wastes that have high oil and grease content, this procedure would be inappropriate. It lacks effectiveness because the oily wastes frequently bind or impede the flow of metals in the extraction medium, thereby yielding artifically low levels of metals. Due to this problem, and because oily wastes likely contain other toxic constituents [many oily wastes were listed for lead and chrome (K048–K052)], such as benzene and polycyclic aromatic hydrocarbons, a separate oily waste EP analytic testing regime has been adopted informally which requires testing for:[66]

1. the four waste characteristics; if the waste contains greater than 1% oil and grease, both the standard EP (261.24) and the oily EP are required when testing for the EP toxicity characteristic;
2. TOC, oil, grease;
3. total metal analysis;
4. specific analysis for 95 constituents.

Multiple Waste Treatment Facilities

Due to the variety and number of incoming wastes, MWTF[67] cannot submit raw material data or use a mass balancing demonstration. In addition, such petitioners must analyze a minimum of 8 weekly composite samples over a 2-month period, and submit a "contingency plan" for testing each batch of treated sludge before it is disposed of for as long as the facility is in operation. In addition to testing for TOC, oil, grease, and the four characteristics, the residue of the treatment process must undergo several other procedures for:

1. prescreening of clients and wastes;
2. total concentrations of EP toxic metal including nickel and cyanide;
3. appropriate leach tests for EP toxic metals, nickel, and cyanide;
4. cyanide: total, free, and leachable;
5. a minimum of the 126 priority pollutants[68] plus the top 10 constituents;
6. an explanation for all Appendix VIII constituents that are not analyzed.

Incorporation of Data into Delisting Decision

Delisting evaluations are both quantitative and qualitative. The Agency has developed an analytical approach to assist in making consistent decisions, and to determine whether a petitioned waste can be excluded. This analytical approach uses a groundwater transport model—the Vertical and Horizontal Spread model (VHS)—to predict a reasonable worst-case contaminant level in groundwater when mismanaged.

The VHS model attempts to simulate the dispersion of toxicants in the vertical and horizontal direction in an aquifer.[69] The model incorporated several reasonable worst-case assumptions by EPA definition such as: saturated soil conditions providing zero attenuation, no precipitation for metals, disposal into an unlined sanitary landfill, continuous toxicant input, and a receptor well (such as a drinking water well) in line with the source and the groundwater flow. The overall approach is used to predict reasonable worst-case contaminant levels in groundwater in nearby receptor wells while estimating the ability of an aquifer to dilute the toxicant from a specific volume of waste. The concentration of listed metal constituents derived from the extraction of a given waste material is then compared to health-based standards for these constituents. Concerns have been raised regarding how representative the reasonable worst-case scenario used in the VHS model really is. While some believe it is too conservative, the model·also assumes that the closest receptor well is 500 feet away, an assumption that potentially allows higher levels of constituents in the extraction leachate, or in general less rigorous treatment prior to land disposal.

Since the model utilizes a maximum allowable contaminant level at the receptor well, and also uses the total volume of waste disposed of into the cell as one of the factors in predicting whether the extraction level will exceed the maximum allowable contaminant level, the net effect of the model is to establish a sliding regulatory scale that suggests a larger yearly volume of waste exhibiting a particular extraction level not be delisted, while a smaller yearly volume of the same waste may be considered non-hazardous. Thus, the model predicts that the larger the waste volume, the higher the level of toxicant in the receptor well.

For delisting wastes, the net effect of the final VHS model and the health-based standards is to lower the previous maximum contaminant levels in the EP from 30 times drinking water standards for listed metal-bearing wastes to a more stringent level of only 6.3 times drinking water standards or lower for these constituents, when the yearly disposal volumes exceed 100,000 tons per year. Consistent with the sliding scale nature of the model, however, if smaller yearly volumes are disposed (such as 5000 tons), the extraction level could approach 32.3 times the current drinking water standards and may still qualify for a delisting. Note that these more stringent levels for delistings only apply to metals contained in listed hazardous wastes. The metals that serve as the basis for listing a waste are the same as those 8 metals that render a waste toxic by virtue of the EP toxicity characteristic. A characteristic metal-bearing waste need only exhibit a metal concentration in the EP leachate equal to or less than 100 times drinking water standards. Thus a listed waste that contained chromium would have to be treated to a level of between 6.3 and 32.3 times (depending on volume) the drinking water standard for chromium in order to be delisted. However, if the waste stream contained chrome but was not a listed RCRA waste it would only have to be minimally treated to a level of 100 times the drinking water standards for chromium to be (Table 2-6) a non-hazardous waste. Furthermore, to delist a listed metal-bearing waste all metal constituents of the waste stream, not only those for which the was originally listed, cannot exceed the 6.3–32.3 range. The extraction procedure used for these demonstrations is the EP, even though listed wastes are involved. This significant discrepancy between the acceptable extraction levels for listed versus characteristic metal-bearing wastes is expected to be redressed in the near future by lowering the regulatory levels for EP metals. In addition, a Guidance Document on the application and use of the VHS is expected shortly.

Other factors may result in the denial of a petition, such as actual field groundwater monitoring data or spot-check verification data. Groundwater monitoring data can be particularly important as a real world validation of the waste's leaching capabilities.

Currently the VHS model only applies to listed metal-bearing wastes that are landfilled. The Agency recently proposed several changes to the VHS model in order to apply it to organic wastes that are landfilled and land-treated, but has not addressed the placement of either metal-bearing or organic wastes into surface impoundments.[70] The most significant among these changes are the following: incorporating persistence and hydrolysis, and failing to take co-disposal with mobilizing solvents into account. These and other factors and assumptions would result in higher levels of organics in delisted material.

Under the proposed revisions to the VHS for organics, only listed organic constituents would be evaluated by this procedure. Characteristic organic constituents, which have been proposed for regulation via the organic toxicity characteristics (OTC), presumably would be evaluated in accordance with the regulatory levels established by the OTC (see discussion above and note 47). Moreover, the proposed evaluation of delisting petitions by the VHS is not a substitute for the "additional factors review" which all delisting petitions are currently subject to.

The VHS model and the development of the OTC for evaluating organic constituent listings/delistings are closely paralleled by the Ageny's development and proposal of the land disposal ban model, and the toxic constituent leaching procedure (TCLP). This model and extraction procedure will be used to determine the acceptability of pre-treated wastes that seek to meet the standard of the land disposal ban (generally 22 times the drinking water standard for constituents). Both the VHS model and the land disposal ban model rely on back calculations from a point of exposure using fate and transport equations to establish a treatment level at the land disposal unit. The major difference is that the VHS model uses an unlined sanitary landfill environment as the basis for predicting potential migration, whereas the land disposal ban model relies on a lined hazardous waste landfill environment. Thus, the VHS will predict more rapid migration and in turn require lower levels of waste constituents in extraction leachate (from either the EP or OTC) than the land disposal ban model.

Chapter 9 examines the land disposal ban model, the new extraction procedure for restricted wastes (the TCLP), and their potential problems. While the actual procedure for determining the land disposal ban levels of constituents in extraction leachate await reconciliation, the acceptable levels for delisted processes will always be significantly lower than those materials that are land disposed as a hazardous waste.[71]

Relationship to Land Disposal Restrictions

The model and approach to evaluating pending temporary exclusions and future petitions are closely paralleled by the activities to develop a model for determining which treated wastes can be land disposed. The land disposal prohibition process establishes "pretreatment standards"; that is, testing to determine whether the waste has been adequate pre-treated so as to prevent migration of hazardous wastes and constituents under a reasonable worst case scenario in a hazardous waste landfill environment (Chapter 9).

While this general land disposal pretreatment model will likely allow for higher extraction levels than those allowed for delistings (due to the more stringent standards for delistings—sanitary, unlined landfill), by incorporating factors such as aquifer recharge and longitudinal dispersion, the land disposal model will also encompass approximately 45 toxic constituents, rather than the limited number of EP toxic metals and pesticides. Once this general land disposal/pre-treatment model is put into use, it is also likely that it will be applied to the delisting process (with lower maximum extraction levels) to establish a single model and quantitative continuum by which both delisting and land disposal acceptability determinations are made. For further discussion see EPA's proposed land disposal prohibition and pretreatment standards.

Impact on State Delisting Programs

Several states have been delegated authority to issue pre-HSWA delistings in their states. The HSWA delisting authorities will eventually be delegated as well, but for now all delistings, including decisions on the 142 outstanding temporary exclusions, will be made by EPA Headquarters (see Chapter 14).

While states do not need to re-evaluate previous final delisting decisions made prior to November 8, 1984, EPA has encouraged them to do so. All states must use the new delisting criteria and methodology for all future delisting applications, once authorized to administer this portion of the program.

Recent Delistings

As of this writing several delisting petitions have been finalized and numerous other previously submitted petitions have been proposed for termination[72] under the new RCRA procedures and standards. Among the delisting petitions that have been finalized is one that has been granted to certain wastes from the Agency's mobile incineration unit.[73]

The significance of the Agency delisting is that it is for the treatment residues (scrubber waters and ash) from the incineration of an acutely hazardous waste—dioxin-contaminated soils—that would otherwise be subject to the "derived from" rule [40 CFR 261.3(c)(2)(i)] as discussed above. In addition, the waste-specific nature of the delisting, the substantial level of detail in the analysis, the extent of sampling, the non-detectability of any organic waste constituent in the residues, and the risk assessment methodology used in this proceeding are indicative of the significant requirements for those seeking future delistings.

NOTES

1. Benjamin Disraeli.
2. 50 *Fed. Reg.* 614 (Jan. 4, 1985) (definition of solid waste).
3. State can be more stringent—3008–3009.
4. U.S. Congress, Office of Technology Assessment, "Technologies and Management Strategies for Hazardous Waste Control," p. 9, Washington, D.C., March 1983.

   Solid Waste Disposal Act (SWDA), section 1004(27). Subtitle C of the SWDA has been designated and is most commonly referred to as the Resource Conservation and Recovery Act (RCRA), after the bill that established the Subtitle C program in 1976, even though such conservation and recovery is a relatively minor part of the SWDA or RCRA program. Also see 42 U.S.C. 6903.

   U.S. House of Representatives, Energy and Commerce Committee, "RCRA Reauthorization," 97th Cong., 2nd Sess., Serial No. 97-69, p. 397 and related testimony, 1982.

   U.S. Senate, Environment and Public Works Committee, "Solid Waste Disposal Act Amendments of 1983," 98th Cong., 1st Sess., S. Hrg. 98-342.
5. U.S. House of Representatives, Engery and Commerce Committee, "Hazardous Waste Control and Enforcement Act of 1983," 98th Cong., 1st Sess., Serial No. 98-32, p. 321, 1983.
6. 45 *Fed. Reg.* 33906 (May 19, 1980) Book 2 of 3. The final regulations promulgated on this date, which became effective on Nov. 19, 1980, represent the first and most significant package of hazardous waste regulations that, among other things, established the interim status program. These regulations are commonly referred to by these dates.

   U.S. Environmental Protection Agency (EPA), Office of Water Regulation and Standards, addendum to "Assessment of the Impacts of Industrial Discharges on POTWs," Feb. 1983. Submitted by JRB Associates, McLean, Virginia (EPA Contract #68-01-5152, DOW 54). Also see note 1, p. 9 (new report).
7. "Report to Congress, Listing Waste Oil as a Hazardous Waste," U.S. EPA, Office of Solid Waste, Report SW-909 (Jan. 16, 1981); Used Oil Recycling Act of 1980 (P.L. 96-463), now Section 3014 of RCRA.
8. U.S. Congress, Office of Technology Assessment, Staff Memorandum, "The RCRA Exemption for Small Volume Hazardous Waste Generators," Washington, D.C., July 1982.

   U.S. Environmental Protection Agency, Office of Solid Waste, "National Small Quantity Hazardous Waste Generator Survey," Feb. 1985 (Contract 68-01-6892) Abt Associates, Cambridge, Mass.
9. 45 *Fed. Reg.* 33090, 33120 (May 19, 1980). Enforcement policy on "sham" burning of low btu waste fuels signed on Jan. 18, 1983. 48 *Fed. Reg.* 11157 (Mar. 16, 1985).
10. See note 4, p. 9; also see Appendix A, "Summary 82 of Damage Incidents Resulting From Recycling of Hazardous Wastes," 50 *Fed. Reg.* 658 (Jan. 4, 1985).
11. 50 *Fed. Reg.* 658 (Jan. 4, 1985).
12. U.S. Congress, *Congressional Record,* Statement of Senator Christopher Dodd, S14205-7, Dec. 8, 1982. Agency proposed to deny numerous previously where they granted temporary delistings. Also see 51 *Fed. Reg.* 2526 (Jan. 17, 1986).
13. RCRA 1004(5); 42 USC 6903(5).
14. RCRA 3004 establishes a standard of regulating "as may be necessary to protect human health and the environment." This basic protection standard makes no reference to costs and is not constrained by economic considerations.
15. Legislative History, 1976 RCRA, S.3622, S. Rpt. 988, 94th Cong., 2nd Sess. 15 (1976) emphasizes that the purpose of the TSD facility standards is to "eliminate

any disposal of a designated hazardous waste in locations or circumstances which might be harmful.'' The House bill H.R. 14496 also states that RCRA Section 3004 standards ''must reasonably protect human health and the environment,'' H. Rpt. No. 1491, 94th Cong., 2nd Sess. 28 (1976). Also see House Floor Debate, on HSWA Statement of Con. Florio (*Cong. Rec.,* 6500, Aug. 4, 1983). Also see discussion of this issue within the context of land disposal ban, Chapter 9.

16. 40 CFR 261.3(a).

17. 40 CFR 261.3(b); 45 *Fed. Reg.* 33095 (May 19, 1980).

18. 40 CFR 261.11(a)(3)(i–ix).

19. 40 CFR 261.11.

20. 40 CFR 261.11(b). Also see multiple chlorinated organic waste proposal and interim final listings 49 *Fed. Reg.* 5308–5813 (Mar. 10, 1984); listing of solvent blends 50 *Fed. Reg.* 18378 (Apr. 30, 1985); 50 *Fed. Reg.* 53316 (Dec. 31, 1985); Section 222(a) of HSWA.

21. U.S. House of Representatives, Hazardous and Solid Waste Amendments of 1984, 98th Cong., 2nd Sess. (to accompany H.R. 2867) Public Law (P.L.) 98-616 (Nov. 8, 1984); Conference Report 98-1133, Section 222(b), pp. 34, 104; U.S. House of Representatives, Energy and Commerce Committee, 98th Cong., 1st Sess.; H. Report 98-198 Part 1, 56–7 (May 17, 1983).

22. 50 *Fed. Reg.* 665 (Jan. 4, 1985); 40 CFR 261.33(a)–(d).

23. 40 CFR 261.7(b)(3).

24. 45 *Fed. Reg.* 76629 (Nov. 19, 1980).

25. 45 *Fed. Reg.* 78539, 78541 (Nov. 25, 1980). For discussion of proposed revisions to current mixture exemption see 51 *Fed. Reg.* 5472 (Feb. 13, 1986). In general, the proposal states that a mixture is acutely hazardous when:

* one or more of the substances listed in 261.33(e)(l) for acute toxicity is included in a commercial chemical mixture;

* the mixture exhibits acute toxicity via one of various inhalation or ingestion measures and exceeds the specified acute toxicity limits for those measures;

* for those mixtures where existing EPA data is inadequate to establish mixture toxicity, the harmonic mean formula (below) is used. Values for acute oral, dermal, or inhalation lethal dose levels must be taken from the National Institute for Occupational Safety and Health Registry of Toxic Effects of Chemical Substances (RTECS). They are then put into the formula and compared to the toxicity limits specified in proposed 261.33(e)(2)(i).

$$\text{Predicted LD50} = \frac{100}{\dfrac{Pa}{\text{LD50 A}} + \dfrac{Pb}{\text{LD50 B}} + \dfrac{Pn}{\text{LD50 N}}}$$

A mixture that does not meet the criteria for an acute hazardous waste is nevertheless subject to RCRA regulation as a non-acutely hazardous commercial chemical product mixture (261.33(f)). These proposed requirements do not apply to mixtures containing substances that were listed in 261.33(e) because they have been found to be fatal to humans in low doses. These latter compounds are newly coded in the proposal, by the hazard code of T*. Mixtures containing such 261.33(e) substances are considered and regulated as acutely hazardous.

26. 50 *Fed. Reg.* 1978 (Jan. 14, 1985). For example, brominated and certain species of chloro-dioxins are not covered, nor are the sludges generated from the use of certain dioxin-containing products.

27. 49 *Fed. Reg.* 49784 (Dec. 21, 1984); 50 *Fed. Reg.* 20238 (May 15, 1985).

28. 45 *Fed. Reg.* 33115 (May 19, 1980). Also see 45 *Fed. Reg.* 76629 (Nov. 19, 1980).

29. Dates represent respective *Federal Register* notices for final and proposed listings. Also see 50 *Fed. Reg.* 44644 (Oct. 29, 1985) (April 21, 1986) (regulatory agendas).

30. HSWA Conference Report 98-1133, p. 113–4.

31. 50 *Fed. Reg.* 49258 (Nov. 29, 1985) (proposed used oil listing). 50 *Fed. Reg.* 49212 (Nov. 29, 1985) (proposed management standards for used oil recycling facilities).

32. 51 *Fed. Reg.* 8206 (Mar. 10, 1986).

33. 50 *Fed. Reg.* (Nov. 29, 1985) (hazardous and used oil fuel specifications).

34. 40 CFR 261.7.

35. RCRA 3001(b)(2)(3) (Bevill Amendment); RCRA 8002(f),(n),(o),(p) (special wastes studies); 50 *Fed. Reg.* 40292 (Oct. 2, 1985) (reinterpretation of mining exclusion).

36. 40 CFR 261.10; 45 *Fed. Reg.* 33119 (May 19, 1980); 45 *Fed. Reg.* 35247, (July 7, 1980).

37. 40 CFR 261.21. Liquids may be tested for ignitability by a Pensky-Martens Closed Cup Tester using ASTM Standard method D-3278-78, or an equivalent test method approved by the Administrator under procedures set forth in 40 CFR 260.20 and 260.21 (rulemaking petition).

38. 49 CFR 173.300 (compressed gases, oxidizing compounds).

39. 40 CFR 261.22.

40. 40 CFR 261.23.

41. 49 CFR 173.151; 49 CFR 173.53; 49 CFR 173.88.

42. Interim Guidance Document for Toxic Gas Generation Reactivity 261.23(a)(5), from Eileen Claussen, Office of Solid Waste, USEPA, July 12, 1985. Also see EPA Guidance Document, "Design and Development of a Hazardous Waste Reactivity Protocol," EPA-6001/2-84-057, NTIS #PB 84-158-807, Feb. 1984.

43. 49 CFR 261.24.

44. Safe Drinking Water Act, sections 1401(i), 1412(b); 42 U.S.C. 300(f) (i), 300(g); 40 CFR 141.11–16, 40 CFR 143.1–4.

45. 45 *Fed. Reg.* 33127 (May 19, 1980); 45 *Fed. Reg.* 72032 (Oct. 30, 1980); 45 *Fed. Reg.* 35247 (July 7, 1980).

46. U.S. Senate, Committee on Environment and Public Works, Solid Waste Disposal Act Amendments of 1983; 98th Cong. 1st Sess,; S. Report 98-284, 32-36 (to accompany S. 757); (Oct. 28, 1983). Also see H. Report 98-198.

47. 51 *Fed. Reg.* 21648 (June 13, 1986).

48. On Dec. 31, 1985 (50 *Fed.Reg.* 53316) EPA listed solvent mixtures containing 10% *or more* solvent by volume (before use) of total listed solvent, and still bottoms from the recovery of these spent solvents. The Spring 1986 draft of this rule identifies wastes and still bottoms with *less than* 10% solvent as hazardous.

49. 40 CFR 261.3(a)(2)(iii), (iv) (mixture rule); 40 CFR 261.3(2)(2)(iii), (iv) (A)–(E) (exceptions).

50. 40 CFR 261.3(a)(2)(E).

51. 40 CFR 261.3(d)(1)(2).

52. See Note 20 for discussion of solvent mixtures. Acutely hazardous waste mixtures are discussed at 51 *Fed. Reg.* 5472 (Feb. 13, 1986) and at 50 *Fed. Reg.* 37338 (Sept. 12, 1985).

53. 50 *Fed. Reg.* 49176 (Nov. 29, 1985).

54. The Agency has established a "de minimus" policy for other wastes—1 ppm for carcinogens, 25 ppm for non-carcinogens. 40 CFR 261.3(iv).

55. 40 CFR 261.3(c)(2)(i).

56. 40 CFR 261.3(c)(2)(ii).

57. 40 CFR 261.3(d)(1).

58. 40 CFR 261.3(d)(2).

59. 45 *Fed. Reg.* 33096 (May 19, 1980); 51 *Fed. Reg.* 19859 (June 3, 1986).

60. 50 *Fed. Reg.* 37338 (Sept. 12, 1985).

61. 50 *Fed. Reg.* 28727 (July 15, 1985) (codification rule).

62. Compton, R., "Delisting Hazardous Wastes: Do the RCRA Amendments Spell Relief?" *Environmental Law Reporter,* Vol. 14, 10374, Oct. 1984. S. Silverman, "Delisting Hazardous Wastes Under RCRA: A Response to Compton and Patterson," *Environmental Law Reporter,* Vol. 15, 10006, Jan. 1985.

63. RCRA, 3001(f); HSWA, Section 222.

64. 40 CFR 260.22(c), (d), (3). Also see 50 *Fed. Reg.* 28742 (July 15, 1985) commonly termed the "codification rule" for the Hazardous and Solid Waste Amendments of 1984, P.L. 98-616, which discussed new section 260.22(c). Also see 261.11(a).

65. U.S. EPA, Office of Solid Waste, "Petitions to Delist Hazardous Wastes: A Guidance Manual," Washington, D.C., April 1984; National Technical Information Service, Document Number PB85-194488, pp. 3–4, 18–20, and Appendices A, G, and J.

66. Ibid., pp. 18–20 and Appendix J.

67. Ibid., pp. 20.

68. Clean Water Act, Section 307(a).

69. 50 *Fed. Reg.* 7883 (Feb. 26, 1985) Appendix I (proposed VHS model). 50 *Fed. Reg.* 48886 (Nov. 26, 1985) (final VHS model).

70. 50 *Fed. Reg.* 48943 (Nov. 27, 1985).

71. 51 *Fed. Reg.* 1736 (Jan. 14, 1986).

72. 50 *Fed. Reg.* 34687 (Aug. 27, 1985); 50 *Fed. Reg.* 37364 (Sept. 13, 1985) (final delistings); 50 *Fed. Reg.* 4886 (Nov. 27, 1985); 51 *Fed. Reg.* 2326 (Jan. 17, 1986) (proposed denials of temporary exclusions).

73. 50 *Fed. Reg.* 23721 (June 5, 1985) (proposed rule); 50 *Fed. Reg.* 30271 (July 25, 1985) (final rule).

CHAPTER THREE

What Materials Are Wastes?

As discussed in Chapter 2, a waste material must first be designated a "solid" waste before it can be designated a "hazardous" waste. In other words, all RCRA hazardous wastes are also RCRA solid wastes. The converse is not true, however.

Significantly, "solid" in the context of RCRA does not refer to a waste's physical form, because a "solid" waste may be either a solid, liquid, semi-solid, or contained gaseous material. Rather, solid waste is an umbrella term that means all waste materials—hazardous and non-hazardous alike—as compared to products, feedstocks, or other non-waste material. The term is frequently used to compare and contrast the universe of RCRA hazardous and RCRA non-hazardous wastes, the latter being referred to as solid waste.

The process of determining whether a given material is a solid and whether it is a hazardous waste involves two separate but related steps: first, it requires knowledge of the waste's generation process and the inherent hazards of a given material, such as its physical and chemical composition; and second, the management practices that are applied to the waste and/or the subsequent uses to which the waste is put. This two-step analysis is particularly important when a hazardous waste is recycled, because the application of some or all of the Federal regulations to a particular waste may depend on whether or how a waste is recycled, as we will see later in this chapter.

For purposes of simplicity, Chapter 2 was largely dedicated to the first half of this equation. Chapter 3 now examines the second half: the impact of various factors—statutory and regulatory exclusions, management and recycling practices—on the designation of a material as hazardous. Due to the wide range of "recycling" and "reuse" practices applied to wastes, Chapter 3 is primarily of importance to those who intend to recycle or reuse wastes, and distinguishes production processes from those that constitute hazardous waste management. If a waste material meeting the definition of "hazardous" in Chapter 2 is not excluded by statute or regulation, then it is generally subject to full regulation if generated in sufficient quantities.

The complexity and diversity of recycling practices themselves, and in turn the scope of Federal jurisdiction and regulation, require first and foremost a familiarity with several key recycling terms. Note that "recycling" is another umbrella term referring to *any* use, reuse, or reclamation of a waste. Similarly, "secondary materials" is a regulatory term that refers to five broad categories of waste materials (discussed below) that may be designated as solid and/or hazardous wastes depending on the type of management practice applied to them.

UNDERSTANDING RECYCLING PRACTICES AND PROBLEMS

The ability to distinguish between materials and management practices that are waste-like, and those materials and practices that represent products or production practices, is the most fundamental requirement to understanding the RCRA hazardous waste regulatory system.

Just about everyone can agree that materials that are discarded or thrown out are "solid wastes" and may be hazardous. And most people can agree that some materials are so intrinsically toxic (e.g., dioxin-containing materials) that they are both solid and hazardous wastes. In addition, most would recognize that "storage" may become a form of disposal where materials are accumulated for extended periods of time and are more like wastes than products or raw materials, thus requiring regulation as either a solid or hazardous waste. All three of these general categories of solid wastes—abandoned, inherently waste-like, and over-accumulated—are for the most part defined by *either* the act itself (abandoning or accumulating) *or* by the intrinsic properties of the waste (inherently waste-like).

"Recycling" presents a much more complex picture. The challenge in identifying and distinguishing between those materials and practices that represent "wastes" and those that reflect "products" or production practices requires a knowledge of *both* the intrinsic properties of the materials involved *and* the management practices involving those materials. In addition, recycling is not one activity, but several.

Recycling is the most loaded and double-edged term in the hazardous waste lexicon. It generally connotes a highly desirable activity such as reclamation (regeneration) of spent solvents. However, it also refers more generally to any use or reuse of a waste, such as burning, to recover energy or materials, or applying materials to the ground as "fertilizer" or "fill material." Depending upon the types of wastes and the nature of the practice such recycling activities can either help protect or harm human health and the environment. (For example, using a waste as a fertilizer may actually aid crop growth or may be little more than disposal, if toxic metals run off in the process or are taken up by crops.)

Prior to the enactment of the 1984 RCRA Amendments, "recycling" was defined in the 1980 regulations in its broadest context, as virtually any use or reuse of a hazardous waste. In addition, any such use or reuse recycling practice was exempt from any RCRA control provided it was deemed "beneficial" by the generator or recycler. The determination of whether a given waste management practice was "recycling" and therefore exempt from RCRA regulation was based solely on the judgment of an individual generator or facility that the recycling practice was "beneficial" to him or her, irrespective of environmental consideration. A beneficial use was defined as any use that accomplished the stated "recycling" purpose. For example, if the waste was intended to control dust and it actually accomplished this purpose, it was exempt, without regard to and even if it caused environmental harm in the process (only "imminent hazards" would have been subject to enforcement action, but not actual regulatory control, before the harm was perpetrated (RCRA 7003)). Moreover, the chances of even the most egregious cases of the "beneficial use" exemption being detected were extremely slim since many of these facilities and operations were not required to notify EPA of their existence or activity due to their exempt status, or they would provide only an interim status notification as a storage facility. In effect, benefit to the generator outweighed harm to the environment. Thus, a facility owner/operator could exempt themselves from control by determining that a given practice was a "beneficial use."[1] No other guidance was provided to distinguish wastes from products, or in any way limit the scope of this regulatory exclusion.

The Agency's rationale for the beneficial use exemption in the original RCRA regulations issued on May 19, 1980, was based on the belief that the intrinsic value of many wastes would ensure recycling in an environmentally sound manner. By 1985, however, the Agency recognized the limitations of this rationale and had completely restructured the definition of "solid waste,"[2] which is the subject of the balance of this chapter. In fact, in defending against several legal challenges to the new and expanded recycling controls and redefinition of "solid waste," the Agency notes that "Unfortunately, experience has shown that merely because a waste has sufficient value to warrant recycling does not mean that it will be managed safely."[3] More often the benefits of cheap and unprotective disposal outweighed the intrinsic value of the waste material.

So-called recycling practices have caused numerous cases of significant environmental harm, including many "Superfund" sites. The Agency has documented 83 specific cases of environmental damage due to waste recycling (use, reuse, or actual regeneration) or accumulation prior to purported recycling.[4] For example, various acts of actual recycling or reuse have had serious adverse affects.

The Times Beach, Missouri, disaster resulted from mixtures of dioxin-containing hazardous wastes and used oil being spread on roads to control dust. This practice, although it occurred prior to RCRA's original enactment in 1976, would have been exempted under the 1980 regulations since the purpose of the spraying was to control dust.[5]

Substantial risks have also been noted from uncontrolled leaching and wind dispersal of hazardous waste being placed on the land, such as a road base, or by mixing with other materials to form waste-derived product, that is then placed on the land as a purported fill material.[6] See more later in this chapter under the discussion of proposed controls on used-oil recycling. (Note: Waste-derived products are by no means universally harmful; the use of certain waste oils in the production of asphalt is allowed provided that it can be demonstrated that hazardous constituents are chemically bound to the road base material.[7])

The burning of hazardous waste as fuels in boilers and furnaces to purportedly recover energy and/or materials also represents a previously exempt recycling practice. This widespread and uncontrolled burning of hazardous wastes has resulted in numerous cases of air pollution and other environmental releases, including several "Superfund" sites such as Laskin's Greenhouse in Jefferson, Ohio.[8] The widespread use of this exemption also prompted the Agency to issue its first limitation on the beneficial use exemption by issuing an enforcement policy declaring that the burning of low btu fuels (5000–8000 btu/pound) constituted "sham recycling" and therefore was not a beneficial use.[9]

Many other damage cases involved in-house, on-site recycling activities, where generators stored their own wastes unsafely before recycling them. The Asarco, El Paso, primary smelting facility stored the byproduct slag from its smelting operations in large, uncovered piles before it was re-smelted. Runoff from these piles is heavily contaminated with toxic metals, and has contaminated surface water with lead, mercury, arsenic, and cadmium.[10]

Byproduct slags from copper smelting were also stored in uncovered piles at Kennecott Copper's Utah facility before being re-smelted. Contaminated seepage, leachate, and runoff from these piles has caused groundwater contamination with the toxic metals lead, arsenic, and copper.[11]

At the same time, the 1980 solid waste definition was beset with deficiencies at the other end of the regulatory spectrum. "Solid waste" was defined as anything that was "sometimes discarded": the net effect of which was to potentially extend RCRA regulation to all waste materials no matter how they were recycled.[12]

These and numerous other recycling damage cases and definitional problems prompted the Congress, through HSWA, to: specifically control certain hazardous waste recycling, and uses and reuses such as the burning of hazardous wastes in non-incinerator devices and place limitations on the waste content of fuels (RCRA, 3004(q),(r), (s)); ban the use of hazardous wastes and mixtures of wastes and waste oil as a dust supressant or for road treatment (RCRA, 3004(1)); specifically control recycling by small generators (RCRA, 3001(d)(2)); and limit the length of storage of hazardous wastes (RCRA, 3005(j)). Even the original RCRA reauthorization bill, H.R. 6307, contained a general statutory directive for the Agency, "to promulgate such regulations as may be necessary to protect human health and the environment ensuring that the use, reuse, recycling, and reclamation of hazardous wastes is conducted in a manner consistent with such protection."[13]

At the same time, the Agency has come to recognize and respond to these shortcomings by issuing several new regulations to generally expand the regulation, and refine the scope and definition, of hazardous waste recycling activities including: the redefinition of solid waste; a specification that limits the hazardous waste content of fuels burned for energy recovery; the listing of used oil as a hazardous waste; the issuance of management standards for burners, blenders, transporters, and marketers of fuels containing hazardous wastes; and standards for generators, transporters, and recyclers of used oil.

The redefinition of solid and hazardous waste places particular emphasis on distinguishing between those recycling or reuse activities that constitute hazardous waste management, and those that are tantamount to production or product storage practices.

"I am made all things to all men." Until recently that quote from the Bible was equally applicable to the "recycling" of hazardous wastes; the recycling regulations were made to mean something different to just about everyone. At the same time, understanding the definitions of the distinctions between solid wastes, hazardous wastes, regulated recycling practices, and production activities constitute the "bible" of hazardous waste management in more ways than one. The reader is cautioned that many of these relationships and definitions are complex and subtle. Nevertheless, the following discussion and analysis attempts to prevent the reader from having to seek divine guidance in understanding the definition of solid waste and its many nuances.

Defining what constitutes solid and hazardous waste management is a dynamic and evolving process. New information and insights are always being developed. For the near future, complete data will not be available on every recycling practice (e.g., wastes used as "fertilizers"), but decisions must be made nevertheless. The perfect cannot be allowed to be enemy of the good. In exercising these judgments, risks are taken—risks that the scope of regulatory coverage is too lenient or too narrow, allowing additional damage to occur. On balance, the Agency has substantially improved the 1980 definition of solid waste by expanding and refining the scope of regulated recycling activities. Areas of potential or predictable difficulty are identified throughout the following discussion.

"SOLID WASTE" DEFINITION AND EXCLUSIONS

The term solid waste is a statutory term that encompasses any: garbage, refuse, or sludge from a waste treatment plant, water supply treatment plant, or air pollution control facility; or other discarded material, including solid, liquid, semi-solid, or contained gaseous material resulting from industrial, commercial mining, or agricultural operations or community activities; but does not include solid or dissolved material in domestic sewage, or solid or dissolved materials in irrigation return flows or industrial discharges that are point sources subject to permits under section 402 of the Federal Water Pollution Control Act, as amended, or source, special nuclear, or byproduct material as defined by the Atomic Energy Act of 1954, as amended.

Three points about this definition are worth noting. First, as noted above "solid waste" is a misnomer, as a waste may be a solid, liquid, semi-solid, or contained gases. Second, Congress has exempted certain materials from the definition of solid waste in RCRA itself. Third, EPA has added additional exemptions in its regulatory definition of a solid waste. The following discussion will examine these statutory and regulatory exclusions, summarized by Figure 3-1.

Statutory Exclusions

There are several industrial processes and management methods that are statutorily excluded from the definition of solid wastes, in some cases because they are governed by other statutes.[14]

1. *Domestic sewage,* including solid or dissolved materials in domestic sewage.

2. *Industrial wastewater discharges* that are point-source discharges subject to regulation under Section 402 of the Clean Water Act, as amended. This exclusion applies only to the actual point-source discharge. It does not exclude industrial wastewaters while they are being collected, stored, or treated before discharge, nor does it exclude sludges that are generated by industrial wastewater treatment.

3. *Irrigation return flows.*[15]

4. *In-situ mining wastes* that are not removed from the ground are not regulated as solid wastes.[16] However, when removed from site they do become subject to RCRA. In addition, other mining wastes such as overburden ore processing wastes are subject to an interim regulatory exemption pending the completion of studies to determine the nature and scope of regulatory control.

5. *Source, special nuclear,* or *byproduct material* as defined by the Atomic Energy Act of 1954, as amended, 42 U.S.C. 2011 et seq.

DOMESTIC SEWAGE   The statutory definition of solid waste specifically excludes "solid or dissolved materials in domestic sewage." In interpreting this phrase, EPA decided that Congress intended to include hazardous waste that *mixes* with domestic sewage in a sewer leading to publicly owned treatment works (POTW). EPA did not assess whether such discharges were adequately regulated under RCRA, the Clean Water Act, or any other environmental law.

An industrial waste stream that never mixes with sanitary wastes in the sewer prior to treatment or storage does not fall within the exemption.[17] A waste falls within the domestic sewage exemption when it first enters a sewer system that will mix with sanitary wastes prior to storage or treat-

Figure 3-1   Statutory and Regulatory Exclusions from Definition of Solid Waste

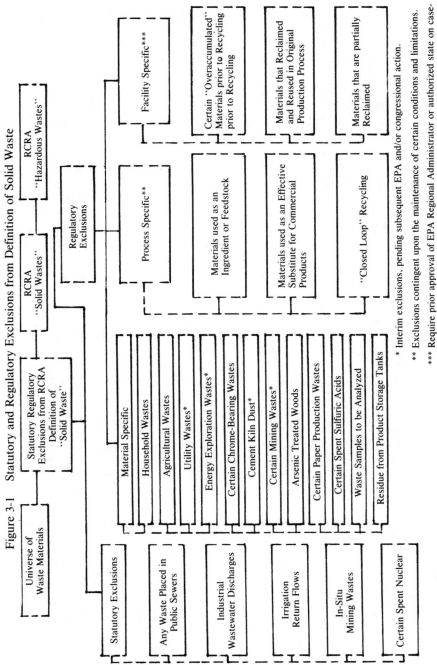

* Interim exclusions, pending subsequent EPA and/or congressional action.

** Exclusions contingent upon the maintenance of certain conditions and limitations.

*** Require prior approval of EPA Regional Administrator or authorized state on case-by-case basis.

ment by a POTW. Until such time as it is mixed, and if it is stored or treated prior to discharge to the sewer, it is subject to RCRA coverage.

The statutory exemption is for domestic sewage rather than for POTWs. The sludges and wastes produced by POTWs in the treatment of these wastes are potentially subject to RCRA control, and must be tested to determine whether they exhibit any characteristics of a hazardous waste. The EP toxicity characteristic is the most likely test a POTW waste would flunk, although EPA believes most POTW sludge would pass the EP test.

While the precise size and impact of this exemption has not been determined, several studies indicate that it is sizable. OTA estimated in 1982 that 5 million tons of hazardous waste were so disposed. A Chemical Manufacturers Survey from 1985 revealed that 50 millions tons of hazardous waste were discharged to POTW lines. In addition, a recent study of small generators revealed that approximately 10% of their wastes were sewered, and for small chemical manufacturers, 20%. This exclusion is one of the most serious impediments to proper treatment of hazardous wastes, particulary in urban areas, where access to public sewers is un-· restrained.[18]

Due to 1) the continuing delays in implementing the CWA's pre-treatment program, 2) the failure of EPA to determine if the pre-treatment program is sufficient once regulations required by the NRDC consent decree[19] have been issued, and 3) the substantial use of the sewer as a legal method of waste disposal, Congress has requested a re-examination of discharges of industrial wastes into POTW lines through the 1984 RCRA Amendments.[20]

Section 3018(a) and (b) of RCRA now contains a directive to report to Congress by February 1986 on the nature and extent of the domestic sewage loophole, and so revise existing regulations under CWA, RCRA, or both to assure that substances listed or identified under 3001 which pass through POTWs are adequately treated to protect human health and the environment by August 1987.[21]

INDUSTRIAL WASTEWATER DISCHARGES   Of course, any discussion of the domestic sewage exemption must include its interface with the Clean Water Act. Many industrial generators do not use public sewer systems for the discharge of their hazardous wastes. Rather, many discharge their wastewaters *directly to surface water* pursuant to permits (NPDES) under Section 402 of the Clean Water Act (CWA). The aforementioned 1985 CMA survey found that over 250 million tons of hazardous wastewaters were treated and discharged to surface waters each year in accordance with CWA standards. Unlike the domestic sewage exemption, where the waste is exempt from RCRA control once it is placed into the sewer system, discharges from wastewater facilities permitted under Section 402 of the CWA are exempt from RCRA only at the point of actual discharge of surface water. Thus all units and facilities that hold, treat, or manage RCRA wastes prior to such permitted discharges are subject to RCRA 3004 standards and 3005 permitting requirements. Despite the considerable controversy over this approach in 1980, the policy governing these units has taken on added significance in light of the fact that 55% of wastewater from the CMA survey was held in unlined surface impoundments prior to discharge.[22]

Industrial facilities that do discharge their hazardous wastewater into a POTW are subject to the treatment requirements of Section 307(b) of the Clean Water Act—frequently referred to as pre-treatment standards. These pre-treatment standards are divided into two broad categories: categorical and general. Categorical standards focus on 34 industries and 129 toxic pollutants frequently termed priority pollutants (many of which are listed or identified hazardous wastes under RCRA 3001) as specified under a consent decree settling a lawsuit brought by several environmental organizations.[23] The aim of these categorical standards is to produce the same level of treatment for each pollutant including toxic, non-toxic, and conventional pollutants prior to discharge from the POTW as that which would have been imposed had the industrial facility been a direct discharger of wastes to navigable waters.

While many so-called categorical pre-treatment standards for firms that discharge to the POTWS have been issued,[24] many important organic waste categories have not had categorical standards issued. Without them, many categories of wastes, such as organic chemical production wastes, can be placed into public sewers with little or no treatment whatsoever. In addition, the variety of generators regulated under RCRA and the wastes which may be designated hazardous are much broader than industries and pollutants covered by the consent decree.

RCRA hazardous wastes that have had no categorical standard issued are nevertheless subject to general pre-treatment requirements[25] directed at protecting the POTW facility rather than insuring proper treatment of wastes that are so discharged. These general pre-treatment standards prohibit discharging to a POTW the following: materials that can ignite or explode; discharges with a pH of 5.0 or less (unless the POTW is designed to handle such discharges); viscous materials that would obstruct sewer system flow; discharges that may upset the treatment process; and discharges whose heat is in excess of 104°F such that it would inhibit the biological activity of the works.

The Agency recently completed the required report to Congress (The Domestic Sewage Study) on the gaps in coverage between CWA and RCRA.[26] It found: existing CWA pre-treatment standards may not adequately control the significant quantities of ignitable, corrosive, and reactive hazardous wastes that are discharged to POTWs; over 30% of all electroplating/metal finishing firms have not complied with categorical standards for various metals and cyanides, requiring more aggressive enforcement; significant sources of organic constituents are not controlled by Federal categorical standards including pharmaceuticals, equipment manufacturing, laundry, and petroleum refining; significant discharges of "non-priority" inorganic and organic pollutants are discharged without prior treatment; major organic industries discharge 2.5 times more non-priority organics than priority pollutant organics including many solvents and are in need of further control; discharges from hazardous waste management facilities have caused operational problems at POTWs.

The report concluded that despite the significant deficiencies in regulatory coverage of hazardous waste being discharged to sewer systems, particularly organic pollutants, sufficient legal and enforcement authority exists to redress existing gaps. Under HSWA, EPA has until August 1987 to close these gaps by instituting additional controls under the CWA and/ or RCRA.

RADIOACTIVE WASTES   In defining solid wastes, Congress specifically exempted "source, special nuclear, or byproduct material as defined by the Atomic Energy Act of 1954," as amended. Issues of interpretation have arisen, however, as to how far this exclusion was intended to reach. The Department of Energy has asserted at various times that this exemption applies to entire facilities with such materials, and to wastes deemed hazardous that are mixed with such materials.

The environmental stake in this issue is great. For example, at the Oak Ridge, Tennessee, Y-12 Plant, four seepage basins have leaked over 4.7 million gallons of hazardous waste per year into the groundwater.[27] DOE initially responded to the statute by asserting a categorical exemption for all of its nuclear weapons plants operated under the Atomic Energy Act. This exemption claim was rejected in Federal court in the suit of *Legal Environmental Assistance Foundation* v. *Hodel*.[28]

Now there are disputes concerning the regulatory status of mixed waste and the meaning of the term "byproduct material" in the statutory exclusion. This issue may be resolved shortly in a lawsuit brought concerning the DOE Savannah River Plant in South Carolina. Although DOE recently acknowledged that its mixed waste is subject to RCRA, the Department now plans to claim that much of its mixed waste is not mixed waste at all, but in fact radioactive byproduct material, which is exempted from RCRA by definition.[29]

MINING WASTES   Mining wastes that are returned or never removed from the original site of their excavation are not subject to RCRA regulation. If wastes from mining operations such as shale oil or metal ore are removed from the original site of excavation and stored or managed elsewhere (e.g., in a surface impoundment or lagoon) they do become potentially subject to RCRA control as either a solid or hazardous waste.[30]

Mining waste (frequently referred to as overburden) from metal ores other than in-situ mining wastes and certain other materials are subject to an interim statutory exemption from control as hazardous wastes pending the issuance of a Report to Congress on studies of "special wastes" to determine the need for regulation of the following waste materials: fly ash, bottom'ash, slag waste, and flue gas emission control waste generated primarily from the combustion of coal or other fossil fuels; solid waste from the extraction, beneficiation, and processing of ores and minerals, including phosphate rock and overburden from the mining of uranium ore; and cement kiln dust. These interim exemptions are specified in RCRA Section 3001(b)(3). The studies of these "special wastes" are mandated in RCRA Sections 8002(f),(n),(o),(p). The Agency recently completed the studies of mining wastes required under 8002(f),(p), and determined that signficant releases of toxic metals and corrosive wastes occurred from virtually all types of mining operations.[31] The Administrator submitted these studies in February 1986, and now has 6 months to determine whether these mining wastes should be subject to RCRA Subtitle C hazardous waste regulation. The Agency has also proposed to re-interpret (or limit) the scope of the interim statutory exclusion for the "extraction and beneficiation" of certain mining waste ores. Previously the Agency extended this exemption even to wastes from primary smelting operations and metals used in the fabrication and alloying of other materials. This re-interpretation would subject several primary smelting wastes to RCRA Subtitle C hazardous waste regulation for the first time.[32] (See further discussion below under Regulatory Exclusions.)

RCRA Section 3001(b)(2) also provides an interim statutory exemption for drilling fluids, produced waters, and other wastes associated with the exploration, development, or production of crude oil, or with natural gas or geothermal energy. Once the Administrator has completed a special study of these wastes under RCRA 8002(m), a separate act of Congress is required before such regulations would take affect.

A new RCRA Section 3004(x) was created by HSWA, which allows the Administrator to vary many of the new minimum technology and other new HSWA requirements (e.g., liners) for mining waste facilities in the event that such wastes are subject to Subtitle C control, provided that such varied requirements assure protection of human health and the environment.

Material-Specific Regulatory Exclusions

Several additional exemptions are contained in the regulations, thereby subjecting the wastes to regulation under Subtitle D of RCRA. In general, RCRA regulatory exemptions complement and supplement the statutory exclusions:[33]

1. *Household wastes,* including garbage, trash, and sanitary wastes from septic tanks derived from households including residences, hotels, and motels. The Agency recently proposed to extend this exclusion to campgrounds and other public places. The 1984 RCRA Amendments

amended 3001(i) to clarify this exclusion for resource recovery facilities that burn only household wastes and solid waste from commercial or industrial sources that does not contain hazardous wastes listed or identified under 3001.[34] The facility would therefore not be considered a hazardous waste treatment facility, but the exemption does not extend to the waste generated by the combustion process itself. Thus, if the ash generated by the combustion process is hazardous at regulated quantities, the facility is a hazardous waste generator.

2. *Agricultural wastes* that are returned to the ground as fertilizer, but does not include silviculture wastes.

3. *Mining overburden* returned to the mine site.

4. *Utility wastes* from coal combustion including fly ash waste, bottom ash waste, slag waste, and fuel gas emision control waste.

5. *Exploration wastes* from oil, natural gas, and geothermal energy drilling.

6. *Various chrome-bearing wastes* that exhibit only the EP toxicity characteristic for chromium due exclusively to the presence of tri-valent chromium if the waste is frequently managed in non-oxidizing environments. These wastes include certain leather tanning wastes, and wastewater treatment sludges from the production of titanium dioxide pigment using chromium-bearing ores by the chloride process. Due to the problems associated with "fertilizer" uses for such wastes, the agency has proposed to reexamine this exclusion in the near future.[35]

7. *Cement kiln dust wastes.*

8. *Solid wastes* from the *extraction, beneficiation, and processing of ores and minerals* (including coal) including phosphate rock and overburden from the mining of uranium ore.

9. *Arsenic treated woods* when discarded, provided that they exhibit only the hazardous waste toxicity characteritic and the waste is used for the generators for the intended purposes.

10. *Black liquor* that is reclaimed in a pulping liquor recovery furnace and then reused in the paper process, unless it is accumulated speculatively as defined in Part 40 CFR 261.1(c)(o). This exclusion does not apply in situations where black liquor is maintained in an impoundment that is releasing hazardous constituents into the environment.

11. *Spent sulfuric acid* used to produce virgin sulfuric acid, unless it is accumulated speculatively as defined in 40 CFR 261.1(c)(o).

12. *Samples* of hazardous waste, or a sample of air, water or soil which is collected for the sole purpose of testing to determine its characteristics or composition, are not subject to any requirements of Subtitle C or the notification requirements of Section 3010 or RCRA. The conditions for samples are specified in the regulations.[36]

13. *A hazardous waste that is generated in a product or raw material storage tank,* a product or raw material pipeline, or in a manufacturing process unit or an associated non-waste-treatment-solids manufacturing

unit, is not subject to regulation under 262–265, 270, 271, or 124, or to the notification requirements of Section 3010 or RCRA *until it exits* the unit in which it was generated, unless the unit is a surface impoundment, or unless the hazardous waste remains in the unit more than 90 days after the unit ceases to be operated for manufacturing, or for storage or transportation of product or raw materials. However, leakage from these process tanks or certain underground storage tanks may be regulated as discussed in Chapter 12.[37]

"SPECIAL WASTES" A number of wastes can best be described as being in regulatory limbo. Their regulatory status depends upon the outcome of studies, the most notable being the mining wastes (discussed above under Statutory Exclusion). Other studies are directed at investigation methods of encouraging resource recovery and recycling. In the interim, these materials are regulated as a solid waste. Due to the fact that the following materials are solid wastes and are under study to be controlled as hazardous wastes (Section 8002 (f),(m),(n),(o),(p) of RCRA), these solid wastes are commonly termed special wastes to indicate their tentative status: glass and plastic, mining waste, sludge, tires, drilling fluids, produced waters, and other wastes associated with the exploration, development, or production of crude oil, natural gas, or geothermal energy: material generated from the combustion of coal and other fossil fuels; cement kiln dust waste; and material generated from the extraction, beneficiation, and processing of ores and minerals, including phosphate rock and overburden from uranium mining.

ALUMINUM POTLINERS: A CASE STUDY ON THE MINING EXCLUSION Several of these exemptions may be revoked in the near future due to the completion of the required mining waste studies. Congress granted these interim statutory exemptions for materials generated from the extraction, beneficiation, and processing of ores and minerals due to the perceived low toxicity and high volume of these waste materials.

Even though these exclusions are interim, they are far from harmless due to the manner in which the Agency has expanded the scope of the "extraction, beneficiation" exclusion. In interpreting these exclusions, EPA even removed from the list of RCRA-regulated wastes several categories of waste that EPA had previously determined to be hazardous![38]

This was accomplished by expanding the interim exclusion to include wastes generated in the smelting, refining, and other processing of ores and minerals. This action brought within the exclusion several materials that EPA knew and acknowledged were hazardous, including spent potliners (i.e., liners of smelting furnace) from primary aluminum production which contain high concentrations of cyanide and have caused much damage (EPA Waste Number K088).[39]

This action, coupled with EPA's failure to complete the studies in a timely manner, and documented exposures of up to 24 parts per million of cyanide in runoff from piles of aluminum potliners, have precipitated additional citizens' suits to redress this glaring delay and exclusion.[40] In response, EPA has proposed a reinterpretation of this exclusion that would list as hazardous waste several waste streams from primary aluminum, lead, chromium, and cadmium smelting and various ferroalloy wastes (Chapter 2).[41]

This case study is instructive because it highlights the fact that weak and unstructured directives can paralyze efforts to control even those wastes that are clearly in need of RCRA hazardous waste regulations. This is one reason HSWA contains many of the minimum regulatory controls, presumptions, and statutory prohibitions, described in Chapters 1 and 9.

Process-Specific Regulatory Exclusions

Once a material is determined not to fall within any of the statutory or regulatory exclusions to the regulatory program, the next step is to determine if the material falls within the regulatory definition of a solid waste. The regulatory definition is aimed at differentiating wastes from products, and determines whether and to what extent certain waste recycling practices will be regulated. If a waste has not been excluded and is not to be recycled (e.g., will be disposed in a landfill or underground injection well), has been designated hazardous (as described in Chapter 2), and has been generated in sufficient quantities to be regulated (see Chapter 4), it is subject to RCRA regulation and the requirements described here.

To a large extent, the definition of solid and hazardous waste attempt to delineate the differences between waste management activities and production processes.[42] Often in the process of making a product, materials are generated that meet the criteria of a solid and hazardous waste. However, when these materials are only intermediates in a production process or are an integral and direct component of a closed production process, it would not be appropriate to regulate such activities as hazardous waste management.

In drawing these distinctions in its January 4, 1985, regulations, the Agency has identified three specific activities that ordinarily do not involve waste management because they are like production operations or ordinary usage of commercial products. These limited exceptions are based on the general principle that the direct use of the material (without reclamation) in either a manufacturing process or as a finished commercial product is not a waste management process.

USE AS AN INGREDIENT OR FEEDSTOCK   Using or reusing secondary materials as ingredients or feedstocks in production processes occurs only when the secondary material is used directly as an ingredient or a feedstock, such as using fly ash in the production of cement, or using distillation bottoms from solvent production in the production of the same or closely related solvent.

When distinct components are recovered, however, the material is not being used, but rather reclaimed and would not be excluded under this provision. In addition, when the material is used as an ingredient in waste-derived fuels or in waste-derived products that will be placed on the land, not only is the original material a solid waste, but the waste-derived product remains a solid waste and potentially subject to RCRA hazardous waste controls.[43]

EFFECTIVE SUBSTITUTE FOR COMMERCIAL PRODUCTS Using or reusing secondary materials as *effective substitutes for commercial products* occurs when materials are directly used as substitutes for commercial products, thus they are deemed to be functioning as raw materials not wastes. Examples include lime sludges that are used as water conditioners, or byproduct hydrochloric acid from chemical manufacture used in steel pickling.

It does not take the most creative of minds to imagine a situation where these feedstock or substitution exceptions could be abused. For example, where only one still bottom is needed, five could be put into the reactor. Situations that would not qualify for this exclusion include:[44]

1. where the material is ineffective or only marginally effective for the claimed use such as a heavy metal sludge being used in concrete;
2. where materials are used in excess of the amounts necessary to operate a process;
3. where a material is not as effective as what it is replacing; and
4. if the material is not handled in a manner consistent with its use as raw material, such as storage in a leaking surface impoundment as commonly occurs with corrosive wastes claimed to be used as neutralizing agents.

CLOSED-LOOP PRODUCTION PROCESSES A closed-loop production process returns materials as feedstock to the original and primary production process prior to any reclamation. (Reclamation means any recovery or regeneration.) Incidental processing prior to reinserting in the original production process is allowed. In implementing this provision, EPA must therefore distinguish between reclamation and incidental processing, and clarify what is meant by returning material to the "original production process." Operations that recover or regenerate materials so as to make them available for further use is considered reclamation and would not qualify. A practical consequence of this distinction is that no secondary materials generated or stored in a lagoon would be eligible for the closed-loop exclusion. Storage of materials in an impoundment is rarely done in a manner to minimize loss, which is why virgin materials (e.g., feedstocks) are rarely if ever stored in this manner.[45]

The production distinctions and definitions encountered often involve very subtle concepts. While the following examples in some contexts may be startling, they are a reflection of the difficulties in distinguishing de facto disposal from beneficial reclamation and production processes. For example, wetting down of dry wastes that have been previously placed on the ground to prevent dispersal would not be deemed to be reclamation and hence would not be regulated. On the other hand, certain processing operations that only de-water waste material to make them amenable for reuse, but do not actually recover or regenerate the materials, nevertheless constitute reclamation and therefore are not closed-loop processes. Emission control dust from a primary zinc smelting furnace could be returned to any part of the process associated with zinc production and qualify as a closed-loop process. However, if the dust waste is sent to byproduct cadmium recovery operations, it would not be considered returned to the same process from which it was generated, even if the cadmium recovery unit was at the same facility because the original production process was zinc not cadmium.

It is important to note that solvent reclamation itself is not deemed to be a "production process," whereas the initial manufacture of solvents from petroleum would be. Solvent reclamation is "reclamation," not production. Therefore, any return of solvents to a reclamation unit is not a production operation and does not qualify for *this* exclusion. Rather, the production output of solvent reclamation operations are excluded from regulation as a hazardous waste by virtue of other changes to the derived from rule (see Chapter 2, and discussion of products of reclamation process below). This policy was first established in the 1980 regulations.[46]

SUMMARY   Materials that are solid and hazardous waste when recycled in certain ways are *not solid wastes* when:

1. use or reused as ingredients in an industrial process to make a product, provided the materials are not being reclaimed; or
2. used or reused as effective substitutes for commercial products; or
3. returned to the original process from which they are generated, without first being reclaimed. The material must be returned as a substitute for material feedstock and the process must use raw materials as principal feedstocks.

However, the following materials *are solid wastes,* even if the recycling involves use, reuse, or return to the original process as described above:

1. materials used in a manner constituting disposal, or used to produce products that are applied to the land; or
2. materials burned for energy recovery or used to produce a fuel, or contained in fuels; or
3. materials accumulated speculatively; or

4. materials listed in 40 CFR 261.2(d)(1)—those materials deemed to be inherently waste-like.

These four limitations will be described in greater detail below.

Facilities and generators that seek to exempt materials from the coverage of the solid waste definition must demonstrate that there is a known market or disposition for the material and that it meets the terms of the exclusion of exemption. In doing so, they must provide appropriate documentation, such as contracts, that a second person uses the material as an ingredient in a production process to show that the material is not a waste, or is exempt from regulation. In addition, owners or operators of facilities claiming that they actually are recycling materials must show that they have the necessary equipment to do so.

Facility-Specific, Case-By-Case Variances

In addition to the previous process-specific exemptions from the solid waste definition, the recent revisions to the solid waste definition provide the Regional Administrators with the authority to evaluate and grant case-by-case facility-specific variances from classification as a solid waste provided that one of three conditions is met. Standards and procedures have been established for rendering determinations on such variance applications, and can be found at 40 CFR 260.31:[47]

Materials accumulated without sufficient amounts (75% within 1 year) being recycled. The opportunity for such variances is provided primarily to accommodate situations where a temporary downturn in the economy may prevent recycling of 75% of the accumulated volume within a given calendar year.[48] The applicant must demonstrate "sufficient" amounts of the material will be recycled in the following year.

Materials that are reclaimed and then reused within the original primary production process. This variance would allow material to be reclaimed before being reused within the original primary production process and still be termed closed-loop recycling.

Materials that are reclaimed but must be reclaimed further before material recovery is complete. This variance would allow a recyclable material to become a non-waste after only one step of a two-step process, if it is "commodity-like" but not yet a commercial product.

DEFINITION OF SOLID WASTE—OVERVIEW

Up to this point we have examined only the statutory and regulatory exclusions from the definition of solid waste. The balance of the chapter will examine those materials that are solid wastes by virtue of being abandoned, overaccumulated, recycled, or inherently waste-like. The extent to which these solid wastes are also RCRA hazardous wastes then depends upon whether the materials are listed or identified as a hazardous waste as discussed in Chapter 2.

The reader will also see that in certain cases even where a combination of management practice and/or the intrinsic hazards of a given solid waste subject it to the jurisdiction of RCRA's hazardous waste regulations under Subtitle C, the imposition of specific controls may be deferred or temporarily suspended. In addition, once regulatory controls are imposed, they may be limited to the transportation and storage of materials prior to the actual management practice, for which there may be no specific controls (e.g., regeneration of spent solvents).

As stated above, the term solid waste is a statutory term which means any garbage, refuse, sludge from a waste treatment plant, water supply treatment plant, or air pollution control facility (or other) discarded material, including solid, liquid, semi-solid, or contained gaseous material resulting from industrial, commercial mining, agricultural operations and from community activities, but does not include solid or dissolved material in domestic sewage, or solid or dissolved materials in irrigation return flows or industrial discharges which are point sources subject to permits under section 402 of the Federal Water Pollution Control Act, as amended, or source, special nuclear or byproduct material as defined by the Atomic Energy Act of 1954, as amended (RCRA, Section 1004).

The statutory definition, as implemented through the January 4, 1985, redefinition of solid waste holds that a "solid waste" is any discarded material that is not specifically excluded by the statute (40 CFR 261.4(a)). A "discarded material" in turn is any material which is either abandoned, inherently waste-like, or recycled in certain ways (use constituting disposal, burning for energy recovery, reclaimed, or overaccumulated). "Overaccumulation" is categorized as a form of "recycling" under the regulations. It may be more convenient, however, to view overaccumulation as a precursor to recycling or disposal.

Figure 3-2 summarizes those waste management activities and materials categories that are RCRA solid wastes.

MATERIALS THAT ARE SOLID WASTES WHEN ABANDONED, OVERACCUMULATED, OR ARE INHERENTLY WASTE-LIKE

EPA has determined that certain wastes should be regulated no matter how they are managed (inherently waste-like), and certain waste management practices should generally be regulated because the practices reflect waste-like activity (abandonment and overaccumulation). These three categories are discussed first because they are management methods and materials that do not usually involve recycling (abandonment, inherently waste-like), or because they are activities that occur prior to recycling (overaccumulation).

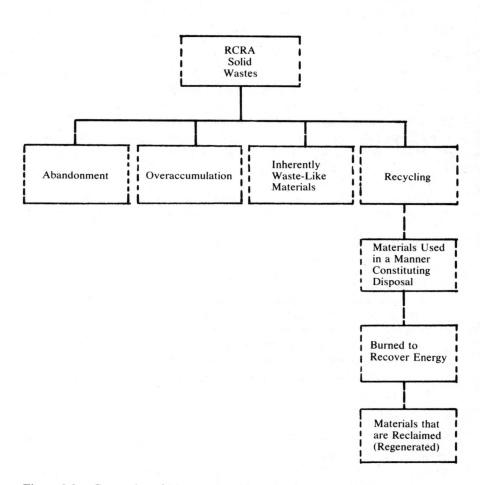

Figure 3-2   Categories of Management Activities and Conditions Constituting
Hazardous and/or Solid Waste Management

Abandonment

Materials that are abandoned are, simply, thrown away or disposed of. Materials that are accumulated, stored, or treated (e.g., incinerated) prior to or in lieu of being thrown away are also solid wastes. However, materials that are recycled in any manner are not considered to be abandoned, even though recycling is a form of treatment.[49]

Inherently Waste-Like

Certain dioxin-containing materials are solid wastes when recycled in *any* manner. These materials are considered too hazardous to be unregulated regardless of how they are managed and are designated with the EPA Hazardous Waste Codes F020–F023 and F026–F028 (see Table 2-2).[50] F020 listed wastes do not include wastes from the production of hexachlorophene from highly purified 2,4,5-trichlorophenol. In addition, neither of these categories of listed wastes includes sludges from the use of these products, such as those generated by the use of dip tanks in the application of preservatives to poles and other wood products, nor do they include situations where such wastes are used as an ingredient to make a product at the site of generation.

The Administrator may use the following criteria to add wastes to the list of materials that are inherently waste-like:[51]

1. materials that are originally disposed of, burned, or incinerated; *or*
2. materials that contain toxic constituents listed in Appendix VIII of Part 261 when these constituents are not ordinarily found in raw materials or products for which the materials substitute (or are found in raw materials or products in smaller concentrations) and are not used or reused during the recycling process; *and*
3. materials that may pose a substantial hazard to human health and the environment when recycled.

Overaccumulation

All materials overaccumulated (also referred to as speculative accumulation) are solid wastes with one exception. Commercial chemical products (as listed in 40 CFR 261.33) may be accumulated for recycling without restriction.

A material is considered to be accumulated speculatively if it is accumulated before being recycled and the person accumulating it cannot show that the material is potentially recyclable or that he has a feasible means of recycling it; and—during the calendar year (commencing on January 1)—the amount of material that is recycled, or transferred to a different site for recycling, equals at least 75% by weight or volume of the amount of that material accumulated at the beginning of the period.[52]

In calculating the percentage of turnover, the 75% requirement is to be applied to each material of the same type (e.g., slags from a single smelting process) that is recylced in the same way (i.e., from which the same material is recovered or that is used in the same way). Wastes otherwise excluded from regulation should not be included in making the calculation, nor should materials that are already defined as solid wastes.

The protection afforded by this definition rests heavily on safeguards against abuses and sham recycling situations. Hazardous wastes that are accumulated with the expectation of eventual recycling but for which no known recycling market exists will be considered hazardous wastes. Demonstrating the existence of a market for the accumulated wastes or the feasibility of recycling is the burden of the accumulator by records demonstrating contracts, location of the recycler, and the relative costs of recycling. In addition, the burden of showing that 75% individual wastes are being recycled within one year rests with the person accumulating the material.[53]

HSWA also contains a provision intended to discourage overaccumulation. The provision prohibits the storage of waste otherwise prohibited from land disposal (see Chapter 9) unless such storage is solely for the purpose of the accumulation of such quantities as are necessary to facilitate proper recovery, treatment, or disposal.[54]

MATERIALS THAT ARE SOLID WASTES WHEN RECYCLED

The recycling of materials can constitute the management of solid and potentially hazardous waste including use constituting disposal, reclamation (regeneration of materials), and burning for energy recovery. Due to the close relationship between these recycling practices and the "abandonment" of secondary materials, which can occur before or after recycling, and "speculative accumulation," which usually occurs before or in lieu of recycling, this discussion should be viewed as a complement to the preceding discussion of these concepts and categories of regulatory control.

Uses Constituting Disposal

Waste materials that are applied to or placed on the land or contained in products that are applied to the land are generally solid wastes. An exception has been made if the waste is listed on the commercial chemical products lists (40 CFR 261.33) and the products are applied to the land in their intended manner.

As a result, fertilizers, asphalt, building foundations, and fill material that use hazardous wastes as ingredients and are applied to the land *are* hazardous wastes under RCRA, unless they do not exhibit the characteristic(s) or do not contain any of the listed wastes that were present in the hazardous waste itself. Conversely, the application of pesticides, fertilizers, or paving products which do not use hazardous wastes as ingredients are not classified as hazardous wastes. As with most general rules anomalies do occur, largely due to previous deficiencies of the delisting process. For example, "certain fertilizers" use tannery wastes as ingredients, wastes that have been excluded from regulation despite the presence of signficant concentrations of chromium. Even if such fertilizers flunked the EP toxicity test for chromium, it would not be a hazardous waste because the fertilizer technically was made from a trivalent chromium waste that was previously excluded from regulation.

This broad jurisdictional claim over recycling that involves uses constituting disposal is traced to the history of the 1984 RCRA Amendments.[55] Numerous documented damage cases have resulted from wastes or "products" derived from these wastes being used in manners analogous to disposal, such as calling a material a fertilizer, fill dirt, paving material, or landscaping bunkers. While the "products" themselves may well fulfill their stated claims, such applications take place without regard to the fate of the toxic constituents in the waste.

"Reclamation" and "Recycling"

"Recycling" is an umbrella term that encompasses any use, reuse, or reclaimation in any manner. "Reclamation" is a subset of "recycling" that refers to a material that is processed to recover or regenerate a usable product, such as the regeneration of spent solvents.

The determination as to whether a reclaimed material (i.e., a waste that has been subjected to a regeneration or recovery process) is considered a hazardous waste is more complicated than the other classifications because it depends heavily on: the physical state of the waste, the reason it was designated hazardous, and the nature of the process reclaiming the material. In addition to the four categories of recycling activities established by the redefinition of solid waste, the Agency has further divided the universe of waste materials into five categories for the purpose of distinguishing between those recycling activity/waste material combinations that represent solid waste management, and those that represent hazardous waste management. While this categorization of waste materials is applicable to all forms of recycling, it is most relevant and important to understanding the scope of hazardous waste controls on reclamation activities. As such, the five material categories are presented below: spent material, byproduct, co-product, sludges, and scrap metal (see Fig. 3-3).

Definition of Terms

SPENT MATERIAL   Spent materials are any materials that have been used and as a result of contamination can no longer serve the purpose for which they were produced *without subsequent processing*. For example, a solvent used to clean circuit boards is no longer pure enough for that continued use and would have to be processed before being used in that application. Therefore, it would be deemed a spent material. However, these contaminated solvents are pure enough to be used as a metal degreaser,

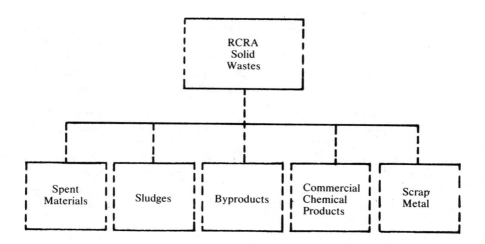

Figure 3-3   Categories of Secondary Materials That are RCRA Solid and Hazardous Waste When Recycled

These five categories of solid wastes are applicable to all forms of recycling activities (use consituting disposal, burning for energy recovery, overaccumulation, and reclamation), but they are most relevant in determining which reclamation (regeneration, recovery) activities constitute hazardous and/or solid waste management. When any of these materials are abandoned or are inherently waste-like, they are solid and hazardous waste.

and would not be designated as spent materials if they were subsequently used in this manner. However, after use in that manner, such contaminated solvents almost invariably would be designated a spent material, for it would be difficult if not impossible for such contaminated solvent to serve the purpose for which it was produced without some form of processing.

BYPRODUCTS AND CO-PRODUCTS Byproducts are materials, generally of a residual nature, that are *not* produced intentionally or separately, and that are unfit for end use *without substantial processing*. Examples include still bottoms, reactor cleanout material, slags, and drosses. However, a byproduct that is used as an intermediate to make a new product would not be considered to be a hazardous waste. A still bottom used in this manner would not be considered a waste due to its manner of recycling (substitute ingredient).

Byproducts need to be distinguished from co-products. *Co-products* are materials produced intentionally, and which in their existing state without further processing *can* ordinarily be used as commodities in trade by the general public. Examples are sulfuric acid from a smelter's metallurgical acid plant, various metals produced in tandem by smelting operations, and co-products from petroleum refining such as kerosene, asphalt, or pitch from petroleum refining. Co-products can also be produced from a variety of processes at a facility. However, co-products that include hazardous wastes as ingredients are classified as hazardous wastes when burned for energy recovery or when placed directly into the land.

A very large grey area in the new definition of solid and hazardous waste exists due to the manner in which the Agency defines and distinguishes between byproducts and co-products.[56] While these provisions make a serious attempt to distinguish between waste generation and production processes, several questions are raised by these definitions. Of particular concern is the requirement that for a material to be a byproduct it must undergo "substantial processing," while a co-product can be generated from multiple processes (which would allow substantial processing and still be exempt from regulation).

A recent independent review of the Agency's distinction between co-products and byproducts also noted that "the regulations may create incentives for manufacturers to classify certain materials as "co" rather than "by" products.[57] Thus it would be left to the Agency to distinguish between these activities on a case-by-case basis. This distinction is of particular significance in identifying cases of waste overaccumulation.

SLUDGES Sludges are any solid, semi-solid, or liquid waste generated from a municipal, commercial, or industrial wastewater treatment plant, water supply treatment plant, or air pollution control facility or any other such waste having similar characteristics of effects.

SCRAP METAL Scrap metal is defined as bits and pieces of metal parts or pieces that are combined with bolts or soldering that, when worn or superfluous, can be recycled. Metal materials that are not scrap include residues generated from smelting and refining operations (i.e., drosses, slags, and sludges), liquid metal wastes, or metal-containing wastes with a significant liquid component such as spent batteries.

COMMERCIAL CHEMICAL PRODUCTS.   See Chapter 2.

SUMMARY   All spent material, listed byproducts, listed sludges, and scrap metal are solid wastes when reclaimed to recover or regenerate a usable product.[58] Conversely, *the following materials are not solid wastes when reclaimed:* non-listed (characteristic) byproducts and sludges when reclaimed, due to the Agency's view that these secondary materials can be routinely processed to recover usable products as part of on-going production operations. However, it is expected that the Agency will be listing many of these materials as hazardous wastes.

In addition, although the Agency considers the reclamation of scrap metal a solid waste management practice, the Agency is temporarily exempting such scrap from hazardous waste regulation pending further study of the controls and requirements.[59] See the third column of Table 3-1 for a summary of these relationships.

Products of Reclamation Process

In Chapter 2 the ''derived from'' rule was discussed. It states that even the residues from the treatment of listed wastes remain hazardous wastes because they were derived from listed wastes.[60] A strict application of this rule would designate reclaimed solvent, metals and the like as hazardous wastes. The derived-from rule has been amended to indicate that commercial products reclaimed from hazardous wastes are products, not wastes.

However, this principle does not apply to reclaimed materials that are not ordinarily considered to be commercial products, such as wastewaters used for cooling or other purposes, nor does it apply when the output of reclamation process is burned for energy recovery or placed on the land. If a spent solvent is treated and blended with oil to sell as a fuel, that fuel is a hazardous waste. In addition, this principle does not apply to wastes that have been minimally or partially processed, but must be reclaimed further before recovery is completed.

Wastes Burned to Recover Energy or Used to Produce a Fuel

Of all the categories of reclamation, burning for energy recovery is perhaps the most complex, and the one which the HSWA has addressed most directly. The following discussion sets forth the distinction between burning for destruction, energy recovery, and materials recovery. Properly identifying a given activity is highly significant because at present: burning for destruction is fully regulated, burning for energy recovery is subject to full or partial regulation depending upon the type of combustion device,

Table 3-1 Matrix of Which Types of Secondary Materials Will be Defined as Solid and Hazardous Wastes When Recycled and Which Types of Recycling Activities Constitute Waste Management

	Use constituting disposal	Burning for energy recovery, or use to produce a fuel	Reclamation	Speculative accumulation
Spent materials (both listed and nonlisted/characteristic).	Yes	Yes	Yes	Yes.
Sludges (listed)	Yes	Yes	Yes	Yes.
Sludges (nonlisted/characteristic)	Yes	Yes	No	Yes.
By-products (listed)	Yes	Yes	Yes	Yes.
By-products (nonlisted/characteristic)	Yes	Yes	No	Yes.
Commercial chemical products listed in 40 CFR § 261.33 that are not ordinarily applied to the land or burned as fuels.	Yes	Yes	No	No.
Scrap metal	Yes	Yes	Yes	Yes.

Yes—Defined as a solid waste
No—Not defined as a solid waste.

and burning solely for materials recovery is presently exempt. The scope of present and future regulatory controls on burning for energy recovery (used oil fuel specification, technical burning standards for boilers and furnaces) and, the mandates of HSWA to control burning for energy recovery will be examined later in this chapter in the section dealing with regulatory controls. Also note that Chapter 2 previously examined the impact of the mixture rule in determining whether a given mixture is a used oil fuel or a hazardous waste fuel.

DESTRUCTION AND ENERGY RECOVERY The "burning" of hazardous wastes refers to the controlled thermal combustion of a material in an enclosed device such as a boiler,[61] industrial furnace,[62] or incinerator.[63] Burning for destruction occurs when hazardous wastes are burned in devices that meet the definition of incinerator or other thermal destruction devices for which the Agency is developing standards (see Chapter 6). Burning for energy recovery occurs when these same wastes are burned in a device like a boiler or industrial furnace, except where the waste being burned is of such a low energy value that little energy recovery is occuring, which is considered "sham" recycling and is subject to control as an incinerator.[64] The practical significance of these differences between burning for destruction and energy recovery may be very small, when EPA issues technical standards for devices that burn for energy recovery as mandated by HSWA.

Under the definition of solid wastes, all secondary materials (sludges, byproducts, spent material, scrap metal) when burned for energy recovery are solid wastes, except for commercial chemical products that are themselves fuels.[65] In addition, readers should note that materials intentionally produced for commercial use without processing, like kerosene or certain grades of fuel oil from petroleum refining, are products, not wastes. Legally, they are called co-products, while wastes are called byproducts.

ENERGY RECOVERY AND MATERIALS RECOVERY A different set of issues is involved in distinguishing between burning that involves energy recovery (a regulated activity)—and that which involves only materials recovery (exempt) or both—(regulated).

Burning hazardous wastes in boilers is by definition energy recovery since this is the sole funciton of such devices. However, when hazardous wastes are burned in industrial furnaces, often an integral part of the furnace's operation is to recover certain materials. For example, cement kilns that burn chlorinated wastes recover both energy and chlorine. Burning a distillation bottom in a steel blast furnace provides both energy and reduction of iron ore. However, in attempting to restrict regulation to waste management processes rather than production processes, the primary concern must be to ensure that de facto disposal practices do not masquerade under the label of materials recovery.

For example, depending upon the scope of this interpretation, a hazardous waste incinerator or other combustion device that recovers calcium carbonate from its air scrubber could claim that it was burning wastes for materials recovery. In addition, a steel blast furnace may burn wastes such as an organic still bottom, which is not normally associated with the furnace, or in concentrations in excess of those ordinarily burned in the furnace, and claim that the material is solely a process ingredient.

Therefore, when an industrial furnace burns any hazardous waste where energy and materials recovery occurs, it too is considered to be burning for energy recovery and is subject to control as a hazardous waste management facility. While the precise nature of the technical and operating requirements may differ from a boiler or an incinerator, it is nevertheless hazardous waste management and the performance standards must be the same. HSWA clearly contemplated this policy and scope of coverage.[66] Several examples and additional detail of how this provision would work are provided in the regulations.[67]

Thus, as with overaccumulation and reclamation, the provision attempts to balance two competing principles: limit control to those activities that constitute hazardous waste management, but at the same time take a broad view of hazardous waste management and err on the side of controls rather than complacency in equivocal situations.

SUMMARY   Table 3-1 and Figure 3-4 summarize those materials that are solid and hazardous waste when recycled, and which type of recycling activities constitute waste management.[68] Table 3-1 shows that secondary materials (all spent materials, sludges, byproducts, commercial chemical products, and scrap metals) when they are either listed or exhibit a characteristic of a hazardous waste are subject to regulation as both a solid and hazardous waste when recycled by a use constituting disposal, when burned for energy recovery, when reclaimed, or when speculatively accumulated *except* for the following situations:

> Sludges and/or byproducts exhibiting a characteristic are exempt from hazardous waste control when reclaimed.

> Commercial chemical products when reclaimed or even when speculatively accumulated are not considered solid or hazardous waste.

ENFORCEMENT OF THE SOLID WASTE DEFINITION

In the context of EPA enforcement actions, if a generator claims that a particular secondary material is not a solid waste or is conditionally exempt because it was recycled in a certain manner, the generator must show that it was indeed recycling the material in the manner specified. Thus parties claiming the benefits of an exemption to a specified scheme have the burden of proof to show that they qualify for it.

Figure 3-4 Decision Tree for Deciding Which Secondary Materials Are Solid Wastes When Recycled

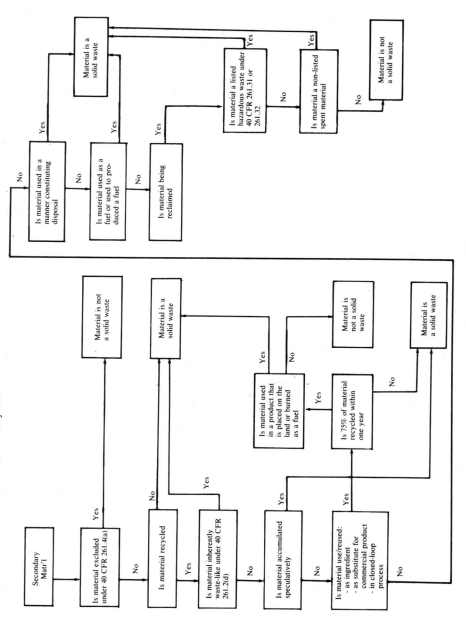

The presumption is that harzardous secondary materials (i.e., spent materials, sludges, byproducts, commercial products, scrap metal) are hazardous wastes unless demonstrations to the contrary can be sustained.[69] In addition to possessing the necessary equipment and producing proper documentation of the way in which the material is being recycled, the facility must also show when challenged (i.e., inspected) that they are not overaccumulating the material.

The exclusions to the definitions of solid waste based on recycling do not limit the Agency's ability to pursue enforcement actions under RCRA Section 3007, 3013, or 7003 (see Chapter 13 and 40 CFR 261.1(b)(2)). The broader statutory definitions of solid waste will be used when these provisions are involved. This is necessary in order to enforce these provisions and conduct inspection of firms that claim exclusions. Enforcement authority extends to all material that *could* be solid wastes under RCRA, not just those defined as solid wastes in the regulations at the time.

REGULATORY REQUIREMENTS FOR MANAGING HAZARDOUS WASTES THAT ARE RECYCLED

The previous sections of this chapter identified those recycling practices that constitute hazardous wastes management when the materials involved are hazardous wastes, and those secondary materials that are not solid wastes or are specifically excluded due to their close resemblence to production processes.

However, merely identifying a given recycling practice as constituting hazardous waste management is but a necessary prelude to establishing specific regulatory standards and requirements for the recycling practice. Identifying these practices and subjecting them to regulation does not mean that they all are regulated to the same extent or in an identical manner.

The regulation of hazardous wastes that are recycled (also referred to as "recyclable materials" in the regulations) at this time largely involves controls on the storage and transportation of such materials, and limitations on the waste content of materials burned or blended as fuels. Unlike specific operating requirements that apply to incineration and land disposal facilities, no technical requirements are presently imposed on processes such as solvent reclamation or burning hazardous waste in boilers or cement kilns. In short, the recycling process itself is not regulated except when recycling is analogous to land disposal or incineration.[70]

Certain recyclable materials and recycling practices are subject to regulatory standards that are not identical to those contained in 40 CFR Parts 262 through 265 for other generators, transporters, and owners/operators of TSDFs. The regulatory standards for these types of recycling activities are contained in 40 CFR Part 266. To a large extent, Part 266 indicates whether all or only some of the generator, transporter, and facility standards of Parts 262-265 apply to facilities engaged in recycling, but in some cases, it also imposes some new or different requirements of its own. Secondary materials that are abandoned or inherently waste-like are subject to full regulation under Parts 262–265 when generated, transported, treated, stored or disposed.

Section 40 CFR 261.6(a)(2) serves as a cross-reference, listing those recyclable materials and recycling activities subject to the: tailored standards of Part 266;[71] generator and transporter requirements of Part 262 and 263,[72] respectively; the facility standards of Parts 264 and 265 (interim status);[73] or whether the recyclable materials, although being a hazardous waste, are not subject to regulation under these provisions due to a decision to defer controls or because the substance is controlled under other statutes or for other reasons.[75] The precise scope of controls imposed on the generation, storage, transportation, and management of recyclable materials are summarized in Table 3-4.

Use Constituting Disposal

Due to the close similarity between a purported recycling practice and direct land disposal, hazardous wastes used in a manner that constitutes disposal are regulated under the interim status standards and final permitting standards (Parts 264, 265 respectively) applicable to land treatment or land disposal. These standards are contained in 40 CFR Part 266, Subpart C. In addition, storage and transportation occurring prior to actual recycling is regulated in a manner identical to other forms of disposal.[76]

In this context, use constituting disposal includes hazardous wastes placed on the land even after mixing the waste with other materials if such mixing doesn't significantly alter the waste's chemical character so as to become "inseparable" from the other materials. With respect to characteristic wastes, presumably mixing recyclable materials until they no longer exhibit a characteristic would not be a use constituting disposal because of the mixture rule. However, if the recyclable material is a listed waste, the regulation is vague as to what constitutes becoming "inseparable."

Application of listed wastes to the land in an "as is" condition must either be delisted prior to their land application or the land application will be considered land treatment subject to the Part 264 and 265 standards.[77]

DUST SUPPRESSION   In addition, the 1984 RCRA Amendments established a *statutory prohibition* on the use of any hazardous waste or hazardous waste mixture for application to the ground as a dust suppressant, except those that are hazardous solely due to ignitability.[78] According to EPA, the prohibition does not apply to used oils that are contaminated with hazardous constituents by normal use, but would restrict the use of any used oil contaminated through hazardous waste adulteration. The Agency's approach to identifying adulteration, which relies on indicator concentrations of contaminants as presumptive evidence of adulteration, is discussed below.

WASTE-DERIVED PRODUCTS   Generally, only products that contain hazardous wastes which have undergone a chemical reaction so as to become inseparable by physical means are presently exempt from hazardous waste regulation. Examples of this "inseparability" are concrete and asphalt that contain hazardous wastes. Conversely, wastes applied to the land after drying or dewatering remain subject to regulation, as would wastes mixed with used oil.

The only exception to this "chemical bonding" principal are commercial fertilizers applied to the land. "Commercial fertilizers" is taken to mean fertilizers produced for the general public's use and not for the exclusive use of the generator. Thus, when a hazardous waste generator or other facility applies its waste, mixed or not, solely to its own land as a fertilizer, this is considered to be a use constituting disposal[79] subject to regulation.

Regulating the *application and use* of commercial fertilizers, whether or not chemical bonding occurs, and other commercial products where they are chemically bonded to hazardous wastes, have both been deferred pending further examination and study of the risks associated with their use. However, the *transportation and storage* of hazardous waste before processing of the waste-derived products that will ultimately be applied to the land are subject to immediate regulation. Similarly, if wastes are placed on the land as a use constituting disposal, they are subject to regulation when transported or stored prior to being placed on the land.[80] For example, when a generator produces a hazardous sludge that contains certain metals beneficial to crop growth and sends it to a fertilizer manufacturer, who in turn produces a fertilizer that is sent to a retail outlet, the fertilizer manufacturer would need a storage permit for the wastes shipped to his facility, even though the product is not currently registered. The Agency recognizes the significant potential for abuse of these regulations in their current form due to the potential for toxic metals to be placed on the ground as "fertilizers" and migrate into ground and surface waters.

Reclamation

For almost every reclamation situation, the Part 262–265 standards apply. Three specific modifications to this general rule are discussed immediately below. In addition, because the reclamation of characteristic sludges and byproducts were not included within the scope for recycling activities that constitute hazardous waste management, there are no regulatory requirements governing these activities. Moreover, commercial chemical products listed on the Part 261.33 lists (Tables 9-1, 9-2, 9-3) that are produced from reclamation processes are not wastes and are not subject to any regulatory requirements.[81]

As of this date, three specific reclamation activities have had tailored standards under Part 266 developed for them; specifically, the reclamation of used oil,[82] precious metals,[83] and spent lead-acid batteries.[84] Other forms of reclamation are subject generally only to generator, transporter, and storage requirements prior to reclamation (40 CFR, Parts 262–265).

USED OIL   The Agency has issued a series of constituent specifications to identify used oil that is subject to hazardous waste controls when burned for energy recovery (discussed below).[85] In addition, the Agency has proposed to list certain used oils as hazardous wastes irrespective of whether they are burned or managed. This was a mandate of RCRA since 1980 and was reinforced by the 1984 Amendments.[86]

In addition to the proposed used-oil listing and final waste fuel constituent specification decisions, the Agency has proposed standards for facilities that reuse and recycle used oils that are either listed or identified as hazardous waste in a manner which "assures that facilities which recyle used oil will need to comply fully with the standards applicable to owners and operators of any hazardous waste TSDF".[87] These *proposed* standards and requirements for generators, transporters, and facilities that manage recycled oil are summarized in Table 3-2 and explained below.

"Recycled oil" is a subset of "used oil" (Chapter 2) and means any used oil that is either burned for energy recovery, used to produce a fuel, reclaimed (including used oil that is reprocessed or redefined) or otherwise recycled, or that is collected, accumulated, stored, transported, or treated prior to recycling. The term includes mixtures of recycled oil containing other materials; however it does not include used oil that is discarded, inherently waste-like, or used in a manner constituting disposal (e.g., road oiling). Mixtures of used oil containing hazardous wastes are "hazardous wastes" not "recycled oil." Used oil containing more than 1000 ppm total halogens is presumed to be mixed with chlorinated hazardous wastes listed in 40 CPR Part 261, and would be regulated under Parts 262–265, rather than the tailored standards for used oil recycling facilities, Part 266 Subpart E.[88] This presumption and the *final* standards that apply to used oil that is recycled by burning (recycled oil) are discussed below. Details of the mixture rule and its relationship to the process of determining whether a given material is a "used oil" (and in turn a "recycled oil" when the used oil is recycled) are discussed in Chapter 2.

The Part 266 recycling standards for used oil largely reflect the Part 262–265 standards with certain limitations. The Part 266 Subpart E standards apply to: recycled oil that is a hazardous waste (except those fuels that are hazardous wastes); household oil used *only* when aggregated at collection centers; and to recycled oil that is recovered from wastewater. Conditional exemptions have been proposed for certain commercial products of used oil reclamation: reclaimed lubricants, asphalt roofing material containing recycled oil, and used oil burned as a fuel that meets the used oil fuel specification (termed "specification fuel," and discussed below).

Table 3-2   Proposed Standards for Generators, Transporters, and Facilities
That Manage Used Oil

Recycled Oil Manager	Proposed Standards
Generators (<1000 kg/mo)	*Part 266.40(c)* - prohibition on dust suppression - if underground tanks used, special measures to prevent corrosion - volume must not exceed 1000 kg/mo or Part 266.41 generator requirement applies - 1000 ppm total halogen presumption - (future controls on burning in space heaters) - oil is subject to 266.42 transportation requirements when shipped off-site
Generators (>1000 kg/mo)	*Part 266.41(c)* - obtain identification number (262.12) - oil must be stored in tanks or containers - containers meet 265.171, 265.173–174, 265.176 regarding condition, handling, ignitable wastes - uncovered tanks must have at least 2' of freeboard, auto cutoffs, or by-pass - conduct daily inspections for leaks, corrosion, drainage, and flow equipment - label all tanks and containers "Recycled Oil" - store wastes for less than 40 days or be subject to 266.43 facility standards - at closure all residue must be removed - leaking tanks must immediately be removed from service, flow stopped, Reg. Admin. notified, and tank drained within 24 hours, contain leakage and tank - (new tanks will be subject to secondary containment at a future date) - phone, fire extinguisher, and absorbents must be present; an employee must be present or on-call at all times, local fire authorities must be familiar with the facility - fires must be reported to Reg. Admin. within 15 days - off-site shipments must comply with pretransportation requirements of 262.30–33, and 262.50 for international shipments - manifest reg of Part 262, Subpart B and exception reporting of 262.42 apply *except* where a written recycling contract exists between the generator and an authorized facility (266.40(e)). The written contract in lieu of a manifest must be maintained at the generator's and receiving facility and be obtained before initiating a shipment. Such notices must be retained for 3 years.
Person that Initiates an Off-site Shipment	*Part 266.41(d)* - as noted above for generators > 1000 kg/mo
Transporters	*Part 266.42* - apply to all transporters, including small quantity recycled oil generators - does *not* apply to transporters of conditionally exempt recycled oil: specification used-oil fuel, asphalt paving uses, lubricant once it is refined. - obtain identification number (263.11) - if a manifested shipment is accepted, Part 263 Subpart B governs - unmanifested shipments are governed by the following in lieu of Part 263: maintain record of acceptance for 3

Recycled Oil Manager	Proposed Standards
	years including name, address, EPA ID number of generator; quantity and DOT shipping code; date accepted; oil delivered within 35 days to an authorized facility (interim status, permitted TSDF, or facility with permit-by-rule); obtain and retain notice that receiving facility is authorized to manage recycled oil.
Owners/Operators	*Part 266.43* -obtain EPA ID number (264.11) - notices (264.12) - standards for use constituting disposal (266.23) - off-site shipments (266.41(d)) - oil analysis requirements (266.43(b)(1)–(3), discussed below) - acceptance of recycled oil from offsite (266.43(e), discussed below) - recordkeeping and reporting (266.43(f), discussed below) - standards for burners (266.44, discussed below)
Owners/Operators (with storage)	- all 264, Subpart B except the 264.13 analysis requirement, which is supplemented by following: analysis for total halogens, used oil fuel constituents, ignitability, and document that no mixing of recycled oil and hazardous waste of recycled oil and hazardous waste occurs at the facility. An analysis plan must be developed specifying the methods and frequencies of oil analysis and maintain records of the analysis. - preparedness and prevention (264 Subpart C) - contingency and emergency plan (264 Subpart D) - acceptance of manifested shipments (264.71–72) when unmanifested shipments accepted same information required of transporters must be obtained and retained for 3 years - reports of unmanifested shipments (264.76) - when analysis reveals the shipment is a hazardous waste, it must be refused or managed by 262–265, 270, 124 - recordkeeping/reporting (264.73–75, 264.77) - closure/post-closure (265 Subparts G, H, F; facility qualifies for permit-by-rule) - closure/post-closure (264 and 265 G&H for all other facilities) - containers (Part 264 Subpart I) - tanks (Part 265 Subpart J) - tanks (Part 264 Subpart J for facilities that are not eligible for permit by rule)
Owners/Operators (recycle in surface impoundments)	-Parts 262–265 Standards - Parts 124, 270 permitting procedures - RCRA 3010 notification
Burners	*Part 266.44* - Part 266.43 facility requirements - (substantive standards for burners of recycled oil will be issued in near future. Final standards for burning of hazardous waste fuels and off-specification used oil fuels are discussed below)
Recycling in a Manner Constituting Disposal	*Part 266.20* - Standards are final, see Table 3-4

Used oil recycled by these processes are neither solid nor hazardous wastes provided that certain records verifying the content of the recycled oil are maintained.[89]

The Agency's proposed abbreviated standards for generators and transporters of recycled oil, under 40 CFR Parts 266.41 and 266.42, respectively,[90] and for owners/operators of used oil recycling facilities[91] are summarized in Table 3-2.

The proposed rule would allow facilities that manage recycled oil in accordance with the Part 266 Subpart E requirements to qualify for a permit-by-rule (Chapter 6) except where recycled oil is: used or reused in a manner constituting disposal; stored or treated in a surface impoundment; or managed at a facility that treats, stores, or disposes of other hazardous wastes. Facilities not eligible for a permit-by-rule must qualify for interim status. Those facilities that are in full compliance with the proposed permit-by-rule requirements upon finalization of the proposed rule would not have to qualify for interim status. Those facilities that are not in full compliance with these proposed conditions would be required either to shut down or to seek interim autorization under 3005(e).[92]

PRECIOUS METAL Due to the perceived inherent value of wastes containing precious metals, tailored standards have been developed that partially exempts reclaimers of "economically significant amounts of precious metals"[93] from most of the regulatory requirements applicable to other reclaimers. Under 40 CFR 266 Subpart F, precious metal reclaimers must comply with: the requirements to notify EPA of their existence under RCRA 3010; standards governing overaccumulation; and manifesting and recordkeeping requirements to document that wastes are being transported to the designated facilities and to ensure that the materials are not being overaccumulated.[94]

For purposes of this provision, precious metals include gold, silver, platinum, palladium, the platinum group metals (iridium, osmium, rhodium), and any combination of these. Beryllium, germanium, gallium, and indium are not included in this definition.

The term "economically significant amounts" is intended to prevent sham operations where only trace amounts, or where amounts too low to be economically recoverable, exist at the facility.[95]

Due to the severe although infrequent damage cases that have occurred at precious metal reclamation facilities, a case-by-case variance procedure allows the Regional Administrator to regulate individual unsafe operations while otherwise maintaining the exemption and not regulating the entire class of such facilities.[96]

Lastly, it is important to note that only the reclaimed precious metal is not hazardous. The waste generated by precious metal reclamation is presumptively hazardous due to the large concentrations of toxic metals and cyanide in the effluent and the presence of spent solvents (e.g., F006).

This is the same standard that applies to any waste "derived from" the treatment storage or disposal of a hazardous waste.[97]

SPENT LEAD-ACID BATTERIES Facilities that reclaim lead-acid batteries are regulated under 40 CFR Part 266 Subpart G and in turn are subject to the full spectrum of Part 262–265 requirements (with certain limited modifications),[98] including 3010 Notification and applicable permitting requirements under Parts 270 or 124. Persons who generate, transport, or collect spent batteries or who store spent batteries but do not reclaim them are not subject to any of these requirements. However, recovered lead would be regulated until it is smelted.

Speculative Accumulation

Any facility that is speculatively accumulating any secondary material (except for 261.33 commercial chemical products) is subject to the requirements of 262–265, the notification requirements of 3010, and all applicable permit requirements of Parts 124 and 270.

Regarding hazardous scrap metal that is accumulated without sufficient amounts being recycled, the Agency has temporarily deferred regulatory controls pending the development of additional information on these practices.

Burning for Energy Recovery

A tailored set of controls has been proposed by the Agency to establish fuel specifications that would distinguish between hazardous waste fuels and used-oil fuels. Due to the complex patterns of regulatory coverage respecting the varied types and numbers of participants involved in the burning and blending of hazardous waste and used-oil fuels, these provisions merit a separate section below. In addition to the fuel specification (termed the Phase I controls), EPA will propose a complementary set of technical standards (Phase (II) governing those devices that burn waste fuels for energy recovery.

HSWA REQUIREMENTS The 1984 Amendments impose several new requirements, including: notification, labeling of waste-derived fuels, recordkeeping, restrictions on certain burning in industrial furnaces, and technical standards and restrictions on the burning of hazardous wastes for energy recovery.

By April 8, 1986, any facility that produces a fuel from hazardous waste, used oil, or used oil in combination with any other material; any facility that burns for purposes of energy recovery any of the materials described above; and anyone who distributes or markets fuels produced from these materials must notify the Agency and their state, if it is an authorized state, that they are engaged in any of these activities. This requirement is contained in RCRA 3010(a). Such notifications must include the location of the facility and provide a general description of the facility, the types of wastes involved, and a description of the production or energy recovery process. EPA has excluded certain small entities, such as households, from the notification requirement. In addition, petroleum coke containing petroleum refining hazardous wastes is exempt so long as it does not exhibit a hazardous waste characteristic.

The notice to be filed must be done in accordance with the requirements of RCRA 3010(a)(1)–(3), and may subject such facilities to interim controls under Part 265. Thus failure to notify places one in non-compliance with several requirements: notification, labeling, recordkeeping, and other applicable interim status standards. *Knowing failure to notify is a criminal offense.*

Any person that produces, distributes, or markets a fuel containing a hazardous waste, or a hazardous waste burned directly as a fuel must include a conspicuous warning *label* in the invoice that reads: "Warning: This Fuel Contains Hazardous Wastes." Such labels must list the hazardous wastes contained therein. While this requirement took effect on February 8, 1985, it has been eclipsed by the manifest and invoice requirements of RCRA 3004(r)(1) as contained in finalized regulations[99] for various waste fuels, since a manifest requirement served the same function as a warning label. The labeling requirement applies to any person required to notify the Agency of their activities to burn, blend, market, or distribute a fuel, including intracompany transfers of such material.

Section 3004(r) also contains several discrete exemptions from the labeling requirements for hazardous waste-derived petroleum coke and for two types of hazardous waste-derived fuels from petroleum refining operations that are generated and reinserted on the site of the refining process.[100]

Coincident with the April 8, 1986, notification, the Administrator must promulgate regulations requiring that all those that notify in accordance with RCRA 3010 maintain records regarding fuel blending and distribution practices and activities.

RCRA Section 3004(q) requires that by November 8, 1986, the Administrator must issue standards applicable to the owners and operators of facilities that:

1. produce a fuel from any hazardous waste or any hazardous waste and any other material;
2. burn for the purpose of energy recovery any such fuel or any fuel that otherwise contains any hazardous waste identified or listed under Section 3001; and,
3. distribute or market any such fuels.

The only statutory exception to these standards, when issued, are petroleum refinery wastes containing oil that are converted into petroleum coke at the same facility at which such wastes were generated, unless the resulting coke product exhibits one or more characteristics of a hazardous waste.

Standards governing the production, distribution, and burning of hazardous waste–derived fuels will be issued in two phases: Phase I includes waste content specifications for used-oil fuels, restrictions on the burning of waste fuels in non-industrial boilers, and storage and transportation standards for the distribution and marketing of waste fuels; Phase II standards will include technical performance and operating standards for the burning of waste fuels in industrial boilers and furnaces, and should be proposed by Summer 1986. These standards and operating requirements are expected to be analogous to those currently required of hazardous waste incinerators.

Lastly, the 1984 Amendments establish specific interim prohibitions on the burning of wastes and waste fuels in certain *cement kilns located in urban areas* with populations greater than 500,000. The prohibition remains in effect until the Agency develops and issues Phase II standards or unless such kilns comply with the standards applicable to hazardous waste incinerators.[101]

FINAL PHASE I STANDARDS ON BURNING AND BLENDING   On November 29, 1985, the EPA finalized a rule to implement Phase I of the two phase plan to control the burning and blending of hazardous wastes for energy recovery.[102] Phase I extends hazardous waste management regulations to transportation, marketing, and burning for energy recovery of hazardous wastes and used oils. The major element of the proposal is the used-oil fuel specification, which establishes permissible limits of hazardous constituents that can be contained in waste fuels, and is used to distinguish between those fuels that are fully regulated as hazardous waste fuels (HWF), those which are subject to lesser levels of control (off-specification used-oil fuels, OUOF) or no controls provided that the fuel does not exceed the spec limits (used oil fuel, UOF). These categories are further distinguished by a presumptive indicator of a hazardous waste fuel—1000 ppm total halogen.

In addition to establishing the used-oil fuel spec, and the presumptive indicator, the Phase I final rule prohibits the burning of hazardous waste fuels and off-specification used oil in all non-industrial boilers. Used-oil fuels can be burned in these boilers only if they meet the fuel spec. Significantly, the rule allows dilution of used oil to bring it within the fuel spec limits for metal and flash point, but not total halogens.

In order to enforce the prohibitions on burning of these materials, the rule also establishes an administrative requirement that creates a tracking system from initial waste fuel marketers, through distributors to burners. These requirements include: notification, receipt of EPA identification number, compliance with manifest (hazardous waste fuels) or invoice system (off-specification used-oil fuels), used-oil analysis for persons claiming to meet the fuel spec (and therefore exempt), certification by the burner to the fuel marketer that his facility is an industrial boiler, and recordkeeping requirements. In addition, the rule would extend the current interim (Part 265) and final (Part 264) storage facility standards to facilities that store, process, or blend hazardous waste fuel.

HAZARDOUS WASTE FUELS AND USED-OIL FUELS   The linchpin of the final rule is the definitions of the hazardous waste fuel (HWF), off-specification used-oil fuel (OUOF), and used-oil fuel (UOF) categories. The category that one's fuel falls within determines the nature and scope of regulatory controls imposed on the material in question.

A "HWF" is any hazardous waste and any fuel produced by processing, blending, or other treatment of hazardous waste, that is burned for energy recovery in a boiler or industrial furnace that is not subject to regulation as a RCRA hazardous waste incinerator. However, used-oil fuel that is also a hazardous waste (i.e., ignitability), provided it is not deliberately mixed with hazardous wastes, is subject to regulation as a used oil fuel.[103] An HWF can be burned only in a hazardous waste incinerator, or in an industrial boiler or furnace until such time as EPA issues Phase II technical standards for such devices. An "industrial boiler" is any boiler located on the site of a manufacturing facility where substances are being transformed into new products or component parts by mechanical or chemical processes (also see notes 61–63).

A "UOF" means any oil that has been refined from crude oil, used, and as a result of such use is contaminated by physical or chemical impurities, which does not exceed the used-oil fuel specification (Table 3-3), and which is subsequently burned for energy recovery. This includes any fuel produced from used oil by processing, blending, or other treatment, and which does not contain hazardous wastes. UOF may itself exhibit a characteristic of hazardous waste provided it has not been mixed with hazardous waste.[104] UOFs can be burned in all boilers and furnaces including residential and commercial.

An "OUOF" is a used-oil fuel that exceeds one or more of the constituent parameters established in Table 3-3. While an OUOF can be processed to meet the fuel spec in Table 3-3 (other than the total halogen level) a hazardous waste fuel cannot. OUOF's are subject to the same restrictions on burning as HWFs; however, OUOFs are subject to an invoice tracking system rather than the manifest system that applies to HWFs.[105] Table 3-3 also presents the recommended procedures for analyzing used oil to determine whether a given sample of waste material meets or exceeds the specification levels.

THE TOTAL HALOGEN REBUTTABLE PRESUMPTION   The problems with using three categories of fuels as the basis of determining the applicability and level of hazardous waste control are several. The most significant is attempting to determine the nature of the original material, and how it came to contain the constituents of concern. Was it an oily waste that had hazardous wastes added to it (and potentially classed as an OUOF rather

Table 3-3   Used-Oil Fuel Specification[1]
Recommended Analytical Procedures

Used Oil Fuel Specification[1]

Constituent/ property	Proposal allowable level	Final rule allowable level
Arsenic	5 ppm maximum	5 ppm maximum
Cadmium	2 ppm maximum	2 ppm maximum.
Chromium	10 ppm maximum	10 ppm maximum.
Lead	10–100 ppm maximum [2].	100 ppm maximum.
PCBs	50 ppm maximum	
Total halogens.		4000 ppm maximum.
Flash point	100 °F minimum	100 °F minimum.

[1] The specification applies only to used oil that is not mixed with hazardous waste other than small quantity generator hazardous waste.

[2] EPA proposed to a select level from the range of 10 to 100 ppm for promulgation. Lead is limited to 100 ppm by today's final rule.

Recommended Analytical Procedures

Parameter	Method		Source
Total halogens	D808–81		ASTM.
Flash point	1010		SW–846 and Proposed Test Methods for Evaluating Solid Waste[*].
	Preparation	*Determination*	
Arsenic	3040*/3050	7060	SW–846 and Proposed Test Methods for Evaluating Solid Waste[*].
Cadmium	3040*/3050	6010 7131 7131	Do.
Chromium	3040*/3050	6010 7191 7191	Do.
Lead	3040*/3050	6010 7420 7421	Do.

Notes:

[*] Recommended only for non-sedimentaceous oils.

'SW–46 (*Test Methods for Evaluating Solid Waste*) is available from the U.S. Government Printing Office. *Proposed Test Methods for Evaluating Solid Waste* is available from NTIS under order No. PB8–103–026.

than a HWF), or was it a hazardous waste that had used oil added to it (presumably a HWF but would be difficult to prove). To remedy this obvious problem of end-use regulation based on the origins of the material, the Agency has established a level of 1000 ppm total halogens (primarily chlorine) as a presumptive indicator of deliberate adulteration and so a cutoff for regulation as a HWF unless the presumption can be successfully rebutted by the generator or facility.[106] The need for a chlorine specification and the adequacy of this safeguard not withstanding, the final rule still allows OUOF to merely be diluted with oil to comply with the fuel spec (except for the 1000 ppm total halogen specification), accomplishing little in the way of removing hazardous constituents from the environment. Several examples of how these provisions would work are provided in the regulations.[107] In addition, the 1000 ppm total halogen rebuttable presumption is the governing principle in identifying and distinguishing between those waste and/or used-oil mixtures that are RCRA hazardous wastes and those that are not. Chapter 2 examines these mixture issues in detail.

REGULATORY REQUIREMENTS The transportation and storage requirements for generators, transporters, blenders, and burners of HWFs prior to actual burning are summarized in Table 3-4. Of particular note is the fact that both generators and transporters of OUOF would be exempt from any hazardous waste regulation. How the Agency plans to prevent transporters from claiming that they are carriers of either UOF or OUOF is unclear.

Recyclable Materials Exempt from Regulation

Unlike the recyclable materials discussed above which had standards and requirements that were tailored to specific recycling applications, other recyclable materials are exempt from regulation entirely,[108] although some are on a temporary basis:

> reclaimed industrial ethyl alcohol
> used batteries returned to a battery manufacturer for regeneration
> used oil exhibiting a hazardous waste characteristic (temporary)
> scrap metal being reclaimed (temporary)

Variances

The Agency has adopted a series of variance standards and procedures that allow the Regional EPA Administrators to either impose or remove regulatory control at a given facility and/or process. To a large extent these provisions serve as means of arbitrating and determining whether or not the recycling regulations apply to a given process.

Due to the severe although infrequent damage cases that have occurred at previous metal reclamation facilities, a case-by-case variance procedure allows the Regional Administrator to regulate individual unsafe operations while otherwise maintaining the exemption and not regulating the entire class of such facilities. A separate set of standards and administrative procedures have been established for the Regional Administrator to impose such case-by-case controls. Due to the broad diversity of flame combustion devices, a variance procedure has also been included which allows the Regional Administrator to classify a given device as a boiler.[109]

IMPACT ON STATE PROGRAMS

Since the revised definition of solid waste and its accompanying recycling regulations are not mandated by HSWA (except for burning and blending controls, waste oil listing, and dust suppression restrictions), the definitions and requirements discussed in this chapter will not apply in authorized states until they revise their programs to include controls for hazardous wastes that are equivalent to or more stringent than EPA's (Table 3-4). In non-authorized states, the regulations became effective July 15, 1985, or when the state lost its authorization, whichever is later (see Chapter 14).

Table 3-4   Regulatory Requirements for Recycling Practices and Materials[1]

Facility/Activity	Material	Regulatory Requirements	Status	Effect Date
Use Constituting Disposal[2]				
Generators, Transporters, TSDFs	All except waste-derived products (WDP), & use for dust suppressants	262–5, 124, 270, 3010	Final (1-4-85)	Auth. State[2] (7-5-85)
Generators, Transporters	Waste-derived Products	262, 263, & storage reg prior to UCD 3010	Final (1-4-85)	Auth. State (7-5-85)
TSDFs	Waste-derived Products (e.g., fertilizers)	264–5, 124, 270, 3010	Deferred	Auth. State (7-5-85)
Any Person using Waste Material for Dust Suppression	Any HW or Hw mixed w/used oil, except ignitable-only mixtures	Prohibited by Statute	Final (1-4-85)	8-15-85
Any Person using Waste Material for Dust Suppression	Ignitable only HW & Waste Mixtures	262–5, 124, 270 3010	Final (1-4-85)	Auth. State (7-5-85)
Overaccumulation				
Generators	All except commercial chemical (CCP)	262, 3010	Final (1-4-85)	Auth. State (7-5-85)
Transporters	All except CCP	263, 3010	Final (1-4-85)	Auth. State (7-5-85)

Continued

Table 3-4 Continued

Piles	All except CCP	264, 265, 124, 270, 3010	Final (1-4-85)	Auth. State (7-5-85)
Tanks, Containers	All except CCP or scrap metal	264, 265, 124, 270, 3010	Final (1-4-85)	Auth. State (7-5-85)
Tanks or Containers storage for > 90 days, or < 90 days w/o complying w/ 266.34	All except CCP	264, 265, 124, 270, 3010	Final (1-4-85)	Auth. State (7-5-85)
Tanks, Containers (261.4(c) Manufacturing unit)	All	None	Final (1-4-85)	Auth. State (7-5-85)
Generators, Transporters, TSDFs (except surface impoundments)	Commercial chemical products	None	Final (1-4-85)	Auth. State (7-5-85)
Surface Impoundments	Commercial chemical products	264, 265, 124, 270, 3010	Final (1-4-85)	Auth. State (7-5-85)
Generators, Transporters, TSDFs	Scrap metal (w/o suffic. amounts being recycled)	None	Final (1-4-85)	Auth. State (7-5-85)
Generators, Transporters, TSDFs	Scrap metal (w/o a known market for recycled product)	262–5, 124, 270, 3010	Deferred	1-4-85
Generators, Transporters, TSDFs	Black liquor from paper processing spent sulfuric acid used to produce virgin sulfuric	262–5, 124, 270, 3010	Final (1-4-85)	1-4-85
Generators, Transporters, TSDFs[3]	Reclaimed industrial ethyl alcohol, used batteries returned to manuf., used oil (character only), scrap metal	None	Final (1-4-85)	1-4-85

Reclamation

Generators, Transporters, TSDFs	All spent materials, listed sludges, listed byproducts, scrap	262, 3010, 263, 264–5, 124, 270, 3010	Final (1-4-85)	Auth. State (7-5-85)
Generators, Transporters, TSDFs	Characteristic sludges, characteristic byproducts, commercial chemical products	None	Final (1-4-85)	Auth. State (7-5-85)
Generators, Transporters, Storage Facilities, Recycling Facilities	Precious metals (266.70)	262, 263.20, 263.21, 265.71, 265.72, 266.70(c)— records, volume limitations, amount reclaimed	Final (1-4-85)	Auth. State (7-5-85)

Table 3-4 Continued

Generators, Transporters, Storage Facilities	Spent lead-acid batteries	None (conditional) 266.30	Final (1-4-85)	Auth. State (7-5-85)
Reclamation Facilities That Store	Spent lead-acid batteries (266.30)	264, 265, except 264.13, 264.71, 264.72, 265.13, 265.71, 265.72, 124, 270	Final (1-4-85)	Auth. State (7-5-85)
Generator, Own Waste	All	262–5	Final (1-4-85)	Auth. State (7-5-85)
Persons Reclaiming Other's Waste	All	262–5	Final (1-4-85)	Auth. State (7-5-85)
Batch Tolling Operations	All	262–5	Final (1-4-85)	Auth. State (7-5-85)
Generators, Transporters, Storage Facilities, Burners, Marketers	Used oil	266.40–4 (see Table 3-2)	Proposed	Upon promulgation in all states

Burning for Energy Recovery

Generator[4]	Hazardous waste fuel	262[5]	Final (11-29-85)	12-09-85
Generator	Off-specification used-oil fuel	None	Final (11-29-85)	12-09-85
Generator	Used-oil fuel	None	Final (11-29-85)	12-09-85
Generators, transporters taking intermediate waste-derived fuels from fuel processors to burners	Used-oil fuels	Exempt	Final (11-29-85)	12-09-85
Transporters	Hazardous waste fuel	263[6]	Final (11-29-85)	12-09-85
Transporters	Off-specification used-oil	Exempt	Final 11-29-85)	12-09-85
Marketers[4]	Hazardous waste fuel	266.34 N, RN, P, M, G, R, S	Final	12-09-85
Marketers	Off-specification used-oil fuel	266.43 N, RN, P, I, C, R	Final	12-09-85
Marketers	Used-oil fuel	Exempt	Final	12-09-85
Burners	Hazardous waste fuel	266.35 N, RN, P, M, C, R, S	Final	12-09-85
Burners	Off-specification used-oil fuel	266.43 N, RN, P, I, C, R	Final	12-09-85
Burners	Used-oil fuels	Exempt	Final	12-09-85

[1] Standards for recyclable materials that are managed in a manner constituting disposal are contained in 266.20–23; for overaccumulation, 261.1(c)(8); for hazardous wastes and used oils burned for energy recovery, 40 CFR Part 266.30 and 266.40, respectively.

Table 3-4   Continued

[2] "Auth. State" signifies that these are non-HSWA requirements that do not take effect in states with authorized RCRA programs until the state has changed its regulations to incorporate them. The "(7-5-85)" indicates the date that these requirements take effect in all other states, usually 6 months after final promulgation (see Chapter 14 for discussion of State Programs).

[3] Exemptions for these materials are specified at 261.6(a)(3).

[4] Hazardous waste and used oil generators are not regulated as marketers unless they market directly to a burner.

[5] Hazardous waste generators who send their waste to a hazardous waste fuel marketer are subject to Part 262 standards as ordinary generators (see 266.32(a)). Generators who market their hazardous waste fuel to burners are subject to the Part 262 generator standards as well as today's hazardous waste fuel marketer requirements (see 266.32(b)).

[6] Hazardous waste fuel transporters are subject to regulation as ordinary hazardous waste transporters. Thus, they are not required to notify or re-notify for their waste-as-fuel activities. However, they must notify for their hazardous waste transportation activities if they have not notified already.

Key: N   - Notification and identification number.
     RN   - Re-notify for waste-as-fuel activities.
     P   - Prohibitions on marketing to, or burning in, non-industrial boilers.
     M,I   - Compliance with manifest (M) or invoice (I).
     C   - Provide or receive certification of compliance with standards for burning.
     R   - Recordkeeping.
     S   - Storage standards.

NOTES

1. 40 CFR 261.6 (beneficial use exemption); 45 *Fed. Reg.* 33091, 33090–33095 (May 19, 1980); 40 CFR 261.3(b) (definition of a hazardous waste); 45 *Fed. Reg.* 33095 (May 19, 1980).

2. 50 *Fed. Reg.* 614 (Jan. 4, 1985) (redefinition of solid waste).

3. Brief of EPA in *American Mining Congress et al.* v. *EPA* Mos 85-1206, 85-1208, 85-1211, 85-1212, Dec. 12, 1985, D.C. Cir., p. 9.

4. 50 *Fed. Reg.* 658 (Jan. 4, 1985) Appendices A, B. Also see 40 CFR Part 300, Appendix B, for current list of "superfund" sites.

5. Supra note 3, p. 10.

6. Ibid.

7. 50 *Fed. Reg.* 49220 (Nov. 29, 1985) (proposed standards for recycling of used oil).

8. Supra note 3, p. 11. Also see 50 *Fed. Reg.* 858 (Jan. 4, 1985) Appendix A.

9. Statement of Enforcement Policy issued Jan. 18, 1983; 48 *Fed. Reg.* 11157 (Mar. 16, 1983).

10. Supra note 3, p. 10.

11. Ibid.

12. 48 *Fed. Reg.* 1447S (April 4, 1983).

13. HR 6307, 97th Cong. 2nd Sess., Sect. 13.

14. 40 CFR 261.4(a)(1)–(5).

15. 40 *Fed. Reg.* 33099 (May 19,1980).

16. Ibid.

17. 45 *Fed. Reg.* 33097–99, 33101–2 (May 19, 1980).

18. "Technologies and Management Strategies for Managing Hazardous Wastes," U.S. Congress, Office of Technology Assessment, p. 9, Washington D.C., March 1983; "The CMA Hazardous Waste Survey for 1983, Final Report, p. 1, Chemical Manufacturers Assoc., Washington, D.C., May 1985; "National Small Quantity Hazardous Waste Generator Survey," p. 41, D-12 U.S. EPA, Office of Solid Waste, Washington, D.C., prepared by Abt Associates Inc., Cambridge, Mass. (contract 68-01-6892), Feb. 1985.

19. 8 E.R.C. 2120 D.D.C. 1975.

20. RCRA, Section 3018; P.L. 98-616, Section 246.

21. EPA Report to Congress on the Discharge of Hazardous Wastes to POTWs," Office of Water, Feb. 1986.

22. 45 *Fed. Reg.* 33097–8 (May 19, 1980); also see supra note 18, CMA Survey, p. 19.

23. *NRDC* v. *Train* 8 E.R.C. 2120 (D.D. Cir. 1976).

24. 40 CFR 403.7.

25. 40 CFR 403.5.

26. Supra note 21, pp. 7-1–7-12.

27. Barbara Finamore, "Regulating Hazardous and Mixed Waste at Department of Energy Nuclear Weapons Facilities: Reversing Decades of Environmental Neglect," *Harvard Environmental Law Review,* Vol. 9, No. 1, p. 85, 1985.

28. *Legal Environmental Assistance Foundation (LEAF)* v. *Hodel,* 586 F. Supp. 1163 (E.D. Tenn. 1984).

29. Supra note 27, p. 86.

30. 45 *Fed. Reg.* 33099–33101 (May 19, 1980).

31. EPA Report to Congress on "Wastes from Extraction and Beneficiation of Metallic Ores, Phosphate Rock, Asbestos, Overburden from Mining Wastes, and Oil Shale." USEPA Office of Solid Waste, December 1985, EPA/530SW-85-033.

32. 50 *Fed. Reg.* 40292 (Oct. 2, 1985).

33. 40 CFR 261.4(b).

34. Senate Report 98-284, p. 61; Conference Report 98-1133, p. 106.

35. 40 CFR 261.4(b)(6). See 50 *Fed. Reg.* 48892 (Nov. 27, 1985), for discussion of chrome study and related problems with chrome waste exclusion.

36. 40 CFR 261.4(d).

37. 40 CFR 261.4(c); 45 *Fed. Reg.* 72028 (Oct. 30, 1980); 45 *Fed. Reg.* 80287 (Dec. 4, 1980).

38. RCRA, 3001(b)(3)(A); 45 *Fed. Reg.* 76618–20 (Nov. 19, 1980).

39. 46 *Fed. Reg.* 4614–15 (Jan. 16, 1981).

40. *Concerned Citizens of Adamstown* v. *EPA,* District Court for Washington, D.C., Civil Action No. 84-3041 (Sept. 28, 1984).

41. 50 Fed. Reg. 40292 (Oct. 2, 1985).

42. 50 *Fed. Reg.* 638 (Jan. 4, 1985).

43. 50 *Fed. Reg.* 633 (Jan. 4, 1985) (definition of reclamation).

44. 50 *Fed. Reg.* 637-8 (Jan. 4, 1985) (sham substitute situations).

45. 50 *Fed. Reg.* 639-40 (Jan. 4, 1985).

46. 45 *Fed. Reg.* 33093–4 (May 19, 1980).

47. 40 CFR 260.30, 260.31–33.

48. 50 *Fed. Reg.* 634, 636–7, 654 (Jan. 4, 1985).

49. 50 *Fed. Reg.* 627–8 (Jan. 4, 1985).

50. 40 CFR 261.2(d).

51. 40 CFR 261.2(d)(2).
52. 40 CFR 261.1(b)(8) (definition of speculative accumulation); 50 Fed. Reg. 634–6 (Jan. 4, 1985).
53. Ibid.
54. RCRA, Section 3004(j).
55. 50 *Fed. Reg.* 628 (Jan. 4, 1985); House Report 98-198, p. 46.
56. 50 Fed. Reg. 618 (Jan. 4, 1985).
57. J. T. Smith and R. W. Fratz, "EPA Revises Solid Waste Definition and Rules," *Legal Times,* vol. III, No. 32, June 15, 1985.
58. 50 *Fed. Reg.* 619 (Jan. 4, 1985).
59. 50 *Fed. Reg.* 649 (Jan. 4, 1985).
60. 40 CFR 261.3(c)(d), 50 Fed. Reg. 634 (Jan. 4, 1985).
61. *Boilers.* The definitions of both boilers and furnaces depend upon the concepts of integral design, combustion efficiency, and energy recovery. The definition of boilers focuses on its physical characteristics that allow for the efficient conversion of fuel to energy.

     A boiler is defined as an enclosed device using controlled flame combustion and has the following characteristics:

     it must physically provide for recovering and exporting thermal energy in the form of steam, heated fluids, or heated gasses; *and*

     the unit's combustion chamber must be of an integral design. To be of an integral design, the primary energy recovery unit must consist of a single unit. In addition, the following units are boilers even though they do not consist of an integral design: process heaters and fluidized bed combusion units: *and*

     the unit must maintain a thermal energy recovery efficiency of at least 60% relative to the thermal value of the fuel; *and*

     the unit must export and utilize at least 75% of the recovered energy calculated on an annual basis: *or*

     the Regional Administrator has determined that the units is properly classified as a boiler subsequent to a consideration of certain standards.
62. *Industrial Furnaces.*These are any enclosed devices that are integral components of manufacturing processes and that use controlled flame devices to accomplish recovery of materials *or* energy: cement kilns; lime kilns; aggregate kilns; phosphate kilns; coke ovens; blast furnaces; smelting, melting and refining furnaces, including pyrometallurgical devices such as cupolas, reverberator furnaces, sintering machines, roasters, and foundry furnaces; titanium dioxide chloride process oxidation reactors; methane reforming furnaces; pulping liquor recovery furances; combustion devices used in the recovery of sulfur values from spent sulfuric acid.
63. *Incinerator.* An incinerator is defined as any enclosed device that is neither a boiler nor an industrial furnace that uses controlled flame combustion to destroy wastes. This approach eliminates the previous approach to defining incinerators, which focused on whether each waste fuel was burned for the primary purpose of destruction (the so-called primary purpose test, which proved impractical and too easily evaded. See also supra note 13, pp. 9, 129.
64. "Sham Burning Enforcement Policy," 48 *Fed. Reg.* 11157 (Mar. 16, 1983).
65. 40 CFR 261.2(c)(2)(C)(ii).
66. See RCRA 3004(q), House Report 98-198 (Part I), pp. 30–32, 38–39, 42.
67. 50 *Fed. Reg.* 631 (Jan. 4, 1985). Also see Intervenor Brief of Hazardous Waste Treatment Council, *AMC* v. *U.S. EPA,* Case No. 85-1206 and consolidated cases, D.C. Cir.; supra note 3, pp. 46–51.
68. Also see "When is a Waste Not a Waste," B. Garelick, *Environmental Forum,* September 1985, p. 26. Note: article contains several inaccuracies regarding intent

of redefinition rule and scope of Agency's jurisdiction to control recycling activities generally. See S. Silverman, letter to the editor, *Environmental Forum,* April 1986.

69. 50 *Fed. Reg.* 642 (Jan. 4, 1985).
70. 45 *Fed. Reg.* 33092–3; H. Rpt. 98-198, p. 46.
71. 40 CFR 261.6(a)(2)(i)–(v).
72. 40 CFR 261.6(b).
73. 40 CFR 261.6(c).
74. 40 CFR Part 270 (124 permitting requirements).
75. 40 CFR 261.6(a)(3).
76. 40 CFR 261.6(a)(2)(i), Part 266, Subpart C.
77. 50 Fed. Reg. 646 (Jan. 4, 1985), "Background Document for July 26, 1982 Regulations—Land Application of Wastes as Fertilizers."
78. RCRA, Section 3004(1); 50 *Fed. Reg.* 28118 (July 15, 1985).
79. 50 *Fed. Reg.* 647 (Jan. 4, 1985).
80. Ibid.
81. 50 *Fed. Reg.* 651 (Jan. 4, 1985).
82. 40 CFR 261.6(a)(2)(iii); 266 Subpart E.
83. 40 CFR 261.6(2)(iv); 266 Subpart F.
84. 40 CFR 261.6(a)(2)(v); 266 Subpart G, Section 3010.
85. 50 *Fed. Reg.* 49164 (Nov. 29, 1985).
86. 50 *Fed. Reg.* 49258 (Nov. 29, 1985).
87. 50 *Fed. Reg.* 49212 (Nov. 29, 1985). Also see Conference Report 98-1133, pp. 113–4.
88. Ibid., pp. 49216–8.
89. Ibid., pp. 49218–9.
90. Ibid., pp. 49252–4.
91. Ibid., pp. 49254–6.
92. Ibid., p. 49242.
93. 50 *Fed. Reg.* 649 (Jan. 4, 1985).
94. RCRA, Section 3010; 40 CFR 261.2(c)(4) (speculative or overaccumulation governed by 262-265); 40 CFR, 264.70, 265.70.
95. 50 *Fed. Reg.* 648–9 (Jan. 4, 1985).
96. 260.40, 260.41 (variance procedures).
97. 50 *Fed. Reg.* 649 (Jan. 4, 1985); 40 CFR 261.3(c)(2) ("derived from" rule).
98. 50 *Fed. Reg.* 667–8 (Jan. 4, 1985); 266.30(b)(1)–(4) provides a minor variance from 264.265 for reclamation of lead-acid batteries.
99. 50 *Fed. Reg.* 49195 (Nov. 29, 1985).
100. RCRA 3004(r)(2)(3); 50 *Fed. Reg.* 28725 (July 15, 1985).
101. 3004(9)(2)(c)(i); 50 *Fed. Reg.* 28724 (July 15, 1985); PL 98-616, Sec. 204.
102. 50 *Fed. Reg.* 49164 (Nov. 29 1985). Originally proposed on Jan. 11, 1985, 50 *Fed. Reg.* 1684.
103. 50 *Fed. Reg.* 49211 (Nov. 29, 1985).
104. Ibid.
105. Ibid.
106. Ibid., pp. 49175–7.
107. Ibid., pp. 49176–8.
108. 40 CFR 261.6(a)(3)(i)–(iv).
109. 40 CFR 260.32, 260.33.

CHAPTER FOUR

Regulating Generators

There are now new HSWA requirements imposed upon generators producing less than 1000 kilograms per month of hazardous waste, often called "small quantity generators." In comparing requirements applicable to large and small quantity generators, this chapter provides a detailed description of regulations for all generators of hazardous waste. Significantly, these requirements can also apply to a facility owner/operator that generates a waste through spill cleanup, rainwater or leachate collection, or as a residue from a treatment process (see Chapter 7).

THE HISTORY OF THE SMALL QUANTITY EXEMPTION

The regulation of small quantity generators has been controversial from the outset of the RCRA program because both the environmental consequences of underregulation and the economic burden of unnecessary regulation can be severe in this area. Caught between a rock and a hard place, EPA could not determine, on a generic basis, a minimum quantity of hazardous waste below which no substantial hazard to human health or the environment would develop from improper waste management.[1] Nor could EPA perform the virtually endless analyses necessary to establish tailored quantity cutoffs for particular types of waste generators in specific types of environmental contexts.[2]

Further igniting the controversy was an inadequate data base, a problem exacerbated by EPA's failure to impose reporting requirements on generators otherwise exempt from regulation. In short, EPA could not develop a technical solution to a thorny political issue.

Consequently, the issue was ultimately resolved by the Congress, an entirely appropriate result given that it called for a legislative rather than technical judgment as to how to balance the need to protect human health and the environment with the administrative and economic burdens imposed by the RCRA program.[3] The 1976 RCRA provided no guidance in this area since it did not differentiate generators by types or quantities of waste generated, thus contributing to the regulatory deficiencies created by EPA.

In 1978, EPA proposed a general quantity cutoff of 100 kg/mo. However, when the regulations were finally issued in 1980, EPA had raised the general exclusion level 10 times, to 1000 kg/mo. The major provisions of the 1980 regulations, codified at 40 CFR 261.5, were as follows:

1. Wastes generated in quantities of less than 1000 kg/mo were not subject to federal hazardous waste regulation as long as the generator: de-

termined if its waste was hazardous; did not accumulate over 1000 kg of hazardous waste at any one time; and managed the waste at either a hazardous waste TSDF, a municipal or industrial solid waste facility licensed or registered with the state, a recycling or reclaiming operation, or a facility treating the waste prior to such beneficial recycling or reclamation.

2. Mixtures of hazardous and non-hazardous waste would not be subject to regulation unless the hazardous waste component of the mixture exceeded 1000 kg/mo.

3. Lower quantity cutoffs were established for products on the 261.33(e) list (1 kg/mo), and contaminated soils and debris from the spills of such products (100 kg/mo). These wastes, sometimes called acutely hazardous wastes, are generally subject to regulation only when disposed of in a pure or off-specification form, and are not considered to represent a significant portion of the waste that is generated.

There were obvious flaws in the 1980 regulations. They did not require that wastes generated below the quantity cutoff be accompanied by manifests, either to warn people handling the waste that the waste was hazardous, or to ensure the waste would arrive at the appropriate facilities. The regulations also allowed the waste to be sent to municipal landfills handling household garbage or other solid waste facilities, many of which need not be designed with liners or leachate collection systems, or monitored for their environmental impacts.

EPA recognized that these regulations did not satisfy the statutory mandate for protection of human health and the environment, and pledged to initiate a second rulemaking within 2 to 5 years to lower the quantity cutoff.[4] Available EPA data indicated that the better quantity cutoff was 100 kg/mo, the level needed to achieve control over single 55-gallon drums of hazardous waste.[5] EPA had reviewed damage incident reports, and concluded that 55-gallon drums of ignitable, reactive, and corrosive waste posed a problem at solid waste landfills because operators were not aware of their contents and employees were not adequately trained to properly handle hazardous waste.[6] Other damage incidents revealed well contamination and illnesses resulting from the improper management of small amounts of hazardous waste.[7]

EPA justified the 1000 kg/mo cutoff in 1980 solely on the basis of federal and state agency resource constraints, arguing that lowering the cutoff to 100 kg/mo in 1980 would interfere with the higher priority application of the regulatory program to larger generators. Support for EPA's justification consisted of several contractor reports on programmatic resource needs and waste generation profiles. According to these reports, only one percent of the hazardous waste produced annually in the U.S. (600,000 tons) was generated by 91% of the generators (690,000) at levels below 1000 kg/mo. Therefore, EPA believed that even with a 1000 kg/mo cutoff, it would still be regulating most of the waste while at the same time avoiding the burden of regulating thousands of additional generators.[8]

Two years passed, and during this time the Agency provided no indication as to when or if the second rulemaking would begin. In July 1982, the Office of Technology Assessment (OTA), a research arm of the Congress, issued a staff memorandum criticizing EPA's prior contractor reports. OTA estimated that as much as five percent of the hazardous waste generated nationally was excluded from regulation by the small quantity exemption, and since larger generators tended to manage waste on-site, the excluded waste amounted to between 10 and 50 percent of the hazardous waste destined for off-site land disposal.[9]

In addition, the resource constraints that EPA had identified in 1980 were apparently not sufficient to discourage a significant number of states from lowering the quantity cutoff to below 1000 kg/mo on their own. The Association of State and Territorial Solid Waste Management Officials (ASTSWMO) surveyed its members and found 16 states with quantity cutoffs below 1000 kg/mo.[10] A number of states, in fact, had no exclusions or exclusions below 100 kg/mo, including Massachusetts (20 kg/mo) and Oregon (25–200 lbs depending on the waste).[11] Other states were clustered at a 100 kg/mo cutoff.[12] However, not all states were capable of lowering the quantity cutoff if EPA did not do so first, because state law prevented their regulations from being more stringent than the federal program.[13]

Acknowledging weaknesses in its existing data base, EPA initiated a second study of small quantity generators in 1983 which it would not complete until early 1985. At the same time, EPA all but abandoned its previously announced intentions to lower the quantity cutoff to 100 kg/mo, and would not propose a schedule for further rulemaking in this area. The same agency that had previously complained about a lack of Congressional guidance on small quantity generators was now seeking to limit Congressional intervention in this area under the guise of the need to retain administrative discretion when new data became available.[14]

Congressional efforts to lower the quantity cutoff began with the passage in 1982 of H.R. 6307 in the U.S. House of Representatives. EPA's reluctance to tighten the exemption and opposition from the regulated community confirmed the need for a legislative provision that would ensure a set of "minimum regulatory controls" over previously exempted waste would be in place by a certain date. These controls, often referred to as "hammers," served as the template for structuring other provisions as HSWA evolved into law during 1983 and 1984.

THE HSWA REQUIREMENTS

Congress adopted a provision (Section 221 of HSWA) that contained substantial minimum requirements for waste generated by small quantity generators and delegated the remaining decisions to EPA to be decided in an

EPA rulemaking mandated for completion by March 31, 1986. The provision is largely based on a compromise written by representatives of the small business and environmental communities.[15] The provision contains six principal components:

1. Beginning August 5, 1985, off-site shipments of non-acutely hazardous waste generated at rates between 100 kg/mo and 1000 kg/mo must be accompanied by the Uniform Hazardous Waste Manifest (UHWM) signed by the generator and filled out as specified in the provision.

2. EPA must issue new regulations by March 31, 1986, which, at a minimum, lower the quantity cutoff to 100 kg/mo for non-acutely hazardous waste and require management of the waste at a permitted or interim status hazardous waste treatment, storage, or disposal facility (TSDF).

3. Should EPA fail to issue regulations by March 31, 1986, minimum regulatory controls (MRCs) are automatically imposed on an interim basis until EPA issues the mandated regulations, including certain waste tracking requirements and the management of the waste at a permitted or interim status hazardous waste TSDF.

4. The lower quantity cutoffs (1 kg/mo) in effect for acutely hazardous wastes remain in effect.

5. EPA is instructed to make special efforts to educate small quantity generators about their new responsibilities.

6. EPA was required to complete the study it had begun regarding small generators by April 1, 1985; and perform three additional studies by April 1, 1987, regarding: hazardous waste generated by high schools and universities, the efficacy of the manifest tracking system as it applies to small quantity generators, and the feasibility of licensing transporters to perform the responsibilities which will be assumed by small quantity generators. A more detailed discussion of the principal components follows.

The August 5, 1985, Manifest Requirement

The August 5, 1985, manifest requirement serves as a warning notice; it was imposed to ensure that handlers of hazardous waste generated in quantities greater than 100 kg/mo, including transporters and TSDF personnel, would know the waste is hazardous, and why, so the waste could be handled safely. To accomplish this immediate goal, Congress did not require that all of the manifest form be filled out, and certain recordkeeping and reporting requirements typically associated with tracking the waste to its ultimate disposal location were *not* triggered by this provision. The manifest merely "accompanies" the waste, and once the generator has properly filled out one copy of the manifest, signed it, and given the manifest copy and the waste to the transporter, the generator's manifest duties under the provision are completed.

The Uniform Hazardous Waste Manifest was issued by EPA and the U.S. Department of Transportation (DOT) on March 20, 1984, a copy of which is provided as Figure 4-1. It is "uniform" because the use of this form is required for all regulated interstate or intrastate hazardous waste shipments after September 20, 1984. Generators seeking copies of the form should consult the state in which the facility receiving the waste is located, the state in which the generator is located, or other printing sources *in that order*. This hierarchy of acquisition is specified in the regulations applicable to larger generators, and while Congress did not specify these regulations apply to the small quantity generator manifest requirements of August 5, 1985, it may be useful to follow these procedures from the outset since they will apply under EPA regulations effective September 22, 1986. The hierarchy was established because many states require the submission of signed manifests to the state shortly after shipment, including submission from out-of-state generators shipping waste to a facility within the state. By requiring generators to use the forms of the state in which the facility receiving the waste is located, out-of-state generators can be made aware if that state imposes manifest submission requirements.

The statute is specific about the information the small quantity generator needs to provide on the UHWM. The information shall include:

1. the name and address of the generator (line 3);
2. the name and address of the facility designated to receive the waste (line 9);
3. the DOT description of the waste, including shipping name, hazard class and UN/NA ID number (line 11);
4. the number and type of containers (line 12);
5. the quantity of waste being transported (lines 13 and 14); and
6. the manifest must also be signed by the generator (line 16).

Between August 5, 1985, and September 22, 1986, the existing federal rules allowing the management of small quantity generated waste at solid waste facilities, or a facility which reuses, recycles or reclaims the waste, or a facility which treats the waste prior to reuse, recycling or reclamation remain in effect. No other new requirements were imposed by HSWA during this interim period. Beginning September 22, 1986, the August 5 manifest requirements are superseded by the new EPA regulations described below.

New EPA Regulations

The EPA regulations mandated by HSWA must require that waste generated at quantities between 100 kg/mo and 1000 kg/mo be managed at a permitted or interim status hazardous waste TSDF. To ease this burden, Congress extended the time that generators can store waste temporarily on-site in tanks or containers for shipment off-site before becoming a stor-

Please print or type. *(Form designed for use on elite (12-pitch) typewriter.)*   Form Approved. OMB No. 2000-0404. Expires 7-31-86

UNIFORM HAZARDOUS WASTE MANIFEST	1. Generator's US EPA ID No.	Manifest Document No.	2. Page 1 of	Information in the shaded areas is not required by Federal law.

3. Generator's Name and Mailing Address

A. State Manifest Document Number

B. State Generator's ID

4. Generator's Phone (   )

5. Transporter 1 Company Name   6.   US EPA ID Number

C. State Transporter's ID

D. Transporter's Phone

7. Transporter 2 Company Name   8.   US EPA ID Number

E. State Transporter's ID

F. Transporter's Phone

9. Designated Facility Name and Site Address   10.   US EPA ID Number

G. State Facility's ID

H. Facility's Phone

11. US DOT Description (Including Proper Shipping Name, Hazard Class, and ID Number)	12. Containers		13. Total Quantity	14 Unit Wt/Vol	I. Waste No.
	No.	Type			
a.					
b.					
c.					
d.					

J. Additional Descriptions for Materials Listed Above   K. Handling Codes for Wastes Listed Above

15. Special Handling Instructions and Additional Information

16. GENERATOR'S CERTIFICATION: I hereby declare that the contents of this consignment are fully and accurately described above by proper shipping name and are classified, packed, marked, and labeled, and are in all respects in proper condition for transport by highway according to applicable international and national government regulations.

Unless I am a small quantity generator who has been exempted by statute or regulation from the duty to make a waste minimization certification under Section 3002(b) of RCRA, I also certify that I have a program in place to reduce the volume and toxicity of waste generated to the degree I have determined to be economically practicable and I have selected the method of treatment, storage, or disposal currently available to me which minimizes the present and future threat to human health and the environment.

Printed/Typed Name   Signature   Month Day Year

17. Transporter 1 Acknowledgement of Receipt of Materials
Printed/Typed Name   Signature   Month Day Year

18. Transporter 2 Acknowledgement of Receipt of Materials
Printed/Typed Name   Signature   Month Day Year

19. Discrepancy Indication Space

20. Facility Owner or Operator: Certification of receipt of hazardous materials covered by this manifest except as noted in Item 19.
Printed/Typed Name   Signature   Month Day Year

EPA Form 8700-22 (Rev. 4-85) Previous edition is obsolete.

Figure 4-1   Uniform Hazardous Waste Manifest

age facility requiring a permit. Larger generators can store up to 90 days without a permit; small generators can store up to 180 days without a permit, or 270 days for quantities up to 6000 kg if the waste must be shipped off-site over 200 miles. Larger generators engaged in non-permitted or temporary storage must comply with 40 CFR 262.34, which imposes a minimum number of operating requirements. HSWA provides EPA with the discretion to determine whether and to what extent 40 CFR 262.34 will apply to small quantity generators. EPA also has discretion to vary other standards applicable to larger quantities of waste but the standards must still be protective of human health and the environment. In particular, Congress authorized EPA to adopt different reporting and recordkeeping approaches where environmental protection would not be sacrificed.

On March 24, 1986, EPA issued the small quantity generator regulations mandated by HSWA. For the most part, generators must be in compliance with these rules beginning September 22, 1986. Generators managing wastes on-site in a manner requiring them to obtain interim status and eventually a permit, have until March 24, 1987, to qualify for interim status and meet interim status standards. Table 4-1 describes the regulations in effect applicable to larger generators, and compares those rules to EPA's regulations for generators producing between 100 kg/mo and 1000 kg/mo of non-acutely hazardous waste. Copies of the small quantity generator rules may be obtained by calling the EPA RCRA Hotline toll-free (800-424-9346) or the EPA Small Business Hotline toll-free (800-368-5888).

MRCs Imposed if EPA Fails to Issue New Regulations

In case EPA failed to issue final regulations for small quantity generators on time, Congress would have imposed minimum regulatory controls on non-acutely hazardous waste generated in quantities of between 100 kg/mo and 1000 kg/mo, effective March 31, 1986. These controls are specified in Section 3001(d)(8) of RCRA. However, since EPA issued the rules on time, this section of the law will *not* be triggered. EPA's timely behavior was, in large part, due to the existence of the minimum regulatory controls provision, thus the provision accomplished its intended purpose.

COMPLIANCE TIPS

In addition to the federal requirements described above, generators must become familiar with state regulations. As mentioned above, many state requirements were more stringent than the federal rules prior to the enactment of HSWA, and are likely to continue to be more stringent even after EPA issued the final rules mandated by HSWA. Where the state regulations are more stringent, generators must comply with the more stringent state rules. These rules may include lower quantity cutoffs, listing or identifying additional wastes as hazardous, tougher standards for non-permitted storage in tanks and containers prior to transport, and manifest

Table 4-1 EPA's Regulations for Large and Small Quantity Generators

	Regulations in Effect for Large Quantity Generators	EPA Rules for Generators Producing Between 100 and 1000 kg/mo of Non-acutely Hazardous Waste
Hazardous Waste Determination 40 CFR 262.11	It is the generator's responsibility to determine if waste is listed as hazardous, or meets the characteristic definitions through testing or knowledge of the waste. Analyses, test results, etc. must be retained for three years from the date waste was last sent off-site or managed on-site.	Same as for large generators.
EPA Identification Number 40 CFR 262.12	Generator must obtain EPA Identification number by filling out and submitting Form 8700-12 to EPA. Generators must ship waste only with transporter that has an EPA Identification number.	Same as for large generators.
Manifest Tracking and Reporting Requirements a) Filling out the Manifest 40 CFR 262.20	Generator must fill out all non-shaded areas of Uniform Hazardous Waste Manifest (shaded areas are information which may be requested by the states).	Same as for large generators although EPA solicited comment on exemption from waste minimization certification. See 51 *Fed. Reg.* 10177 (Mar. 24, 1986).
b) Acquisition of Manifest 40 CFR 262.21	Generator is required to obtain copies of UHWM from state to which waste will be shipped, if provided, and its use requested by state; if not, then from state in which generator is located; and if neither state supplies the manifest, from any other source.	Same as for large generators.
c) Number of Copies 40 CFR 262.22	Sufficient number of copies required which will provide generator, each transporter, and TSDF owner/operator with one copy; as well as one copy to be sent to the generator after TSDF owner/operator receives the waste shipment.	Same as for large generators.
d) Use of Manifest 40 CFR 262.23	Generator signs the manifest, obtains transporter's signature on manifest, dates the manifest, retains one copy and gives remaining copies to the transporter.	Same as for large generators.

Continued

Table 4-1 Continued

	Regulations in Effect for Large Quantity Generators	EPA Rules for Generators Producing Between 100 and 1000 kg/mo of Non-acutely Hazardous Waste
e) Manifest Retention 40 CFR 262.40	Three years.	Same as for large generators.
f) Exception Reporting 40 CFR 262.42	When waste arrives at designated TSDF, owner/operator signs manifest and returns one copy to generator so generator knows waste arrived. If generator fails to receive a signed manifest within 35 days of shipment, it must investigate waste's whereabouts. If signed manifest not received within 45 days, it must file "Exception Report" with EPA or authorized state. Copy of report must be retained by the generator for three years.	No exception report requirement. Generators are "encouraged" to inform EPA or authorized state of lost shipments.
g) Exemptions from Manifesting	None.	Exemption provided where: 1) waste is reclaimed under contractual agreement; 2) agreement specifies type of waste and frequency of shipments; 3) transportation of the waste is in a vehicle owned and operated by the reclaimer; and 4) the generator retains a copy of the contract for three years after termination of the agreement.
Pre-transport Requirements 40 CFR 262.30–33	Generator must package, label, mark, and ensure the placarding of container or package according to Department of Transportation Regulations. Each container of 110 gallons or less must be marked: "Hazardous Waste—Federal Law Prohibits Improper Disposal. If found, contact the nearest police or public safety authority or U.S. Environmental Protection Agency." The generator's name, address, and manifest document number must also be provided on the container.	Same as for larger generators.

On-site Accumulation ("Temporary Storage") 40 CFR 262.34		
a) Maximum Duration and Quantity Allowed without Obtaining TSDF Permit/Interim Status	Duration limit of ninety days, extendable for up to 30 additional days due to unforeseen, temporary, and uncontrollable circumstances at the discretion of EPA (or an authorized state). No limitation as to quantity of waste.	HSWA established a duration limit of 180 days, or 270 days if the generator must ship waste over 200 miles. This period may be extended by up to 30 days as provided for larger generators. There is a quantity limit of 6000kg.
b) Types of Units	Only tanks and containers.	Same as for larger generators.

c) Container Standards*	Date of accumulation period initiation must be marked on each container.
	Container must be labeled "Hazardous Waste."
	Compliance with 40 CFR 265 Subpart I required:
	  a) containers must be kept in good condition and leaking containers replaced;
	  b) containers must be compatible with waste stored in them;
	  c) container must be closed except when waste is added or removed, and cannot be handled in a way causing them to rupture or leak;
	  d) containers must be inspected at least weekly for leaks and signs of corrosion;
	  e) containers holding ignitable or reactive wastes must be at least 50 feet from property line (may be changed—see June 5, 1984, proposal); and
	  f) incompatible wastes cannot be placed in same container to cause fires, leaks, or other releases.
		Same as for larger generators, except exemption provided from 50-foot buffer zone requirement for ignitable and reactive wastes.

d) Tank Standards Note: Significant changes to	Tank must be labelled "Hazardous Waste." Compliance with most of 40 CFR 265 Subpart J required:	Same as for larger generators. When EPA modifies tank standards (see **Continued**

119

Table 4-1 Continued

Regulations in Effect for Large Quantity Generators	EPA Rules for Generators Producing Between 100 and 1000 kg/mo of Non-acutely Hazardous Waste
these tank standards were proposed by EPA on June 26, 1985 (see Chapter 12).	a) waste capable of causing ruptures, leaks, corrosion, or otherwise causing the tank to fail cannot be placed in tank; b) uncovered tanks must have at least 2 feet of freeboard or a secondary containment dike or trench to prevent overfilling spillage; c) where waste is continually fed into tank, tank must be equipped with a means to stop the inflow; d) at least once per operating day, generator must inspect, if present, waste inflow cutoff systems, drainage systems, data from monitoring equipment such as pressures and temperature gauges to ensure proper operation, and level of waste in tank to ensure compliance with freeboard requirement; e) at least weekly, generator must inspect tank and immediate area around tank for corrosion or leakage; and f) special requirements for ignitable, reactive, and incompatible wastes, as specified in 40 CFR 265.198–199, must be met (may be changed—see June 5, 1984, proposal).	Chapter 12), EPA will consider whether modified standards will apply to this class of generators.
e) Other Requirements Applicable to All Temporary Storage	Preparedness and Prevention (40 CFR 265 Subpart C) a) facilities must be maintained and operated to minimize possibility of fire, explosion, or other accidental releases; b) unless none of the waste requires this kind of equipment, the facility must be equipped with an internal communications or alarm system, a radio or telephone readily available to request outside emergency assistance (i.e., help from police or fire depts.), portable fire extinguishers and other release control equipment, and an adequate water supply; c) the above equipment must be tested and maintained; d) all persons involved in waste handling must have immediate access to alarm system or emergency	Same as for larger generators.

communication device, where device is required;

e) aisle space must be maintained to allow the unobstructed movement of people and equipment to any area in case of emergency, unless aisle space not required for emergency response.

f) the owner/operator must attempt to make emergency arrangements with police, fire departments, hospitals, etc., as appropriate for the waste at the site. Refusals by such entities to enter into emergency arrangements must be documented.

Contingency Plans and Emergency Procedures (40 CFR 265 Subpart D)

a) a contingency plan to minimize releases from fires, explosions, and other accidents must be developed which includes responsibilities of facility personnel, arrangements agreed to by persons providing outside assistance, the designation of person or persons as emergency coordinator, a list of emergency equipment, and an evacuation plan for facility personnel if potentially necessary;

b) copies of the plan must be maintained at the facility and submitted to outside parties providing emergency assistance;

c) an emergency coordinator must be at the facility or on call, and in emergency situations activate alarms, seek outside assistance, determine nature and extent of release including potential health and environmental risk posed by the release, notify federal (National Response Center at 800-424-8802) and local authorities, take such actions as necessary to minimize the release and ensure that recovered waste and contaminated materials are managed properly.

1) Emergency coordinator(s) must be selected and be on-site or on call;

2) The name and telephone number of the coordinator; location of fire extinguishers, fire alarm (if present) and spill control equipment; and fire department phone numbers (unless facility has direct alarm); must be posted next to the telephone;

3) All employees must be familiar with waste handling and emergency procedures relevant to their facility responsibilities; and

4) Coordinator must respond to emergencies to minimize the release, and must notify the National Response Center and file a report whenever release could threaten human health outside the facility, or if a spill has reached surface water.

Continued

Table 4-1 Continued

	Regulations in Effect for Large Quantity Generators	EPA Rules for Generators Producing Between 100 and 1000 kg/mo of Non-acutely Hazardous Waste
	Personnel Training (40 CFR 265.16) a) classroom or on-the-job training required on regulatory responsibilities, directed by person trained in hazardous waste management procedures; b) personnel must annually review training; c) records must be maintained with respect to job title, description, and training provided for each employee related to hazardous waste management; training records must be retained for all current employees and for 3 years after employee no longer works at facility.	Not required.
Biennial Report 40 CFR 262.41	By March of each even number year, the generator must submit to EPA (or an authorized state) a report which includes information identifying the generator and the facilities where the generator's waste was managed, identifying waste transporters, describing the waste sent off-site, and a description of the efforts undertaken to reduce the volume and toxicity of wastes generated and the results of those efforts.	Not required.
Regulations Applicable for Storage in Tanks and Containers beyond Quantity and Duration Allowed for "Temporary Storage," and All Other Treatment, Storage, or Disposal Performed by the Generator (40 CFR Parts 264 and 265)	Compliance with the full TSDF standards. Regulations typically become effective six months after publication in final form.	Same as for larger generators but small quantity generators managing waste on-site will be allowed one year from publication of the regulations to achieve compliance with interim status standards. This includes requirements for filing a Part A permit application, as described in Chapter 6 and 40 CFR 270.10.

*A generator may accumulate, without a maximum time limit, up to 55 gallons of non-acutely hazardous waste or one quart of acutely hazardous waste in containers at locations where the waste initially accumulates at the facility (so-called satellite storage areas). For such storage, generators must comply with (a) and (b) cited above, ensure the containers are closed except when waste is added or removed, and mark the container with the words "Hazardous Waste" or the equivalent. If these maximum quantities are exceeded, the generator must comply with the temporary storage requirements within 3 days for all wastes in excess of the satellite storage quantity limitations. See *49 Fed. Reg.* 49568 (Dec. 20, 1984), 40 CFR 262.34(c).

submissions to the state at the time or shortly after the waste is shipped off-site. Generators are urged to contact state agencies for additional information, and to contact the states and the EPA Small Business Hotline (800-368-5888) for assistance in complying with these regulations. A list of state offices is provided as Appendix A.

Second, generators must determine if the byproducts or materials they produce are hazardous waste as defined by federal or state regulations. To make this determination, a generator needs to determine if the byproducts or materials it produces are considered a solid waste. (The statutory and regulatory definition of a solid waste is discussed in Chapter 3.)

The generator also needs to ascertain if the solid wastes are *hazardous* wastes. This may require a better understanding of the materials used in the generator's process, including lubricants and degreasing solvents not normally associated with the production process. The generator is responsible for determining if its waste is hazardous by checking the list of wastes EPA and the states have designated hazardous, and either testing or applying its knowledge of the waste to determine if the waste is hazardous by virtue of a characteristic (see Chapter 2). Appendix B lists the types of businesses which EPA believes contains significant numbers of generators producing greater than 100 kg/mo of hazardous waste. Appendix C lists the types of hazardous waste three of those businesses commonly generate (vehicle maintenance, printers, and dry cleaners) as determined by EPA. EPA has developed similar materials for the remaining businesses listed in Appendix B, and they can be obtained by calling EPA's Small Business Hotline. Generators in businesses producing relatively similar wastes nationwide should also contact their trade association for further information, or perhaps to arrange cooperative testing.

Third, a generator should determine if the hazardous waste it generates is above the quantity cutoff for regulation under state and federal law. Perhaps a change in raw material or production process can reduce the amount of hazardous waste generated to levels below the quantity cutoff. Trade associations, universities, state agencies, and suppliers or manufacturers could be consulted to achieve such a goal. Generators producing below 100 kg/mo of non-acutely hazardous waste will remain subject to the 1980 regulations in 40 CFR 261.5, unless a state imposes more stringent requirements. If such generators accumulate more than 1000/kg at any one time, however, they become subject to the new EPA regulations for generators producing between 100–1000 kg/mo.

In assessing the amount of hazardous waste a generator has produced in a given month, the generator should note EPA regulations which exempt certain hazardous wastes from the quantity cutoff determination. These regulations apply where the particular waste is destined for reuse, recycling, or reclamation. For example, EPA has specifically excluded from the quantity cutoff determination the type of used oil that is considered hazardous only because it is ignitable, and spent lead-acid batteries, provided they will be recycled by someone else off-site.[16] In its 1985 study on small quantity generators, EPA estimated that more than 60% of the waste generated at quantities below 1000 kg/mo was lead-acid batteries, 90% of which was reclaimed.[17] Excluding lead-acid batteries from the quantity cutoff determination reduced by almost half the number of generators producing between 100 kg/mo and 1000 kg/mo of hazardous waste.[18]

Other hazardous wastes which do not count toward the 100 kg/mo cutoff are industrial ethyl alcohol destined for reclamation, other used batteries returned to a battery manufacturer for regeneration, scrap metal, and certain hazardous waste designated ignitable only which will be burned for energy recovery. In addition, waste reclaimed on-site but not stored or treated prior to reclamation does not count toward the quantity cutoff. The residues or sludges resulting from the reclamation process may count however.[19]

Generators should realize they may be subject to different requirements depending on how much waste they generate each month. They are not allowed to take an average of the quantities generated over time to reduce their regulatory requirements. Accordingly, it may be necessary to be prepared for the requirements applicable to a higher generation rate in the event such quantities are actually generated in a given month. Generators should also note that if they mix waste subject to full regulation with waste subject to reduced regulation, all the waste is subject to full regulation.

Fourth, generators producing hazardous waste above the quantity cutoff will need to evaluate how to manage the waste. Since for most small quantity generators, off-site management will be the economically preferable option, the generator will need to hire a responsible waste transporter or management firm.

Generators and TSDFs shipping hazardous waste off-site for further management must become familiar with U.S. Department of Transportation (DOT) requirements for hazardous materials transportation. Waste designated hazardous by EPA is a subset of hazardous materials regulated by DOT under the Hazardous Materials Transportation Act.

To comply with DOT requirements, a generator must first "classify" the waste, because DOT requirements vary depending on the waste's classification. A waste may be listed in DOT's Hazardous Materials Table found at 49 CFR 172.101 or it may fall within general hazard classes (i.e., explosives, compressed gases, flammable and combustible liquids, flammable solids, oxidizers and organic peroxides, poisons, radioactive materials, and corrosives).[20] If it is not listed and does not fall within one of these hazard classes, the waste is classified "ORM," meaning other regulated materials. There are five groups of ORM materials (ORM-A through ORM-E), and ORM-E is the group for wastes designated hazardous by

EPA which do not fit within any other hazard class or ORM grouping. This classification process will yield the DOT description of the waste required by line 11 of the Uniform Hazardous Waste Manifest.

Based on the waste's classification, DOT requirements impose packaging (49 CFR 171.3(e) and Part 173), marking (49 CFR Part 172 Subpart D),[21] labeling (49 CFR Part 172 Subpart E), placarding (49 CFR Part 172 Subpart F), and documentation (49 CFR Part 172 Subpart C) requirements on the generator shipping hazardous waste off-site. Significantly, DOT documentation requirements may be satisfied for any hazardous waste shipment by complying with EPA's manifest regulations. However, generators of all sizes should note that some DOT requirements have their own quantity cutoffs, which are different from EPA's. In some cases, therefore, generators exempt from EPA regulations will *still* be subject to DOT transportation requirements and vice versa.

Generators managing waste on-site in a manner requiring a permit may need to devote significant resources to meeting permitting standards and submitting a permit application. This is likely to be particularly true for on-site management in a land disposal facility or underground tank that cannot be entered for inspection. All generators now subject to regulation should become familiar with the development of land disposal restrictions as described in Chapter 9, so an appropriate long-range waste management plan can be developed.

HAZARDOUS WASTE EXPORT REQUIREMENTS

Prior to the passage of HSWA, generators exporting hazardous waste to a foreign country were subject to extremely limited reporting requirements and few controls. Briefly, the generator's chief responsibilities were to notify EPA in writing four weeks before the initial shipment each calendar year and then confirm the delivery of the waste to the foreign country using a slight variation of the manifest tracking system. It was not necessary for the generator to obtain the consent of the receiving country prior to shipment, nor was it necessary to inform EPA or the receiving country of the amount of waste to be exported, the expected frequency of export shipments, the management methods proposed for the waste in the receiving country, or the ultimate destination of the waste. In one reported instance, an American citizen had dumped hazardous waste into an abandoned mine in Mexico without that government's knowledge or consent.[22] This incident, and the potential for increasing exports due to stricter regulatory controls in the United States, raised congressional concerns that EPA procedures were inadequate to satisfy either environmental protection or foreign policy objectives.[23]

Therefore, Congress enacted new Section 3017 of RCRA, which established new procedures and controls over hazardous waste exports. Beginning November 8, 1985, persons intending to export hazardous waste must notify EPA by providing the following information:

1.   the name and address of the exporter;
2.   the types and quantities of hazardous waste to be exported;
3.   the frequency of future export shipments;
4.   the ports of entry;
5.   a description of how the waste will be managed in the receiving country; and
6.   the name and address of the facility in the foreign country which will receive the waste.

This notification will be forwarded by EPA to the Department of State, which has the responsibility to provide the foreign country with information regarding the waste shipment and to determine whether that country objects or consents to receiving the waste shipment. Beginning November 8, 1986, hazardous waste cannot be exported unless EPA has received prior notification, the written consent of the receiving country is attached to the manifest accompanying each waste shipment, and the shipment conforms to the terms of consent set by the receiving country. A limited exception to this prohibition is provided where the United States and the foreign country have reached an agreement regarding waste exports establishing notice and enforcement procedures, and the shipment conforms to the terms established by such agreement.

Congress also required, beginning March 1, 1985, and by every March 1 thereafter, all hazardous waste exporters to file annual reports to EPA summarizing the types, quantities, frequency, and destination of all exports during the previous calendar year. This requirement has been codified by EPA at 40 CFR 262.50. EPA proposed regulations governing the remaining requirements newly imposed by Section 3017 of RCRA on March 13, 1986.[24]

Finally, Congress explicitly established that the export of hazardous waste without the consent of the receiving country or in violation of an agreement reached between the United States and a receiving country is a criminal offense, subject to fines and/or imprisonment as provided in Section 3008(d) of RCRA (see Chapter 13).

NOTES

1.   45 *Fed. Reg.* 33103 (1980).
2.   Ibid. In 1985, EPA concluded that it could not rely upon waste characteristics, management practices, or location criteria to make meaningful distinctions between large and small quantity generators, because the Agency believed there were not significant differences in any of these areas. See 50 *Fed. Reg.* 31285 (Aug. 1, 1985).
3.   43 *Fed. Reg.* 58970 (1978).
4.   45 *Fed. Reg.* 33103 (1980).

5. Ibid., pp. 33103-4.
6. Section 261.5 Special Requirements for Hazardous Waste Generated by Small Quantity Generators (Background Document), EPA Office of Solid Waste, April 28, 1980, p. IV-21.
7. Ibid., pp. III-2, 3.
8. 45 *Fed. Reg.* 33102-3 (1980).
9. The RCRA Exemption for Small Volume Hazardous Waste Generators; Staff Memorandum, Materials Program, Office of Technology Assessment, July 1982, pp. 2, 14.
10. State Small Quantity Hazardous Waste Generator Survey, Final Report (Draft), Sept. 1983, p. 6.
11. Ibid.
12. Ibid. See also Lennett and Greer, State Regulation of Hazardous Waste, *Ecology Law Quarterly,* Vol. 12, pp. 201–5.
13. ASTSWMO Report, supra note 10, p. 27.
14. Statement of Lee Thomas *et al.* before the Subcommittee on Commerce, Transportation and Tourism, Committee on Energy and Commerce, U.S. House of Representatives, March 24, 1983, reprinted in Hazardous Waste Control and Enforcement Act of 1983—Hearings before the Subcommittee on Commerce, Transportation and Tourism of the Committee on Energy and Commerce, 98th Congress, 1st Session, Ser. No. 98-32, pp. 349, 370.
15. 129 Cong. Rec. H 6501, H 6514-6517 (Aug. 4, 1983).
16. 51 *Fed. Reg.* 10152. (Mar. 24, 1986). In its proposed regulations governing the recycling of used oil, and the listing of used oil as a hazardous waste, EPA proposed to subject used oil to a separate quantity cutoff determination. See 50 *Fed. Reg.* 49212 (Nov. 29, 1985) and Chapter 2.
17. National Small Quantity Hazardous Waste Generator Survey, prepared for EPA's Office of Solid Waste by Abt Associates Inc., Feb. 1985, p. 36.
18. Ibid., p. 47.
19. 40 CFR 261.6(a)(3), 266.36; 51 *Fed. Reg.* 10152 (Mar. 24, 1986).
20. In some cases, these classes are further divided into subclasses. Definitions of these classes and subclasses can be found in Appendix D. Unfortunately, the DOT classes and subclasses differ from EPA's four hazardous waste characteristics. Thus, a waste designated reactive by EPA could be classified as an explosive or a poison (i.e., irritating material) by DOT. Wastes falling within more than one DOT hazard class or subclass should be handled according to procedures specified in 49 CFR 173.2. For more information regarding federal transportation requirements, contact your trade association or the Office of Hazardous Materials Transportation at DOT, or obtain the guidance manual on compliance with transportation requirements cited in Chapter 5.
21. A proper DOT shipping name for a hazardous waste that is listed in the DOT Hazardous Materials Table or falls into a DOT hazard class is the name of the material as listed or classified, preceded by the word "waste." ORM-E materials are named "Hazardous Waste N.O.S." (not otherwise specified).
22. 129 *Congressional Record* H8163 (Oct. 6, 1983) (Statement of Rep. Mikulski).
23. Senate HSWA Report, p. 47.
24. 51 *Fed. Reg.* 8744.

CHAPTER FIVE

Transporter Requirements

The transportation of hazardous waste is jointly regulated at the federal level by EPA and the U.S. Department of Transportation (DOT). The authority for DOT regulation is the Hazardous Materials Transportation Act.[1] Wastes designated hazardous by EPA are a subset of hazardous materials regulated by DOT under that law.

EPA REGULATIONS

EPA's regulations, codified at 40 CFR Part 263, are principally manifest tracking and discharge cleanup requirements. EPA intentionally did not issue detailed requirements related to the actual transportation of the waste to avoid problems of duplication or conflict with DOT requirements.

Before transporting hazardous waste, a transporter must obtain an EPA identification number. A number can be obtained by filling out EPA Form 8700-12 and submitting it to EPA.

Compliance with the manifest tracking system generally requires the hazardous waste transporter to:

1. accept only waste shipments from generators that are accompanied by a signed manifest;
2. sign the manifest upon acceptance of the waste and return a signed copy of it to the generator;
3. ensure the manifest accompanies the waste;
4. upon arrival at the facility designated (or an alternate also designated) on the manifest, obtain the signature of the owner/operator; and
5. retain one copy of the manifest for three years and give the remaining copies to the facility owner/operator.

Rail and bulk water transporters face slightly different manifest tracking requirements. States may also adopt more stringent standards. Finally, non-acutely hazardous waste generated in quantities between 100 and 1000 kg/mo may be exempt from manifest tracking requirements if transported off-site pursuant to a reclamation agreement (see Chapter 4). In such instances, the transporter must instead utilize a log or shipping paper containing the information specified in 40 CFR 263.20(h) which accompanies the waste shipments and is retained for at least 3 years after the reclamation agreement terminates.

EPA regulations also require the transporter to undertake cleanup or take other action requested or approved by federal, state, or local officials to abate any hazard to human health or the environment caused by a discharge during transportation. EPA regulations incorporate DOT notification requirements in the event of a discharge during transportation, which will be described further below.

Transporters will also be subject to EPA's generator or facility standards if they conduct certain activities. For example, transporters importing hazardous waste from abroad or mixing hazardous wastes of different types into one container are considered waste generators and must comply with 40 CFR Part 262 (see Chapter 4). The same is true for transporters engaged in cleanup activities due to a discharge occurring during transportation. Transporters storing hazardous waste, except for manifested shipments in containers at a transfer facility stored for no longer than 10 days, are also regulated as owners/operators of storage facilities (see Chapters 6 through 8).

DOT REGULATIONS

DOT's transportation requirements are sufficiently lengthy and complex to warrant a separate guide for complying with them. They vary substantially depending on the type of waste and how they are transported. Readers seeking more detailed information than what is provided below are urged to contact DOT's Office of Hazardous Materials Transportation and obtain the compliance guidance manual jointly prepared by EPA and DOT.[2] There may also be additional state regulations, particularly with respect to routing; permitting or registration of transporters; and pre-notification of shipments. Contact your state agency and/or state trucking associations for additional information on state requirements.

The DOT regulations are codified in volume 49 of the CFR. They apply to shippers, carriers, and container manufacturers.[3] Shippers are the persons who prepare the wastes for shipment, and under the RCRA program are the generators of the hazardous waste. The carriers are the persons who physically transport the waste, by rail, highway, water, or air. They are the hazardous waste transporters.

The proper characterization of the waste is the critical first step in compliance with DOT requirements. Only when a waste is properly characterized can generators and transporters determine the procedures they must follow to comply with the law. The generator is initially responsible for characterizing the waste as a necessary prerequisite for preparing the waste for transport. The transporter requires a proper characterization because he is only allowed to accept hazardous waste properly prepared for transportation, and the transporter standards also vary depending on the classification of the waste. Furthermore, since characterization of the waste influences packaging, marking, and emergency response procedures, improper classification can be dangerous.

There are three steps to the classification process. First, the waste may be listed in DOT's Hazardous Materials Table found at 49 CFR 172.101. If it is not listed there, the waste should be compared to DOT's hazard classes. The classes and their definitions can be found in Appendix D. Wastes falling within more than one hazard class should be classified according to procedures specified in 49 CFR 173.2. Finally, if the waste is not listed and does not fall within a DOT hazard class, the waste is designated "ORM," meaning other regulated materials. There are five groups of ORM materials (ORM-A through ORM-E), and ORM-E is the group for hazardous wastes that do not fit within any hazard class or other ORM grouping. Appendix D also includes the definition of each ORM category.

As discussed in Chapter 4, the generator prepares the waste for shipment by characterizing the waste; packaging, marking, labeling, and placarding the waste; and preparing the waste manifest.

Placarding is actually the joint responsibility of the generator and transporter. Generators offering waste for highway shipment are required to provide the transporter with the placards unless the transporter has already properly placarded the vehicle. In the case of rail transport, the generator must affix the placard to the rail car unless the transport container is already properly placarded. Significantly, all hazardous waste identified in Table 1 of 49 CFR 172.504 must be placarded, regardless of quantity (including waste from generators producing less than 100 kg/mo), while waste identified in Table 2 of 49 CFR 172.504 requires placarding for shipments of over 1000 lbs. The tables also specify the type of placard required depending upon the waste's classification. Placard specification and requirements applicable to rail, and highway shipments, as well as freight containers, cargo tanks, and portable tanks are also codified in 49 CFR 172 Subpart F.

The DOT transporter regulations are generally organized by mode of shipment: rail (40 CFR Part 174), air (49 CFR Part 175), water (49 CFR Part 176), and highway (49 CFR Part 177). Since most hazardous waste is transported by highway or rail, regulations applicable to these two modes will be described.

Truck transporters must comply with general motor carrier safety regulations (49 CFR Parts 301-399),[4] and regulations specifically pertaining to hazardous materials transportation. Included in the hazardous materials requirements are loading and unloading requirements (49 CFR Part 177 Subpart B), and a list of materials that cannot be transported together (49 CFR 177.848). The reporting of spill incidents is governed by 49 CFR 177.807, and 171.15, 171.16 and 171.17. Those provisions specify where, how, and to whom notice is required of a discharge or other problem arising during transportation of the waste. Procedures for handling broken or leaking packages, and for disabled vehicles are specified in 49 CFR 177.854. Additional regulations contain procedures to follow for accidents involving explosives, flammables, corrosives, compressed gases, poisons, and radioactive materials.

Rail transporter requirements specify time constraints for the movement of hazardous waste once accepted by the transporter (49 CFR 174.14), which is generally within 48 hours or one week depending on the train schedule. As with highway transport, loading and unloading procedures are also specified (49 CFR Part 174 Subpart C). They include a list of materials which must be segregated from each other (49 CFR 174.81). Subparts E–L of 49 CFR 174 contain special handling procedures for explosives, gases, flammables, oxidizers, poisons, corrosives, and radioactive materials. Special information on billing papers (i.e., waybill, switching order) and other switching documents is required so that shipments of hazardous materials can be easily tracked and transport personnel are alerted when cars are loaded or unloaded (49 CFR 174.25). Additional informational requirements govern the transportation of explosives. As with highway transport, the spill incident reporting procedures of 49 CFR 171.15-17 apply. Leaking packages (other than tank cars) may not be forwarded until the packages are repaired or reconditioned, or placed in a salvage drum meeting certain specifications (49 CFR 173.3(c), 174.48). Leaking tank cars may not be unnecessarily moved until corrected, must be protected against ignition, and trigger other marking, removal, and moving requirements (49 CFR 174.50). Procedures for handling damaged shipments can be found in 49 CFR 174.103.

FEDERAL ENFORCEMENT

Since both EPA and DOT regulate shipments of hazardous waste, the two agencies executed a Memorandum of Understanding (MOU) to delineate areas of responsibility.[5] Under the terms of the MOU, EPA provides DOT with a list of hazardous waste transporters and their ID numbers as well as information on violators of DOT regulations; investigates DOT reports on RCRA violations; and brings enforcement actions involving an imminent and substantial endangerment to human health and the environment. DOT conducts inspections of hazardous waste generators and transporters to monitor compliance with DOT requirements, and informs EPA of potential violations of RCRA the agency may become aware of during such inspections. DOT also investigates EPA reports of violations of DOT requirements. Both agencies have agreed to attempt to coordinate investigation and enforcement efforts to avoid duplication of effort.

The bottom line, however, is both EPA and DOT can generally enforce the regulations promulgated pursuant to RCRA and the Hazardous Materials Transportation Act where such regulations have been promulgated or incorporated by both agencies in the CFR. Exceptions to joint jurisdiction over hazardous waste shipments are the discharge cleanup requirements (limited to EPA) and general motor vehicle safety regulations (limited to DOT).

NOTES

1. P.L. 93-633, 49 U.S.C. 1801 *et seq.*
2. Environmental Protection Agency/Department of Transportation: *Hazardous Waste Transportation Interface: Guidance Manual,* November 1981, available from the National Technical Information Service, document # PB82-182361.
3. Container fabrication and testing specifications are in 49 CFR Part 178; detailed specifications for rail tank cars are in 49 CFR Part 179.
4. Special motor carrier regulations pertaining to hazardous materials transportation include parking, operating, routing, and financial responsibility requirements. See 49 CFR 387, 397.
5. 45 *Fed. Reg.* 51645 (August 4, 1980).

CHAPTER SIX

Permit Applications and Procedures for TSDFs: Interim Status and Final Permits

While currently there are about 200,000 generators and transporters subject to certain RCRA requirements, the vast majority of RCRA is devoted to the regulation of the approximately 5000 treatment, storage, and disposal facilities (TSDFs) that ultimately manage hazardous wastes. The current universe (as of March 1, 1986) of TSDFs is expected to grow as a result of new waste listings, the listing of used oil as a hazardous waste, and other RCRA actions that will subject management facilities to RCRA control for the first time.

Section 3005 of RCRA requires owners/operators of TSDFs to obtain an operating permit, which specifies the operating and technical design and performance requirements applicable to that type of TSDF. Until a final permit is issued, existing facilities can continue operating through a grandfather provision in RCRA granting them "interim status." New facilities must obtain a final permit before they can begin operation. The process of issuing final operating permits is now underway and is expected to continue through 1992.

Chapter 6 examines the process of applying for a TSDF permit, exclusions from the permit process, and the Agency's administrative procedures for processing and evaluating permit applications. Permits are issued and determinations of compliance are based on a series of general and technical operating requirements depending upon the type of TSDF involved. In addition, these permitting standards and requirements vary and change depending upon what phase of the permitting process a given TSDF is in: interim status or has a final operating permit. Due to the complex nature of the TSDF requirements under interim status, and the final permitting requirements, the next seven chapters are devoted to this subject.

Chapters 7 and 8 examine both the general and technical requirements that apply to TSDFs under interim status and final operating permits, respectively. Chapters 9, 10, 11, and 12 respectively examine the highly detailed standards and technical requirements governing: land disposal restrictions; minimum technology requirements; groundwater monitoring and corrective action; and standards for hazardous waste tanks and underground tanks generally. These general and technical standards, upon which permitting and compliance are based, are contained in 40 CFR Parts 264 (final permits—also referred to as the permitting standards), 265 (interim status requirements), 266 (recycling and special facility standards), 268 (land disposal restrictions), and 280 (underground product storage tank requirements).

The federal permit application and evaluation procedures are contained in Part 270 and Part 124 of the regulations, respectively. Part 270 contains the basic permit application requirements, general permit conditions, and provisions governing permit duration, modification, and termination. Part 124 contains the Agency's administrative procedures for evaluating and issuing such permits. Taken together, these sections comprise the entire federal permitting process for RCRA TSDFs starting with the application and extending through Agency processing, issuance, appeal, and final determination. Many states, however, have additional permitting procedures, including a siting process for new or major facilities.

It may be useful to view the relationship between the permitting process discussed here (40 CFR Parts 270 and 124 of the regulations) and the discussion in Chapters 7–12 (Parts 264–268) as analogous to the relationship between building permits and building codes. Part 270 is equivalent to the blueprints and the building permit application. Part 124 is equivalent to a review by the public and the building inspector to ensure that the blueprints conform to established building and zoning codes. Parts 264–268 are analogous to the material specifications, and building and zoning codes themselves.

The standards and requirements for RCRA TSDFs are divided into those that apply once a facility has been granted interim status, and those that apply after.a final operating permit has been issued. Consistent with this scheme, the permit application process is divided into two parts: *Part A,* which requires very basic information to be filed prior to qualifying for interim status, and the more extensive *Part B* application for a final operating permit.

Technically, interim status is just that, a status granted by the statute to virtually all facilities that meet three statutory criteria established by the Congress (discussed below) until final permits are issued. Recognizing that development of final permitting regulations and the issuance of final permits based on these regulations would take several years, Congress established "interim status" in RCRA Section 3005(e) to: identify the hazardous waste TSDFs in existence; begin the process of imposing some level of control on TSDFs in the interim; and to prevent facilities from having to close because they had no permit upon RCRA's enactment. Thus, unlike Part B applications and final operating permits, interim status is not a "permit" because the Agency does not *selectively* or *formally* grant interim status. Once a valid Part A is submitted, and all required notifications (RCRA Section 3010) are filed, the facility is generally granted interim status unless and until the Agency takes action on the Part B application.

The Agency complemented the statutory provisions of RCRA 3005(e) by developing a series of interim status standards. These were first issued in May 1980, along with the original waste listings and permit procedures,[1] and consisted largely of administrative and recordkeeping requirements. "Interim" in this context does not necessarily mean that these requirements will be suspended or superseded, but rather that they are the only applicable requirements in the interim period until final permits are issued. The final permitting standards for TSDFs complement and build on those required during interim status by improving on or imposing additional requirements that were not contained in the interim status standards. Interim status standards are nonetheless highly significant because it is now clear that many TSDFs will be solely governed by them for many years to come.

Compliance with interim status standards, upon proper qualification, or compliance with the terms and requirements of a final operating permit upon its issuance constitutes compliance with RCRA Subtitle C for purposes of enforcement. Compliance with permit conditions "shields" an owner/operator from suits brought by EPA, states, or citizen groups for failure to comply with regulations. However, a permit does not provide a defense against a suit for imminent hazards that may be caused even if such facility is in full compliance with all permit conditions and requirements. In addition, a permit may be modified, revoked, reissued, or terminated for cause during its term. A permit does not convey any property right or exclusive privilege, nor does it authorize any injury to persons or property or infringement of state or local laws or regulations.[2]

THE RCRA PERMIT PROGRAM

Facilities Subject to and Excluded From Permit Proceedings

The RCRA permitting process is primarily directed at the treatment, storage, and disposal of hazardous wastes listed or identified under Part 261 (Chapters 2 and 3). However, facilities that are solely engaged in the generation or transportation of hazardous wastes may also become subject to TSDF requirements depending upon the nature and duration of the waste management activity at the facility. These situations are noted throughout Chapters 6–8.[3] In addition, facilities that must conduct post-closure care and related corrective actions must procure post-closure permits under certain circumstances.

There are several important *exclusions* from this general rule. The following persons and facilities are exempt unless otherwise specified:[4]

1. Generators, provided that they do not accumulate hazardous waste on site for more than 90 days, at which time they must apply for a storage permit (see Chapter 4 for further discussion including more liberal rules for small quantity generators).[5]

2. Farmers who dispose of hazardous waste pesticides from their own use as provided.[6]

3. Generators and persons who operate facilities solely for the treatment, storage, or disposal of hazardous wastes excluded from regulations (Chapter 3).[7]

4. Owners and operators of totally enclosed treatment facilities.[8]

5. Owners and operators of elementary neutralization units or enclosed wastewater treatment units.[9]

6. Transporters, provided that hazardous wastes are not stored at the transportation terminals for more than 10 days. The transporter must seek a permit, however, if they dispose of hazardous waste spill residue, or engage in any treatment, storage, or disposal activities.[10]

7. A person engaged in a treatment or containment activity undertaken as an immediate response to any of the following situations: a discharge of a hazardous waste, an imminent and substantial threat of a discharge of hazardous wastes, and a discharge of material which, when discharged, becomes a hazardous waste. The wastes generated and managed in these situations are nevertheless subject to all regulatory requirements and restrictions that apply to such wastes. Anyone who continues or initiates hazardous waste treatment or containment activities after the immediate response has been completed is fully subject to all application requirements.[11]

8. A wide range of facilities that reclaim certain types of hazardous wastes including ethyl alcohol, used batteries returned to a battery manufacturer, used oil that only exhibits a particular characteristic, and scrap metal. Some of these "reclamation" exemptions may be changed or modified in the near future. See Chapter 3 for further discussion.

OBTAINING INTERIM STATUS

Interim status was established in the 1976 law with the original RCRA program, and subsequently modified by amendments to RCRA in 1980 and by HSWA in 1984. It was originally envisioned to be a brief period during which TSDFs could continue to manage hazardous wastes until a final permit was obtained, provided that the following three statutory criteria are met.[12]

First, the TSDF must have been "in existence" on November 19, 1980 (the effective date of RCRA's interim status regulations referred to as Phase I regulations or the "May 1980 package");[13] *or* in existence on the effective date of statutory or regulatory changes under RCRA that render the facility subject to Section 3005 permit requirements. Second, the owner/operator must have complied with the 3010(a) notification requirement (discussed below); and third, the owner/operator must have applied for a permit by submitting a Part A application (discussed below).

EPA has broadly defined "in existence" and "existing hazardous waste management facility" to include planned facilities provided there exists a binding contract to construct the facility prior to November 19, 1980, or prior to the date of regulations that initiate RCRA control at a facility. When new regulations take effect that expand the scope of RCRA coverage, new interim status application deadlines are listed in the respective *Federal Register* notice.[14]

Interim status has taken on a significance far beyond that which was originally expected, due to the time required to issue permitting standards (Part 264), and to issue final TSDF permits based on these regulations. To date, 10 years after RCRA's original enactment, only a relative handful of final permits have been issued. Thus the interim status facilities still represent the largest segment of the regulated TSDFs.

In addition, due to several provisions of HSWA that expand the scope of wastes and facilities subject to RCRA control, many TSDFs will be subject to control for the first time and must apply for interim status to continue to manage hazardous wastes.[15] For example, when EPA lists a new hazardous waste under Part 261 (e.g., solvent, pesticide production residue) generators, transporters, and owners/operators of TSDFs that manage the newly listed hazardous waste will usually be required to submit a section 3010 notification within 90 days after the promulgation of such regulation.

For a TSDF where the newly regulated waste is the first and/or only hazardous waste it manages, a Part A application must also be filed usually within 6 months after issuance of the listing regulation (those facilities that already have applied and been granted interim status must submit a Part A modification in order to manage the newly regulated waste—see discussion below). Facilities that have notified and submitted a Part A application by the specified deadlines qualify for interim status, and can continue operating until they close or a decision on their final permit application is made. Facilities with interim status must comply with interim status standards in Part 265 (Chapters 7 and 8) or with analogous provisions of State programs. Interim status commences once the three statutory criteria are satisfied. No formal Agency approval of the Part A is required; however, the Agency may act to deny or grant interim status due to an incomplete or inaccurate application.[16]

A TSDF that is newly subject to RCRA and which fails to comply with the Part A application deadline is prohibited, with limited exception, from managing the newly regulated waste until it receives a RCRA permit (or in the case of an existing interim status facility, until it modifies its Part A). For facilities that fail to submit a timely Part A application due to oversight or excusable neglect, EPA can allow a facility to be treated as if it had interim status and to continue operation by issuing Interim Status Compliance Letters (ISCLs) where the Agency determines that continued operation is in the public interest. The ISCL protects the facility from federal enforcement actions during the time it is valid, but does not shield the facility from a citizen's suit under 7002 (see Chapter 13). During the effective period of the ISCL, the facility must comply with all applicable interim status standards regardless of whether they are allowed to qualify for interim status.[17]

A facility, or unit at a facility, that has previously been denied a RCRA permit or had its interim status terminated (such as those subject to the "Loss of Interim Status" provision of HSWA—Chapter 13) cannot subsequently qualify that facility or unit for interim status.[18] Such facilities and/or units can resume operation only after a Part B permit has been submitted and approved by the Agency or an authorized state.

Notification

RCRA Section 3010(a) requires that any person who manages a hazardous waste must file a notification with EPA within 90 days after regulations are promulgated identifying the waste as hazardous. The statute explicitly states that unless a person complies with the notification requirements, it is unlawful for that person to transport, treat, store, or dispose of that hazardous waste.[19] Notification requirements take on added significance with the enactment of HSWA, with many facilities subject to RCRA coverage for the first time due to waste listings and expanded regulatory coverage.

The notification must identify the hazardous waste that is handled and provide the location and a general description of the hazardous waste management activity. The Agency has issued a specific form (No. 8700-12, see Fig. 6-1) to be used in complying with the 3010(a) notification requirements.[20] However, a firm may use its own format provided that it contains all the information required on the EPA form. This information includes the following for each site or facility at which the waste is managed: name and location of the facility, and EPA Hazardous Waste Number for *all* the listed or characteristic wastes managed at the facility (e.g., F005, K022, D002).

To determine whether a notification must be filed, a company must review its hazardous waste activity at each site for 3 months prior to a required notification.[21] Any hazardous waste handled during the 3-month period must be included on the notification, including wastes that may have been exempted due to a regulatory exclusion that has been revoked. If a company expects to manage a hazardous waste in the future, the notification should be filed in advance of the management practice to ensure timely processing of the notice and issuance of an EPA facility ID number. Such advanced notification is particularly important for generators that intend to store hazardous wastes on-site without having to obtain a storage permit (Chapter 4). The 3010 notification must be filed with the EPA Regional Administrator or the state, if it has been authorized.[22]

Merely filing a RCRA 3010 notification does not compel a company to immediately submit to RCRA regulation. Only when a company actually manages a hazardous waste is it subject to RCRA requirements.

Form Approved OMB No. 158-S79016
GSA No. 0246-EPA-OT

⊕EPA

U.S. ENVIRONMENTAL PROTECTION AGENCY
NOTIFICATION OF HAZARDOUS WASTE ACTIVITY

INSTRUCTIONS: If you received a preprinted label, affix it in the space at left. If any of the information on the label is incorrect, draw a line through it and supply the correct information in the appropriate section below. If the label is complete and correct, leave Items I, II, and III below blank. If you did not receive a preprinted label, complete all items. "Installation" means a single site where hazardous waste is generated, treated, stored and/or disposed of, or a transporter's principal place of business. Please refer to the **INSTRUCTIONS FOR FILING NOTIFICATION** before completing this form. The information requested herein is required by law *(Section 3010 of the Resource Conservation and Recovery Act).*

INSTALLATION'S EPA I.D. NO.	
I. **NAME OF INSTALLATION**	
II. **INSTALLATION MAILING ADDRESS**	PLEASE PLACE LABEL IN THIS SPACE
III **LOCATION OF INSTALLATION**	

FOR OFFICIAL USE ONLY

COMMENTS

C

INSTALLATION'S EPA I.D. NUMBER | **APPROVED** | **DATE RECEIVED** *(yr., mo., & day)*

F

I. NAME OF INSTALLATION

II. INSTALLATION MAILING ADDRESS

STREET OR P.O. BOX

3

CITY OR TOWN | ST. | ZIP CODE

4

III. LOCATION OF INSTALLATION

STREET OR ROUTE NUMBER

5

CITY OR TOWN | ST. | ZIP CODE

6

IV. INSTALLATION CONTACT

NAME AND TITLE *(last, first, & job title)* | PHONE NO. *(area code & no.)*

2

V. OWNERSHIP

A. NAME OF INSTALLATION'S LEGAL OWNER

8

B. TYPE OF OWNERSHIP *(enter the appropriate letter into box)*

F = FEDERAL
M = NON—FEDERAL

VI. TYPE OF HAZARDOUS WASTE ACTIVITY *(enter "X" in the appropriate box(es))*

☐ A. GENERATION ☐ B. TRANSPORTATION *(complete item VII)*
☐ C. TREAT/STORE/DISPOSE ☐ D. UNDERGROUND INJECTION

VII. MODE OF TRANSPORTATION *(transporters only – enter "X" in the appropriate box(es))*

☐ A. AIR ☐ B. RAIL ☐ C. HIGHWAY ☐ D. WATER ☐ E. OTHER *(specify):*

VIII. FIRST OR SUBSEQUENT NOTIFICATION

Mark "X" in the appropriate box to indicate whether this is your installation's first notification of hazardous waste activity or a subsequent notification. If this is not your first notification, enter your installation's EPA I.D. Number in the space provided below.

☐ A. FIRST NOTIFICATION ☐ B. SUBSEQUENT NOTIFICATION *(complete item C)* C. INSTALLATION'S EPA I.D. NO.

IX. DESCRIPTION OF HAZARDOUS WASTES

Please go to the reverse of this form and provide the requested information.

EPA Form 8700-12 (6-80) **CONTINUE ON REVERSE**

Figure 6-1a

IX. DESCRIPTION OF HAZARDOUS WASTES *(continued from front)*

A. HAZARDOUS WASTES FROM NON—SPECIFIC SOURCES. Enter the four—digit number from 40 CFR Part 261.31 for each listed hazardous waste from non—specific sources your installation handles. Use additional sheets if necessary.

1	2	3	4	5	6
7	8	9	10	11	12

▲ DETACH ▲

B. HAZARDOUS WASTES FROM SPECIFIC SOURCES. Enter the four—digit number from 40 CFR Part 261.32 for each listed hazardous waste from specific industrial sources your installation handles. Use additional sheets if necessary.

13	14	15	16	17	18
19	20	21	22	23	24
25	26	27	28	29	30

C. COMMERCIAL CHEMICAL PRODUCT HAZARDOUS WASTES. Enter the four—digit number from 40 CFR Part 261.33 for each chemical substance your installation handles which may be a hazardous waste. Use additional sheets if necessary.

31	32	33	34	35	36
37	38	39	40	41	42
43	44	45	46	47	48

D. LISTED INFECTIOUS WASTES. Enter the four—digit number from 40 CFR Part 261.34 for each listed hazardous waste from hospitals, veterinary hospitals, medical and research laboratories your installation handles. Use additional sheets if necessary.

49	50	51	52	53	54

E. CHARACTERISTICS OF NON—LISTED HAZARDOUS WASTES. Mark "X" in the boxes corresponding to the characteristics of non—listed hazardous wastes your installation handles. *(See 40 CFR Parts 261.21 — 261.24.)*

☐ 1. IGNITABLE (D001) ☐ 2. CORROSIVE (D002) ☐ 3. REACTIVE (D003) ☐ 4. TOXIC (D000)

X. CERTIFICATION

I certify under penalty of law that I have personally examined and am familiar with the information submitted in this and all attached documents, and that based on my inquiry of those individuals immediately responsible for obtaining the information, I believe that the submitted information is true, accurate, and complete. I am aware that there are significant penalties for submitting false information, including the possibility of fine and imprisonment.

SIGNATURE	NAME & OFFICIAL TITLE *(type or print)*	DATE SIGNED

▲ DETACH ▲

EPA Form 8700-12 (6-80) REVERSE

Figure 6-1b

Contents of a Part A Application

The Part A application is comprised of Forms 1 and 3 of the application forms contained in EPA's consolidated permits regulations.[23] Form 1 requests very general information on the nature of the business, location, and regulated activities. Form 3 requests more specific information on the TSDF's hazardous waste activities including process descriptions, waste codes, and scale drawings of present and future TSDFs units on the property.

All Part A's must be signed by a "responsible corporate officer," meaning any officer performing functions similar to a vice president. A plant manager or operations person can sign such applications provided that the facility employs more than 250 persons and has sales or expenditures in excess of $25 million per year. Liability for untrue, inaccurate, and/or incomplete applications may accrue to both the facility and the individual officer who signs the application. Where the facility is owned by one person and operated by another, a responsible officer of both the owner and operator must sign the permit application. A specific certification form with the required language is provided in the regulations.[24]

Operation, Changes, and Expansions During Interim Status

During the interim status period the facility shall comply with all applicable interim status standards as specified in Part 265 and shall not:

1. treat, store or dispose of hazardous wastes not specified in the Part A of the permit application;
2. employ processes not specified in the Part A;
3. exceed the specified design capacities as specified in the Part A.[25]

The extent to which a facility can institute changes in the facility's management practices depend on both the nature and scope of those changes.[26] If a facility decides to handle additional or other wastes not previously specified, only a revised Part A is required. Increases in the design capacity of processes used at a facility must be approved by EPA or an authorized state and justified because of a lack of available capacity at other TSDFs. Similarly, changes in the processes used for treatment, storage, and disposal must be approved by EPA or an authorized state and justified on the basis that such changes are necessary to protect human health or the environment, or they are necessary to comply with federal, state, or local laws.

Changes in the ownership or operational control of a facility may be made if the new owner or operator submits a revised Part A no later than 90 days prior to the scheduled change. When such changes occur, the old owner or operator is required to comply with the financial responsibility requirements (Part 265; Chapter 7) until the new owner or operator can demonstrate compliance with these requirements.

Expansions under interim status that amount to reconstruction are prohibited. However, "reconstruction" does not occur until the capital investment in the changes exceeds 50% of the capital cost of a comparable entirely new state-of-the-art hazardous waste management facility. In addition, the cost of capital improvements to bring a facility into compliance with new RCRA requirements (e.g., secondary containment for hazardous waste storage tanks) is exempted from these expansion restrictions.[27]

Subsequent to the enactment of HSWA, expansions or replacements of interim status waste piles, landfills, and impoundments may be subject to specific minimum technology requirements for wastes received at such facilities. Chapter 10 discusses these and other interim status requirements in detail, including potential limited waivers from the minimum technology requirements at certain facilities.

Termination of Interim Status

Prior to the enactment of HSWA, EPA regulations specified two ways to lose interim status: obtain a final operating permit, or fail to furnish a requested Part B application on time or to furnish in full the information required by the Part B application.[28] Submitters of deficient Part A applications are served with a notice of deficiency and provided with an opportunity to redress them before being denied interim status or being subject to an enforcement action for operating without a permit.[29] Noncompliance with interim status standards can also result in the loss of interim status where the Agency believes such violations justify this type of sanction.

HSWA contains a number of new conditions that can result in the loss of interim status as discussed in Chapter 13, including:

1. the failure of owners/operators of land disposal units to submit a Part B permit application and to certify compliance with all applicable Part 265 groundwater monitoring and financial responsibility requirements by November 8, 1985. For those land diposal facilities in existence on the effective date of a statutory or regulatory change that makes the facility subject to RCRA for the first time after enactment of HSWA (November 8, 1984), this requirement takes effect 12 months after the date on which the facility first becomes subject to the permitting requirements (see Chapter 13);[30]

2. owners/operators of incinerators that fail to submit a Part B application by November 8, 1986, will lose interim status for those units on November 9, 1989, and must cease operation unless they have received a RCRA permit; and

3. owners/operators of any other treatment or storage facility that have not submitted its Part B by November 8, 1988, will lose interim status for those units on November 8, 1992, and must cease operation unless they have received a RCRA permit.[31]

FINAL RCRA PERMITS

National Permit Strategy

The Agency has developed a new national permit strategy which, while not a specific HSWA provision, anticipates the needs and demands of the new law for alternative treatment capacity. The strategy states the following goals:

1. Establish as the highest priority, the permitting of incineration, recycling, and other treatment facilities including research and development facilities (discussed below) that provide alternative capacity to land disposal as required by HSWA.
2. Actively encourage treatment and incineration alternatives to land disposal.
3. Enhance public education and involvement in the permitting process.[32]

Contents of a Part B Application

All facilities that seek a final RCRA operating permit must submit a Part B. In certain cases, facilities that are not certified closed prior to January 26, 1983, are subject to the Part B post-closure permit requirements (see Chapter 11).

The submission of a Part B application either because of a statutory deadline or a voluntary Agency "call in" involves a very detailed series of submissions regarding all aspects of facility operation. There is no specific Part B application form. Rather, each Part B information requirement is related to a specific requirement of the Part 264 regulations for that type of TSDF. Thus every time a 264 standard is promulgated or amended, the Part B application requirements for the TSDF are similarly affected.

The information requirements of a Part B do not apply uniformly to each facility. A data requirement may be waived by the Agency on a case-by-case basis provided the owners/operators of the facility can demonstrate that the information cannot be provided to the extent required. Certain technical data such as design drawings, specifications, and engineering studies must be certified by a registered, professional engineer.[33]

GENERAL INFORMATION REQUIREMENTS   A Part B application is usually divided into two parts: general information required of *all* TSDFs, and information specific to the type and location of the TSDF. The following represents the general information requirements of a Part B application:

1. A general description of the facility including detailed information of the facility's location, topographical description, seismic characteristics, and an identification of whether the facility is within the 100-year flood plain.
2. A chemical and physical analysis of the wastes to be handled including

all information which must be known to treat, store, or dispose of the wastes properly and in accordance with Part 264.

3. A copy of the facility's analysis plan.
4. A description of the security procedures and equipment and structures used at the facility to prevent runoff, employee exposure, contamination of water supplies, and spills or other releases to the environment.
5. A copy of the general inspection schedule for the facility.
6. A contingency plan and personnel training program.
7. Information on traffic volume, patterns, and control.
8. The closure and post-closure plans, including a copy of the most recent closure cost estimate and the financial assurance mechanism adopted for the facility.

SPECIFIC INFORMATION REQUIREMENTS   The specific information requirements of a Part B application differ according to the Part 264 final standards applicable to the various TSDFs, and in many cases would require a separate text to fully detail these permit application requirements. These requirements are codified at 40 CFR 270.14–22. The EPA RCRA Hotline (800-424-9346) can provide the available EPA permitting guidance documents for each of the following facilities: containers, tanks, surface impoundments, incinerators, land treatment facilities, and landfills. Chapters 7–12 discuss and analyze the RCRA requirements and standards that TSDF permit applications must address.

A new HSWA amendment explicitly provides that an Administrator may modify or review an individual TSDF permit at any time during its term. Such reviews are required to consider improvements in control and measurement technology and changes in applicable regulations. This new HSWA requirement also allows the Administrator to impose additional permit requirements that are not contained in the regulations as necessary to protect human health and the environment (see Chapter 10). Thus, regulatory requirements serve as a floor, not a ceiling for permit conditions.[34] The Agency has recently proposed regulatory amendments to reflect those changes in potential permit and application conditions.

Conditions Applicable to All Permits

The following conditions apply to all RCRA permits and are incorporated into the permits either expressly or by reference.[35] These requirements include:

1. compliance with all conditions of the permit;
2. proper operation and maintenance including the operation of back-up or auxiliary units when necessary to achieve compliance;

3. halting production when necessary to ensure compliance, and taking all reasonable steps to minimize releases to the environment;

4. providing all relevant information requests by the Agency regarding facility operation including the reporting of any noncompliance that may endanger health or the environment within 24 hours of the time the owner or operator becomes aware of such conditions (note: a notice of anticipated noncompliance does not suspend or negate any permit condition);

5. allowing authorized representatives to inspect the facility upon presentation of credentials;

6. maintaining and reporting all records and monitoring information necessary to document and verify compliance including data such as continuous-strip chart recordings from monitoring instruments;[36]

7. reporting all planned changes and anticipated periods of noncompliance.[37]

Facilities that comply with all conditions and terms of their permits are deemed to be in compliance with the statute. This "shield provision" insulates the facility against suits for noncompliance or inadequacy of permit conditions provided the facility is in compliance. However, it does not provide a defense against "imminent hazard" actions brought under RCRA's emergency provisions (7003 and 7002(a) (1) (B)).[38] See further discussion below.

Schedules of compliance also may be incorporated into final permits provided that actual compliance is achieved usually within one year from the date of issuance. Compliance schedules that extend beyond one year require yearly timetables detailing the levels of compliance to be achieved in that interval.

Partial Permits and Permit Duration

The Agency may issue or deny a final permit for one or more *units* at a facility without simultaneously issuing or denying a final permit to all units at the facility. The interim status of any unit for which a permit has not been issued or denied is not affected by the Agency's action on other units at the facility.[39]

No RCRA TSDF permit can exceed 10 years. HSWA also requires the Agency to review all land disposal permits every 5 years to modify such permits to incorporate new Parts 260–268, 270, and 124 standards that have been issued during that period. The Agency also has the authority to issue permits for less than 10 years, and to review and modify a permit at any time. States may also issue permits of shorter duration.[40] The relationship between permit duration and the modification process is both complex and subtle, and is discussed in further detail immediately below.

Changes to Permits and the "Shield Provision"

MAJOR MODIFICATIONS   The duration of a RCRA permit (discussed above) may also be affected by modifications during the permit's extent. These modifications may include a HSWA provision, a non-HSWA RCRA regulation, or a change initiated by the facility owner/operator.

As discussed at the beginning of this chapter, the purpose of a permit is to specify the exact conditions and requirements for compliance with RCRA for the duration of that permit (i.e., 10 years or less). The permit "shields" or protects the owner/operator from suits (other than those for imminent hazard) that claim non-compliance with RCRA, provided that all permit conditions are indeed being complied with. Without this type of protection, suits for non-compliance could be brought in an attempt to claim non-compliance even where the basis for the suit (e.g., a desire for four synthetic liners rather than the required two) was not a permit condition at the time of final permit issuance. Without the shield provision, facility operations could be interrupted virtually at will, depending upon individual desires.

Thus prior to the enactment of HSWA in November 1984, any new TSDF requirement that was promulgated by EPA after the issuance of a fixed-term "final" permit would not be required at that facility until the permit was renewed at the end of its term (e.g., 10 years) or when and if the permit was re-issued prior to its stated duration for other reasons. One exception to this situation is where the permittee requests that the modifications be included prior to the permit's term. However, facilities that had applied for, but had not yet received, a final permit would have these new conditions imposed at the time of final permitting.

HSWA has substantially changed this relationship between final permit duration and the timing of compliance with new regulations at that facility. Virtually all HSWA requirements and provisions become conditions of permit compliance at the affected universe of facilities on the effective date of the requirement (e.g., land disposal ban for solvents and dioxins on November 8, 1986) irrespective of whether the affected TSDFs have received a fixed duration final permit or are still interim status facilities. Moreover, the Administrator is authorized to review and modify any RCRA permit at any time during its duration in order to incorporate new requirements or technological developments.

Until recently, the Agency has interpreted this new authority very narrowly and has chosen not to re-open final permits or modify them until they have expired. However, EPA recently proposed that any new requirement it decides to issue may become a permit compliance condition at facilities that received a final, fixed-term permit prior to permit renewal. In addition, RCRA 3005(c)(3) now states that land disposal facilities are subject to modifications every 5 years, to incorporate new regulatory requirements (e.g., location standards or vulnerable hydrogeology criteria for disposal facilities).[41]

In general, a final RCRA permit may be modified subsequent to issuance only for specific reasons. Most facility modifications that affect the capacity or operation of the facility are currently classed as "major modifications" and as such are subject to a new permit proceeding including public participation and hearing (Part 124 discussed below). Thus a facility's discretion to modify operations once it obtains its final or Part B permit is much more limited than under interim status. Either EPA, citizens, authorized state, or the facility owner/operator can trigger a major modification proceeding because of: material and substantial alterations to the facility; the discovery or existence of new information about the facility that was not available at the time of permitting; the effects of unpredictable events such as floods, materials shortages, or acts of God on a compliance schedule. Significantly, when land disposal facilities must adjust their groundwater monitoring programs from detection monitoring to compliance monitoring (due to the presence of significant contamination), or from compliance monitoring to corrective action, these permit modifications are also considered major modifications (40 CFR 264.98–100).[42] (See Chapter 11 for further discussion.) As noted above, land disposal facilities are subject to modifications every 5 years to incorporate new regulatory requirements; such modifications are also considered major. New requirements that are due to a specific HSWA provision, rather than this general and discretionary authority to reopen permits at any time, are not considered to be, nor do they trigger, major modifications to each affected facility.

When a permit is subject to a major or minor permit modification (discussed below), only the conditions subject to modification are reopened. Conversely, if a permit is revoked or reissued (discussed below) the entire permit is reopened and subject to revision to incorporate all new regulatory requirements. The permit is then reissued for a new term.

Suitability of the facility location is not considered at the time of permit modification, revocation, or reissuance unless new information or standards indicating that a threat to human health or the environment exists which was unknown at the time of permit issuance. For example, HSWA now requires that the EPA issue guidance criteria identifying areas of "vulnerable hydrogeology." The 5-year review for land disposal facilities may incorporate a review for "vulnerable hydrogeology" at that time, and a major permit modification.[43]

MINOR MODIFICATIONS   There are also a number of "minor" modifications to RCRA TSDF permits that are not subject to full and formal repetition of the permitting process. These include very minor changes in things such as compliance schedules (less than 120 days), trial burns, land treatment demonstrations, and contingency plans.[44] Defining the limits of "major" and "minor" permit modifications has taken on greater significance since the enactment of HSWA. HSWA has created a need for expansion of proper treatment capacity. At the same time, even minor facility changes such as adding an additional storage tank with no other change in the treatment process is currently classed as a "major" modification and subject to a full and formal repetition of the permit process.

The potential conflict between the need for additional treatment capacity and the constraints imposed by the current "major modification" regulations is punctuated by the fact that many Part B applications were submitted in advance of HSWA, or certainly before the specific nature of a firm's future treatment needs could be established. For example, a facility's choice of treatment technologies will depend upon the pretreatment requirement of the land disposal ban (Chapter 9). While Part B permit applications can be modified to a certain degree at any time prior to final permit issuance, many of the quantitative and qualitative treatment needs of firms will not come into final focus until this rule is finalized in late-1986, and are likely to continue evolving for several years to come even after Part B or final operating permits are issued. Part Bs for most major facilities were submitted many months and even years prior to the unfolding of the HSWA provisions. EPA has issued a proposal to address some of these impending conflicts between the permit process and the near-term need for additional treatment capacity.[45] In addition, the Agency has decided to undertake a "negotiated rulemaking" with all interested parties on the major/minor permit modification issue in an attempt to develop a consensus position on future revisions to these regulations.

TRANSFERS OF PERMITS   A permit may be transferred by the permittee to a new owner or operator as a minor permit modification provided the Agency determines that no other change in the permit is necessary, and a written agreement containing a specific date for transfer of permit responsibility, coverage, and liability between current and new permittees is submitted to the Agency. At the same time, notification of a proposed transfer of the permit is cause for the Agency to simultaneously modify the permit.

TERMINATION OF PERMITS   The Agency's authority to terminate a permit once issued is very broad and can occur for failure to comply with any permit condition. If a permit is terminated the facility is not only subject to enforcement action, but it may no longer conduct the business of waste management activity allowed by the permit. The failure to fully disclose all relevant facts in a Part A or B application, or threats to human health and the environment from TSDF operations are the leading reasons for potential termination.[46] A formal evidentiary hearing must precede any RCRA permit termination if requested by the TSDF owner/operator.

While HSWA specifically terminated interim status for certain land disposal facilities, it did not affect the Agency's discretionary authority to terminate final operating permits.

CONTINUATION OF EXPIRED PERMITS   All permits, whether issued by EPA or authorized states, are limited to a maximum of 10 years. At the time of permit renewal, a problem may occur if a new permit is not issued by the expiration date of the original permit. The permitting regulations provide for an automatic continuation of an EPA issued permit until the effective date of an authorized state's decision to issue or deny the state RCRA permit, provided that the facility submits a timely complete state permit application.[47]

Preconstruction Ban

All new hazardous waste management facilities (other than research facilities, discussed below) must submit a Part B application before they begin construction of the facility, and are not eligible for interim status. "New" is defined as those facilities which began operation or for which construction began after November 19, 1980. For facilities that are subject to RCRA for the first time (e.g., new waste listing), "new" facility would generally be defined as those that were not in existence within 3 to 6 months of the effective date of the regulation that initially subjected the facility to RCRA jurisdiction. In addition, all new facility construction and all existing facility expansions and modifications that exceed the limitations of interim status (50% expansion/reconstruction rule, discussed above) fall within this requirement. This so-called preconstruction ban affects all facilities that must submit a Part B, except PCB incinerators that are permitted and constructed in accordance with the Toxic Substances Control Act.[48] In addition, facilities that qualify for research, development, and demonstration permits (RDD) (see discussion below) are only subject to the preconstruction ban as it pertains to breaking ground or set-up at a specific site. The construction and assembly of such units at the factory or other areas is not subject to the preconstruction ban. The provision is intended to prevent the construction of TSDFs that do not or cannot satisfy the Part 264 final permitting standards for the type of facility in question, and to prevent potential bias in the permitting process.

SPECIAL FORMS OF PERMITS

Permits-by-Rule

Virtually all RCRA TSDFs are subject to an individual permit application and proceeding. However, the RCRA permitting regulations also provide a mechanism for the Agency to simultaneously issue a RCRA permit to a TSDF through other federal permits. This is accomplished through the issuance of a regulation, describing the class or group of facilities that will be deemed to have a RCRA permit if they meet certain conditions. Usually these conditions are operating and permitting standards specified by other environmental statutes for that class of facilities.

RCRA permits-by-rule are a formal method of deferring primary permitting responsibility for certain TSDFs to other statutes, where such statutes provide equivalent or greater protection than would be afforded under RCRA. To date, permits by rule have been authorized for: ocean disposal barges and ocean incineration vessels (proposed) with permits under the Marine Protection, Research and Sanctuaries Act; operators of Class I & IV underground injection wells with UIC permits issued under the Safe Drinking Water Act; and publicly owned treatment works (POTWs) regulated under the Clean Water Act. Compliance with permits issued under these statutes and selected additional requirements as specified in 40 CFR 270.60 constitutes compliance with RCRA. In 1980 the Agency also proposed to issue permits-by-rule to wastewater treatment tanks and elementary neutralization tanks under RCRA, a variation on the standard use of this mechanism. To date no final rule has been issued, meanwhile these units remain exempt from all RCRA permit requirements.[49] Chapter 8 discusses the extent to which interim status or other RCRA requirements apply to these facilities under the terms of the permit-by-rule.

Permits-by-rule serve a useful purpose by allowing the Agency to focus its permitting resources on major facilities and/or waste management activities that are not governed by other statutes. However, such permits have posed significant problems because frequently they have omitted important substantive requirements which would have applied to the TSDF had they been individually permitted under RCRA. Ocean incineration ships have been the source of a major controversy due largely to attempts to permit these units without following the RCRA public hearing process or by using destruction and removal efficiency standards less stringent than those which apply to RCRA land-based incinerators. The hazardous waste injection regulations under the Safe Drinking Water Act (SDWA) fail to impose RCRA's financial responsibility or groundwater monitoring requirements for land disposal facilities. However, HSWA specifically imposes the RCRA corrective action requirements as a permit condition for these facilities, as well as all other types of RCRA TSDFs.[50] Deep wells are also subject to the land disposal restrictions of HSWA. A facility's permit-by-rule can be terminated by EPA where special environmental concerns warrant.[51]

Class Permits

Another variation on the group permitting theme is the class permit. These allow the Agency to process and facilities to submit a shortened, standardized permit application form for reasonably similar facilities (e.g., storage pads). Such permit applications are nevertheless accompanied by the procedural requirements attendant to site-specific permits. It is anticipated that this implicit Agency authority would be used only in situations where large numbers of relatively non-controversial and similar facilities are involved. The Agency is currently developing such a class permit for on-site storage facilities.[52]

Emergency, Operational Readiness Permits

In situations where the Administrator determines that an imminent and substantial endangerment to human health and the environment exists, a temporary emergency permit may be issued to a previously unpermitted TSDF or to a permitted TSDF to allow a waste management activity not covered by the original permit.[53] Such permits are limited to 90 days, are revocable at will, and may be issued orally (for a maximum of 5 days) or in writing. Emergency permits must also be publicly noticed.

An owner/operator is not required to have an emergency permit to immediately contain or treat a spill of hazardous waste, such as a commercial chemical product spill. However, an emergency permit would be required to treat, store, or dispose of the spilled material or debris. A generator that contained the spill of a commercial chemical product on the 261.33(e) or (f) list could still store the spilled material for 90 days before having to submit a storage facility permit application.

Similar short-term permits can also be granted for the purpose of conducting an incinerator trial burn or to demonstrate the effectiveness of a land treatment operation. Both of these short-term permits are nevertheless subject to very specific and detailed requirements.[54]

Research, Development, and Demonstration Permits

HSWA provides the Agency with new authority to issue permits for experimental treatment facilities or innovative uses of existing technologies without first issuing standards for such units. Such permits are limited to 365 operating days, but are renewable up to 3 times.

The provision was directed at eliminating the "catch-22" that has existed in the permitting of research and development treatment facilities for which Part 264 and 265 operating standards have not been issued. Only incinerator standards and cursory requirements for treatment in tanks have been issued. For other research and development treatment units, a permit could not be issued unless it was shown to meet a given performance standard. However, such a unit could not meet a performance standard that didn't exist. Thus, the provision was enacted.

The Agency has the authority to prescribe any and all requirements and safeguards to ensure proper operation of RDD treatment facilities during the research period. Public review of the permit prior to operation is required; however, all other permit requirements may be waived other than the financial responsibility requirements (see Chapter 7).

The provision is not intended to provide de facto commercialization of a facility. It is essentially a stepping stone to a final permit, provided that the data from early tests verify the efficacy of the technology. The Agency is currently developing guidance which defines the scope and permit application procedures for implementing this important provision. Of particular concern are definitions of "research," "innovation," "demonstration," the relationship of this provision to the state authorization process, the role of the pre-construction ban, and the streamlining of the permit application process.[55]

In addition to this effort, the Agency is also developing final Part 264 permit standards for all other technologies. These so-called "Subpart X" standards should complement the research permit process for successfully demonstrated technologies. The Subpart X standards are anticipated to consist of a general environmental performance standard.

Portable Treatment Unit Permitting

One of the most promising technological developments in recent years is the emergence of modular or portable treatment units that can be brought to the site and scaled to meet the daily and/or remedial treatment needs of that particular site.

Such portable units are anticipated to play a major role in waste minimization, phase separation, chemical destruction (particularly PCBs), biological degradation, groundwater reclamation, and in the redressing of the ongoing releases from land disposal facilities (particularly impoundments) that are either seeking a final permit or which are closing. In fact, the RCRA Conference Report reflects Congress' desire to expedite the use of such units by varying the standard RCRA permit process for such units: "EPA is encouraged to use its existing authority to develop a permit program for mobile treatment units. Individual permits for each site that will be visited shall not be required although a unit-specific permit should anticipate and specify the type of site and general location where such treatment unit is authorized to operate."[56]

If the full RCRA permit process were to be required each time a portable, modular unit is moved, irrespective of how brief the duration at the site, or how basic the treatment operation (e.g., dewatering, phase-separation) the use of these units would be drastically curtailed and the needed treatment and/or remedial action either delayed or rendered inaccessible to that site. In fact, situations have already arisen where the procedural impediments to using portable incineration units on the site of an impoundment closure (e.g., interim status "reconstruction" rule discussed above, and the site-specific nature of the permit process) has resulted in the prolonged migration of hazardous constituents from the site. The Hazardous Waste Treatment Council has formally petitioned the Agency for review and modification of the site-specific permit process for certain portable treatment units. The petition seeks to conform or adjust the site-specific nature of RCRA permit process to the nature and duration of the unit's operation at a specific site. Simultaneous with this petition the Agency has initiated an internal review of portable unit permitting.[57] An Agency proposal to modify these permitting procedures for certain mobile units is expected by late-Spring 1986.

PERMITTING PROCEDURES

The EPA procedures for issuing, denying, modifying, revoking, reissuing, or terminating RCRA permits are specified in Part 124 of the regulations. The requirements discussed below also apply to the application and review process in state RCRA programs, but state programs may have different and more elaborate procedures.

The Agency first reviews the permit application for completeness. If deficiencies exist the Agency will send a "Notice of Deficiency" to the facility, which details the inadequacies. The facility owner/operator is then usually provided 90 days in which to respond to the Notice. Once the application is considered complete, EPA will then prepare a "project decision schedule," which specifies target dates for preparing a draft permit, completing the public comment process, and issuing a final permit.[58]

The next step in the permitting process is the issuance of a draft permit, which incorporates all applicable conditions, compliance schedules, and monitoring requirements. The draft permit is based on an administrative record, and made available for public comment and hearing in accordance with RCRA 7004(b). The draft permit must also be accompanied by a document entitled "statement of basis" for the permit or a permit "fact sheet." The former document is used in uncontroversial permit proceedings and for uncomplicated permits where only a minimum amount of information is needed to describe how the conditions of the draft permit were derived. The fact sheet is a detailed document used for major facilities where significant public interest is expected. The fact sheet must include a discussion of the principal facts and legal findings used in the preparation of a draft permit.[59]

All RCRA permits also require public notice. A 45-day comment period on the draft permit is required, during which anyone can submit written comments and request a public hearing. Whenever anyone submits a written notice of opposition and requests a public hearing, the Agency is required to honor the request. RCRA public hearings are not full evidentiary hearings. Cross-examination of witnesses by other parties to the proceeding is usually not allowed. Rather, witnesses offer testimony, and the hearing officer may then question the witness.[60]

After the close of the comment period and the public hearing, if any, the Agency (or authorized state) must decide whether to issue or deny the permit. The permit decision must be accompanied by a response to public comments. While no time limit is placed on the Agency's decision, once a final decision is reached it becomes effective 30 days later, unless challenged. During this 30-day period, anyone that commented on the draft permit or participated in the public hearing may petition for review of any permit condition to the EPA Administrator, if EPA is issuing the permit.

This petition or administrative appeal is a requirement for subsequent judicial review of the Agency's determination. Once challenged, the effectiveness of the permit is automatically stayed. Thus, an unpermitted TSDF may not begin operation, but a facility with a pre-existing permit or interim status can continue operating under the terms of the prior permit or interim status standards. The Agency is allowed "a reasonable time" to either grant or deny the petition. If granted, parties to the proceeding submit briefs to the Agency for a final determination on the appeal.[61]

The Administrator's determination is also subject to judicial review under RCRA 7006 in the jurisdiction where the permittee or person resides or transacts business. Petitions for judicial review must be submitted within 90 days after the Administrator rules on the administrative appeal. The same administrative appeals procedures apply to actions that would modify, revoke, or terminate a RCRA permit. However, authorized state programs frequently have different appeals procedures.[62]

NOTES

1. 45 *Fed. Reg.* 33066 (May 19, 1980), The "May 19, 1980 Package."
2. 40 CFR 270.4.
3. 40 CFR 270.1. See 270.2 for definition of treatment, storage, and disposal. See 50 *Fed. Reg.* 28710-12 (July 15, 1985) for a discussion of post-closure permits to conduct corrective action; also see Chapter 11.
4. 40 CFR 270.1(c)(2).
5. 40 CFR 262.34.
6. 40 CFR 262.51.
7. 40 CFR 261.5 (small generators); 40 CFR 261.4 (statutory and regulatory exclusions).
8. 40 CFR 260.10. A totally enclosed treatment facility treats hazardous waste that is directly connected to an industrial production process and is contructed and operated in a manner that prevents the release of any hazardous waste or any of its constituent into the environment during treatment. An example is a pipe in which waste acid is neutralized. Also see 45 *Fed. Reg.* 33218 and July 1981 regulatory interpretation memo.
9. 40 CFR 260.10. Elementary neutralization unit is a device which is used for neutralizing wastes that are hazardous only because they are corrosive or listed solely due to corrosivity and meets the definition of tank, container, transport vehicle, or vessel. Wastewater treatment unit is a device that is part of a wastewater treatment facility that is subject to regulation under either Section 402 or Section 307(b) of the Clean Water Act, and receives, treats or stores a hazardous waste, or generates a wastewater treatment sludge that is hazardous under RCRA.
10. 40 CFR 270.1(c)(2)(vi).
11. 270.1(c)(3).

12. RCRA, Section 3005(e)(1).

13. 45 *Fed. Reg.* 33154 (May 19, 1980).

14. 40 CFR 270.2. For example, also see the "Waste-as-Fuel" final rule regarding facilities newly subject to interim status, 50 *Fed. Reg.* 49164 (Nov. 29, 1985).

15. 50 *Fed. Reg.* 28753 (July 15, 1985); 40 CFR 270.70(a).

16. 40 CFR 270.1(b); 270.70(e)(11)(ii).

17. 45 *Fed. Reg.* 76632, 11-19-80 (ISCL letters); 48 *Fed. Reg.* 52718 (Nov.22, 1983).

18. 40 CFR 270.70(c); 50 *Fed. Reg.* 28753 (July 15, 1985).

19. RCRA 3010(a); 45 *Fed. Reg.* 47832 (July 16, 1980).

20. 45 *Fed. Reg.* 12746 (Feb. 26, 1980).

21. Ibid.

22. Ibid. Also see *RCRA Hazardous Waste Handbook,* R. Hall, T. Watson, J. Davidson, D. Case, and N. Bryson, Government Institutes, 1985, pp. 3–5.

23. 40 CFR 270.13 (contents of Part A); 40 CFR 270.1(b).

24. 40 CFR 270.11; 48 *Fed. Reg.* 39622 (Sept. 1, 1983).

25. 40 CFR 270.71.

26. 40 CFR 270.72.

27. 40 CFR 270.72(e); 45 *Fed. Reg.* 33324 (May 19, 1980); 50 *Fed. Reg.* 26504 (June 26, 1985) (hazardous waste tank example). Also see (July 30, 1982) interpretive memo of Bruce Weddle, Deputy Director, Office of Solid Waste, U.S. EPA, and (July 20, 1982) letter from Rita Lavelle to Con. Mikulski on interim status expansions.

28. 40 CFR 270.73; 270.10(e)(5).

29. 40 CFR 270.10(e)(5) (failure to provide timely Part B); 49 *Fed. Reg.* 17716 (April 24, 1984) (incomplete Part A).

30. 40 CFR 270.73(c),(d); 50 *Fed. Reg.* 28724 (July 15, 1985).

31. 40 CFR 270.73(e) (incinerators); 40 CFR 270.73(f) (all other facilities).

32. "Revised National Permit Strategy," Office of Solid Waste, U.S. EPA, April 9, 1985.

33. 40 CFR 270.14(a).

34. RCRA, 3005(c)(3); HSWA, Section 212, This new HSWA provision is codified at 40 CFR 270.32, 50 *Fed. Reg.* 28722 (July 15, 1985). The Agency has recently proposed to amend the permit application requirements to include such additional conditions beyond those in the current regulations that the Administrator believes necessary at the time of permit application (proposed section 270.10(k). 51 *Fed. Reg.* 10715 (March 28, 1986). An additional proposed regulation would codify the authority to modify a permit once it has been issued, but before its term is expired. See note 41 and related discussion (proposed 270.41(a)(3).).

35. 40 CFR 270.30.

36. 40 CFR 270.30(j); 40 CFR 270.31.

37. 40 CFR 270.30(1).

38. 40 CFR 270.4.

39. 40 CFR 270.1(c)(4); 50 *Fed. Reg.* 28752 (July 15, 1985). The Codification Rule amends Sections 270.41 and 270.50 to require review of land disposal permits every 5 years.

40. RCRA, Section 3005(c)(3); 40 CFR 270.50(a)–(c); HSWA, Section 212.

41. 40 CFR 270.4, HSWA Section 212, RCRA Section 3005(c)(3), 40 CFR 270.41, 50 *Fed. Reg.* 28752 (July 15, 1985). Also see the proposed rule to allow EPA to modify permits before their term is expired without the prior approval of the permitee (51

Fed Reg. 10714 (March 28, 1986; proposed 270.41(a)(3)) and previously proposed rule on this subject (48 *Fed. Reg.* 10715 (Feb. 8, 1983))

42. 40 CFR 270.41(a).

43. RCRA 3004(o)(7); HSWA, Section 202.

44. 40 CFR 270.42.

45. 49 *Fed. Reg.* 9850 (March 15, 1984).

46. 40 CFR 270.43–45 *Fed. Reg.* 33316 (May 19, 1980). The Agency expressed its policy to seek permit terminations only in extreme situations.

47. 40 CFR 270.51; 48 *Fed. Reg.* 39672 (Sept. 1, 1983).

48. RCRA, Section 3005(a); HSWA, Section 211; 40 CFR 270.10(f)(1).

49. 40 CFR 270.60. 40 CFR 264.1; 265.1 (10)(exclusions for wastewater and neutralization tanks).

50. 50 *Fed. Reg.* 28752 (July 15, 1985); P.L. 98-616, Section 206.

51. 40 CFR 270.60(b)(c) (injection wells and POTWs subject to 264.101 corrective action); 45 *Fed. Reg.* 76076 (Nov. 17, 1980).

52. 50 *Fed. Reg.* 44681 (Oct. 29, 1985) (regulatory agenda); 49 *Fed. Reg.* 29524 (July 20, 1984) (comments on class permits).

53. 40 CFR 270.61.

54. 40 CFR 270.62 (incinerators); 40 CFR 270.63 (land treatment).

55. RCRA, Section 3005(g); HSWA, Section 214; 40 CFR 270.65; 50 *Fed. Reg.* 28728 (July 15, 1985); "Draft EPA Guidance Document on Research, Development, and Demonstration Permits," Office of Solid Waste, U.S. EPA, October 5, 1985.

56. HSWA, Conference Report 98-1133, p. 95.

57. Rulemaking Petition of Hazardous Waste Treatment Council to the U.S. EPA to Establish a Permitting Program for Portable Hazardous Waste Treatment Units, January 15, 1986, Petition Number XXX, addressed to Mr. Lee Thomas, Administrator. The petition would utilize two existing permitting mechanisms to expedite and conform the extent of site-specific permitting to the nature and duration of portable unit operation. The petition identifies five major obstacles to the timely permitting of such units: 1) current EPA regulations are structured to permit only fixed-site facilities, 2) the permit process itself may take years and frequently lasts longer than the treatment process itself, 3) the regulatory requirement for "local" notice of opportunity for public comments, 4) the current structure of the major/minor permit modification regulations (40 CFR 270.41–42), and 5) the Agency's reluctance to use enforcement authorities, to require the use of portable units to achieve permanent cleanup at RCRA remedial sites (i.e., RCRA 3008(h)).

58. 40 CFR 124.3(c),(g).

59. 40 CFR 124.6–124.8.

60. 40 CFR 124.10, 124.12, 124.13.

61. 40 CFR 124.14–124.21.

62. 40 CFR 271.14. Authorized states are not required to adopt the RCRA appeals procedures in order to receive final authorization.

CHAPTER SEVEN

General Requirements Applicable to All RCRA TSDFs

The stringency and scope of the RCRA requirements for TSDFs differ according to whether the facility has been granted interim status or issued a RCRA final operating or post-closure permit. Existing RCRA facilities are initially subject only to the interim status standards of 40 CFR Part 265, which consist largely of general administrative and "housekeeping" regulations. These general requirements include, for example, waste analysis, personnel training, manifesting, and financial responsibility. For the most part these requirements will continue to apply once a facility receives a final permit. During interim status, a facility is also subject to a limited set of facility-specific technical standards, such as groundwater monitoring at land disposal facilities.

Once the owner/operator of a facility obtains a final operating permit, an additional set of specific or technical regulatory requirements found in Part 264 are applied to TSDFs in accordance with the management practice. Unlike the largely administrative nature of the interim status requirements, the standards of Part 264 are generally more specific and vary according to the type of TSDF involved. They consist of specific technical requirements and standards such as destruction and removal efficiency standards for incinerators, and secondary containment for container storage areas.[1]

This chapter will examine the general standards applicable to RCRA TSDFs. Chapter 8 will examine the specific technical standards that apply to various TSDFs during interim status and final permitting, with the exception of the specific standards for recycling facilities (Chapter 3), and hazardous waste tank standards (Chapter 12). The standards and requirements discussed in Chapters 7–12 are the basis for evaluating permit applications and determining whether a given facility is in compliance with its respective requirements. The eligibility criteria for interim status and final permits, and the process of submitting permit applications based on these regulatory requirements were discussed in Chapter 6.

GENERAL REGULATORY STANDARDS

The following series of general regulatory standards apply to all RCRA TSDFs that require a RCRA permit, regardless of whether they are storage, treatment, or disposal facilities. Those hazardous waste management facilities that have been explicitly exempted from the RCRA permitting process were discussed in Chapter 6. These regulatory standards have been termed "general" because they apply with general uniformity to all TSDFs and for the most part do not involve technical requirements. Individual state regulations are frequently more stringent, particularly in the areas of manifesting and financial responsibility.[2]

Administrative Requirements

ID NUMBER AND REQUIRED NOTICES Owners/operators of all hazardous waste TSDFs must apply to EPA for an EPA identification number by filing a notification with EPA using Form 8700-12. This I.D. number application/notification must be filed by the date specified in the regulation that first subjects the facility to RCRA coverage. Among other things, the application must include the name and location of the facility and the specific types of wastes managed at the facility. (Note: generators also must have an ID number before shipping wastes off-site.)[3] Facilities that have arranged to ship a hazardous waste to a foreign country may be subject to additional notification and other shipping requirements. See Chapter 4 for further discussion.[4]

Before transferring ownership or operation of a facility during the operating life (under interim status or as a permitted facility), closure, or post-closure care period (applicable to certain land disposal facilities), the current owner/operator must notify the Administrator or authorized state no later than 90 days prior to the scheduled change. When the ownership transfer occurs, the old owner/operator must also comply with all applicable financial requirements until the new owner/operator has demonstrated compliance with these requirements. All other interim status duties are transferrable effective immediately upon the date of the change in ownership or operational control of the facility. The failure of the previous owner to provide such notification does not relieve the new owner of the obligation to comply with all applicable requirements.[5]

GENERAL WASTE ANALYSIS Before a waste is treated, stored, or disposed of at a given TSDF, the owner/operator must conduct a chemical and physical analysis of a representative sample of that waste. Such analysis must contain all the information necessary to treat, store, or dispose of that waste in accordance with the regulations (e.g., waste incompatibilities such as ignitability and reactivity characteristics), and must be accurate and current. The analysis must be repeated when any new waste is managed or there is any change in the character of wastes that were previously analyzed. This requirement takes on added significance once the land disposal restrictions take effect (Chapter 9), because of the need to ensure that prohibited wastes are either properly pre-treated or not land disposed at all in the event that the waste cannot be pre-treated. When the generator does not supply such information to a facility that accepts the waste for off-site shipment, the analysis must be conducted by the receiving facility prior to managing the waste.[6]

SECURITY   Owners and operators must install security systems to prevent unknowing entry and to minimize the potential for unauthorized entry of people or livestock to the active portion of the TSDF. This requirement may be satisfied by a 24-hour surveillance system or a barrier around the the facility, including a means to control entry and posted "Danger" signs. An exemption from these requirements can be granted where the facility demonstrates that unauthorized or unknowing entry will not result in injury to individuals, livestock, or the environment. These requirements may continue to apply during the post-closure care period for land disposal facilities.[7]

GENERAL INSPECTION   Operators are required to prepare and implement an inspection schedule specific to the nature of the waste management practices at the facility. In general, inspections must be often enough to identify problems in time to correct them before they harm human health or the environment. The inspection schedule must specify the types of defects, malfunctions, and operating errors for which all operating, monitoring, structural, and safety equipment is to be inspected. Only the inspection requirements applicable under interim status are discussed here. Other final permit inspection requirements, such as weekly inspections of leak detection systems for surface impoundments, are discussed in Chapter 8.

The frequency of inspection may vary based on the rate of possible deterioration of equipment and the probability of human error resulting in an "environmental incident." Areas subject to spills such as loading docks must be inspected daily when in use. At a minimum the inspection schedule must include the following items and frequencies:

1. Containers: weekly for deterioration and leakage.
2. Monitoring, discharge, and control devices associated with hazardous waste tanks: each operating day.
3. Hazardous waste tank integrity and confinement area structures: weekly.
4. Free board and dikes associated with surface impoundments: weekly.
5. Combustion and emission control instruments at incinerators and thermal destruction devices: every 15 minutes.
6. The complete incinerator or thermal destruction devices and associated equipment: daily.
7. Discharge control, safety, and monitoring equipment associated with chemical, physical, and biological treatment must be inspected each operating day, while construction materials associated with such treatment units must be inspected weekly.[8]

Inspection records must be kept on file at the facility for 3 years. Although not a Part 264 or 265 requirement, RCRA now requires that all TSDFs be inspected at least once every 2 years beginning 12 months after the enactment of HSWA, or November 8, 1985. Federal and State operated facilities must be inspected yearly.[9] (See Chapter 13 for further discussion of these inspection requirements).

PERSONNEL TRAINING Operating personnel at TSDFs are required to be competent in the areas to which they are assigned in order to minimize the possibility that inadequate training might cause or fail to prevent an accident at the facility. The training can be formal classroom instruction or on-the-job training, but at a minimum must ensure that personnel are able to respond effectively to emergencies, including ability to: operate emergency equipment and automatic waste cut-off systems; respond to fires, explosions, and groundwater contamination; and shutdown the facility operations. Personnel must be trained within 6 months of the date they begin employment, and must review their training annually. Personnel records, including job and training descriptions, must be retained for each employee for at least 3 years after the employee leaves the facility.[10]

IGNITABLE, REACTIVE OR INCOMPATIBLE WASTES The regulations also require that special procedures and precautions should be instituted when managing ignitable, reactive, or incompatible wastes. (Chapter 2 defines these categories of wastes.) In addition an appendix to the Part 265 regulations provide examples of waste mixtures that should be avoided, and is reproduced here for the reader's convenience (Table 7-1).

Ignitable and reactive wastes must be separated and protected from sources of ignition or reaction including open flames, hot surfaces, cutting and welding areas, and radiant heat. "No Smoking" signs must be placed wherever there is a hazard from ignitable or reactive wastes.

Any deliberate mixing of reactive, ignitable, and/or incompatible wastes must be conducted so that it does not: generate extreme heat, fire, explosion, or violent reaction; produce dusts, fumes, gases, or toxic mists; produce uncontrolled flammable fumes or gasses which pose a risk of fire or explosion; damage the structural integrity of the device; or through other means threaten human health or the environment. Specific restrictions on the management of these wastes apply to each facility type as well.[11] Owners/operators of finally permitted facilities must separately document their compliance with these requirements.

LOCATION STANDARDS Three types of location standards are contained in the requirements that apply to RCRA TSDFs. Seismic and floodplain restrictions apply only to finally permitted facilities. A ban on the placement of hazardous wastes into salt domes or underground mine locations apply to both interim status and finally permitted TSDFs (Chapter 9).

The seismic location standards apply only to new TSDFs (i.e., TSDFs not in existence when similar TSDFs first were subject to RCRA regulation). The seismic location standard specifies that new facilities or portions thereof that treat, store, or dispose of hazardous wastes may not be located within 200 feet of faults that have moved in the recent geologic

Table 7-1

Table 7-1

EXAMPLES OF POTENTIALLY INCOMPATIBLE WASTE

Many hazardous wastes, when mixed with other waste or materials at a hazardous waste facility, can produce effects which are harmful to human health and the environment, such as (1) heat or pressure, (2) fire or explosion, (3) violent reaction, (4) toxic dusts, mists, fumes, or gases, or (5) flammable fumes or gases.

Below are examples of potentially incompatible wastes, waste components, and materials, along with the harmful consequences which result from mixing materials in one group with materials in another group. The list is intended as a guide to owners or operators of treatment, storage, and disposal facilities, and to enforcement and permit granting officials, to indicate the need for special precautions when managing these potentially incompatible waste materials or components.

This list is not intended to be exhaustive. An owner or operator must, as the regulations require, adequately analyze his wastes so that he can avoid creating uncontrolled substances or reactions of the type listed below, whether they are listed below or not.

It is possible for potentially incompatible wastes to be mixed in a way that precludes a reaction (e.g., adding acid to water rather than water to acid) or that neutralizes them (e.g., a strong acid mixed with a strong base), or that controls substances produced (e.g., by generating flammable gases in a closed tank equipped so that ignition cannot occur, and burning the gases in an incinerator).

In the lists below, the mixing of a Group A material with a Group B material may have the potential consequence as noted.

Group 1-A	Group 1-B
Acetylene sludge	Acid sludge
Alkaline caustic liquids	Acid and water
Alkaline cleaner	Battery acid
Alkaline corrosive liquids	Chemical cleaners
Alkaline corrosive battery fluid	Electrolyte, acid
Caustic wastewater	Etching acid liquid or solvent
Lime sludge and other corrosive alkalies	
Lime wastewater	Pickling liquor and other corrosive acids
Lime and water	Spent acid
Spent caustic	Spent mixed acid
	Spent sulfuric acid

Potential consequences: Heat generation; violent reaction.

Group 2-A	Group 2-B
Aluminum	Any waste in Group 1-A or 1-B
Beryllium	
Calcium	
Lithium	
Magnesium	

Potassium
Sodium
Zinc powder
Other reactive metals and metal hydrides

Potential consequences: Fire or explosion; generation of flammable hydrogen gas.

Group 3-A	Group 3-B
Alcohols	Any concentrated waste in Groups 1-A or 1-B
Water	Calcium
	Lithium
	Metal hydrides
	Potassium
	SO_2Cl_2, $SOCl_2$, PCl_3, CH_3SiCl_3
	Other water-reactive waste

Potential consequences: Fire, explosion, or heat generation; generation of flammable or toxic gases.

Group 4-A	Group 4-B
Alcohols	Concentrated Group 1-A or 1-B wastes
Aldehydes	Group 2-A wastes
Halogenated hydrocarbons	
Nitrated hydrocarbons	
Unsaturated hydrocarbons	
Other reactive organic compounds and solvents	

Potential consequences: Fire, explosion, or violent reaction.

Group 5-A	Group 5-B
Spent cyanide and sulfide solutions	Group 1-B wastes

Potential consequences: Generation of toxic hydrogen cyanide or hydrogen sulfide gas.

Group 6-A	Group 6-B
Chlorates	Acetic acid and other organic acids
Chlorine	Concentrated mineral acides
Chlorites	Group 2-A wastes
Chromic acid	Group 4-A wastes
Hyphochlorites	Other flammable and combustible wastes
Nitrates	
Nitric acid, fuming	
Perchlorates	
Permanganates	
Peroxides	
Other strong oxidizers	

Potential consequences: Fire, explosion, or violent reaction.

Source: "Law, Regulations, and Guidelines for Handling of Hazardous Waste." California Department of Health, February 1975.

past. Such earth movement faults are termed Holocene faults. Appendix VI to the Part 264 regulations identifies political subdivisions that have a history of actual or potential seismic activity. If a new TSDF is located in one of these areas, it must comply with the 200-foot seismic location standard.[12]

The floodplain location standard prohibits a new or existing TSDF from operating in a 100-year floodplain unless it is designed, constructed, and operated so as to prevent washout of hazardous wastes by a 100-year flood (a flood with a 1% chance of occurring in any given year) through the use of dikes or floodwalls. A limited exemption from the floodplain standard is allowed if the facility can demonstrate that wastes can be safely removed before flood waters reach the facility; or for existing facilities, that no adverse effects on human health and the environment will result if a washout occurs. In many areas of the country 100-year floodplains have been identified by the Federal Insurance Administration (FIA). Since the floodplain standard applies to both new and existing facilities at the time of final permitting, those interim status TSDFs so located may be required to retrofit the facility in order to comply or be denied a final permit.

The third location standard applicable to TSDFs currently prohibits the placement of any hazardous waste, whether containerized or bulk, into salt domes and underground mines, caves, or shafts. This prohibition was instituted by HSWA, which allows the total ban to be lifted for containerized hazardous wastes at such time as permitting standards and requirements are issued for such facilities under Part 264. Until that time, however, the total ban applies (Chapter 9).

HSWA also requires the Agency to issue location standards based on identifying areas of vulnerable hydrogeology by May 8, 1986. This and other potential location criteria, such as proximity to wetlands, are discussed in Chapter 10. Requirements pertaining to other Federal laws (such as the Endangered Species Act and the Wild and Scenic Rivers Act) which affect the location and permitting of facilities also must be addressed by EPA at the time of permitting.[13]

Preparedness and Prevention

In keeping with RCRA's preventive approach, additional measures are imposed to minimize the likelihood of an accident during the management of hazardous wastes, including the use of the following equipment, unless it can be demonstrated to the Regional Administrator that none of the hazards posed by waste handled at the facility could require such equipment or safeguards: internal alarm or communications systems; a device capable of summoning emergency assistance from local agencies; fire and spill control equipment; decontamination equipment, and sufficient aisle space to allow the unobstructed movement of such equipment.

The regulations also require that emergency equipment be maintained and tested to ensure proper function and that adequate aisle space be maintained at all times to allow unrestricted movement of emergency equipment to any area of the facility. The facility must also make arrangements with local emergency officials and hospitals to ensure familiarity with the facility. Where state and/or local authorities decline to enter into such arrangements, the facility must document the refusal in the operating record.[14]

Contingency Plan and Emergency Procedures

Owners/operators are required to prepare a contingency plan, which identifies a prepared set of responses to a series of anticipated emergencies including personnel duties, equipment to be used, and plans for evacuation if such action is necessary. The plan must be maintained at the facility and submitted with the Part B application. The contingency plan must be implemented whenever there is a fire, explosion, or release of hazardous wastes that could threaten human health and the environment. Each facility must designate an employee as the Emergency Coordinator, who must be on call at all times. Subsequent to such an event, the Emergency Coordinator must file a written report with the EPA Regional office within 15 days after the incident that triggers implementation of the plan.[15]

The regulations do not specify what amount of spilled material triggers a contingency plan implementation. It is also unclear whether the spill of a hazardous waste in amounts that must be reported under "Superfund" are considered sufficient to trigger the contingency plan.

Manifest System, Recordkeeping, Reporting

Hazardous waste produced by a generator or a TSDF in regulated quantities that are shipped off-site (except waste samples shipped for analysis) generally must be accompanied by a manifest. The manifest is a waste shipment invoice that accompanies the waste from point of origin to point of final disposition.

Using the Uniform Hazardous Waste Manifest (Chapter 4), owners/operators of facilities that receive hazardous wastes by truck shipment must:

1. Sign and date each copy of the manifest to certify that the hazardous waste covered by the manifest was received.
2. Note any significant discrepancies in the manifest on each copy of the manifest form. "Significant discrepancies" can be for both waste type and quantity. Quantitative discrepancies include variations of greater than a 10% weight difference (bulk wastes), and any variation in piece count, such as a discrepancy of one drum per truck load. Significant discrepancies in type are obvious differences that can be discovered by inspection or waste analysis such as waste solvent substituted for acids, or toxic constituents not reported on the manifest or shipping paper.

3. Immediately give the transporter at least one copy of the signed manifest.
4. Within 30 days of delivery, send a copy of the manifest to the generator. In the event that the generator has not received a copy of the manifest, large quantity generators must investigate and file an exception report with EPA or the State (Chapter 4).
5. Retain at the facility a copy of each manifest for at least 3 years from the date of delivery.

Significantly, off-site shipments are not required by Federal regulation to use EPA Hazardous Waste Codes on the manifest or to specify all the reasons that a waste is hazardous (e.g., a F001 solvent mixed with D002 corrosives). Only the Department of Transportation codes are required for off-site shipments; however, state laws frequently require use of all applicable Hazardous Waste Codes.

Where wastes are shipped by rail or water transportation, special manifest requirements apply (Chapter 4). TSDFs that become generators via spill cleanup, by generating treatment residues, or by otherwise processing hazardous wastes are also subject to the manifest requirements when they ship wastes off-site.[16]

The regulations also require that all TSDFs maintain a complete operating record until closure. The operating record or facility "diary" must include the following information:[17]

1. the type, quantity and location of each hazardous waste received; the method used to treat, store, or dispose of that waste; and when such management occurred;
2. waste analysis results;
3. incidents where the contingency plan was implemented;
4. results of facility inspections, monitoring, and testing carried out by the operator. Groundwater monitoring data for land disposal facilities generally must be kept through the post-closure period;
5. closure estimates, and post-closure cost estimates where applicable;
6. in the case of hazardous waste generators that treat, store, or dispose of wastes on the site where it was generated, an annual certification that the facility has established a program to reduce the volume and toxicity of wastes generated to the degree determined economically practical by the generator. This "waste minimization" certification is a new requirement instituted by HSWA to complement and supplement the statute's prohibitions on land disposal. It should be noted that irrespective of whether a generator deems a given volume or toxicity minimization program at his facility "economically practical" has no bearing on the requirement to comply with all land disposal bans and minimum technology requirements. Compliance with these latter provisions are not predicated on any form of cost consideration.[18]

There are three recordkeeping reports that the TSDF operator must file with the EPA Regional Administrator, or authorized states. The first is the biennial report to be filed by March 1 of every even-numbered year covering hazardous waste activities during the preceding odd-numbered year. This report is filed using EPA Form 8700-13B. The second report is the unmanifested waste report, which must be filed within 15 days of accepting any hazardous waste that is not accompanied by a manifest form, unless the wastes were shipped by unregulated generators. To ensure waste is properly considered "unregulated," the Agency suggests that the owner/operator obtain from each generator a certification that the waste qualifies for an exclusion. Where the owner/operator cannot obtain assurances, the Agency suggests that an unmanifested waste report be filed.[19] In addition, reports must be filed with the Regional Administrator when the following events occur: releases, fires, and explosions; groundwater contamination; and facility closure.[20]

Facility Closure and Post-Closure Requirements

EPA regulations contain procedures and standards for closing a facility, and in some cases for monitoring and maintenance after closure. "Closure" is the period after which hazardous wastes are no longer accepted by a TSDF and during which time the operator completes treatment, storage, or disposal operations. "Post-closure" is the period (usually 30 years) after closure when owners/operators of disposal facilities are subject to various monitoring and maintenance requirements. Generally, where treatment and storage units are dismantled and removed, and other contaminated materals (including soils) are removed or decontaminated, the owner/operator is not required to perform post-closure care. Where waste remains on-site after closure, however, post-closure care is generally required.

The performance of post-closure care for TSDFs that were not certified as "closed" prior to January 26, 1983, will require a post-closure permit and subject the TSDF to the permitting procedures described in Chapter 6. The facility closure and post-closure requirements also take on added significance because of HSWA. Stricter regulations and stronger enforcement provisions will result in the closure of numerous facilities in the coming months and years. In many cases, these facilities will be subject to increased monitoring and cleanup requirements, due to a number of HSWA provisions. Chapter 11 discusses these HSWA provisions as they affect the closing of facilities. Chapter 11 also examines how the permit application requirements (including applications for post-closure permits) relate to the closure and post-closure regulations and HSWA.[21]

CLOSURE PLANS   All existing TSDFs are required to have closure plans. TSDFs that subsequently become subject to a new RCRA regulation (e.g., new waste listing) must prepare such plans by the effective date of that regulation. The closure plan must identify the steps necessary to completely or partially close the TSDF at any point during the facility's intended life, and to completely close at the end of the operating life. Facilities must close in a manner that minimizes the need for further maintenance, and eliminates hazardous waste releases and runoff from the facility after closure. All TSDFs are subject to certain general closure requirements. There are additional requirements for each specific type of TSDF (Chapter 8). Only the general closure requirements will be discussed here.[22]

Requirements of the closure plan include but are not limited to the following:

1. a description of how and when the facility will be partially or completely closed;
2. an estimate of the largest inventory of wastes in storage or treatment at any given time during the facility's life, and a description of how equipment will be decontaminated; and,
3. an estimate of the expected year of closure, and a schedule for final closure.

Generally, the closure plan for interim status facilities must be submitted to the Regional Administrator or the authorized state for approval at least 180 days before the last volume of hazardous wastes will be managed at the facility (or at a particular unit at the facility). If the plan is rejected, the owner/operator must submit a new plan within 30 days. The second plan is either accepted or modified by EPA or the state. The public must be provided with the opportunity to submit written comments on the plan, and to request a hearing on it.

For facilities that seek a final operating permit, the closure plan must be submitted with the Part B permit application. The closure plan becomes part of the permit. Since closure plans are included in the permit, it does not have to be resubmitted for approval at the time of closure. However, a closure plan must be amended within 60 days of the date of any changes in waste management activities that affect the terms of the plan. For a permitted TSDF, such modifications or other changes to the closure plan initiated by the operator are subject to the permit modification procedures specified in the regulations (Chapter 6).

The operator must complete closure activities by 180 days after approval of the closure plan, or 180 days after the final volume of waste is received at the closing unit, whichever is later. The Regional Administrator (or authorized state) may extend these time limits if the owner/operator demonstrates that the closure will necessarily take longer, or a new owner/operator begins operations anew.

When closure is completed all facility equipment and structures must have been properly disposed of, or decontaminated by removing all hazardous wastes and residues. Upon completion of closure activities, the owner/operator and an independent registered professional engineer must submit a certification to the Regional Administrator that the facility has been closed in accordance with the specifications in the approved closure plan.

On March 19, 1985, the EPA proposed several major revisions to the interim status and final permitting standards governing facility closure, post-closure, and financial responsibility requirements, including several key definitions.[23] Significant proposed changes to these requirements may include: all partial and final closures must contain additional information on such activities as groundwater monitoring, leachate collection, and run-on and runoff controls; a description of steps and methods to decontaminate all equipment and/or remove contaminated structures and soils; a prohibition on further modifications to closure plans once closure has begun; permission to remove contaminated soils and structures from the facility prior to a notification of partial or final closure; allowance for extensions to the 90-day deadline for handling all hazardous wastes received at the facility and for the 180-day deadline for completing closure of a hazardous waste management at the facility; numerous changes to the procedures for paying into trust funds and otherwise verifying compliance with the financial responsibility requirements; and elimination of the "independence" requirement for the engineer certifying closure. (A final rule was issued in the May 2, 1986, *Fed. Reg.*).

POST-CLOSURE PLANS AND REQUIREMENTS   All land disposal facilities are subject to additional groundwater monitoring, facility security, and general maintenance requirements where wastes remain on-site subsequent to facility closure. Such monitoring and maintenance must continue for 30 years post-closure. This compliance period can be reduced or extended by the Regional Administrator or authorized state subject to certain conditions (Chapter 11). As with closure plans, all existing disposal facilities must have a written post-closure plan. Land disposal facilities that become subject to RCRA because of new regulations must have such plans by the effective date of the new regulation.[24]

As with closure plans, interim status land disposal facilities must submit the post-closure plan to the Regional Administrator for approval at least 180 days prior to beginning closure. This review process also includes public notice and comment, and potentially a public hearing on the post-closure monitoring plan which may occur simultaneously with the closure plan. For permitted facilities, the post-closure plan is reviewed at the same time as the rest of the final permit application.

At a minimum the post-closure plan must contain the following: a description of the groundwater monitoring program, the planned maintenance activities that will ensure the integrity of the final cover or other waste containment structures, and the name, address, and phone number of the person to contact concerning the post-closure care period.

Owners/operators of disposal facilities have additional reporting responsibilities. Within 90 days after closure the operator must submit a survey plat to local land authorities (i.e., zoning authorities, or the authority with jurisdiction over local land use) and to the Regional Administrator or authorized state. The survey plat must show the location and dimensions of the landfill cells or other disposal areas with respect to permanently surveyed landmarks, and a record of the types and quantities of hazardous wastes disposed of in the facility. Pursuant to state law, the operator must also record a notation on the deed to the facility property, or some other instrument which is normally examined during a title search, that in perpetuity will notify any potential purchaser of the property that the land has been used for disposal of hazardous wastes, and that its future use is restricted to activities which will not disturb the facility's cover and containment system.[25]

The operator must amend the post-closure plan within 60 days of any changes in operating plans or facility design or other events during the active life of the facility that affect the post-closure plan. The operator may voluntarily amend the plan during the operating life, provided it is subjected to the applicable review processes.

During the post-closure care period, the plan can or must be modified through several mechanisms. The owner/operator may amend the plan at any time during the post-closure period. However, he must amend the plan any time changes in monitoring or maintenance plans or events which occur during the post-closure care period affect the plan. In the latter instance, the owner/operator must petition the Regional Administrator (or authorized state) within 60 days of the changes or events, under a specified set of petition procedures. In addition, the Regional Administrator (or authorized state) may also initiate or require changes to the plan or do so in response to a citizen's petition. Such amendments are subject to a level of review and public involvement virtually equivalent to that of the original plan submission (Chapter 6).[26]

Financial Requirements

The financial responsibility requirements refer to a facility's ability to demonstrate that it has sufficient financial resources to compensate for harm to third parties caused by TSDF operations, and to conduct all necessary closure and post-closure monitoring and maintenance responsibilities. All interim status and finally permitted TSDFs (other than those exempted from permitting—see Chapter 6) must demonstrate financial responsibility for third-party liability for sudden events and final closure. All land disposal facilities must also demonstrate financial responsibility for third-party liability for non-sudden events or releases. Land disposal facilities closing in a manner requiring post-closure care (e.g., those that leave hazardous wastes at the site) must also demonstrate assurances for post-closure monitoring and maintenance.[27] These requirements, however, do not apply to state and federally operated facilities because EPA believes that such entities will have sufficient resources to compensate individuals and cover the costs of closure and post-closure. The financial requirements contained in the Federal regulations apply to companies or firms, not individual facilities. States frequently impose more stringent financial requirements.

THIRD-PARTY LIABILITY   All TSDFs (until closure certification) must have third-party liability insurance for *sudden* and accidental occurrences (i.e., spills, explosions) in the amount of 1 million dollars per occurrence with a 2 million dollar annual aggregate. Operators of landfills, surface impoundments, and land treatment units must also obtain insurance for *nonsudden* occurrences such as gradual groundwater leakage and contamination in the amount of 3 million dollars per occurrence with a 6 million dollar annual aggregate. At present, these limits must exclude legal defense cost and explicitly reference the RCRA requirements they are intended to satisfy.[28]

Certain firms may satisfy either or both of these requirements by an alternative mechanism, a self-insurance test, if they can meet one of two sets of criteria:

1. net working capital and tangible net worth at least 6 times the amount of aggregate liability coverage to be demonstrated ($12 million for sudden coverage, and/or $36 million for nonsudden coverage); *and*
2. tangible net worth of at least $10 million; *and*
3. assets in the U.S. amounting to either: 90% of total assets; or at least 6 times the amount of aggregate liability coverage to be demonstrated; *or*
1. a current Standard and Poor's rating for the firm's most recent bond issuance of AAA, AA, A, or BBB, or a Moody's rating of Aaa, Aa, A, or Baa; *and*
2. tangible net worth of $10 million; *and*
3. tangible net worth at least 6 times the amount of aggregate liability coverage to be demonstrated; *and*
4. assets in the U.S. of at least 90% of total assets, or at least 6 times the amount of aggregate liability coverage to be demonstrated.

Irrespective of which of the two sets of self-insurance criteria an operator chooses, three items must be submitted to the Regional Administrator: a letter signed by the owner's or operator's chief financial officer and worded as specified in the regulations[29]; an independent CPA's financial statement for the latest complete fiscal year; and a special report from the independent CPA stating that his review of the financial officer's letter revealed no matters that would cause the data to be adjusted.

The liability assurance regulations also contain variance and adjustment provisions. In general, these provisions allow the Regional Administrator to lower or increase the level of liability coverage required based on a demonstration by the operator that the degree and duration of risk associated with the facility is inconsistent with level of coverage required for the facility.[30] A public hearing may be required by the Regional Administrator (or authorized state) prior to granting a variance or waiver of these requirements. In addition, readers should note some state requirements are more stringent than the Federal regulations, including higher liability amounts, limitations on self-insurance, and expanded application of these requirements to underground injection wells.

In recent months it has become increasingly difficult for some firms to secure the necessary insurance for third-party liability coverage due to the receding and changing scope of the commercial environmental insurance industry. In light of the anticipated long-term difficulties and transition within the environmental insurance market, and the fact that many firms cannot meet the self-insurance test, the Agency has proposed authorizing other financial responsibility mechanisms such as the corporate guarantee. The corporate guarantee is currently available for satisfying the closure and post-closure care financial requirement.[31]

CLOSURE AND POST-CLOSURE   Owners/operators of TSDFs must have written estimates of the cost of closing the facility. Owners/operators of land disposal facilities must also have written estimates of the cost of closing the facility and the annual cost of a post-closure monitoring and maintenance program. The closure and post-closure plans are the basis for developing the financial reaponsibility cost estimates for closure and post-closure. The estimated cost of the post-closure program is the annual cost multiplied by the number of years mandated for post-closure care (e.g., 30 years).

These estimates must be modified whenever a change in the closure or post-closure plan would affect the estimate of closure or post-closure costs. The operator must also adjust the closure and post-closure cost estimates for inflation within 30 days after each anniversary of the date on which the first post-closure estimate was prepared. Such inflation estimates must use a specified formula.[32]

After preparing the plan and developing cost estimates, the operator must choose one of the 5 financial instruments provided by the regulations to assure financial responsibility: trust fund (including a surety bond form of payment into a trust fund), letter of credit, insurance policy, financial worth test, or a corporate guarantee. An owner/operator may also use a combination of the trust fund, surety bond, letter of credit, and insurance mechanisms to satisfy those requirements.

The trust fund is a mechanism that allows an interim status facility to gradually accumulate the full amount of closure and post-closure costs over the expected life of the facility or over a 20-year period, whichever is shorter. For permitted facilities the pay-in period is the duration of the permit (i.e., 10 years) or the expected life of the facility, whichever is shorter.[33] The annual payment into the trust fund must be adjusted for inflation, changes in closure and post-closure cost estimates, and changes in the value of any securities owned by the trust. The regulations specify the exact wording of the trust agreement and must be accompanied by a formal certification of acknowledgment by the operator.[34]

Surety bonds and letters of credit made payable to the EPA Regional Administrator (or authorized state) are administered like the trust fund; however, they are required to be issued for the full amount of the expected costs, rather than accumulated over time. Specific forms for these agreements are provided for issuance of these mechanisms as well.[35] A supplemental trust fund must be established if either of these instruments is used so that any funds drawn on the accounts can be placed into a trust fund which then makes payments for closure and post-closure costs. The institutions issuing such instruments must in the case of surety bonds be among those listed as acceptable on the U.S. Department of Treasury Circular 570, and in the case of letters of credit must be an institution that is regulated by Federal or State agencies.[36]

An insurance policy may also be obtained from a qualified insurer for an amount at least equal to the full amount of its closure and post-closure cost estimates, and must be adjusted to reflect increases in the closure and post-closure cost estimates.[37] Such policies must be non-cancellable except for non-payment of premium. The failure to comply is a major violation of this requirement and can result in termination or revocation of interim status or the operating permit.

The final mechanism that may be used to demonstrate such financial assurance is the financial test. It can be satisfied in the same manner as those seeking to self-insure for third-party liability coverage: meet one of the two 4-part financial tests available discussed above. An operator of a subsidiary can also obtain a corporate guarantee from a parent corporation if the parent meets one of the 4-part financial tests. Under the corporate guarantee, if the operator fails to perform final closure or post-closure responsibilities, the corporate guarantor is required to perform these responsibilities directly or establish a trust fund to do so. The wording of the guarantee must be identical to that specified in the regulations.[38]

In addition, HSWA now provides that in cases of bankruptcy as defined by the Federal Bankruptcy Code, or where court jurisdiction cannot be obtained over any owner or operator that is likely to be solvent at the time of judgment, a claim for performance of closure, post-closure care, or third-party liability may be asserted directly against the guarantor of financial responsibility. The guarantor's liability is limited to the aggregate amount of the insurance policy, corporate guarantee, or other instrument used to satisfy the requirements.[39]

Those with a need to have additional detail on the various financial instruments should refer to EPA's guidance document.[40]

CORRECTIVE ACTION   HSWA established a new financial assurance requirement—demonstrating the financial capability to conduct corrective action for continuing releases from solid waste management units—as a condition of permitting under Section 3004(u) of RCRA.[41] EPA is planning to write regulations implementing these requirements, which should be finalized in early 1987.[42] EPA is also developing financial responsibility corrective action regulations for "regulated units" (land disposal units that received hazardous wastes after July 26, 1982) which should be finalized in late 1987.[43] (See also Chapter 11.)

NOTES

1. EPA's initial promulgation of the largely administrative interim status program (40 CFR Part 265) and the general facility standards applicable after final permitting occurred on May 19, 1980 (45 *Fed. Reg.* 33066); the two are frequently referred to as the Phase I regulations or the May 1980 package.

2. Hazardous waste management facilities or units that are exempt from RCRA requirements are at Part 270.2(c)(2). Also see Chapter 6 for discussion of permit-by-rule.

3. RCRA, Section 3010(a); 40 CFR 264.11, 265.11.

4. RCRA, Section 3017 (hazardous waste export); HSWA Section 245. Also see proposed rule to establish standards for waste export 51 *Fed. Reg.* 8744 (March 13, 1986).

5. 40 CFR 264.12, 265.12; also see 40 CFR 270.72.

6. 40 CFR 264.13, 265.13.

7. 40 CFR 264.14, 265.14.

8. 40 CFR 264.15, 265.15.

9. RCRA, Section 30017; HSWA, Section 229 (Federal), 230 (state), 231 (TSDF).

10. 40 CFR 264.16, 265.16.

11. 40 CFR 264.17, 265.17.

12. 40 CFR 264.18(a) (seismic zones); 40 CFR 270.14(b)(11).

13. 40 CFR 264.18(b) (floodplains); RCRA, 3004(b); 40 CFR 264.18(c), 265.18(c) (salt domes); HSWA, Section 201; RCRA, Section 3004(o)(7); HSWA, Section 202 (vulnerable hydrogeology); 40 CFR 270.3 (location criteria, other statutes).

14. 40 CFR 264.30–37, 265.30–37.

15. 40 CFR 264.50–56, 265.50–56.

16. 40 CFR 264.71–72, 265.71–72.

17. 40 CFR 264.73, 265.73.

18. RCRA, Section 3002; HSWA, Section 224; 40 CFR 264.73(b)(9); 50 *Fed. Reg.* 28746 (July 15, 1985).

19. 40 CFR 264.75–.76, 265.75–.76.

20. 40 CFR 264.77, 265.77 (additional reports); 40 CFR 264.56(j), 265.56(j) (emergency reports); 40 CFR 264.93–94, 265.93–94 (groundwater monitoring); 40 CFR 264.114, 265.115 (closure).

21. 50 *Fed. Reg.* 28711-12 (July 15, 1985). Still to be resolved is the mechanism for ensuring proper care of the TSDF beyond the post-closure period. The 1980 Superfund, 42 U.S.C. 9601 *et seq.*, established a Post-Closure Liability Fund (PCLF) which would assume *all* the liabilities of a permitted owner/operator if the

firm complies with applicable closure and post-closure requirements, and if up to 5 years of monitoring data after closure indicates "there is no substantial likelihood that any migration off-site or releases from confinement of any hazardous substance or other risk to public health or welfare will occur." The PCLF is financed by a $2.13 per dry weight ton tax on the receipt of hazardous waste at a disposal facility, with a $200,000,000 ceiling imposed on the size of the fund. The PCLF as enacted has serious shortcomings, including a substantial likelihood of future insolvency as a result of inadequate size and the inability of only 5 years of post-closure monitoring data to reveal meaningful information about the integrity of the facility. The PCLF also assumes the long-term liability for the facility regardless of the financial status or capabilities of the owner/operator. The PCLF therefore subsidizes land disposal, the least preferred method of managing hazardous waste, and eliminates individual accountability, which would otherwise encourage firms to take stronger steps to minimize risk than is required by federal or state regulations. For these reasons and others, Congress is reconsidering the 1980 PCLF, and as part of Superfund reauthorization, will request EPA to study a variety of options to ensure proper long-term care of land disposal facilities. See Sections 201 of H.R. 2817 and 161 of S. 51 as passed by the U.S. House of Representatives (Dec. 10, 1985) and the U.S. Senate (Sept. 26, 1985) respectively.

22. 40 CFR 264.112(a), 265.112(a) (closure plans); 40 CFR 265.197 (tank closure).
23. 40 CFR 264.112–115, 265.112–115 (closure plans); 50 *Fed. Reg.* 11068 (March 19, 1985).
24. 40 CFR 264.117–120, 265.117–120.
25. 40 CFR 264.117(c), 265.117(c).
26. 40 CFR 264.118, 265.118.
27. 40 CFR 264.140–151, 265.140–150 (financial req.); 40 CFR 264.142–.144, 265.142–.144 (post-closure).
28. 40 CFR 264.147(g), 265.147; 265.147(f)(3)(i) cross-references wording of trust instruments contained in 264.151.
29. 40 CFR 264.151 (wording of instruments); 40 CFR 264.147(f) (self-insurance).
30. 40 CFR 264.147(b)(4), 265.147(b)(4).
31. 40 CFR 265.145(e) (corporate guarantee for post-closure); 40 CFR 265.143(e) (corporate guarantee for closure); 50 *Fed. Reg.* 33902 (Aug. 21, 1985).
32. 40 CFR 264.144(b) 265.144(b).
33. 40 CFR 264.145(a)(3), 265.145(a)(3).
34. 40 CFR 264.143(a), 265.143(a); 40 CFR 264.151 (wording of trust fund instruments).
35. 40 CFR 264.151(b) (wording of surety bond); 40 CFR 264.151(d) (wording of letter of credit).
36. 40 CFR 264.143(b), 265.143(b) (surety bond); 40 CFR 264.143(d), 265.143(d) (letter of credit).
37. 40 CFR 264.143(e), 265.143(d).
38. 40 CFR 264.143(f), 265.143(e) (financial test, corporate guarantee for closure); 40 CFR 264.151(h) (wording of corporate guarantee).
39. RCRA, Section 3004(t)(2),(3); HSWA, Section 205.
40. "Financial Assurances for Closure and Post-Closure Care: A Guidance Manual," EPA SW-955; NTIS PB 83-237-595; "Liability Coverage: A Guidance Manual," EPA SW-961; NTIS PB 83-144-675.
41. RCRA, Section 3004(u); Section 206.
42. 50 *Fed. Reg.* 44683 (Oct. 29, 1985).
43. Ibid. p. 44682.

CHAPTER EIGHT

Technical Requirements Applicable to RCRA TSDFS

Chapter 7 examined the administrative and general requirements that apply to TSDFs when under interim status (40 CFR 265) and when they receive a final RCRA permit. At the time of final permitting these requirements are retained and strengthened by the imposition of additional specific technical requirements for each type of TSDF (40 CFR Part 264). This chapter examines technical standards applicable to the various types of TSDFs under interim status and the final permitting standards including: containers; hazardous waste tanks (also see Chapter 12); surface impoundments; landfills; waste piles; land treatment units; incinerators; other thermal treatment units; chemical, physical, and biological treatment units; and underground injection wells.

The general nature of most interim status standards in relation to the more specific and technical requirements was discussed in Chapters 6 and 7. These distinctions will be readily evident with the ensuing discussion. It must also be noted, however, that several of HSWA's new requirements blur the clear distinctions that previously existed between interim status and the permitting standards by requiring minimum technology requirements for many types of interim status facilities that previously applied only to units that received final permits (e.g., liners, leak detection, retrofitting of impoundments, corrective action through enforcement orders).

Chapter 8 seeks to provide the reader with an understanding of the technical and operating requirements for permitted TSDFs, how they differ from those imposed under interim status, and the impact of HSWA on final permitting requirements. The Agency has published a complete list of available guidance documents to assist in preparing permit applications and complying with various permit conditions. This document is available through the RCRA Hotline 202-382-3000 (800-424-9346), or the RCRA Permitting Division 202-382-4746.

CONTAINERS

Interim Status Standards

Containers are used for storage or under certain circumstantces, treatment. The interim status management standards for hazardous waste containers largely consist of requirements to ensure that containers are: handled to prevent rupture or leakage, visually inspected for integrity on a weekly basis, and mixed in a manner that does not create violent or acute releases to the environment.[1] If inspections reveal leaks or deterioration, the wastes must be transferred to another container or managed by other methods. When wastes are stored in containers they must be kept closed to prevent emissions. Containers holding ignitable or reactive wastes must be located at least 50 feet from the facility property line.[2] Incompatible wastes cannot be placed in the same containers unless special precautions are observed. Interim status container storage areas are allowed to hold listed dioxin wastes under more stringent conditions (Chapter 2).[3] The reuse of containers in transportation is governed by Department of Transportation regulations.[4]

These standards also apply to generators that temporarily store wastes in containers on-site for up to 90 days (Chapter 4). When closure occurs under interim status, all hazardous waste containers, liners, bases, and contaminated soils must be removed from the site (or decontaminated), subjecting the owner/operator to generator standards. The wastes must be managed and transported in accordance with the requirements for hazardous wastes (Parts 262–266). While this closure requirement has only been proposed by the Agency, it largely represents a clarification of EPA's view of the existing rule.[5]

Under certain circumstances a container may itself be a hazardous waste unless it is "empty." A container is determined to be "empty" depending upon the extent of waste removal after it is has been used. Only those containers that fail to meet the following criteria for an "empty container" are regulated as hazardous. In general, for non-acutely hazardous wastes, all wastes must be removed using the practices commonly employed to remove materials from that type of container (e.g., pouring, pumping, aspirating). No more than one inch of residue may remain at the bottom of the container, or no more than 3% by weight of the total capacity of the container may remain in the container or inner liner, for containers less than or equal to 110 gallons (0.3% for containers larger than 110 gallons).

For wastes determined to be acutely hazardous (40 CFR 261.31, 261.32, 261.33(e)), the container or inner liner must be triple rinsed using an appropriate solvent, or the wastes must be removed from the container or inner liner using another method that has been shown in the scientific literature or by the generators test to achieve equivalent removal. For all kinds of wastes a container is "empty" if the inner liner that prevented contact between the waste and the container is removed and managed as a hazardous waste.[6]

Because acutely hazardous wastes are listed wastes (Chapter 2), the rinsate from containers of such wastes remain and must be managed as acutely hazardous wastes. Rinsate of non-acutely hazardous listed wastes also retain this classificaiton. However, where the containerized waste is hazardous solely due its exhibiting a hazardous characteristic (Chapter 2), the rinsate from such containers is hazardous only if it still exhibits the characteristic(s).

Final Permitting Standards

The permitting standards require that containers holding hazardous wastes must be kept closed during storage, and must be not be opened, handled, or stored in a manner that may rupture the container or cause it to leak.[7]

Storage areas holding containers of hazardous wastes that contain free liquids must have secondary containment systems capable of holding and collecting any spills, leaks, or accumulated rainfall. Storage areas where none of the containers hold wastes with free liquids do not require a secondary containment system provided either that: the storage area is sloped or designed to facilitate proper drainage from precipitation, or the containers are elevated or otherwise protected from contact with accumulated liquid. All storage areas that hold containers of listed dioxin wastes (F020, F021, F022, F023, F026, F027) must have secondary containment. The containment systems must be designed to include:

1. A base underlying the containers that is sufficiently impermeable to hold any leaked or spilled wastes or accumulated precipitation for removal.

2. A drainage system so that spilled wastes or precipitation does not remain in contact with the containers, or a mechanism such as elevation to minimize contact between spilled wastes liquids and the containers.

3. Sufficient capacity to contain 10% of the volume of all the containers, or the volume of the largest container, whichever is greater. Run-on into the containment system must be prevented unless the collection system has sufficient excess capacity (in addition to the 10% volume buffer) to contain any run-on which might enter the system.

4. Spilled or leaked waste and accumulated precipitation must be removed from the sump or collection area in as timely a manner as is necessary to prevent overflow.

In the event that the collected material is a listed, identified, or hazardous waste mixture (Chapter 2), all generator and other management standards apply. If the collected material, hazardous or otherwise, is discharged to any surface waters of the U.S., it must be permitted under the Clean Water Act NPDES program. If discharged to a sewer system, a local or state permit it may be required, and it may also be subject to the pretreatment standards of the CWA.[8]

In addition to the general requirements for containers holding ignitable, reactive, and incompatible wastes, (i.e., waste analysis, trial tests for compatability) containers with ignitable and reactive wastes must be located at least 50 feet from the facility property line.[9] Stored containers of wastes that are potentially incompatible with wastes in other containers, piles, open tanks, or surface impoundments must be separated or protected from them by a dike, wall, berm, or other device.

At closure, all hazardous waste and hazardous residues must be removed from the secondary containment system. Remaining containers, liners, bases, and soil containing hazardous wastes or hazardous waste residues must be decontaminated or removed. No post-closure care is required because contaminated materials cannot remain on-site after closure.

HSWA has also instituted a new provision that requires *all TSDFs* that receive a final permit to conduct cleanup actions for dangerous releases at the time of or as a condition of final permitting (Chapter 11).[10]

HAZARDOUS WASTE TANKS

Interim Status and Final Standards

Unlike containers, which are transportable, a tank is a stationary device designed to contain hazardous wastes and is constructed primarily of non-earthen materials. Types include above-ground and underground, covered and uncovered tanks.[11] Prior to the enactment of HSWA, the Agency had formally deferred issuing permitting standards for underground hazardous waste tanks that could not be entered for inspection.[12] HSWA now requires the issuance of final regulations governing all forms of hazardous waste tanks, and the establishment of a separate regulatory program for underground tanks storing petroleum and many toxic chemicals (i.e., those tanks with more than 10% of the total volume (inclusive of piping) below ground level).[13]

The design and general operating requirements for hazardous waste tanks currently serve as the only permitting standards for non-thermal waste treatment processes. These requirements focus on the integrity of the tank and the ability of the treatment process or management activity to conform with practices that prevent corrosion, overflows, or uncontrolled releases to the environment.

All facets of the hazardous waste and underground tank programs are examined in Chapter 12 including: the existing interim and final permitting standards for above-ground hazardous waste tanks, the Agency's recent proposal to modify the hazardous waste tank standards and initiate regulation of underground hazardous waste tanks, and HSWA's new mandate to regulate underground tanks including those used for the storage of petroleum and toxic chemicals.

SURFACE IMPOUNDMENTS

Interim Status Standards

A surface impoundment is a natural topographical depression, man-made excavation, or diked area formed primarily of earthen materials, which is designed to hold an accumulation of liquid wastes or wastes containing free liquids, and which is not an injection well. Surface impoundments may be used for treatment, storage, or disposal and include units such as holding ponds, settling ponds, seepage and aeration pits, and lagoons.[14]

The interim status standards for surface impoundments are minimal. An impoundment must maintain at least 2 feet of freeboard (buffer space) to prevent overflow of the pond by overfilling, wave action, or a storm. The 2-foot freeboard requirement can be waived if the operator obtains a certification by a qualified engineer that an alternative design will prevent overflow of the dike. Earthen dikes around the impoundment must have a protective cover such as grass to prevent erosion and maintain structural integrity. Weekly inspections of the dikes and daily inspection of the freeboard level are required.

A special waste analysis is required when interim status impoundments are used to treat wastes substantially different from those previously contained in the impoundment. The analysis involves demonstrations such as bench-scale tests or written analysis to verify operational efficacy. In general, ignitable or reactive wastes cannot be placed into an impoundment unless the material no longer displays these characteristics before or immediately after placement in the impoundment.

The interim status groundwater monitoring and corrective action requirements for surface impoundments are discussed in Chapter 11. HSWA's minimum technology requirements regarding liners, leachate collection, and early leak detection systems for new, expansion, and replacement units, and the scheduled retrofitting (or phaseout) of most existing surface impoundments due to inadequate design are discussed in Chapter 10.

Ignitable or reactive wastes may not be placed in a surface impoundment unless: the waste is treated, rendered, or mixed before or immediately after placement in the impoundment so that the resulting waste, mixture, or dissolution of material no longer meets the definition of a ignitable or reactive waste (Chapter 2); or a waste so placed is protected from any material or condition that may cause it to react or ignite. Surface impoundments that are used only for emergencies are exempt from these restrictions.[16] Incompatible wastes, or incompatible wastes and other materials (Table 7-1) must not be placed in a surface impoundment unless compliance with the general restrictions such wastes are satisfied.[17]

No listed dioxin wastes (F020–F023, F026, F027) may be managed at any interim status surface impoundment unless it is a wastewater treatment sludge that is generated in a surface impoundment as part of the plant's wastewater treatment system.[18]

The impending land disposal bans (Chapter 9) apply to all forms of surface impoundments. While the Administrator may distinguish between various forms of land disposal when issuing the restrictions, it is not anticipated that impoundments will qualify for separate consideration because of the large volumes of hazardous liquids that are usually found in these lagoons, and the high potential for migration. However, in HSWA Congress established specific exceptions for impoundments used for the treatment of restricted wastes, provided that the impoundments meet the minimum technology requirements applicable to new impoundments at the time the waste prohibitions are effective (provided that they were not otherwise exempted from the technology requirements). In addition, hazardous treatment residues must at a minimum be removed from the impoundment for subsequent management within one year of the entry of the waste into the impoundment.[19] Chapters 9 examines the relationship between the timing of the waste banning and the minimum technology requirements for surface impoundments. Chapter 10 examines the technical aspects of the minimum technology requirements, the retrofitting requirements of existing interim status lagoons, and the potential waivers from these requirements.

Prior to HSWA, existing surface impoundments could be expanded or replaced during interim status without meeting the more stringent design standards such as the liner and leachate collection systems that applied to finally permitted units. However, HSWA now requires that each new unit, replacement, and lateral expansion of most existing units must comply with the liner and leachate collection system requirements applicable to new or finally permitted units. The original unit undergoing lateral expansion, termed the "existing portion," is also subject to retrofitting requirements.[20] Chapter 10 examines these HSWA requirements in detail.

At closure of an interim status impoundment, if all wastes, standing liquids, liners, and underlying and surrounding contaminated soils are removed and properly managed (including compliance with generator standards), then the impoundment is no longer subject to hazardous waste requirements since no hazardous wastes would remain on the site. If wastes remain on the site but are no longer hazardous, then the facility may still be subject to solid waste management requirements (40 CFR Part 257). If the hazardous wastes and other materials identified above are not removed, the impoundment must be closed as a landfill and must provide the requisite post-closure care.[21] Chapter 11 discusses many important aspects of interim status surface impoundment closure, including the interrelationship between the closure, post-closure, and the corrective action provisions of current regulations and HSWA's new requirements.

Final Permitting Standards

As under interim status, permitted surface impoundments must be designed, constructed, operated, and maintained to prevent overflow of the impoundment due to normal and abnormal operations, precipitation, wind and wave action, run-on, malfunctions of level controllers, and problems resulting from human error. Rather than the specific 2-foot freeboard requirement and 24-hour, 25-year flood criteria, lagoons must have dikes that are designed, constructed, and maintained with sufficient structural integrity to prevent their massive failure. In establishing the necessary structural integrity, it may not be presumed that the liner system will function with leakage during the active life of the unit.

The final permitting standards also contain more detailed requirements regarding inspections, emergency repairs, removal from service, dioxin wastes, and closure and post-closure.[22] Units must be inspected weekly and after storms for sudden drops in the level of the impoundment, for the presence of liquids in the leak collection system, and for erosion.

A surface impoundment must be removed from service when the level of liquids suddenly drops for reasons unrelated to flow into and out of the impoundment or when the dike around the unit leaks. Under such circumstances, the owner/operator must: immediately shut off the waste flow and contain any surface leakage; immediately stop the leak and take any other necessary steps to contain the leak; and empty the impoundment if the leak cannot be stopped. The Regional Administrator or authorized state must be notified in writing within 7 days of detecting the problem. The contingency plan for such events should the specify the procedures to be followed in such cases, including the use of alternative or back-up impoundments.

Impoundments that were removed from service due to actual or threatened dike failure may not be restored to service unless the failed portion of the impoundment is repaired and the structural integrity restored through reconstruction if necessary and consistent with the design standards for new lagoons. Impoundments that were removed from service due to a sudden drop in the liquid level must install liners that conform to the new facility requirements. For other previously lined portions, the liner repairs must be certified by a qualified engineer as meeting the design specifications approved in the permit. Lagoons that have been removed from service and are not repaired must be closed in accordance with the closure requirements for permitted lagoons (Chapter 11).

Due to several new HSWA requirements, more comprehensive groundwater monitoring and cleanup requirements apply to surface impoundments under final permitting standards. All TSDFs receiving final permits must undertake cleanup activities for dangerous releases from any hazardous *and* solid waste management unit even when the release has crossed the facility boundary (Chapter 11).

HSWA standards also contain the technical specifications for the dual-liner and leachate collection systems to be used at all new impoundment units. The liner system specified in these regulations (discussed in Chapter 10) also may be applicable to the retrofitting of existing units and lateral expansions and replacement of existing units.

Ignitable or reactive wastes cannot be managed in a surface impoundment unless the waste is treated, rendered, or mixed before or immediately after placement in the impoundments so that the resulting waste, mixture, or dissolved material no longer meets the definition of a ignitable or reactive waste (Sections 261.21, 261.23, respectively), and the general requirements for management of such wastes are complied with (Chapter 6).

Alternatively, an impoundment could be used to manage such wastes provided it is done in a manner that protects them from any other material or condition that causes them to ignite or react, or if the surface impoundment is used solely for emergencies.

The dioxin wastes currently listed as hazardous (F020–F023, F026, F027) cannot be managed in any permitted surface impoundment without prior approval of the Regional Administrator. Such approval will be based on an evaluation of: the potential for wastes to migrate or volatilize; the attenuative properties of the underlying soils; the effects of other wastes in the impoundment on the mobilization properties of the dioxin wastes, and the effectiveness of additional treatment, design, or monitoring techniques.

The owner/operator may close the impoundment without performing post-closure care by removing or decontaminating all waste residue, contaminated liners, and contaminated soils and equipment. In the event that the operator chooses to leave contaminated materials on-site after closure, all free liquids in the impoundment must be eliminated, remaining wastes must be stabilized, and a final cover must be designed, constructed, and maintained to prevent rainwater from migrating into the closed unit. The Agency has issued a Guidance Manual to assist in the closure of surface impoundments.[23] Chapter 11 provides a detailed discussion of land disposal closures.

LANDFILLS

Interim Status

A landfill is defined as a disposal facility or part of a facility where hazardous waste is placed in or on the land and which is not a land treatment facility, an impoundment, or an injection well. A waste pile used as a disposal facility is a landfill and is also governed by these regulations. The specific interim status requirements emphasize the need to prevent liquids from running onto and off of the facility, control wind dispersal, and ensure collection of a water volume that would result from a 24-hour, 25-year storm.[24] The liquids so collected likely will require management as a hazardous waste. As with surface impoundments, if these liquids are discharged to surface waters, a NPDES permit may be required. There are no interim status inspection requirements.

A waste, hazardous or not, is defined as a liquid waste according to its performance on the Agency's Paint Filter Test (Chapter 9). Wastes that fail the test by releasing liquids are defined as "liquids" for the purpose of these regulations. Beginning May 8, 1985 the placement of bulk or noncontainerized liquid hazardous wastes or hazardous wastes containing free liquids in landfills is prohibited, whether or not absorbents have been added.[25]

By February 1986, regulations to implement a related ban on the disposal of containerized hazardous wastes where certain forms of absorbents have been added are also mandated by HSWA. These regulations are not expected to be reissued until early 1987. Until that time, the existing prohibition on landfilling of containers with free-standing liquid is maintained. Effective November 8, 1985, the placement of non-hazardous liquids is also prohibited with minor exception. Chapter 9 examines these issues in greater depth; including the Agency's Guidance on implementation of this ban on the landfill disposal of bulk liquid and/or the use of absorbents as a sole means of treatment.

Unless the containers are very small, such as an ampule, containers must be either 90% full when landfilled; or crushed, shredded, or otherwise reduced in volume to the maximum extent practical before burial. This is to ensure that wastes are tightly packed so as to minimize the amount of subsidence (or collapse) once a disposal cell has been filled.

Small containers of hazardous waste in overpacked drums (e.g., lab packs consisting of numerous small containers as would be generated by a laboratory) may be landfilled if the following requirements are met: the inside containers must neither leak, or react or ignite with the waste; the inner containers must be tightly secured and placed in a metal shipping container in conformance with all applicable DOT requirements;[26] the metal shipping container must be overpacked with sufficient non-reactive, non-ignitable absorbent material to absorb all liquid in the drum; incompatible wastes are not placed inside the drum (Chapter 7); and reactive wastes other than certain cyanide or sulfide-bearing wastes must be treated or rendered non-reactive prior to packaging.

Cyanide and sulfide-bearing reactive wastes may be packaged in accordance with the above procedures without first being rendered non-reactive. Absorbent materials may continue to be added to lab packs that conform with these and applicable DOT requirements. It is anticipated that the Agency will initiate rulemaking in the near future to specify additional requirements and restrictions on lab pack disposal. In addition, the pending development of regulations to prohibit the use of compressible and biodegradable absorbents may affect their use in lab pack applications.

Ignitable or reactive wastes other than those disposed of in lab packs may not be landfilled unless the waste is treated to eliminate this property(s) or must be disposed of into separate landfill cells that minimize the potential for ignition or reaction. Incompatible waste mixtures (Table 7-1) cannot be landfilled unless done in the manner as specified in the general facility standards. Listed dioxin wastes may not be placed into interim status landfill units.[27]

Hazardous wastes that are accumulated in the leachate collection system must be managed in accordance with all management and generator standards. If the collected leachate is discharged to surface waters, it is subject to the NPDES requirements of the Clean Water Act and a separate permit may be required.

The groundwater monitoring, liner, leachate collection system, corrective action, and interim status expansion requirements for landfills are virtually identical to those for surface impoundments and are also discussed in Chapters 10 and 11. Chapter 9 discusses the applicable land disposal restrictions.

Since landfills are used solely for disposal, there is no exception from the land disposal prohibitions for treatment of banned wastes in landfills, as is allowed for impoundments that meet the minimum technology requirements.

At final closure of a landfill or an individual cell, the owner/operator must cover the landfill or cell with a final cover designed and constructed to minimize migration of liquids through the closed landfill and erosion or abrasion of the cover, and to promote drainage and accommodate settling so that the cover's integrity is maintained. The closure plan must also address how the migration of pollutants from the facility by groundwater, surface water, and air will be controlled. The top cover must have a permeability less than or equal to that of the bottom liner or natural subsoils present.

After final closure, the owner/operator must comply with the general post-closure requirements (Chapter 7) and must: maintain the function and integrity of the final cover as specified in the closure plan; maintain and monitor the leachate collection, removal, and treatment system (if one is present at the facility) to prevent excess accumulation of leachate in the system; maintain and monitor the gas collection system (if one is present) to control the vertical and horizontal escape of gasses; protect and maintain the surveyed benchmarks; and restrict access to the landfill as appropriate for its post-closure use. As with liquids collected from tank, container, and impoundment containment areas, landfill leachate that is hazardous (Chapter 2) must be managed as a hazardous waste in accordance with all applicable generator, transporter, and other interim status requirements. If discharged through a point-source to waters of the U.S. it is subject to requirements of Section 402 of the Clean Water Act. Chapter 11 examines the groundwater monitoring and cleanup requirements associated with the closure and post-closure care for interim status landfills. A separate Guidance Manual also has been issued to assist operators close landfill cells.[28]

Final Permitting Standards

Permitted landfill units are subject to requirements similar to those discussed above for surface impoundments and elsewhere in the text: prohibitions against land disposal (Chapter 9), the minimum technology requirements respecting liners and leachate collection systems (Chapter 10), and groundwater monitoring and corrective action (Chapter 11).[29]

Final permitting standards for landfills also contain the following interim status requirements: controlling run-on and run-off resulting from a 24-hour, 25-year storm; surveying and recordkeeping; restrictions on ignitable, reactive, incompatible wastes, bulk and containerized wastes, containers generally, and lab packs; emptying all run-on and run-off holding tanks as soon as possible after a storm; controls on wind dipsersal of particulate from the facility; and the option of the Regional Administrator to specify all design and operating practices necessary to ensure that other permit requirements are met. The restrictions on the management of dioxin wastes in permitted surface impoundments also apply to landfills.

Unlike the interim status landfill standards, however, a significant number of additional monitoring and inspection requirements are imposed by final permitting. During and immediately following construction or installation of liners or cover systems, inspections must be conducted to ensure integrity of the materials, seams, and joints. While in operation, the facility must be inspected weekly to detect: evidence of deterioration malfunction or improper operation of the run-on and run-off control systems; the presence of liquids in the leak detection system; proper functioning of wind dispersal systems; and the presence of leachate in and proper functioning of leachate collection and removal systems.

WASTE PILES

Interim Status

A waste pile is defined as any non-containerized accumulation of solid, non-flowing hazardous waste that is used for treatment or storage.[30]

Interim status waste piles must comply with the following requirements: protect the pile from wind dispersal; analyze or ensure that each waste added to the pile is compatible with the existing wastes; and control and collect run-off from the pile. Where hazardous run-off has occurred or is likely to occur, the operator must either place the pile on an impermeable pad and properly manage the hazardous run-off or protect the pile from contact with precipitation and avoid placing liquid wastes or wastes containing free liquids in the pile.

Interim status waste piles must comply with special requirements for ignitable and reactive wastes unless the waste or mixture no longer meets the definition of these characteristics when added to the pile, provided the generally applicable restrictions on management of such wastes are satisfied (Chapter 7). Additional restrictions on the placement of incompatible wastes require that a pile of hazardous waste that is incompatible with any waste or other material stored nearby in other containers, piles, open tanks, or surface impoundments must be separated from the other material or protected from them by a dike, berm, wall, or other device. An area that previously contained a waste pile must be decontaminated prior to placement of other wastes to ensure compliance with the generally applicable reactive waste restrictions. Interim status waste piles that store or treat dioxin wastes (F020–F023, F026, F027) may or do so only if the pile is enclosed or otherwise protected from precipitation and the pile meets all other management standards to control contact with liquids and wind exposure that are applicable as specified in the final permit requirements.

As with other land disposal facilities, waste piles are subject to the waste banning provisions. At closure, all wastes, residues, and contaminated soils must be removed from the facility or decontaminated. If all contaminated soils cannot be practicably removed or decontaminated, the facility must close and perform post-closure care in accordance with landfill requirements. Pile expansions or replacements are subject to HSWA's minimum technology requirements (Chapter 10). Further discussion of the closure and corrective action requirements for interim status waste piles is provided in Chapter 11.

Final Permitting Standards

Like landfills, there is no general retrofitting requirement for existing waste piles. However, permitted waste piles are subject to HSWA's land disposal prohibitions and minimum technology requirements. Piles that received hazardous wastes after July 26, 1982, must also comply with the groundwater monitoring and corrective action requirements applicable to finally permitted facilities (40 CFR Part 264), unless specifically exempted. The groundwater monitoring and corrective action requirements applicable to permitted waste piles are discussed in Chapter 11.

As with other land disposal facilities, new, replacement, or lateral expansions of a waste pile must have a liner system (single rather than double) and a leachate collection system, but can be exempted if the operator can prove that design, operating, and location characteristics will prevent migration into ground or surface water at any future time. Dry, indoor waste piles may be exempted from all groundwater, liner, and leachate collection requirements. As with interim status closures, waste piles that fail to remove all contaminated soil at closure must comply with the post-closure care and monitoring requirements applicable to landfills.[31]

The following standards for interim status waste piles also apply to permitted units: run-on and run-off controls; wind dispersal; waste analysis; and controls for ignitable, reactive, dioxin, and incompatible wastes. The final permit requirements for landfills regarding inspections during and after liner installation, and weekly inspections during the operating life also apply to permitted waste piles.

LAND TREATMENT UNITS

Interim Status

A land treatment unit is a facility at which hazardous waste is applied onto or incorporated into the soil surface. The aim of land treatment is to utilize naturally occurring microorganisms in the soil to degrade and/ or immobilize the hazardous wastes (e.g., petroleum sludges).[33] Unless properly controlled, this "treatment" could easily become de facto disposal with a high probability for migration. Thus, hazardous wastes cannot be placed in or on a land treatment unit unless the waste can be made less hazardous or non-hazardous by biological degradation or chemical reactions occurring in or on the soil.

In addition to the general waste analysis required of all TSDFs (Chapter 7) a special waste analysis prior to land placement is required to determine: whether the waste exceeds any of the limits for EP toxicity (Chapter 2), the presence of any listed waste, including commercial chemical products; and, if food chain crops are grown in the treatment zone, determine the concentrations in the waste of each of the following constituents: arsenic, cadmium, lead, and mercury.

An interim status land treatment facility must design, construct, operate, and maintain a run-on and run-off management system, including collection and holding facilities capable of controlling a water volume at least equivalent to a 24-hour, 25-year storm. Liquids collection and holding areas must be emptied as expeditiously as possible after storms. If the treatment zone contains particulate matter which may be subject to wind dispersal, the owner/operator must manage the unit to control such releases. The special management requirements and principles for ignitable, reactive, and incompatible wastes as they apply to interim status surface impoundments also apply to interim status land treatment units. No materials containing listed dioxin wastes may be placed in an interim status land treatment unit.

If food chain crops are grown in the land treatment unit the operator must notify the Regional Administrator or authorized state. Food chain crops cannot be grown in the land treatment unit unless the operator can demonstrate, based on field testing, that: arsenic, lead, mercury, or any of the other listed or identified wastes discussed above will not be transferred to the crop by uptake or direct contact and will not be ingested by grazing animals; or that these wastes will not occur in concentrations greater than in crops grown in untreated soils. Very specific limitations are placed on any farming in the land treatment unit when the wastes contain cadmium.[34]

Specific requirements for monitoring of the unsaturated zone to detect migration of wastes are also required. Owners/operators of interim status land treatment units are also required to perform monitoring of the unsaturated zone below the treatment zone to determine if the treatment process is working. The monitoring consists of soil core monitoring to determine the extent to which degradation of the waste is occurring, and soil pore monitoring to ensure that the absence of hazardous waste constituents in the soil core sample is due to degradation and not rapid migration through the soil. The regulations, codified at 40 CFR 265.278, do not specify particular procedures or protocols to be followed. Rather they require that a plan be developed and implemented which is capable of determining the concentrations and migrations of selected constituents in the waste (see 40 CFR 265.273(a) and (b)) in the soil underlying the treatment zone and establishing background values for those constituents through testing of similar untreated soil. The plan must specify the frequency and timing of sampling based on rates of waste application, proximity to groundwater, and soil permeability. There are no response requirements specified in the event that soil contamination is detected.

While liners are not required for these units, HSWA's directives for land disposal prohibitions (Chapter 9), and for groundwater monitoring (Chapter 11) also apply to interim status land treatment units. There are no general inspection requirements for such units. Records must be maintained that reflect the date and rates of waste application, and unsaturated zone monitoring data must be kept and maintained in the facility's operating record (Chapter 7).

The interim status closure and post-closure requirements for land treatment units are extensive and require: control of the migration of hazardous wastes into groundwater, continued groundwater and unsaturated zone monitoring, maintenance of run-on and run-off controls, continued soil core sampling and analysis, continued compliance with food chain crop uptake restrictions, and control of wind dispersal.[35] The owner/operator must also consider removal of contaminated soils and placement of a final cover over the units. These closure and post-closure requirements can impose substantial cleanup requirements on the owner/operator of the land disposal units as explained in Chapter 11.

Final Standards

The final permitting requirements incorporate all the interim status requirements respecting waste analysis, operation, and ignitable, reactive, and incompatible wastes. However the standards and requirements for the treatment program, treatment demonstration, and operating requirements are much more stringent and specific.[36] For example, finally permitted units must demonstrate prior to application of the waste that hazardous *constituents* (rather than "wastes," Chapter 2) in the waste can be *completely degraded, transformed, or immobilized* in the treatment zone. Rates and methods of waste application are specified, and the unsaturated zone must be monitoring for principal hazardous constituents (PHC) in the waste. PHCs are hazardous constituents contained in the wastes to be applied at the unit that are the most difficult to treat, considering the combined effects of degradation, transformation, and immobilization. The Regional Administrator establishes these PHCs if he or she finds, based on waste analysis and treatment demonstrations that effective degradation, transformation, or immobilization of the PHCs will assure equivalent or better treatment for other hazardous constituents in the wastes.[37] This same concept is used in determining the effectiveness of incineration treatment (discussed below).

Owners/operators of permitted land treatment units are also required to perform unsaturated zone monitoring to ensure that the waste treatment process is occurring as anticipated. As under interim status, both soil core and soil pore monitoring is required, but the regulations under 40 CFR

264.278 are much more specific than the interim status counterparts. In addition, the range of constituents to be monitored is much larger, because it may include any of the Appendix VIII constituents that must be degraded, transformed, or immobilized in the treatment zone. If the permit writer determines that there are a smaller number of hard-to-treat constituents, he may require monitoring only for the smaller number of constituents (called "principal hazardous constituents") and assume the constituents more amenable to treatment will not be found in the soil where the principal hazardous constituents are also not found.

Background values must be obtained for each constituent to be monitored. Soil pore samples must be based on at least quarterly samples, but soil core samples may be a one-time sampling.

Monitoring frequencies below the treatment zone will be specified in the permit, as well as the appropriate statistical procedures to be employed in comparing background and below treatment zone constituent values. If a statistically significant increase in the presence of hazardous constituents below the treatment zone is detected, the owner/operator must:

1. notify the Regional Administrator (or authorized state within 7 days and

2. submit a permit modification to alter existing operating practices at the treatment facilities within 90 days.

The owner/operator may also choose to demonstrate that the source of soil contamination is not the treatment unit, or that the increase resulted from an error in sampling, analysis, or evaluation. However, he must do so within the same 90 days and is not relieved of the responsibility to submit the operating practices modification unless and until the demonstration is successful.

The soil contamination itself caused by the land treatment units is not addressed by the regulations. Instead, EPA relies on the groundwater monitoring and response requirement that would be triggered when the contamination migrates into groundwater.

Other permitting requirements for land treatment units follow:

1. Specifications must exist on the vertical and horizontal dimension of the treatment zone (that portion of the unsaturated zone below and including the land surface in and on which the owner/operator intends to maintain the conditions necessary for effective degradation, transformation, or immobilization of hazardous constituents).

2. The treatment zone must be no more than 1.5 m from the original soil surface and more than 1 m above the seasonal high water table.

3. Any field test or laboratory analysis conducted to demonstrate "complete degradation" must accurately simulate the characteristics and operating conditions of the proposed land treatment unit, including showing that the wastes will react with and/or not migrate from the treatment zone.

4. The facility must be designed, constructed, operated, and maintained in a manner to ensure performance in accordance with the treatment demonstration.

5. Such facilities must observe the dioxin waste restrictions applicable to all other land disposal facilities.

6. The rate and method of waste application in the treatment zone must be documented.

7. Measures to control soil pH and enhance microbial or chemical reactions and the moisture content of the treatment zone must exist.

8. Measures to control the run-on, run-off, wind dispersal, and liquid collection requirements applicable to interim status land treatment units must exist.

9. The unit must be inspected weekly and after storms to detect evidence of deterioration, malfunction, or improper operation of the run-on, run-off, and wind dispersal control systems.

HSWA's land disposal prohibitions also apply to land treatment units (Chapter 9). Closure and post-closure care and monitoring, and corrective action requirements for these units (Chapter 11) are discussed below in greater detail.

INCINERATORS

Interim Status

An incinerator is an enclosed device using controlled flame combustion that neither meets the criteria for classification as a boiler nor is listed as an industrial furnace (Chapter 3). "Incinerators" are identified in part by their construction and in part by the type of wastes or materials they burn. The interim status requirements and most of the final operating requirements in permitting standards for incinerators also apply to boilers and industrial furnaces that burn hazardous wastes for destruction rather than energy recovery.

There are no performance standards (such as destruction efficiency of the wastes burned) which govern an interim status incinerator's operation. Moreover, industrial boilers and furnaces that burn hazardous wastes remain exempt from virtually all incinerator, interim status, or final permitting standards. Destruction and removal efficiency standards (discussed below) have been developed for permitted incinerators, and will likely apply to boilers and industrial furnaces that burn hazardous wastes when such technical standards are issued in late 1986. In anticipation of this forthcoming rule, many owners/operators of these units have applied for final permits using the permitting standards for incinerators. Non-industrial boilers and furnaces are currently prohibited from burning any hazardous wastes. Chapter 3 provides more detailed discussion of and differentiate between these three categories of waste combustion devices.[38]

Incinerators, boilers, and industrial furnaces that meet the following restrictions are not subject to incinerator standards except for closure requirements: they burn wastes that do not contain any Appendix VIII constituents; *and,* they burn wastes that are hazardous solely because they are ignitable, corrosive, or both, or are reactive.[39]

Any waste that has not been previously burned in the incinerator to establish steady state conditions and to determine the type of pollutants likely to be emitted must be evaluated for: heating (btu) value of the waste; and halogen, sulfur content, and lead and mercury concentrations (unless the operator can document that the waste does not contain these metals). The results from each such waste analysis must be placed in the facility's operating record.

Wastes cannot be fed into an incinerator unless the unit is at steady state operating conditions. The operator must inspect the combustion and emission control instruments every 15 minutes, and the entire incinerator every day. At closure, the owner/operator must remove all hazardous wastes and hazardous residues from the incinerator, including but not limited to ash, scrubber waters, and scrubber sludges. These materials are presumed hazardous waste unless it is demonstrated otherwise through the delisting process. In addition, the owner/operator becomes a generator and must manage the wastes in accordance with the requirements for waste generators (Chapter 4).[40]

Before dioxin wastes (F020–F023, F026, F027) can be burned at any incinerator, the unit must be certified by the Regional Administrator that they can meet the performance standard demonstrating the unit's destruction and removal efficiency (DRE) applicable to finally permitted units (99.9999%). A public notice and 60-day comment period are provided whenever the Assistant Administrator (AA) for Solid Waste and Emergency Response issues a tentative decision as to whether the facility can meet the 99.9999% DRE performance standard. A public hearing may also be held during this time. After the close of the public comment period, the AA will issue a decision whether or not to certify the incinerator.[41]

Final Standards

In addition to the interim status requirements, the final operating standards establish facility-specific operating requirements based on trial burns of the expected waste feeds at the unit.[42] Each set of operating requirements specifies the composition of the waste feed, including acceptable variations in the physical or chemical properties which will not affect compliance with the performance standards (discussed below). For each waste feed, the permit will specify acceptable operating limits for the following conditions: carbon monoxide in the stack exhaust gas; waste feed rate; combustion temperature; an indicator of combustion gas velocity; allowable variations in incineration design and operating procedures; and such other conditions as necessary to ensure the performance standards are met.

Uncontrolled (or fugitive) emissions from the combustion zone must be controlled by sealing the combustion zone, maintaining a combustion zone pressure lower than atmospheric pressure, or by an alternative means of maintaining such negative pressure. The incinerator must be operated with a system of automatic cutoffs, which can be triggered when operating conditions deviate from the operating limits discussed above. An incinerator is required to cease operation when changes in waste feed, incinerator design, or operating conditions exceed limits designated in the permit.

The permitting standards contain several important new operating and analytical requirements. The most notable of these requirements are the incinerator performance standards. When operating in accordance with the operating requirements specified above, the unit must also meet the following performance standards.

1. For all non-dioxin–containing wastes it must achieve a destruction and removal efficiency (DRE) of 99.99% for each principal organic hazardous constituent (POHC) designated for the facility (discussed below) in accordance with the following equation:

$$DRE = \frac{(W_{in} - W_{out})}{W_{in}} \times 100\%$$

W_{in} = mass feet rate of one principal organic hazardous constituent (POHC) in the waste stream feeding the incinerator and
W_{out} = mass emission rate of the same POHC present in exhaust emissions prior to release to the atmosphere.

HSWA established the 99.99% DRE as a minimum technology requirement for permitted incinerators.[43]

2. For dioxin-containing wastes the incinerator must achieve a DRE of 99.9999% for each POHC designated in the permit. This performance must be demonstrated on wastes that are more difficult to incinerate than the dioxin and dibenzofuran wastes to be incinerated.

3. The unit must not exceed a hydrochloric acid stack emission of more than 1.8 kg/hr (4 lb) or 1% of the HCL in the stack gas prior to entering any pollution control equipment, whichever is larger.

4. The unit must not emit particulate matter (P_m) in excess of 180 mg per dry std. cubic m (0.08 grains per dry std. cubic ft.) when corrected for oxygen (Y) in the stack gas in accordance with the following equation:

$$P_c = P_m \times \frac{14}{21 - Y}$$

Where P_c is the corrected concentration of particulate matter, P_m is the measured concentration of particulate matter, and Y is the measured concentration of oxygen in the stack gas, using the Orsat method for oxygen analysis of dry flue gas, presented in Part 60, Appendix A (Method 3).

For purposes of permit enforcement, compliance with the operating requirements specific to the permit will be regarded as compliance with the performance standards. However, where evidence of compliance with permit conditions is insufficient to ensure compliance with the performance standards, it may justify modification, revocation, or reissuance of the permit (Chapter 6).

Verification that the unit can meet its DRE performance standard is based on its ability to achieve the standard for specified Principal Organic Hazardous Constituents (POHC) listed on the Appendix VIII list, and which are contained in the hazardous wastes to be incinerated. These POHCs are specified in the trial burn and reflect the unit's ability to properly incinerate a wide range of difficult to incinerate wastes containing these POHCs. Waste constituents are more likely to be designated as POHCs if they are present in large quantities or concentrations in the waste to be incinerated.[44]

The trial burn precedes the issuance of a final permit and is conducted pursuant to the conditions of a special trial burn permit. Trial POHCs are designated for performance of trial burns in accordance with the procedures specified for trial burn permits (Chapter 6).[46] A trial burn plan must be prepared with detailed information on the waste feed, design, performance, sampling, and monitoring. Trial burns are usually limited to 720 hours (30 days) but may be extended or repeated once for up to that long when a good-cause showing can be made to the Regional Administrator. The incinerator may burn only those wastes specified in the permit and only under operating conditions specified for those wastes. New wastes can be burned only after a new permit has been issued.

The incinerator must monitor combustion temperature, waste feed rate, combustion gas velocity, and carbon monoxide on a continuous basis. Generally, the presence and concentrations of hazardous constituents in the airborne emissions is not routinely monitored. However, the Regional Administrator (or/and authorized state) may require additional sampling and analysis of the waste and exhaust emissions to verify that the operating requirements established in the permit achieve the performance standard.

The incinerator and associated pumps, valves, cutoffs, conveyors, and pipes must be visually inspected at least daily for signs of leaks, spills, fugitive emissions, and signs of tampering. Emergency waste-feed cutoff systems and alarms must be tested weekly, unless the owner/operator demonstrates to the Regional Administrator that weekly testing will unduly upset operations. All monitoring and inspection data must be recorded and the records placed in the operating log. Throughout normal operation the owner/operator must conduct sufficient waste analysis to verify that waste feed to the incinerator is within the limits specified by the operating requirements. Closure and other monitoring requirements are identical to those under interim status.

OTHER THERMAL TREATMENT UNITS

Thermal treatment units are those that treat hazardous waste in a device that uses elevated temperatures as the primary means to change the chemical, physical, or biological character or composition of the hazardous waste. Examples include molten salt, pyrolysis, and calcination incinerators, wet oxidation, and infrared destruction.[46]

The current interim status requirements and standards for other thermal destruction devices are virtually identical to those for incinerators. These regulations note, however, that open burning and detonation of hazardous wastes do not qualify as thermal treatment. Open burning and detonation are prohibited except when waste explosives are detonated in accordance with minimum buffer zones between the explosives and the nearest property. Final permit standards for non-incinerator, thermal destruction units are under development and are expected to contain a general environmental performance standard similar to the incinerator DRE (RDD Permits, Chapter 6). Moreover, until such standards are issued, the operating and performance standards applicable to incinerators will govern the permitting of such other thermal destruction units.

CHEMICAL, PHYSICAL, AND BIOLOGICAL TREATMENT UNITS

A cursory set of interim status regulations have been developed for facilities that treat hazardous wastes by chemical, physical, and biological methods in units other than containers, tanks, surface impoundments, and land treatment facilities.[47] The interim status operating requirements specify only that wastes placed into the treatment process or equipment should not cause a rupture or leak from the equipment before the end of its intended life.

Until more specific final operating requirements are issued, it is anticipated that the new authority to issue research, development, and demonstration permits will be used to tailor requirements specific to those units that seek to operate under these standards in the future (Chapter 6).

RECYCLING FACILITIES

The regulatory standards for facilities that recycle hazardous wastes by reclamation, burning for energy recovery, use constituting disposal, and overaccumulation are discussed in Chapter 3.

DEEP-WELL INJECTION

Shared Jurisdiction: RCRA and the Safe Drinking Water Act (SDWA)

In general, Class I hazardous waste injection wells ("deep wells") are those that inject hazardous wastes through pressurized pipes into a formation that is *below* an underground source of drinking water (USDW), or *into* a USDW that has been exempted by separate regulation. They are subject to the permit-by-rule provisions of RCRA. Under this approach, these facilities are required to obtain individual RCRA permits only for their surface operations (e.g., storage tanks), and instead are deemed to have a RCRA permit if they meet the conditions of the permitting program prescribed under the Safe Drinking Water Act (SDWA) (discussed below) and a small set of RCRA requirements.

Permits-by-rule are intended to be granted to those facilities where regulation and facility controls will satisfy RCRA's mandate to impose such controls "as may be necessary to protect human health and the environment" (RCRA, Section 3004). This has not been the case for deep-well injection under the SDWA program. For example, prior to HSWA, the SDWA regulations did not require financial responsibility for third-party liability, closure and post-closure care, or corrective action. In addition groundwater monitoring of any kind is not required for these facilities. Other deficiencies of the current deep-well regulations and state actions to restrict this practice are discussed below.

As a result of the 1984 Amendments, however, additional controls and restrictions on deep-well injection have been instituted. Class I deep-well injection facilities are subject to the land disposal restrictions under the same general presumptions (i.e., statutory self-implementing prohibition) and to the same extent as any other land disposal facility, although the Agency is provided with additional time to make prohibition decisions. Similarly, the requirement to conduct corrective actions for continuing releases (including demonstrations of financial responsibility to conduct these actions) are fully applicable to deep wells.[48] Finally, in the event that deep-well facilities fail to certify compliance with applicable state requirements respecting financial responsibility and groundwater monitoring (where states have imposed more stringent requirements than the minimal federal program), these facilities are also subject to the loss of interim status directive of the 1984 Amendments (Chapter 13).

Class I deep wells must comply with several interim status standards as a condition of their permit-by-rule: general facility standards, preparedness and prevention, contingency plan and emergency procedures, and manifesting, recordkeeping, and reporting. EPA has stated that it will issue additional interim status standards for deep wells, but has not yet done so.[49]

SDWA Permitting Requirements

Unlike the anticipatory "as may be necessary to protect" standard of RCRA, regulations under Part C of the SDWA are designed to prevent "endangerment" of underground sources of drinking water (USDW) as defined by regulation.[50] The difference in the standard is significant because as a general rule RCRA's protection standard can be triggered with a threat of a release, whereas an endangerment standard usually relies on a determination of the significance of harmfulness of a release once it has occurred. This is the only provision of the SDWA that currently addresses groundwater protection, other than the sole-source aquifer protection requirements.[51]

The statute's underground injection control program (UIC) directs EPA to establish the minimum requirements for underground injection of wastes, and to delegate "primacy" for administration and enforcement of the program to states that are qualified and desire to administer the program. If a state does not seek or does not qualify to implement the minimum federal requirements, EPA must implement the UIC program for that state.[52]

The permitting requirements[53] for deep wells specify that:

1. They may not be located near another known well penetrating the injection zone within the "area of review" (zone expected to be influenced by the Class I well–¼ mile under Federal Law), if the other wells could act as a means for migration of the injected wastes.

2. Prior to permitting, operators must also identify all other injection wells within the area of review and plug any abandoned or insecure wells that could serve as a conduit for migration to a USDW. However, there are no standards for proper plugging.

3. Wells must: inject *below* the lowest underground source of drinking water, be cased and cemented, and have an approved fluid seal or packer set between the injection tubing and the casing immediately above the injection zone.

4. The mechanical integrity of the well must be determined from both construction logs and mechanical integrity testing, and must be redetermined at least every 5 years.

5. Injected wastes must be sampled prior to initial injection. Data on physical, chemical, and other characteristics of the waste must be recorded; however, no analysis is required to determine compatibility with the injection equipment or formation.[54]

6. The rate of injection of fluid, and the pressures of the injected fluid in the injection tubing and the annular fluid (filling the area between the injection tubing and the well casing), must be monitored and recorded.

7. Changes or drops in injection pressure must be addressed to maintain a positive pressure on the injection system. Where positive pressure cannot be maintained or where leaks in the system are detected, injection must be interrupted.

8. Wells must be plugged at the end of their useful life to prevent wastes migrating from the injection well. The requirements do not address migration from the injection zone.[53]

Regulatory Deficiencies and State Actions

It is clear that deference to the SDWA for substantive regulation of deep-well injection has resulted in significant disparities between the controls imposed on land disposal facilities under RCRA and the limited technical and preventive controls imposed on deep-well injection under the Drinking Water program, as summarized below:[56]

1. failure to prohibit the injection of wastes that are incompatible with well material, and injection zone and confining layers;
2. failure to require monitoring of underground sources of drinking water to determine whether contaminants have migrated: where the wellbore passes; the injection zone itself, or the confining layers;
3. reliance on highly speculative assumptions about the migration of waste in the subsurface;
4. insufficent safeguards against potential pressure effects;
5. insufficient mechanical integrity testing to detect damage to the wellbore before significant leaking occurs;
6. failure to require post-closure care and a demonstration of financial assurance for post-closure care, third-party liability, and cleanup of contaminated groundwater;
7. the authority to use USDWs as depositories for hazardous wastes;
8. failure to prohibit underground injection of specified wastes or requiring the pretreatment of waste prior to injection, or to provide criteria for compability testing.

Due to the many and different failure modes of deep-well injection,[57] some states have prohibited deep-well injection outright (Florida, Alabama). Other states such as California have developed a stringent program of prohibitions and restrictions, which prohibits injection of hazardous wastes unless the Regional Water Quality Control Board finds that: no migration from the well will occur; the waste to be injected cannot be reasonably reduced, treated or disposed of by other methods; and a stringent monitoring program has been established. Other states are expected to develop similar individual restrictions in the near future.[58]

NOTES

1. 40 CFR 265.170–265.177.
2. 40 CFR 265.176; Also see 49 *Fed. Reg.* 23290, June 5, 1984. Proposed rule would allow greater flexibility in the 50-foot buffer zone requirement for ignitable and reactive wastes, and would allow fire-resistive construction as an alternate to the distance requirement.
3. 40 CFR 265.177 (c). General requirements under 265.17 for incompatible wastes also apply. 40 CFR 265.1 (d) (dioxin in containers).
4. 49 CFR 173.28.

5. 50 *Fed. Reg.* 11073 (March 19, 1985).
6. 40 CFR 261.7.
7. 40 CFR 264.170–264.178; 40 CFR 264.175 (containment).
8. CWA, Section 402, NPDES; CWA, Section 307, pretreatment requirements.
9. See note 2.
10. RCRA, Section 3004 (u), (v); HSWA, Section 206, 207; 50 *Fed. Reg.* 28711 (July 15, 1985).
11. 40 CFR 260.10 (a) (definition of tank); 40 CFR 265.190–265.199; 49 CFR 264.190–264.200; RCRA, Section 3004 (w) directs EPA to issue final permitting standards for underground hazardous wastes tanks by March 1, 1985. Although this deadline has been missed, the Agency proposed such standards in 50 *Fed. Reg.* 26444 (June 26, 1985). [Final rule: 51 *Fed. Reg.* 25422 (July 14, 1986).]
12. 46 *Fed. Reg.* 2831 (Jan. 12, 1981).
13. RCRA, Section 3004 (w) (hazardous waste tanks); RCRA, Section 3004 (o) (4) (leak detection); RCRA, Section 9000, Subtitle I (non-hazardous underground storage tanks); HSWA, Section 202 (hazardous waste tanks); HSWA, Section 601 (underground tank provisions).
14. 40 CFR 265.220–265.230.
15. See notes 32 and 38 of Chapter 11.
16. 40 CFR 265.229.
17. 40 CFR 265.230.
18. 40 CFR 265.1 (d) (1) (i).
19. RCRA, Section 3005 (j) (11) (A), (B); HSWA, Section 215. Although one of the subsections refer to storage *and* treatment, the Agency has stated that the exemption only applies to those impoundments where treatment is occurring. Storage impoundments are not eligible (51 *Fed. Red.* 1608 (Jan. 14, 1986).
20. The codification rule (50 *Fed. Reg.* 28707 (July 15, 1985)) states that to qualify as an "existing portion," and therefore exempt from the minimum technology requirements, a unit must be "operational" as of November 8, 1984. To be operational, a unit must have begun accepting hazardous wastes, and been constructed to comply with all Federal, state, and local laws including lisences and permits in effect prior to enactment of HSWA, such that as of November 8, 1984, there was no legal impediment to the operation of the unit.
21. Chapter 11 discusses the general interim status closure and financial post-closure requirements of 40 CFR Part 265.110–265.120. The landfill closure requirements are at 265.310; surface impoundment closure at 265.228.
22. 40 CFR 264.220–264.230; 40 CFR 264.221; 50 *Fed. Reg.* 28701 (July 15, 1985).
23. "Guidance Manual on Closure of Hazardous Waste Surface Impoundments," SW-873 discusses many of the technical aspects of closure.
24. 40 CFR 265.300–265.316.
25. RCRA, Section 3004 (c); HSWA, Section 201; 50 *Fed. Reg.* 28706-709 (July 15, 1985).
26. 40 CFR 265.316; 49 CFR 173, 178, 179 (Dept. of Transportation).
27. 40 CFR 265.1 (d) (1).
28. 40 CFR 265.310 (closure, post-closure); 50 *Fed. Reg.* 16048 (April 23, 1985) (closure guidance document).
29. 40 CFR 264.300–264.316.
30. 40 CFR 265.250–265.258; 50 *Fed. Reg.* 28750 (July 15, 1985) discusses requirements for synthetic liners. Also see EPA proposal of July 23, 1985, on waste pile requirements.

31. 40 CFR 264.250–264.258.

32. 40 CFR 265.1 (d) (1); 40 CFR 264.250 (c). Special requirements for dioxin waste piles include all applicable requirements of 264.250–264.258.

33. 40 CFR 265.270–265.282.

34. 40 CFR 265.176 (c).

35. 40 CFR 265.280.

36. 40 CFR 264.270–264.283.

38. 50 *Fed. Reg.* 49164 (Nov. 29, 1985)—hazardous waste fuel specification. Also see 50 *Fed. Reg.* 666 (Jan. 4, 1985), definition of solid waste.

39. 40 CFR 265.341 specifies that the reactive waste exemption is limited to those that are not listed in 261.23 (a) (4) (5) and will not be buried when other hazardous wastes are present in the (confinement) zone. Also see 265.341 (b) (3) (4).

40. 40 CFR 265.340–265.352; 40 CFR 265.347 (monitoring and inspections).

41. 50 *Fed. Reg.* 2005 (Jan. 14, 1985). See also 40 CFR 265.352 regarding dioxin burning restrictions.

42. 40 CRR 264.340–264.351. Amended by 50 FR 665 (Jan. 4, 1985). See also 48 *Fed. Reg.* 36582, Guidance Manual.

43. RCRA, 3004 (o) (i) (B); HSWA, Section 202; 50 *Fed. Reg.* 28726 (July 15, 1985).

44. 40 CFR 264.342.

45. 40 CFR 270.62 (trail burn permit).

46. 40 CFR 260.10 (a); 40 CFR 265.370–265.382. See also 40 CFR 265.383 for dioxin burning restrictions.

47. CFR 265.400–265.405.

48. 50 *Fed. Reg.* 28178 (July 15, 1985).

49. 40 CFR 265.430.

50. Safe Drinking Water Act (SDWA), Section 1421 (b).

51. The recently enacted Safe Drinking Water Act of 1986 (P.L. 99-339) requires continuous migration detection at Class I wells.

52. 40 CFR 142; 40 CFR 144.1–144.41; 40 CFR 145–147.

53. 40 CFR 144.51–146.70; 40 CFR 146.1–146.15.

54. 40 CFR 146.13 (c) (i).

55. 40 CFR 146.10.

56. "Deeper Problems," J. Bloom, W. Gordon. A publication by the Natural Resources Defense Council, NY, NY. 1985. p. 40.

57. See OTA Report, Chapter 9, note 10.

58. Assembly Bill 2058, Calif. Legislature 1985–86, Regular Session, Signed by Gov. Duckmejian, October 7, 1985. See also "Deep Dumps," an Assessment of Waste Injection in Calif., Assembly Office of Research, Sept. 1985.

CHAPTER NINE

Land Disposal Restrictions

EVOLUTION OF THE RESTRICTIONS

The most fundamental deficiency of the RCRA regulations prior to 1984 was the absence of any preference or priority for protective methods of hazardous waste management. With few exceptions the generator exercised complete discretion to use either a landfill or a treatment process for the same waste. This policy of neutrality existed despite EPA acknowledgments that land disposal facilities could not ensure permanent containment. To make matters worse, the myriad deficiencies in the land disposal permitting standards issued by EPA (see Chapters 10 and 11) encouraged additional land disposal by failing to reflect the long-term societal costs and uncertainties associated with disposal, contributing in essence to a regulatory subsidization of land disposal. The resulting price differentials between land disposal and more permanent management options thereby encouraged additional land disposal.

Fortunately, in the void left by EPA there emerged a variety of public and private sector organizations prepared to shape a national waste management policy. Concurrent with the beginning of the reauthorization process in January 1982, with the introduction of HR 6307, a number of major studies and state government actions collectively served to crystallize the long-felt need for change in national hazardous waste policy and regulation.

For example, a landmark study was issued by the State of California's Office of Appropriate Technology, which stated that over 75% of the waste generated in California should be restricted or prohibited from landfill disposal.[1] This study led to the issuance of an Executive Order by Governor Jerry Brown, which established an explicit policy favoring treatment over land disposal, and to the enactment of a specific schedule of restrictions of a wide range of wastes. California's general restrictions and their failure to effectively cover surface impoundments and injection wells both played a key role in shaping HSWA's provisions.[2]

Closely following the California study were reports from the U.S. Congress' Office of Technology Assessment and the National Academy of Sciences confirming the desirability of substantial reductions in the use of land disposal. These studies demonstrated that there was no shortage of methods to treat wastes by alternative technologies, and that their use was stifled by the existence of massive regulatory loopholes.

The National Academy of Sciences study concluded that there exists technology capable of dealing with every hazardous waste so as to eliminate concern for future hazards. The report went on to note that no new major and cost-effective technology exists or is likely to be developed that could be a panacea to dispose of *all* hazardous wastes.[3]

Similarly, the Office of Technology Assessment report concluded that a number of pre-HSWA regulatory policies and practices may serve as disincentives for waste reduction and treatment activities, and that the available capacity for off-site management of wastes is not a barrier to shifting management away from land disposal. Lastly, the report concluded that until the private sector perceives the regulatory structure as not containing a bias in favor of land disposal technologies, investment in new treatment technology research and development and commercial development may be limited.[4]

Juxtaposed to these technology-oriented reports was a series of studies confirming the environmental risks posed by land disposal. A key study issued in September 1982 demonstrated that four state-of-the-art land disposal facilities in the study leaked, despite utilization of the best available dual liners and leachate collection systems.[5] SCA Chemical Services, Inc., discovered that its state-of-the-art landfill in Wilsonville, Illinois, was leaking large volumes of organic solvents, resulting in a virtually unprecedented court-ordered exhumation of the entire landfill. This event was pivotal in the transformation of SCA from a landfill-oriented firm to one that strongly advocated legislative restrictions on the land disposal of a wide range of hazardous wastes. Dow Chemical Co. confirmed that in 1982 over 99% of their wastes were incinerated, recycled, or treated.[6]

EPA itself issued a report in 1983 which found there were over 180,000 surface impoundments (pits, ponds, and lagoons) used for the management of wastes, over 30,000 of which were used for the management of industrial wastes.[7] Of these industrial waste lagoons, 70% were operating without any liner or retention system whatsoever, and 39% were determined to have a high potential to contaminate groundwater. Ironically, many of these de facto groundwater discharge lagoons were and are being used for purposes of treating and discharging industrial wastewater into surface waters in accordance with permits issued under the Clean Water Act. Other studies confirmed that over 30% of current "Superfund" sites were caused by leaking lagoons.[8]

In late 1984, EPA also issued its most comprehensive survey of waste generation and management practices to date, which opened many eyes to the true magnitude and scope of this nation's patterns of hazardous waste generation and mismanagement. This study revealed that a mere 4% of the nation's hazardous waste was recycled in 1981. Only 5% of the nation's 250 million tons of hazardous waste was disposed of in landfills, while injection wells and lagoons accounted for 58% (10 billion gallons) and 38% of the hazardous waste managed, respectively.[9] In addition, other surveys revealed that hazardous waste injection facilities, or deep wells so-called for their injection of wastes below the drinking water aquifer, were associated with some of the most significant uncertainties and vast areas of environmental contamination[10] from any management method. Moreover, the largest hazardous waste fine in history ($10 million) was levied at a deep well site in Ohio for the release of an estimated 45 million gallons of hazårdous waste from the facility's deep well and surface impoundment operations.[11]

The growing consensus regarding the need to utilize management technologies not subject to the uncertainties of land disposal highlighted by these surveys and reports was not lost on certain segments of the hazardous waste treatment industry or the states. Firms that had invested in permanent treatment technology bore witness to the absence of demand for more protective management, and served notice of their intent to withhold further investment until the law provided greater certainty that protection would take priority over tradition. As Congressman Dennis E. Eckart (D-OH), the leading sponsor of HSWA's land disposal and minimum technology requirements noted at the time of House Commerce Committee approval, "For far too long land disposal has been the bargain basement way of doing things. There is currently no incentive for recycling."[12] In addition to California, a number of states were embarking on regulatory efforts to minimize land disposal. Illinois required persons wishing to dispose of waste after January 1, 1987, to prove the waste could not be reused, treated, or incinerated.[13] Similar policies emerged in Massachusetts, Arkansas, Oregon, and Arizona. In addition, states were identifying wastes appropriate for land disposal prohibitions. Illinois was evaluating restrictions on chlorinated solvents, while New York was utilizing the permitting process to restrict wastes containing high concentrations of carcinogens and highly toxic organic contaminants.

Additional support for major reform came from several EPA actions and the performance of several programs. The "liquids in landfill" debacle, the suspension of major regulations, and the Agency's enforcement record (see Chapter 1) provided major impetus for reform. In addition, the ease with which many early "delistings" were granted (Chapter 2), and the failure to complete any of the RCRA "special waste" studies after 5 years of open-ended statutory directives to do so (Chapter 3) supported the need for more proscriptive solutions. Conversely, the prohibitions that Congress placed on the production and management of PCBs under the Toxic Substances Control Act in 1976 proved itself to be the sole reason behind the expansion of existing capacity to incinerate PCBs.

Despite this burgeoning evidence and support for fundamental change, EPA was actively pursuing its own brand of regulatory reform. In response to an inquiry from Congressman John Lafalce (D-NY), whose Congressional District includes the Love Canal area, EPA Administrator Gorsuch stated that "Landfilling represents the lowest risk option currently available for dealing with the large quantities of hazardous wastes generated each year. . . ."[14]

Furthermore, the Assistant Administrator for EPA's hazardous waste program, Rita Lavelle, testified before the Congress that "we believe that most wastes can be satisfactorily managed in the land and that it can be done with a reasonable margin of safety more cheaply in this manner . . . it may be that recycling or destruction is preferable from a strictly health and environmental protection standpoint, but for many wastes, the reduction in risk achieved is probably marginal and may not be worth the cost."[15]

These and other Administration actions, while important, did not themselves drive the reauthorization process. Rather, they served to catalyze a series of Congressional investigations (see notes 5, 6, 12, and 15) that revealed the true scope of the nation's hazardous waste problem, and the fundamental deficiencies in the statute itself.

Lacking more than better leadership, the Agency also needed new proscriptive regulatory tools and Congressional backing to redress past deficiencies and undertake the task of restricting wastes from land disposal in a timely manner. These new tools also had to make it clear to the regulated community that their interest was best served by assisting the Agency. The first of these tools involves a presumptive prohibition against the land disposal of all RCRA wastes (i.e., wastes automatically prohibited by statute), while reserving authority for Agency override (via regulation) in specific situations where it believes the prohibition is not required in order to be protective (such as pretreated wastes). Second, if the Agency fails to make the necessary determinations by specified dates, the prohibitions nevertheless take effect so the status quo will not persist. These two mechanisms are frequently termed "hammers" or minimum regulatory controls (MRCs).

In conclusion, ten years after the original enactment of RCRA we have only now defined the full nature and scope of our hazardous waste management problem, and can now apply the lessons of a decade's pioneering efforts and failures to reform the national controls. The 1984 RCRA Amendments mark the end of the beginning for our national hazardous waste program by declaring the beginning of the end for unrestricted land disposal practices.

STATUTORY LAND DISPOSAL RESTRICTIONS

This chapter is an examination of those portions of the 1984 Amendments which impose restrictions on the land disposal of previously listed and identified RCRA hazardous wastes. Other HSWA provisions related to land disposal are described elsewhere in the book, such as requirements pertaining to groundwater monitoring and exposure assessments (Chapter 11), corrective action (Chapter 11), minimum design standards (Chapter 10), and general permitting and other operating requirements (Chapters 6–8). The original RCRA reauthorization bill from 1982, H.R. 6307 (97th Congress, 2nd Session), laid the groundwork for these landmark provisions, including land disposal restrictions, the self-implementing restrictions ("hammers") on small quantity generators, corrective action for all hazardous waste releases, prohibitions on the unrestricted burning and blending of hazardous wastes and used oils as fuels, and a general directive to control other hazardous waste recycling practices deemed to be unprotective.

National Policy

For the first time, Congress established an explicit national policy which identified a hierarchy of waste management preferences beginning with waste minimization and utilizing the "best treatment, storage, and disposal techniques for each waste." Specifically HSWA states: "The Congress hereby declares it to be the national policy of the U.S. that wherever feasible, the generation of hazardous waste is to be reduced or eliminated as expeditiously as possible. Waste that is nevertheless generated should be treated, stored, or disposed of so as to minimize the present and future threat to human health and the environment."[16]

In selecting the "best" management methods for each waste, Congress provided overall guidance in amendments to the findings and objectives sections of RCRA, Sections 1002 and 1003. Specifically, Congress made the following new findings with respect to hazardous waste:

1. the placement of inadequate controls will result in substantial risks to human health and the environment;
2. if hazardous waste management is improperly performed in the first instance it is likely to be expensive, complex, and time-consuming; and
3. certain classes of land disposal facilities are not capable of assuring long-term containment of certain hazardous wastes, and to avoid substantial risk to human health and the environment, reliance on land disposal should be minimized or eliminated, and land disposal, particularly land and surface impoundment, should be the least-favored method for managing hazardous wastes.

In accordance with these findings, Congress provided EPA with complementary objectives for implementing RCRA, particularly the 1984 amendments and the land disposal restrictions:

1. assuring that hazardous waste management practices are conducted in a manner which protects human health and the environment;
2. requiring that hazardous waste be properly managed in the first instance thereby reducing the need for corrective action at a future date; and
3. minimizing the generation of hazardous waste and the land disposal of hazardous waste by encouraging process substitution, materials recovery, properly conducted recycling and reuse, and treatment.

As the HSWA Conference Report states, these amendments to the findings and objectives of RCRA are intended to "convey a clear·and unambiguous message to the regulated community and EPA: reliance on land disposal of hazardous waste has resulted in an unacceptable risk to human health and the environment. Consequently, the Conferees intend that through the vigorous implementation of the objectives of this Act, land disposal will be eliminated for many wastes and minimized for all others, and that advanced treatment, recycling, incineration and other hazardous waste control technologies should replace land disposal. In other words, land disposal should be used only as a last resort and only under conditions which are fully protective of human health and the environment."

Significantly, these findings and objectives are not dependent upon the cost of changes and technology that are necessary to achieve long-term certainty and protection in the management of hazardous wastes. This is a policy continued from the original 1976 law.

Liquids in Landfills

BULK LIQUIDS   RCRA Section 3004 now contains provisions devoted to prohibiting and minimizing land disposal through a series of phased land disposal restrictions.[17] The earliest restrictions involve the disposal of liquids in landfills.

Beginning May 8, 1985, Congress prohibited the "placement" of bulk or non-containerized liquid hazardous waste (or hazardous waste containing free liquids). Congress focused on the presence of liquids initially because of their propensity to leak from the containment areas into the environment.

To comply with this prohibition, it is first necessary to determine whether a waste is liquid or contains free liquid. EPA has issued a test, known as the "paint filter test," for making such a determination.[18] Briefly, the test requires that a 100 ml or 100 g sample of all wastes intended for land disposal (including those that are ignitable or corrosive) be placed on a paint filter (mesh number of 60) for a period of 5 minutes. Any portion of the waste that passes through and drops from the filter is considered to be a free liquid, and may not be land disposed unless the liquids are decanted, suctioned, and chemically or physically separated or treated (other than solely with the use of absorbents) such that the wastes do not pass through the filter.

The new provision also bans bulk liquid placement "whether or not absorbents have been added." This additional prohibition on absorbents was added due to the prevalent use of absorbents as a means of temporarily transforming bulk liquids into bulk solids, only for the mixed waste and absorbent mixtures to yield wastes under pressure when placed in a landfill.

On May 9, 1985, EPA issued draft guidance implementing the bulk liquid ban.[19] It states that, "The Agency is convinced that Congress did not want materials that function solely as an absorbent to be used in the treatment of bulk liquid hazardous wastes that are allowed to be placed in landfill." Common examples of absorbents are vermiculite, fullers earth, bentonite, fly ash, fine-grained sands, shredded paper, and sawdust. "Absorbents" does not include: any treatment technology that does not involve absorption; a treatment technology that chemically stabilizes, encapsulates, or solidifies a bulk liquid hazardous waste; or an *ad*sorbent (such as activated carbon or other material) that binds the liquid through a chemical reaction (such as hydration) rather than through a physical process.

The guidance does not identify acceptable materials for use in chemical stabilization, and acknowledges that determining whether a material solely functions as an absorbent (no chemical reaction) is both difficult and subtle. However, in distinguishing between stabilization and absorption the guidance states that fly ash, for example, used alone is an absorbent, but used in conjunction with lime or Portland cement may constitute an element of the stabilization process.[20] Accordingly, EPA is developing an additional test to determine whether the material mixed with a waste is merely absorbing the liquids, or whether chemical binding is occurring. The test is expected to be proposed by June 1986.

Significantly, this absolute statutory ban is on the "placement" of bulk liquids in landfills, not on their disposal. Placement is sufficiently broad to encompass not only disposal, but treatment or storage in the landfill as well. Thus, prohibited activities include placing bulk liquids into a landfill cell where liquids are solidified and then transferred to another landfill cell, and placing treated bulk liquids still in liquid form into a landfill cell prior to solidification.[21]

CONTAINERIZED LIQUIDS   Congress has required EPA to issue regulations by February 8, 1986, which would

1. "minimize" the disposal of containerized liquid hazardous waste in landfills; and
2. "minimize" the presence of free liquids in containerized hazardous waste to be disposed in landfills.[22]

Until EPA issues these new regulations, existing restrictions on the landfilling of containerized liquid hazardous waste remains in effect. (These restrictions were discussed in Chapter 8.) (See 40 CFR 269.314.)

While relying upon EPA to issue regulations minimizing containerized liquid wastes, Congress imposed a ban stautorily on bulk liquids. The difference in approach is necessary because of the tendency of wastes to leak when they are simply poured into a landfill cell and when they are exposed directly to rainwater and other wastes.

Congress also used the term "minimize" rather than "prohibit" for containerized liquid placement because of the difficulties in achieving a total prohibition. A small amount of liquid may result, for example, as the waste settles during transport, despite the use of decanting or other techniques to limit liquid formation.

However, Congress also reaffirmed its concern about undue reliance on the use of absorbents as a way of getting around liquid minimization. Specifically, Congress expressly rejected the use of absorbents "that biodegrade or that release liquids when compressed as might occur during routine landfill operations." Conversely, absorbents seem to be an appropriate liquid minimization technique during transportation or in spill cleanups as an adjunct to other liquid minimization techniques such as chemical solidification.

In August 1985, EPA did not believe it could meet the February 1986 deadline for issuing these regulations, indicating instead a date of "early 1987."

NON-HAZARDOUS LIQUID WASTES   Another direct acting statutory prohibition has been imposed on the disposal of non-hazardous liquid wastes into either interim status or fully permitted landfills effective on November 8, 1985. The purpose of this provision was to prevent the mixing of hazardous waste with non-hazardous liquids. If placed in a land disposal cell, non-hazardous liquids can mobilize hazardous wastes that otherwise would remain stable and immobile, thus defeating the purpose of the bulk hazardous liquids restrictions. An exception to this statutory prohibition has been provided for situations where the only "reasonably available alternative" for these non-hazardous liquids is a landfill or unlined surface impoundment which already contains hazardous waste, and the disposal of the non-hazardous liquids in the owner's landfill will not present a risk of contamination to any underground source of drinking water. This exception is designed to prevent shifting of non-hazardous liquids from Subtitle C facilities to potentially dangerous sanitary landfills and unlined impoundments. The implications of this provision for controlling rainwater or for the redisposal of liquid wastes have not been addressed by specific guidance at this time.[23]

Criteria and Chronology for Specific Waste Prohibitions

For all other forms and types of hazardous wastes, Congress established a framework of prohibitions phased over a 6½-year period. All pre-HSWA listed and identified wastes are potentially covered by the prohibitions, however the timing differs depending on the waste type, concentration, and the form of land disposal involved. For example, restrictions on certain dioxins and solvent wastes take effect on November 8, 1986 for all forms of land disposal except deep well injection, which takes effect on August 8, 1988.

The limitations described above for bulk and containerized liquids applied only to placement in landfills. In this broader framework, identifying whether the waste is a "liquid" or "solid" is only one phase in the process of determining the acceptability of landfill disposal for a given waste. Furthermore, the remaining restrictions apply to all forms of land disposal.

Congress defined the term "land disposal" in an attempt to minimize ambiguity arising from the fine line which often exists between long-term storage and disposal. The term "land disposal" includes, but is not limited to, any placement of such hazardous waste in a landfill, surface impoundment, waste pile, injection well, land treatment facility, salt dome formation, salt bed formation, or underground mine or cave.[24] Disposal into above-ground vaults and open detonation of all types are also defined as land disposal. In addition, the storage of any hazardous waste that is prohibited from one or more methods of land disposal is itself prohibited unless such storage is solely for the purpose of the accumulation of such quantities of prohibited hazardous waste as are necessary to facilitate proper recovery, treatment, or disposal once the prohibitions are effective.[25]

Significantly, the restrictions described above concerning liquids in landfills remain in effect regardless of subsequent determinations concerning particular listed or identified wastes.

LAND DISPOSAL RESTRICTIONS   One of the most fundamental and significant changes instituted by the 1984 Amendments are the statutory presumptions against the land disposal of specific hazardous wastes. Those presumptions against the land disposal of specific wastes and the high level of pre-treatment required are intended to be the primary source of public health protection, and relieve the dependence on liners and location standards to prevent environmental releases. These presumptions place the burden on EPA to justify the continued use of land disposal, rather than to justify the imposition of restrictions. Specifically, the Administrator is directed to prohibit wastes from land disposal unless he or she determines that one or more methods of land disposal of a hazardous waste is not required in order to protect human health and the environment for as long as the waste remains hazardous. In addition, in the event that the Administrator fails to issue regulations justifying the continued use of land disposal in a timely manner, the wastes are generally prohibited from land disposal.[26] There are variations on this basic theme for certain listed wastes, injected wastes, and contaminated soils.

While the statute presumptively prohibits the land disposal of virtually all hazardous wastes (e.g., the California list uses concentration cutoffs in defining "prohibited wastes"), the presumption can be overcome by *pre-treatment* that "substantially diminishes the toxicity" or substantially reduces the likelihood of migration; *or* by a waste-specific *petition* that demonstrates there will be "no migration . . . for as long as the waste remains hazardous." Both the pre-treatment and petition processes are discussed below in greater detail.

In determining whether the prohibition against land disposal of a hazardous waste is not required to protect human health and the environment, the Administrator is directed to apply three criteria: 1) the long-term uncertainties associated with land disposal; 2) the goal of managing wastes in an appropriate manner in the first instance; and 3) the persistence, toxicity, mobility, and propensity to bioaccumulate of such hazardous wastes and their hazardous constituents. These three criteria were intentionally selected to heavily disfavor the land disposal of many wastes.

The first criterion is intended to highlight the lack of information available on the fate and transport of hazardous wastes, and the inability of existing land disposal facilities to assure long-term containment. Included in the latter category are liner failures, the inability to maintain adequate leachate collection and removal systems well beyond closure, the complexity of monitoring groundwater contamination, and the institutional uncertainties associated with ensuring protection of human health and the environment from waste migration for hundreds or thousands of years.

The second criterion is intended to encourage the use of management technologies less reliant on containment and cleanup once containment fails, recognizing the complexity and cost of that approach. Through this criterion, Congress emphasizes reducing the need for future cleanup activity and greater reliance on waste minimization, pretreatment, and detoxification.

Finally, "persistence, toxicity, mobility, and propensity to bioaccumulate" are the intrinsic properties that may cause a waste to be prohibited. Wastes that remain hazardous for a long period of time, are mobile in the air, soil, or groundwater, or are highly toxic; or wastes that increase the mobility of other wastes are "prime candidates" for land disposal restrictions. Significantly, a waste may exhibit only one or a combination of some or all of these properties to be prohibited.[27]

The threshold for deciding when a waste is "toxic enough" is not specified in the statute. However, the threshold for such decisions is low, relative to the provision as it was structured originally in the Senate bill. The Senate bill stated that wastes would have to be "highly toxic, highly persistent" in order to be prohibited, rather than merely toxic and persistent, but the modifier "highly" was eliminated from the final law. Thus, while HSWA obviously could not establish a quantitative mechanism for integrating these properties into a decision rule, it does provide a lower threshold for making such determinations than the original Senate version.

A significant debate has ensued over the proper interpretation of this statute as it pertains to the three criteria, including the four waste characteristics in the decision rule governing the prohibitions. Some have argued that using the four characteristics to identify candidate wastes for the prohibitions, EPA can and must establish a health threshold for human exposure to wastes to identify those wastes and pre-treated residues that can and cannot be land disposed. Thus, those hazardous wastes that naturally meet the acceptable levels of toxicity, mobility, persistence, and bioaccumulation would not have to be pre-treated or have a waste-specific petition submitted to allow the waste to be land disposed. Only those wastes that exceed a health threshold, derived from a collective consideration of the four characteristics, would have to be pre-treated or have a petition submitted. But it is expected that most if not all wastes would have to be pre-treated or "petitioned," and even then that stringent pre-treatment and petition standards will drive most wastes, particularly organics (e.g., solvents, still bottoms) to alternative treatment. The aim of the provision was not to devise a pre-treatment scheme such that all wastes could continue to be land disposed, but rather to ensure that only the wastes that had to be land disposed (e.g., metal-bearing sludges) were so placed, and then using only the best available pre-treatment technology.

The statute authorizes only the use of these three criteria (including the four intrinsic characteristics) in one particular instance, where an individual petitioner seeks a variance from the prohibition (see discussion below). Earlier versions of HSWA provided EPA with discretion to set concentration levels, to establish other criteria or characteristics to generically prohibit some wastes and not prohibit others. The final version of the law does not contain similar explicit authority. Instead, the final version prohibits all waste from land disposal without prior treatment, unless an individual variance is obtained.

One justification for this approach is that Congress saw few candidates obtaining legitimate variances under the strict standard it had developed, and wished to place the burden of proof on the petitioner to justify that its claim for a variance was appropriate. Second, Congress sought to apply these factors on a site-specific basis, where a specific waste management context could be analyzed with these factors in mind. To obtain a variance, the petitioner must demonstrate to the Administrator "to a reasonable degree of certainty that there will be no migration of hazardous constituents from the disposal unit or injection zone for as long as the wastes remain hazardous."

Irrespective of the debate, for those that use a petition to attempt to demonstrate the acceptability of continued land disposal, the EPA must apply these criteria to a particular waste stream for a time "as long as the waste remains hazardous." This means forever in the case of many persistent organic wastes and metals, thereby further emphasizing the bias against land disposal of criteria one and two. Significantly, the House Committee report had suggested that a period of two hundred years might be a proper time frame of concern.[28] However, in order to ensure that the most protective approach and most certain and permanent methods of treatment were utilized, a uniform time frame was not adopted. Instead, the HSWA approach objectively relates the intrinsic hazard posed by the waste to the period of time that the waste continues to pose that threat when placed in and while residing in a land disposal setting. The provision was not intended to allow "migration that may be harmful." Rather it was intended to prevent "any migration from the disposal unit" until such time as the waste was non-hazardous at the point and place where it was placed into the unit.

The three criteria are applied to each waste stream to determine whether a "prohibition on one or more methods of land disposal" is appropriate. "One or more methods of land disposal" means that the Administrator may vary the nature of the prohibitions or restrictions for a given waste depending upon the method of land disposal. For example, an organic oily waste that could not be land disposed into an impoundment, landfill, or injection well may be suitable for land treatment provided that the level of biological degradation that occurs is sufficient to meet the standard of "complete degradation, transformation, and immobilization within the treatment zone."[29] However, land disposal facilities that differ solely on the basis of liner systems—single or multiple—are not considered to be different types of land disposal facilities.

Readers should note the factors Congress did not want EPA to consider in making land disposal prohibition determinations. First and foremost, conspicuously absent is any consideration or factoring of *cost* in the imposing of land disposal restrictions or choosing among management alternatives. In addition, Congress did not incorporate site-specific exemptions into the prohibition determinations, except in a limited instance (also see discussion below regarding deadline extension criteria). Once a waste is prohibited from one or more methods of land disposal, an interested person may petition the Administrator for a facility-specific waiver by demonstrating the waste will not migrate from the disposal unit or injection zone for as long as the waste remains hazardous. (This petitioning process will be described further below.) In addition, Congress did not authorize the use of comparative risk assessments between land disposal and treatment methods to determine the acceptability of land disposal for a given waste.

WASTE PROHIBITION SCHEDULE By November 8, 1986, the Agency must schedule for land disposal prohibitions all RCRA listed and identified hazardous wastes that are not included on the "Dioxin and Solvents" or "California" Lists discussed below.[30] The issuance of the schedule by itself does not prohibit any specific wastes. Rather, it specifies which of the remaining listed and identified wastes will be scheduled for determinations at one of the following three junctures: 45, 55, or 66 months after enactment. Thus, the schedule does not by itself prohibit any wastes; rather it establishes priorities for prohibition determinations of the balance of listed and identified hazardous wastes that are to be issued at a later date.

The schedule is to be based on a ranking of the listed and identified wastes, which considers their intrinsic hazard and their volumes such that decisions regarding the large-volume wastes with a high intrinsic hazard shall be scheduled first, and low-volume wastes with a lower intrinsic hazard shall be scheduled last. The issuance of this schedule is not subject to judicial review nor the requirements of the Paperwork Reduction Act.

The schedule is intended to provide a clear and early signal to generators of these listed and/or characteristic wastes that the day of determination, and likely restriction or imposition of a pretreatment standard, is coming, so that the firm can plan for either waste minimization, process change, and/or necessary form and level of treatment.

On May 31, 1985, the Agency proposed a schedule determination of all remaining listed and identified wastes that are not solvents, dioxins or on the California list.[31] Significantly, the proposal notes that EPA is not precluded from banning land disposal or requiring treatment for any scheduled wastes before the scheduled deadline. The Agency is also considering the possibility of making separate determinations for individual hazardous constituents in each waste. If so, the ban or treatment standard for a specific constituent could apply to all scheduled hazardous wastes containing that constituent. Therefore, the Agency may address a waste prior to the deadline assigned to it (Final rule, 5-28-86 *Fed. Reg.*).

The methodology proposed by the Agency would rank hazardous wastes by multiplying a toxicity score for each waste, which represents the waste's inherent toxicological properties, by a volume score (TxV). Due to a lack of uniform environmental fate and effects data for RCRA wastes, the toxicity component of the model represents a composite of acute toxicity date (LD 50), subchronic toxicity data, and chronic toxicity data (Allowable Daily Intake, and Unit Carcinogen Risk), where a higher score is given to wastes that score higher for chronic toxicity. Scores are not adjusted for concentration because of the wide variation in constituent concentrations that sometimes exist within a single waste code. Data on volume of given wastes that are being land disposed are taken from the Westat Survey (see note 9). Additional information on the methodology and scoring procedures is available from the Agency.[32]

Tables 9-1 through 9-3 represent the wastes that are scheduled for prohibition determinations at 45, 55, and 66 months after enactment. For wastes that are listed or identified as hazardous after November 8, 1984, the Agency is required to make land disposal determinations within 6 months of that identification or listing. In the event the Agency misses the 6-month deadline for prohibition determination and/or pretreatment standard, the waste is not automatically prohibited; rather, it is subject to an interim restriction requiring the use of only dual-lined landfills and impoundments until such a determination is made for these wastes.

DIOXINS AND SOLVENTS   Also on November 8, 1986, the Administrator is required to issue final regulations prohibiting from one or more methods of land disposal (except for underground injection) both dioxin-containing (F020–F023, F026, F027) and listed solvent wastes (F001–F005, plus various

Table 9-1

§ 268.10 Identification of wastes to be evaluated by August 8, 1988.

EPA will take action under sections 3004(g)(5) and 3004(m), of the Resource Conservation and Recovery Act, by August 8, 1988, for the following wastes (for ease of understanding the wastes have been listed by the section of 40 CFR Part 261 under which they were listed):

§ 261.31 Wastes

F006—Wastewater treatment sludges from electroplating operations except from the following processes: (1) Sulfuric acid anodizing of aluminum; (2) tin plating on carbon steel; (3) zinc plating (segregated basis) on carbon steel; (4) aluminum or zinc-aluminum plating on carbon steel; (5) cleaning/stripping associated with tin, zinc and aluminum plating on carbon steel; and (6) chemical etching and milling of aluminum.

F007—Spent cyanide plating bath solutions from electroplating operations.

F008—Plating bath sludges from the bottom of plating baths from electroplating operations where cyanides are used in the process.

F009—Spent stripping and cleaning bath solutions from electroplating operations where cyanides are used in the process.

F019—Wastewater treatment sludges from the chemical conversion coating of aluminum.

§ 261.32 Wastes

K001—Bottom sediment sludge from the treatment of wastewaters from wood preserving processes that use creosote and/or pentachlorophenol.

K004—Wastewater treatment sludge from the production of zinc yellow pigments.

K008—Over residue from the production of chrome oxide green pigments.

K011—Bottom stream from the wastewater stripper in the production of acrylonitrile.

K013—Bottom stream from the acetonitrile column in the production of acrylonitrile.

K014—Bottoms from the acetonitrile purification column in the production of acrylonitrile.

K015—Still bottoms from the distillation of benzyl chloride.

K016—Heavy ends or distillation residues from the production of carbon tetrachloride.

K017—Heavy ends (still bottoms) from the purification column in the production of epichlorohydrin.

K018—Heavy ends from the fractionation column in ethyl chloride production.

K020—Heavy ends from the distillation of vinyl chloride in vinyl chloride monomer production.

K021—Aqueous spent antimony catalyst waste from fluoromethanes production.

K022—Distillation bottom tars from the production of phenol/acetone from cumene.

K024—Distillation bottoms from the production of phthalic anhydride from naphthalene.

K030—Column bottom or heavy ends from the combined production of trichloroethylene and perchloroethylene.

K031—By-products salts generated in the production of MSMA and cacodylic acid.

K035—Wastewater treatment sludges generated in the production of creosote.

K036—Still bottoms from toluene reclamation distillation in the production of disulfoton.

K037—Wastewater treatment sludge from the production of disulfoton.

K044—Wastewater treatment sludges from the manufacturing and processing of explosives.

K045—Spent carbon from the treatment of wastewater containing explosives.

K046—Wastewater treatment sludges from the manufacturing, formulation and loading of lead-based initiating compounds.

K047—Pink/red water from TNT operations.

K048—Dissolved air flotation (DAF) float from the petroleum refining industry.

K049—Slop oil emulsion solids from the petroleum refining industry.

K050—Heat exchange bundle cleaning sludge from the petroleum refining industry.

K051—API separator sludge from the petroleum refining industry.

K052—Tank bottoms (leaded) from the petroleum refining industry.

K060—Ammonia still lime sludge from coking operations.

K061—Emission control dust/sludge from the primary production of steel in electric furnaces.

K062—Spent pickle liquor from steel finishing operations in chlorine production.

K069—Emission control dust/sludge from secondary lead smelting.

K071—Brine purification muds from the mercury cells process in chlorine production, where separately prepurified brine is not used.

K073—Chlorinated hydrocarbon waste from the purification step of the diaphragm cell process using graphite anodes

K083—Distillation bottoms from aniline production.

K084—Wastewater treatment sludges generated during the production of veterinary pharmaceuticals from arsenic or organo-arsenic compounds.

K085—Distillation of fractionation column bottoms from the production of chlorobenzenes.

K086—Solvent washes and sludges; caustic washes and sludges, or water washes and sludges from cleaning tubs and equipment used in the formulation of ink from pigments, driers, soaps, and stabilizers containing chromium and lead.

K087—Decanter tank tar sludge from coking operations.

K099—Untreated wastewater from the production of 2,4-D.

K101—Distillation tar residues from the distillation of aniline-based compounds in the production of veterinary pharmaceuticals from arsenic or organo-arsenic compounds.

K102—Residue from the use of activated carbon for decolorization in the production of veterinary pharmaceuticals from arsenic or organo-arsenic compounds.

K103—Process residues from aniline extraction from the production of aniline.

K104—Combined wastewater streams generated from nitrobenzene/aniline production.

K106—Waste water treatment sludge from the mercury cell process in chlorine production.

§ 261.33(e) Wastes

P001—Warfarin, when present at concentration greater than 0.3%

P004—Aldrin

P005—Allyl alcohol

P010—Arsenic acid

P011—Arsenic (V) oxide

P012—Arsenic (III) oxide

P015—Beryllium dust

P016—Bis-(chloromethyl) ether

P018—Brucine

P020—Dinoseb

P030—Soluble cyanide salts not elsewhere specified

P036—Dichlorophenylarsine

P037—Dieldrin

P039—Disulfoton

P041—Diethyl-p-nitrophenyl phosphate

P048—2,4-Dinitrophenol

P050—Endosulfan

P058—Fluoracetic acid, sodium salt

P059—Heptachlor

P063—Hydrogen cyanide

P068—Methyl Hydrazine

P069—Methyllactonitrile

P070—Aldicarb

P071—Methyl parathion

P081—Nitroglycerine

P082—N-Nitrosodimethylamine

P084—N-Nitrosomethylvinylamine

P087—Osmium tetraoxide

P089—Parathion

P092—Phenylmercuric acetate

P094—Phorate

P097—Famphur

P102—Propargyl alcohol

P105—Sodium azide

P108—Strychnine and salts

P110—Tetraethyl lead

P115—Thallium (I) sulfate

P120—Vanadium pentoxide

P122—Zinc phosphide, when present at concentrations greater than 10%

P123—Toxaphene

§ 261.33(f) Wastes

U007—Acrylamide

U009—Acrylonitrile

U010—Mitomycin C

U012—Aniline

U016—Benz(c)acridine

U018—Benz(a)anthracene

U019—Benzene

U022—Benzo(a)pyrene

U029—Methyl bromide

U031—n-Butanol

U036—Chlordane, technical

U037—Chlorobenzene

U041—n-Chloro-2,3-epoxypropane

U043—Vinyl chloride

U044—Chloroform

U046—Chloromethyl methyl ether

U050—Chrysene

U051—Creosote

U053—Crotonaldehyde

U061—DDT

U063—Dibenz o (a, h) anthracene

U064—1,2:7,8 Dibenzopyrene

U066—Dibromo-3-chloropropane 1,2-

U067—Ethylene dibromide

U074—1,4-Dichloro-2-butene

U077—Ethane, 1,2-dichloro-

U078—Dichloroethylene, 1,1-

U086—N,N Diethylhydrazine

U089—Diethylstilbestrol

U103—Dimethyl sulfate

U105—2,4-Dinitrotoluene

U108—Dioxane, 1,4-

U115—Ethylene oxide

U122—Formaldehyde

U124—Furan

U129—Lindane

U130—Hexachlorocyclopentadiene

U133—Hydrazine

U134—Hydrofluoric acid

U137—Indeno(1,2,3-cd)pyrene

U151—Mecury

U154—Methanol

U155—Methapyrilene

U157—3-Methylcholanthrene

U158—4,4-Methylene-bis-(2-chloroaniline)

U159—Methyl ethyl ketone

U171—Nitropropane, 2-

U177—N-Nitroso-N-methylurea

U180—N-Nitrosopyrrolidine

U185—Pentachloronitrobenzene

U188—Phenol

U192—Pronamide

U200—Reserpine

U209—Tetrachloroethane, 1,1,2,2-

U210—Tetrachloroethylene

U211—Carbon tetrachloride

U219—Thiourea

U220—Toluene

U221—Toluenediamine

U223—Toluene diisocyanate

U226—Methylchloroform

U227—Trichloroethane, 1,1,2-

U228—Trichloroethylene

U237—Uracil mustard

U238—Ethyl carbamate

U248—Warfarin, when present at concentrations of 0.3% or less

U249—Zinc phosphide, when present at concentrations of 10% or less

Table 9-2

Table 9-2

§ 268.11 Identification of wastes to be evaluated by June 8, 1989.

EPA will take action under sections 3004(g)(5) and 3004(m) of the Resource Conservation and Recovery Act, by June 8, 1989, for the following wastes (for ease of understanding the wastes have been listed by the section of 40 CFR Part 261 under which they were listed):

§ 261.31 Wastes

F010—Quenching bath sludge from oil baths from metal heat treating operations where cyanides are used in the process.

F011—Spent cyanide solutions from salt bath pot cleaning from metal heat treating operations.

F012—Quenching wastewater treatment sludges from metal heat operations where cyanides are used in the process.

F024—Wastes including but not limited to, distillation residues, heavy ends, tars and reactor clean-out wastes from the production of chlorinated aliphatic hydrocarbons, having carbon content from one to five, utilizing free radical catalyzed processes. [This listing does not include light ends, spent filters and filter aids, spend desiccants, wastewater, wastewater treatment sludges, spent catalysts, and wastes listed in § 261.32.].

§ 261.32 Wastes

K009—Distillation bottoms from the production of acetaldehyde from ethylene.

K010—Distillation side cuts from the productions of acetaldehyde from ethylene.

K019—Heavy ends from the distillation of ethylene dichloride in ethylene dichloride production.

K025—Distillation bottoms from the production of nitrobenzene by the nitration of benzene.

K027—Centrifuge and distillation residues from toluene diisocyanate production.

K028—Spent catalyst from the hydrochlorinator reactor in the production of 1,1,1-trichloroethane.

K029—Waste from the product steam stripper in the production of 1,1,1-trichloroethane.

K038—Wastewater from the washing and stripping of phorate production.

K039—Filter cake from the filtration of diethylphosphoro-dithioic acid in the production of phorate.

K040—Wastewater treatment sludge from the production of phorate.

K041—Wastewater treatment sludge from the production of toxaphene.

K042—Heavy ends or distillation residues from the distillation of tetrachlorobenzene in the production of 2,4,5-T.

K043—2,6-Dichlorophenol waste from the production of 2,4-D.

K095—Distillation bottoms from the production of 1,1,1-trichloroethane.

K096—Heavy ends from the heavy ends column from the production of 1,1,1-trichloroethane.

K097—Vacuum stripper discharge from the chlordane chlorinator in the production of chlordane.

K098—Untreated process wastewater from the production of toxaphene.

K105—Separated aqueous stream from the reactor product washing step in the production of chlorobenzenes.

§ 261.33(e) Wastes

P002—1-Acetyl-2-thiourea
P003—Acrolein
P007—5-(Aminoethyl)-3-isoxazolol
P008—4-Aminopyridine
P014—Thiophenol
P026—1-(o-Chlorophenyl)thiourea
P027—Propanenitrile, 3-chloro
P029—Copper cyanides
P040—O,O-Diethyl o-pyrazinyl phosphorothioate
P043—Diisopropyl fluorophosphate
P044—Dimethoate
P049—2,4-Dithiobiuret
P054—Aziridine
P057—Fluoroacetamide
P060—Isodrin
P062—Hexaethyltetraphosphate
P066—Methomyl
P067—2-Methylaziridine
P072—Alpha-naphthylthiourea (ANTU)
P074—Nickel cyanide
P085—Octamethylpyrophosphoramide
P098—Potassium cyanide
P104—Silver cyanide
P106—Sodium cyanide
P107—Strontium sulfide
P111—Tetraethylpyrophosphate
P112—Tetranitromethane
P113—Thallic oxide
P114—Thallium (I) selenite

§ 261.33(f) Wastes

U002—Acetone
U003—Acetonitrile
U005—o-Acetylaminofluorene
U008—Acrylic acid
U011—Amitrole
U014—Auramine
U015—Azaserine
U020—Benzenesulfonyl chloride
U021—Benzidine
U023—Benzotrichloride
U025—Dichloroethyl ether
U026—Chlornaphazine
U028—Bis-(2-ethylhexyl)phthalate
U032—Calcium chromate
U035—Chlorambucil
U047—Beta-chloronaphthalene
U049—4-Chloro-o-toluidine, hydrochloride
U057—Cyclohexanone
U058—Cyclophosphamide
U059—Daunomycin
U060—DDD
U062—Diallate

U070—o-Dichlorobenzene
U073—Dichlorobenzidene, 3,3-
U080—Methylene chloride
U083—Dichloropropane, 1,2-
U092—Dimethylamine
U093—Dimethylaminoazobenzene
U094—Dimethylbenz(a)anthracene,7,12-
U095—Dimethylbenzidine,3,3'-
U097—Dimethylcarbamoyl chloride
U098—Dimethylhydrazine, 1,1-
U099—Dimethylhydrazine, 1,2-
U101—Dimethylphenol, 2,4-
U106—Dinitrotoluene, 2,6-
U107—Di-n-octyl phthalate
U109—1,2-Diphenylhydrazine
U110—Dipropylamine
U111—Di-N-Propylnitrosamine
U114—Ethylenebis-(dithiocarbamic acid)
U116—Ethylene thiourea
U119—Ethyl methanesulfonate
U127—Hexachlorobenzene
U128—Hexachlorobutadiene
U131—Hexachloroethane
U135—Hydrogen sulfide
U138—Methyl iodide
U140—Isobutyl alcohol
U142—Kepone
U143—Lasiocarpine
U144—Lead acetate
U146—Lead subacetate
U147—Maleic anhydride
U149—Malononitrile
U150—Melphalan
U161—Methyl isobutyl ketone
U162—Methyl methacrylate
U163—N-Methyl-N-nitro-N-nitrosoguanidine
U164—Methylthiouracil
U165—Naphthalene
U168—Napthylamine, 2-
U169—Nitrobenzene
U170—p-Nitrophenol
U172—N-Nitroso-di-n-butylamine
U173—N-Nitroso-diethanolamine
U174—N-Nitroso-diethylamine
U176—N-Nitroso-N-ethylurea
U178—N-Nitroso-N-methylurethane
U179—N-Nitrosopiperidine
U189—Phosphorus sulfide
U193—1,3-Propane sultone
U196—Pyridine
U203—Safrole
U205—Selenium disulfide
U206—Streptozotocin
U208—Teracholoroethane, 1,1,1,2-
U213—Tetrahydrofuran
U214—Thallium (I) acetate
U215—Thallium (I) carbonate
U216—Thallium (I) chloride
U217—Thallium (I) nitrate
U218—Thioacetamide
U235—Tris (2,3-Dibromopropyl) phosphate
U239—Xylene
U244—Thiram

Table 9-3

Table 9-3

§ 268.12 Identification of wastes to be evaluated by May 8, 1990.

EPA will take action under sections 3004(g)(5) and 3004(m) of the Resource Conservation and Recovery Act, by May 8, 1990, for the following wastes (for ease of understanding, the wastes have been listed by the section of 40 CFR Part 261 under which they were listed):

§ 261.32 Wastes

K002—Wastewater treatment sludge from the production of chrome yellow and orange pigments.
K003—Wastewater treatment sludge from the production of molybdate orange pigments.
K005—Wastewater treatment sludge from the production of chrome green pigments.
K006—Wastewater treatment sludge from the production of chrome oxide green pigments (anhydrous and hydrated).
K007—Wastewater treatment sludge from the production of iron blue pigments.
K023—Distillation light ends from the production of phthalic anhydride from naphthalene.
K028—Stripping still tails from the production of methyl ethyl pyridines.
K032—Wastewater treatment sludge from the production of chlordane.
K033—Wastewater and scrub water from the chlorination of cyclopentadiene in the production of chlordane.
K034—Filter solids from the hexachlorocyclopentadiene in the production of chlordane.
K093—Distillation light ends from the production of phthalic anhydride from ortho-xylene.
K094—Distillation bottoms from the production of phthalic anhydride from ortho-xylene.
K100—Waste leaching solution from acid leaching of emission control dust/sludge from secondary lead smelting.

§ 261.33(e) Wastes

P006—Aluminum phosphide
P009—Ammonium picrate
P013—Barium cyanide
P017—Bromoacetone
P021—Calcium cyanide
P022—Carbon disulfide
P023—Chloroacetaldehyde

P024—p-Chloroaniline
P028—Benzyl chloride
P031—Cyanogen
P033—Cyanogen chloride
P034—4,6-Dinitro-o-cyclohexylphenol
P038—Diethylarsine
P042—Epinephrine
P045—Thiofanox
P046—Alpha, alpha-Dimethylphenethylamine
P047—4,6-Dinitro-o-cresol and salts
P051—Endrin
P056—Fluorine
P064—Methyl isocyanate
P065—Mercury fulminate
P073—Nickel carbonyl
P075—Nicotine and salts
P076—Nitric oxide
P077—p-Nitroaniline
P078—Nitrogen dioxide
P088—Endothall
P093—N-Phenylthiourea
P095—Phosgene
P096—Phosphine
P099—Potassium silver cyanide
P101—Propanenitrile
P103—Selenourea
P109—Tetraethyldithiopyrophosphate
P116—Thiosemicarbazide
P118—Trichloromethanethiol
P119—Ammonium vanadate
P121—Zinc cyanide

§ 261.33(f) Wastes

U001—Acetaldehyde
U004—Acetophenone
U006—Acetyl chloride
U017—Benzal chloride
U024—Bis(2-chloroethoxy)methane
U027—Bis(2-chloroisopropyl)ether
U030—Benzene, 1-bromo-4-phenoxy
U033—Carbonyl fluoride
U034—Chloral
U038—Ethyl-4-4'-dichlorobenzilate
U039—4-Chloro-m-cresol
U042—Vinyl ether, 2-chloroethyl
U045—Methyl chloride
U048—o-Chlorophenol
U052—Cresols
U055—Cumene
U056—Cyclohexane
U068—Methane, dibromo
U069—Dibutyl phthalate
U071—m-Dichlorobenzene
U072—p-Dichlorobenzene

U075—Dichlorodifluoromethane
U076—Ethane, 1,1-dichloro-
U079—1,2-Dichlorethylene
U081—2,4-Dichlorophenol
U082—2,6-Dichlorophenol
U084—1,3-Dichloropropene
U085—2,2'-Bioxirane
U087—O,O,-Diethyl-S-methyl-dithiophosphate
U088—Diethyl phthalate
U090—Dihydrosafrole
U091—3,3'-Dimethoxybenzidine
U096—alpha,alpha-Dimethylbenzylhydroxyperoxide
U102—Dimethyl phthalate
U112—Ethyl acetate
U113—Ethyl acrylate
U117—Ethyl ether
U118—Ethylmethacrylate
U120—Fluoranthene
U121—Trichloromonofluoromethane
U123—Formic acid
U125—Furfural
U126—Glycidylaldehyde
U132—Hexachlorophene
U136—Cacodylic acid
U139—Iron dextran
U141—Isosafrole
U145—Lead phosphate
U148—Maleic hydrazide
U152—Methacrylonitrile
U153—Methanethiol
U156—Methyl chlorocarbonate
U160—Methyl ethyl ketone peroxide
U166—1,4-Naphthaquinone
U167—1-Naphthylamine
U181—5-Nitro-o-toluidine
U182—Paraldehyde
U183—Pentachlorobenzene
U184—Pentachloroethane
U186—1,3-Pentadiene
U187—Phenacetin
U190—Phthalic anhydride
U191—2-Picoline
U194—1-Propanamine
U197—p-Benzoquinone
U201—Resorcinol
U202—Saccharin and salts
U204—Selenious acid
U207—1,2,4,5-tetrachlorobenzene
U222—o-Toluidine hydrochloride
U225—Bromoform
U234—Sym-Trinitrobenzene
U236—Trypan blue
U240—2,4-D, salts and esters
U243—Hexachloropropene
U246—Cyanogen bromide
U247—Methoxychlor

K, U, and P wastes), except for methods of land disposal which the Administrator determines will be protective of human health and the environment. A method of land disposal is prohibited unless the Administrator determines that the prohibition of one or more methods is not required in order to protect human health and the environment for as long as the waste remains hazardous, taking into account the three criteria discussed above.[33]

A method of land disposal may not be determined to be protective of human health and the environment unless they can meet the pretreatment standards for wastes prior to land disposal, or the Administrator determines that to a reasonable degree of certainty there will be no migration of hazardous constituents from the disposal unit or injection zone for as long as the waste remains hazardous. These deadlines apply to all forms of land disposal by November 1986, except for wastes injected into deep wells and contaminated soils. The EPA issued its proposed land disposal ban framework on January 14, 1986 (51 *Fed. Reg.* 1602), and proposed specific prohibitions, pre-treatment levels, and a petition process for those solvent and dioxin wastes. This proposal and its many attendant issues are discussed at the end of the chapter.

THE "CALIFORNIA" LIST   By July 8, 1987, the Administrator must evaluate another list of wastes and issue regulations respecting the acceptability of their continued land disposal, using the same criteria, presumptions, process, and deferrals for injection wells, and soils as required for dioxins and solvent wastes discussed above.[34] This list is so named because it was patterned after the landfill restrictions previously imposed by the State of California.

The hazardous wastes listed or identified under 3001 of RCRA (Table 9-4) are subject to the prohibitions of this section when present at concentrations equal to or greater than those specified, provided that the wastes have been listed or identified under RCRA by July 1987 (i.e., PCBs are not currently listed under RCRA). These allowable concentrations of hazardous wastes in land disposed materials generally reflect 10,000 times the current drinking water standards for these waste contaminants. Where necessary to protect human health and the environment, the Administrator shall substitute more stringent concentration levels than the levels specified in Table 9-4.

SCHEDULED CHARACTERISTIC AND LISTED WASTE PROHIBITIONS   By 45, 55, and 66 months after enactment or August 8, 1988, June 8, 1989, and May 8, 1990, the Administrator must issue final regulations prohibiting those RCRA listed and characteristic wastes from one or more methods of land disposal according to the schedule described above.[35] Decisions regarding the remaining RCRA listed and characteristic wastes are to be roughly divided into thirds, with characteristic waste determinations that are not on the California list reserved for the 66-month deadline. Wastes subject

Table 9-4   The California List

(A) Liquid hazardous wastes, including free liquids associated with any solid or sludge, containing free cyanides at concentrations greater than or equal to 1,000 mg/l.

(B) Liquid hazardous wastes, including free liquids associated with any solid or sludge, containing the following metals (or elements) or compounds of these metals (or elements) at concentrations greater than or equal to those specified below:

(i) arsenic and/or compounds (as As) 500 mg/l;
(ii) cadmium and/or compounds (as Cd) 100 mg/l;
(iii) chromium (VI and/or compounds (as Cr VI)) 500 mg/l;
(iv) lead and/or compounds (as Pb) 500 mg/l;
(v) mercury and/or compounds (as Hg) 20 mg/l;
(vi) nickel and/or compounds (as Ni) 134 mg/l;
(vii) selenium and/or compounds (as Se) 100 mg/l; and
(viii) thallium and/or compounds (as Th) 130 mg/l.

(C) Liquid hazardous waste having a pH less than or equal to two (2.0).

(D) Liquid hazardous wastes containing polychlorinated biphenyls at concentrations greater than or equal to 50 ppm.

(E) Hazardous wastes containing halogenated organic compounds in total concentration greater than or equal to 1,000 mg/kg.

When necessary to protect human health and the environment, the Administrator shall substitute more stringent concentration levels than the levels specified in subparagraphs (A) through (E).

to those prohibition determinations are hereafter referred to as "scheduled wastes."

The same criteria, pretreatment requirements, and petition processes are employed for these listed and characteristic waste prohibitions; however, the consequences of a failure by EPA to make the required determinations differs slightly from the approach that applies to the dioxins, solvents, and California wastes.

If by 45 months and 55 months after November 8, 1984, for those wastes respectively designated on the Schedule, the Administrator fails to issue regulatory determinations regarding the prohibitions and/or conditions (pretreatment) on land disposal, such hazardous wastes may only be disposed of into a landfill or surface impoundment if:

1. such impoundments and landfills fully comply with the dual liner and other containment requirements applicable to new facilities (Chapter 10); and

2. prior to such disposal the generator has "certified" to the Administrator that such generator has investigated the available treatment capacity and has determined that the use of such landfill or surface impoundment is the only "practical" alternative to treatment currently available to the generator.[36]

This "minimum regulatory control" continues in effect until the Administrator issues such regulations or at the very latest until 66 months after enactment (May 8, 1990). At that time all wastes listed and identified on the Schedule, including those scheduled for prohibition at 66 months for which a determination has not been made, are prohibited from all forms of land disposal. Thus, unlike dioxins, solvents and the California wastes, where the prohibitions take effect by statute if the Administrator fails to determine whether their continued land disposal is protective of human health and the environment, the wastes scheduled for prohibitions at 45 and 55 months are not fully prohibited from one or more method of land disposal until EPA makes a determination, or May 8, 1990 (66 months) whichever comes first. The EPA has taken the suspect position that the MRC does not apply to characteristic wastes at 66 months.

These modified sanctions, however, may offer little relief to waste generators. The generator's ability to certify that he has investigated and was unable to find the necessary treatment capacity for his waste will be substantially affected and limited by the approach that the Agency takes to making available capacity determinations for land disposal prohibitions generally (see further discussion below). Congress expressed a clear policy that available capacity determinations be made on a national basis.[37] Otherwise, one could seek a waiver from a prohibition simply because such treatment was not convenient by the generator's definition.

In addition, it is expected that the evaluation of generator certifications and claims of practicality will be conducted by EPA, and will not be delegated to authorized state programs.

DEEP-WELL INJECTION   As a first step in re-examining the environmental impacts of this technology, Congress requested from EPA a report on the nation's deep-well injection practices and problems by May 8, 1985. While this report has been submitted, it has left many questions unanswered regarding failures and the types of wastes being injected.[38] For example, the survey failed to provide basic data as required by law on the specific types and volumes of wastes being injected during calendar year 1984.

Also within 45 months of enactment the Administrator is required to make a determination regarding the disposal by underground injection of solvents, dioxins, and the wastes on the California list. The Administrator shall issue final regulations prohibiting the disposal of such wastes into such wells "if it may reasonably be determined that such disposal may not be protective of human health and the environment for as long as the waste remains hazardous," taking into account the same criteria used for other methods of land disposal. If the Administrator fails to make a determination by the specified dates, these wastes are prohibited from any deep injection well.

Other listed and characteristic wastes subject to prohibition determinations at 45, 55, and 66 months when injected into deep wells are subject to prohibition on those dates, and are subject to the same sanction mechanism and decision rule and petition procedure that would apply to these scheduled wastes when disposed of by other land disposal methods: "prohibit such wastes except for methods of land disposal which the Administrator determines will be protective of human health and the environment for as long as the waste remains hazardous." Thus the language of the ban provision governing the prohibition of the scheduled wastes that are injected differs slightly from the ". . . reasonably determined . . . may not be protective" language for solvents, dioxins, and California wastes when injected.

While the provisions for various types of injected wastes are stated in slightly different terms, the distinctions are semantic rather than substantive. Both standards are anticipatory and favor protection of human health over continuation of the practice. Both standards presume that land disposal practices, including injection, are not protective of human health. Thus injection, like all other forms of disposal, is banned unless a timely determination is made that it is protective of human health and the environment, including such conditions and prior treatment as may be necessary. In addition, under either decision rule the Administrator must determine that the continued injection of scheduled or other wastes will be protective of human health and the environment for as long as the wastes remain hazardous; a difficult burden under either decision rule. Finally, the provision defines protection of human health to mean demonstrations that wastes would not migrate from the disposal unit *or the injection zone* for as long as the waste remains hazardous, and retains the self-implementing approach (or "hammer") as a backup implementation tool in the event EPA fails to issue timely implementing regulations.

The major difference between the approach to prohibition determinations for injected or other wastes is one of timing rather than substance. A longer evaluation period prior to the imposition of prohibitions was needed due to massive volumes of wastes that are injected and a Congressional desire for EPA to obtain additional data regarding the practice. As Congressman James J. Florio (D-NJ), a principal House sponsor of HSWA, stated during the House debate that the structure of the deep-well injection provision was to give injectors of hazardous waste "an additional 20 months in which to prove that this method is safe with respect to the wastes that would otherwise be banned in 12 months."[39] Thus the burden to provide data and information necessary to demonstrate that the practice is protective falls on those desiring to continue the practice.

In summary, at 45 months, solvents, dioxins, and California wastes are prohibited from further injection if the Administrator determines that such injection may not be protective of human health and the environment for as long as the waste remains hazardous. Also at 45 months, the first third of scheduled wastes are subject to prohibition determinations using the decision rule that applies to the scheduled wastes. Subsequent determinations on scheduled wastes at 55 and 66 months are to be conducted in accordance with the decision rule for scheduled wastes without distinction for land disposal method. EPA will be proposing a separate methodology for determination on deep-well prohibition by fall 1986.

SHALLOW-WELL INJECTION   On May 8, 1985, prohibitions were imposed on so-called shallow-well injection, or injection into Class IV wells. Class IV wells inject wastes above or directly into formations that contain (or are within ¼ mile of) an underground source of drinking water as defined by the Safe Drinking Water Act. This is in contrast to Class I wells, or deep wells, which inject hazardous wastes below such formations.[40] Section 405 of HSWA prohibits the use of Class IV wells unless the injection is part of a groundwater cleanup program. Specifically, the injection must be part of CERCLA 104 or 106 action or part of a corrective action under RCRA (Chapter 11). The contaminated groundwater is treated to substantially reduce hazardous constituents prior to reinjection, and such response action or corrective action will upon completion be sufficient to protect human health and the environment.

CONTAMINATED SOILS   Until November 8, 1988, certain contaminated soils or debris which would otherwise be prohibited from land disposal because they fell within the solvent, dioxin or California waste groupings are not subject to the land disposal restrictions. Specifically, this temporary exemption from the restrictions applies to contaminated soil or debris resulting from cleanup of a site under Superfund response authorities or corrective action authorities under RCRA described in Chapter 11. This exemption was provided to ensure cleanup responses could proceed in an orderly fashion.

Beginning November 8, 1988, these wastes are subject to the land disposal restrictions. In addition, soils contaminated with other listed or characteristic wastes are subject to the restrictions when they become effective.

For the purposes of applying the exemption, it is not clear from the statute whether corrective action under RCRA encompasses merely enforcement of corrective action orders under Sections 3008(h) and 7003, or also involves corrective action taken as part of a post-closure and/or operating permit under 3004(u) or in accordance with an approved closure plan (see Chapters 11 and 13). It would be a strained interpretation, however, for Congress to require the cleanup and closure of most impoundments while allowing the soils from these actions to merely be land disposed. The Senate Report, where this provision originates, refers only to orders under Section 7003 of RCRA.[41]

DUST SUPPRESSION   Effective November 8, 1984, the use of waste or used oil or any other material, including hazardous waste alone, that is contaminated with any listed or identified dioxin waste or any other identified or listed hazardous waste for dust suppression is prohibited unless the waste is hazardous solely on the basis of ignitability. (See Chapter 3 for further discussion.)

Pretreatment and the Petition Process

The statute provides two mechanisms by which a waste can qualify for a permanent exemption from the ban.

The first is the petition process whereby an interested party may attempt to demonstrate to the Administrator, to "a reasonable degree of certainty," that there will be "no migration" of "hazardous constituents" from the disposal unit or injection zone for as long as the wastes remain hazardous. This petition process is available for all wastes otherwise subject to land disposal prohibitions (except for the restrictions on dust suppression, liquids in landfills, Class IV wells, and salt domes) for any or all methods of land disposal.[42]

"Reasonable degree of certainty" is intended to place the burden on the petitioner to consider all predictable events for as long as the waste remains hazardous. For persistent wastes, certain geologic events likely to occur over a long period of time such as floods and earthquakes must be considered when predicting whether wastes will migrate. Unpredictable events, such as acts of war, need not be taken into account.[43] The burden is on the petitioner to meet this certainty standard, therefore information gaps operate against the granting of the petition.

The "no migration" standard is a prediction as to whether the wastes will *remain contained* in the disposal unit for as long as they are hazardous. Significantly, Congress did not allow migration to occur *even if it would not result* in harmful exposures to human health and the environment. Such a "no harm" demonstration would have been easier for a petitioner to make because of the long-term containment problems associated with land disposal. But Congress rejected this approach because of all the difficulties and uncertainties associated with demonstrating harm from a specific waste in a multiple exposure environment over very long periods of time. For example, merely estimating the size and nature of the potentially exposed population at some date several hundred years in the future would be a difficult task yielding highly questionable results. This site-specific exemption was instead intended to grant relief where hazardous wastes lost their "hazardousness" in the disposal unit or where the hydrogeology of the site prevented waste migration. An example of the former would be certain neutralization impoundments, while an example of the latter might be a desert location where the wastes would be photo-degraded.

The term "hazardous constituents" refers to the list of about 375 chemicals contained in Appendix VIII of 40 CFR Part 261 (see Chapter 2). It involves a broader range of releases than the more limited universe of materials identified or listed as hazardous wastes.

The second method of "relief" from the absolute prohibitions involves applying a pretreatment process(es) to a given waste prior to its placement in a land disposal environment so as to minimize migration and both short-term and long-term threats to human health and the environment.[44] The decision to ban a given waste from one or more methods of land disposal is separate from the decision on the nature and level of pretreatment that will be required in order to render the placement of such pretreated waste protective of health and the environment. However, subjecting a waste to the specified level of pretreatment can allow a waste to be land disposed which would have been prohibited in an untreated state. The Administrator is required to issue these pretreatment regulations simultaneous with the promulgation of regulations governing the various prohibition determinations.

Since treatment standards will accompany the prohibition decisions, the efficacy of the treatment required by EPA will ultimately determine the impact of the land disposal restrictions. The statute requires that these treatment processes "substantially diminish the toxicity of the waste" or "substantially reduce the migration of hazardous constituents" so that short-term and long-term threats to human health are "minimized."

While the legislation could not specify the exact types and levels of treatment for each waste, the Senate history of this provision provides considerable guidance on the manner in which this provision is intended to operate.[45] Technology specific and/or general performance tests could be used to establish the necessary level of pretreatment. For example, a technology standard could be established that prescribes the maximum allowable concentrations of constituents in the waste that the treatment process must attain. Alternatively, all hazardous wastes of a certain class, such as solvents, could be prohibited from land disposal, irrespective of pretreatment, and directed to incineration or recycling. The statute prohibits the use of dilution as a method of meeting the pretreatment standards, and directs the Administrator to prescribe such additional standards, waste analysis, testing, recordkeeping, or other requirements as necessary to prevent dilution and ensure compliance with the treatment standards. Where wastes are hazardous solely due to exhibiting a characteristic (e.g., ignitability), mixing the waste with other materials or diluting the waste is allowed as a means of treatment provided such mixing removes or eliminates the hazardous characteristic.

Variances and Extensions

The land disposal prohibitions on dioxins, solvents, the California list, and the Scheduled wastes are effective on the dates contained in the statute or on the dates of regulatory promulgation, as explained above. However, the Administrator may establish an effective data different from that which would otherwise apply to these wastes if he or she determines that adequate alternative treatment, recovery, or disposal capacity that protects human health and the environment will not be available by the dates of the respective prohibitions.[46] The statute assumes that such capacity will be available unless the Administrator makes an affirmative finding to the contrary.

The provision, however, places limitations on the granting of capacity waivers. Nationally applicable capacity waivers established by the Administrator cannot last for more than 2 years after the effective date of the prohibition that would otherwise apply to the wastes affected by such variances. In addition, the Administrator may also grant case-by-case extensions of the effective dates for up to one year, where an applicant demonstrates that there is a binding contractual commitment to construct or otherwise provide such alternative capacity but due to circumstances beyond the control of such applicant, the necessary alternative capacity cannot reasonably be made available by the effective date(s) of the prohibitions. An individual facility extension may be granted only after opportunity for public notice and comment, consultation with appropriate State agencies, and publication of such findings. Such case-by-case extensions are renewable once for no more than one additional year, thereby resulting in a maximum extension of 2 years generally and 2 additional years on a case-by-case basis.

Where a general variance or case-by-case extension is granted during the period in which the variance or extension is in effect, the affected hazardous wastes may be disposed of in a landfill or surface impoundment only if such facilities meet the minimum technology requirements for new facilities (Chapter 10).

"Alternative capacity" must be for treatment or recovery, including legitimate use, re-use, and recycling, or disposal into facilities that meet the minimum technology requirements. Disposal is included in the alternative capacity determinations because such capacity will be needed for ultimate disposition of several treated wastes such as metal-bearing sludges.

"Adequate" capacity refers to the national availability of treatment, recycling, and disposal capacity that is protective of human health and the environment.

In making decisions on the availability of adequate alternative storage capacity, storage either in or on the land or in tanks and containers cannot be considered by the Administrator for the purpose of determining whether adequate alternative capacity exists.[47] The regulated community may store a restricted waste, however, but solely for the purpose of accumulating volumes necessary for conducting efficient treatment, recovery, or disposal.

Claims of inadequate capacity merit careful scrutiny. As the Senate Report notes, "Claims of inadequate capacity can become a self-fulfilling prophecy if the regulated community believes that land disposal deadlines will normally be extended and that immediate investment in development of alternative capacity will be premature and economically non-productive."[48]

Of particular significance is the fact that there are no cost considerations, either general or facility specific, involved in the variances or extensions from the land disposal determinations. A limited "severe economic hardship" variance was included in the House bill,[49] but was rejected by the Conferees.

Surface Impoundments

The 1984 Amendments take particular aim at unlined and leaking surface impoundments by requiring that in general such facilities must either be retrofitted with dual-liner systems and come into line with other minimum technology requirements within 4 years of enactment, November 8, 1988, or closed. (These provisions, which were sponsored by Congressmen John Breaux (D-LA) and Edwin B. Forsythe (R-NJ), are discussed in detail in Chapters 10 and 11 dealing with minimum technology requirements, and cleanup and monitoring, respectively.)

Owners and/or operators of such facilities, however, must be aware of the fact that the land disposal restrictions for dioxins, solvents, the California list, and the first third of the Scheduled wastes apply to these facilities on the specified dates of these restrictions, well in advance of the 48 months allowed for retrofitting.

Thus, even if an owner/operator fully intends to retrofit or close a unit within 4 years, it may not manage restricted wastes in those units beginning with the effective date of the prohibitions that apply to surface impoundments generally, unless it meets the minimum technology standard at the time of the prohibition and the impoundment is used solely for treatment, not disposal or storage (assuming no variance is granted). Given the breadth of wastes included on the California list, as a practical matter decisions on retrofitting such surface impoundments and utilizing alternative technologies, tank systems, or dual-lined impoundments may need to be made well in advance of the 4-year deadline for retrofitting. In addition, HSWA requires that impoundments used for the treatment of wastes otherwise prohibited from land disposal must meet minimum design standards (unless they qualify for a waiver) when the prohibitions become effective. Significantly, treatment impoundments handling restricted wastes are eligible for fewer waivers from the minimum design standards than other impoundments that handle non-restricted wastes (see also Chapter 10). In other words, an impoundment qualifying for a waiver from the general retrofit requirements may not continue to qualify for a waiver when the wastes it receives are otherwise prohibited from land disposal.

In several ways, therefore, the land disposal prohibitions significantly impact the use and design of surface impoundments to be employed prior to November 1988. Surface impoundments may be used for the treatment of prohibited wastes provided that: the impoundment meets the minimum technology requirements by effective date of the applicable prohibitions (or qualifies for one of the exclusions—Chapter 10); and hazardous treatment residues are removed for subsequent management within one year of the entry of the waste into the impoundment. Storage-only impoundments for restricted wastes are prohibited.[50]

Salt Domes

Irrespective of the waste-specific prohibitions determinations, an immediate prohibition effective on November 8, 1984, is imposed on the placement of any bulk of non-containerized hazardous waste in any salt dome, salt bed formation, underground mine, or cave until such time as: the Administrator has determined that such placement is protective of human health and the environment; the Administrator has promulgated performance and permitting standards under Subtitle C; and a final permit has been issued to the facility under Section 3005(c). The process of approving such placement also requires public hearings in the affected area. In addition, neither interim permits nor interim status can be granted to such facilities.

Containerized liquid and bulk solid form hazardous wastes are also prohibited from salt dome placement effective on November 8, 1984, until such time as the final permit has been issued under 3005(c) of RCRA.

A specific exemption is provided for the Department of Energy's Waste Isolation Project in New Mexico. The inclusion of this exemption acknowledges that the provisions of RCRA, including the land disposal restrictions, apply to Department of Energy facilities managing RCRA listed or identified wastes unless specifically exempted by statute.

Rolling Deadlines

In recognition of the fact that many new wastes will be added to the lists of RCRA listed and identified hazardous wastes (Chapters 2 and 3) and that many new facilities will be subject to the retrofitting requirements, a series of rolling deadlines have been added to ensure that these newly affected facilities are subject to the land disposal restrictions.

For these hazardous wastes identified or listed under section 3001 after November 8, 1984, the Administrator is required to determine whether such waste shall be prohibited from one or more methods of land disposal in accordance with the decision rule and procedures applicable to Scheduled wastes within 6 months after the date of such identification or listing.[51] (The impact of new listings on the retrofitting of surface impoundments is discussed in Chapter 10.)

EPA'S PROPOSED LAND DISPOSAL BAN

On January 14, 1986, EPA issued a proposed rulemaking to implement the Congressionally mandated land disposal prohibitions of HSWA.[52] The ban proposes a framework to establish: treatment standards for hazardous waste; procedures by which EPA will evaluate site-specific petitions for acceptability of land disposal; nationwide variances from statutory effective dates based on capacity findings; extensions of effective dates on a case-by-case basis. In addition, the Agency proposed treatment standards and an effective date for the first class of hazardous waste to be evaluated under this framework: certain dioxin-containing hazardous wastes and solvent-containing hazardous wastes. This proposal is particularly important since it establishes a framework under which the land disposal prohibitions of all hazardous wastes will be evaluated in accordance with the scheduled discussed above, other than those that are disposed of by deep-well injection.

While the Agency has many issues to deal with when establishing a decision framework for the land disposal prohibitions, there are three primary responsibilities that the Agency must fulfill under the statutory scheme. First is to issue treatment standards ensuring that long-term and short-term threats to human health and the environment from continued land disposal of restricted wastes are minimized (RCRA 3004(m)). Second is to evaluate site-specific petitions for those who believe they can successfully demonstrate the continued land disposal of a specific hazardous waste as protective of human health and the environment for as long as the waste remains hazardous (RCRA 3004(d)(1)). Third, the Agency is responsible for establishing variances and extensions from the statutory effective date based upon determinations of "available treatment capacity."

Treatment Standards

Treatment standards govern the quality of wastes or treatment residuals that are placed in a land disposal unit, such as a maximum acceptable concentration level for individual chemical constituents in the waste leachate, or in the wastes themselves. Recall that the standard governing the pre-treatment process requires it to "substantially diminish toxicity (and) substantially reduce migration," as opposed to the "no migration" standard of the petition process. Essentially, EPA had three approaches from which to choose in developing a treatment standard for dioxin and solvent wastes.

1. Health-based thresholds that project an acceptable level of human exposure using an environmental fate and transport model which relies on the behavior of waste in a state-of-the-art hazardous waste land disposal environment.

2. Performance-oriented technology standards using treatment levels based on the efficiencies and performance of "best demonstrated achievable treatment" (BDAT). (For example, all solvent-containing wastes must be treated to the level achieved by incineration, reclamation, or other technologies that yield equal or better levels of treatment.)

3. Technology-specific standards that require the use of specific technologies for various wastes (i.e., solvents must be treated only by incineration or reclamation).

The agency used a combination of the health-based threshold approach and the performance characteristics of BDAT technologies in the development of numeric treatment standards and levels for solvents and dioxins. The Agency has not stipulated that certain wastes must be managed by specific technologies. The proposal notes that the Agency will be devloping these technology-specific treatment standards at a later date, with the listed dioxin wastes as the most likely candidates.

Effective November 8, 1986, the wastes listed in Table 9-5 are prohibited from land disposal (except in an underground injection well, and except for solvent contaminated soils) unless the wastes are treated to meet specified extraction levels or the waste is subject to a successful petition or an extension has been granted on the basis of available capacity.[53] The prohibitions only affect the following listed solvent-containing wastes *containing greater than 1% by weight* total organic constituents.

At the same time, EPA has delayed the effective date for the land disposal prohibitions for all wastes contained in Table 9-5 from November 8, 1986, to November 8, 1988, based upon a lack of available capacity for all solvent containing wastes in Table 9-5 as well as the listed dioxin wastes (F020-F023, F026, F027) *where they contain less than 1% by weight total organic constituent.* In effect, listed dioxins are not subject to the prohibition until November 8, 1988, and any solvent and dioxin waste present in a mixture of less than 1% total organic constituent is not subject to prohibition until November 8, 1988.[54]

For any of the wastes in Table 9-5, including the listed dioxin wastes, the concentration of hazardous constituent(s) in the waste extract after subjecting the treated material to the specified extraction procedure must not equal or exceed the value given for any hazardous constituent listed in Table 9-7. In addition, if none of the concentrations of hazardous constituent in the waste extract equal or exceed the specified concentrations, the waste may be land disposed without further treatment. If the concentration of any hazardous constituent in the waste extract equals or exceeds the level for that constituent, the waste must undergo treatment to bring the level below the applicable concentration level before being land disposed, or be treated by an alternative method. Dilution to meet the treatment level is explicitly prohibited.

The Agency has also deferred on the development of treatment standards expressed as direct waste concentrations as opposed to constituent concentrations in the waste extract.

The Agency surveyed the universe of technologies for their capability to treat solvent and dioxin wastes. Treatment technologies that could not achieve the standard of "substantial reductions in toxicity or mobility" as specified by RCRA pretreatment provision 3004(m) were not considered to be available technologies.

Included in the technology survey were steam stripping, carbon absorption, biological treatment, a combination of the preceeding three, and fuel substitution and incineration. The results of the performances achieved by these technologies are summarized in the middle column of Table 9-6. In virtually every case the best demonstrated available treatment level was less than a tenth of a part per million.

In addition to developing a technology-based standard, the Agency has also developed a series of health-based thresholds. These thresholds have been developed for individual hazardous constituents and identify the maximum concentration at which such constituents will be protective of human health and the environment when land disposed. These health-based thresholds are developed using procedures that commence with a "safe" dose at a point of potential exposure and back calculate using fate and transport equations for each medium to derive maximum acceptable concentrations of individual constituents in releases from hazardous waste.

Table 9-5

(b) Prohibited are the following solvent containing wastes containing greater that 1 percent (by weight) total organic constituents, except for solvent contaminated soils:

F001—The following spent halogenated solvents used in degreasing: tetrachloroethylene, trichloroethylene, methylene chloride, 1,1,1-trichloroethane, carbon tetrachloride, and chlorinated fluorocarbons; all spent solvent mixtures/blends used in degreasing containing, before use, a total of 10 percent or more (by volume) of one or more of the above halogenated solvents or those solvents listed in F002, F004, and F005; and still bottoms from the recovery of these spent solvents and spent solvent mixtures.

F002—The following spent halogenated solvents: tetrachloroethylene, methylene chloride, trichloroethylene, 1,1,1-trichloroethane, chlorobenzene, 1,1,2-trichloro-1,2,2-trifluoroethane, ortho-dichlorobenzene, and trichlorofluoromethane; all spent solvent mixtures/blends containing, before use, a total of 10 percent or more (by volume) of one or more of the above halogenated solvents or those solvents listed in F001, F004, and F005; and still bottoms from the recovery of these spent solvents and spent solvent mixtures.

F003—The following spent non-halogenated solvents: xylene, acetone, ethyl acetate, ethyl benzene, ethyl ether, methyl isobutyl ketone, n-butyl alcohol, cyclohexanone, and methanol; all spent solvent mixtures/blends containing, solely the above spent non-halogenated solvents; and all spent solvent mixtures/blends containing, before use, one or more of the above non-halogenated solvents, and a total of 10 percent or more (by volume) of one or more of those solvents listed in F001, F002, F004, and F005; and still bottoms

from the recovery of these spent solvents and spent solvent mixtures.

F004—The following spent non-halogenated solvents: cresols and cresylic acid and nitrobenzene; all spent solvent mixtures/blends containing, before use, a total of 10 percent or more (by volume) of one or more of the above non-halogenated solvents or those solvents listed in F001, F002, and F005; and still bottoms from the recovery of these spent solvents and spent solvent mixtures.

F005—The following spent non-halogenated solvents: toluene, methyl ethyl ketone, carbon disulfide, isobutanol, and pyridine; all spent solvent mixtures/blends containing, before use, a total of 10 percent or more (by volume) of one or more of the above non-halogenated solvents or those solvents listed in F001, F002, and F004; and still bottoms from the recovery of these spent solvents and solvent mixtures.

P022—Carbon disulfide
U002—Acetone
U031—n-Butyl alochol
U037—Chlorobenzene
U052—Cresols and cresylic acid
U057—Cyclohexanone
U070—o-Dichlorobenzene
U080—Methylene chloride
U112—Ethyl acetate
U117—Ethyl ether
U121—Trichlorofluoromethane
U140—Isobutanol
U154—Methanol
U159—Methyl ethyl ketone
U161—Methyl isobutyl ketone
U169—Nitrobenzene
U196—Pyridine
U210—Tetrachloroethylene
U211—Carbon tetrachloride
U220—Toluene
U226—1,1,1-Trichloroethane
U228—Trichloroethylene
U239—Xylene

Table 9-6

Constituent	Screening/ Liner protection threshold	Technology-based level	Treatment standard
Acetone	2.0	[1] <0.050	2.0
n-Butyl alcohol	2.0	[1] <0.100	2.0
Carbon disulfide	2.0	[1] <0.010	2.0
Carbon tetrachloride	0.1	<0.010	0.1
Chlorobenzene	2.0	<0.062	2.0
Cresols	2.0	[1] <0.100	2.0
Cyclohexanone	2.0	[1] <0.100	2.0
1,2- Dichlorobenzene	2.0	0.053	2.0
Ethyl acetate	2.0	[1] <0.100	2.0
Ethylbenzene	2.0	<0.010	2.0
Ethyl ether	2.0	[1] <0.100	2.0
Isobutanol	2.0	[1] <0.050	2.0
Methanol	2.0	[1] <0.100	2.0
Methylene chloride	1.2	<0.011	1.2
Methyl ethyl ketone	2.0	[1] <0.050	2.0
Methyl isobutyl ketone	2.0	[1] <0.100	2.0
Nitrobenzene	0.09	<0.010	0.09
Pyridine	0.7	[1] <0.500	0.7
Tetrachloroethylene	0.015	<0.010	0.015
Toluene	2.0	0.016	2.0
1,1,1- Trichloroethane	2.0	0.457	2.0
1,1,2-Trichloro-1,2,2-trifluoroethane	2.0	[1] 0.457	2.0
Trichloroethylene	0.1	<0.019	0.1
Trichlorofluoromethane	2.0	[1] 0.457	2.0
Xylene	2.0	<0.005	2.0

[1] Estimated value.

Table 9-7

Hazardous constituent	Concentration (in mg/l)
Acetone	2.0
n-Butyl alcohol	2.0
Carbon disulfide	2.0
Carbon tetrachloride	0.1
Chlorobenzene	2.0
Cresols	2.0
Cyclohexanone	2.0
Ethyl acetate	2.0
Ethyl benzene	2.0
Ethyl ether	2.0
HxCDD—All Hexachlorodibenzo-p-dioxins	.001 (1ppb)
HxCDF—All Hexachlorodibenzofurans	.001 (1ppb)
Isobutanol	2.0
Methanol	2.0
Methylene chloride	1.2
Methyl ethyl ketone	2.0
Methyl isobutyl ketone	2.0
Nitrobenzene	0.09
PeCDD—All Pentachlorodibenzo-p-dioxins	.001 (1ppb)
PeCDF—All Pentachlorodibenzofurans	.001 (1ppb)
Pentachlorophenol	1.0
Pyridine	0.7
TCDD—All Tetrachlorodibenzo-p-dioxins	.001 (1ppb)
TCDF—All Tetrachlorodibenzofurans	.001 (1ppb)
Tetrachloroethylene	0.015
2,3,4,6 Tetrachlorophenol	2.0
Toluene	2.0
1,1,1-Trichloroethane	2.0
1,2,2-Trichloro- 1,2,2-tyrifluoroethane	2.0
Trichloroethylene	0.1
Trichlorofluoromethane	2.0
2,4,5 Trichlorophenol	8.0
2,4,6 Trichlorophenol	0.04
Xylene	2.0

Using the test methods described in SW–846 or equivalent methods approved by the Administrator under the procedures set forth in §§ 260.20 and 260.21 of this chapter, the extract from a representative sample of a waste identified in Subpart C of this part, or from the residue of treatment of such a waste, must not contain any of the constituents listed in Table CCWE at a concentration greater than the respective value given in that table. Where the waste contains less than 0.5 percent filterable solids, the waste itself, after filtering, is considered to be the extract for the purposes of this section.

These levels are expressed by constituent concentrations in the waste extract (Table 9-7). As one can see from examining Table 9-7, it is these levels (based upon the environmental model) that have been established as *the* treatment standard (Table 9-6, third column). These treatment standard levels are in every case higher than the technology based treatment levels and frequently by two and three orders of magnitude. For example, in Table 9-6 one can see that for cresoles the technology-based level yielded by the use of BDAT was less than a tenth of a part per million. However, the treatment standard established by health-based thresholds is two parts per million.

An additional component of the health-based thresholds is the use of a "liner protection threshold." This was done because the back-calculation model used to establish the health-based threshold does not explicitly address the fact that solvents can mobilize other constituents and have adverse effects on liners. To complicate matters further, the health-based thresholds have accounted for these effects through the use of an overriding "liner protection threshold." This level is based on the application of a one hundred-fold safety factor on the levels known to adversely effect liners. Thus, thresholds are established for solvents based on the more stringent of either the health-based or "liner protection threshold." The modeling of "health-based" thresholds frequently allowed the land disposal of wastes that actually attacked synthetic liner systems.

These screening levels are supposed to serve three major functions. First, the screening or concentration level will be used to override the technology-based standard, where more stringent treatment levels would be required by the technology standard. In some cases, according to EPA, available technologies may be capable of achieving greater reductions in toxicity and/or constituent mobility than are actual necessary to provide protection of human health and the environment in subsequent land disposal of hazardous waste (as is the case with both dioxins and solvents). Second, in some cases the reverse may occur. The application of BDAT or technology-based treatment levels may not be able to achieve concentrations low enough to fully protect human health and the environment. Thus, the screening levels truly serve as the ceiling or maximum constituent concentration which cannot be exceeded in a waste to deem it acceptable for subsequent land disposal.

Third, in the event that EPA concludes that no candidate treatment technologies provide the "substantial" reductions in toxicity and mobility as required by the statute's pretreatment provisions, the Agency would determine that there are no treatment technologies available upon which to base the treatment standards.

The relationship of the technology-based standards and the health-based screening-level approaches to meeting the pretreatment requirements of HSWA can be summarized as follows. If application of BDAT treatment (technology-based treatment standards) results in concentration levels equal to or more stringent than the screening levels, then the Agency will issue the screening level as the treatment standards capping off required BDAT treatment at these protective levels. If application of BDAT treatment results in levels that are less stringent than the screening level but BDAT does realize substantial reductions in toxicity and mobility and does not pose greater risk than land disposal, then the technology-based level becomes the treatment standard and the screening level remains as the goal that may be reached as new technology emerges. If no technology exists that results in substantial reductions in toxicity and mobility or all treatment technologies pose greater risk than land disposal, then EPA will not be able to specify a technology-based level and the screening level becomes the treatment level. Wastes that naturally meet the treatment levels without having to actually undergo treatment would be exempt from the ban under the proposed EPA methodology.

In establishing the screening levels for pre-treated wastes, the Agency has adapted the statutory standard for the petition process—"no migration" to pre-treated wastes:

a method of land disposal may not be determined to be protective of human health and the environment for hazardous waste unless upon application by an interested person it has been demonstrated to the Administrator to a reasonable degree of certainty that there will be no migration of hazardous constituents from the disposal unit or injection zone for as long as the wastes remain hazardous.

However, in promulgating the standard, the EPA is not reading the statutory definition of "protective" as an absolute, no-migration standard. The quantitative procedures that have been developed to calculate the screening levels involve the use of constituent fate and transportation models through air, groundwater, and surface water. The models are designed to assess the process of constituent migration (e.g., advection, diffusion, dilution, dispersion, chemical transformation, or degradation that occur during transportation) from their point of release to points of potential human exposure downstream from the disposal unit. Models are employed to back-calculate the maximum concentration that could be present in a hazardous waste extract directly above, below, or adjacent to a land disposal unit, from a point of potential human exposure that is not expected to exceed a human health risk level for the contaminants.

The Petition Process

The second major method by which a firm or a generator can qualify their waste as "acceptable for land disposal" or "protective of land disposal" is through the site-specific petition process, using the statutory standard discussed above. This demonstration is made in the form of petition to the EPA Regional Administrator or authorized state program director. The petition may be submitted by any interested person, including generators of hazardous waste, to the Agency any time prior to the effective date of the ban or at any time after the ban becomes effective.

The statutory requirement for an application is intended to place the burden on the applicant to demonstrate to a reasonable degree of certainty there will be "no migration of hazardous constituents from the land disposal units or injection zone for as long as the waste remains hazardous." EPA has interpreted this to mean that the nature of the facility and the waste must assure that hazardous constituents do not migrate in harmful quantities, as with the screening process above. The Agency has developed a protocol with a tiered approach to the risk assessment process required in petition demonstrations.

Several critical issues are involved in the Agency implementation of the petition process. These include the protocol to be used in evaluating petitions; the "no migration" performance standard; the meaning of "reasonable degree of certainty"; evaluations of the period over which migration is measured; the role of artificial barriers in making the no-migration determination; the role of environmental effects; the significance of "hazardous constituents" rather than hazardous waste; and the meaning of the terms disposal unit and injection zone.

The components of the demonstration include several ill-defined components governing: waste analysis, human and environmental exposure risk assessment, and site characterization. In establishing levels of acceptable risk to human health and lifetime risk to human health in the petition process, the Agency is proposing a range of risks from 1 in 10,000 to a 1 in 10,000,000 chance of developing cancer, depending upon the number of people at risk; the lower the number at risk, the higher the acceptable exposure. In the petition process, the Agency is also seeking to consider the design operation and maintenance and expected performance of engineered systems with the disposal units in making such demonstrations.

Treatment Standards and Effective Dates for Dioxins and Solvents

The EPA is proposing to establish a threshold concentration of 2 parts per million for various "F," "U," and "P" series solvent-containing wastes as the maximum allowable concentrations of these levels for land disposal environments.

The effective date of these prohibitions for solvent wastes is November 8, 1986, for all but three categories of solvent wastes. The proposal would grant a 2-year national variance to: solvent water mixtures containing less than one percent of total organic constituents; inorganic sludges and solids containing less than one percent total organic constituents; and solvent-contaminated soils.

The screening levels for dioxin are essentially a no-detection limit. The technology standard for treating dioxin wastes is the 99.9999% DRE. A 2-year extension is granted dioxin wastes on the basis of the lack of available capacity. In making this determination, the Agency admits that it has only surveyed existing unused commercial capacity.The Agency is in the process of conducting a survey of both on-site and off-site TSDFs regarding present and future treatment plans.

Problems with the Proposed Approach

On balance, the EPA-proposed land disposal ban approach for certain solvents and dioxin wastes raises numerous serious problems regarding protection of public health, existing capacity for alternative treatment, and adherence to statutory requirements. These problems include: establishing unprotective health-based or screening levels where technology is capable of delivering more protective levels of treatment; the inappropriate use of a national model which does not accurately reflect anticipated environment conditions and migration potential, making decisions despite a lack of toxicity data, unprotective and liberal assumptions in the model used to develop the screening standards including the 1 in 10,000 risk level and acceptance of significant migration distances to allow for attenuation of wastes during the back calculation; the use of a "no harm" standard in the petition process rather than a no-migration standard; and the delays in the effective dates for aqueous solvent wastes despite an absence of data confirming a capacity shortfall.

The Agency raises several additional concerns by allowing wastes with less than 1 % solvent concentration to be land disposed. There is no technical or capacity basis for allowing what amounts to 90% of all solvent wastes (i.e., dilute wastewaters) to be exempted from the ban. While "dilution" is prohibited as a means of treatment, very few guidelines are specified to limit its use. Additional opportunities to evade the ban are anticipated due to the absence of a requirement on generators to specify all reasons that a waste may be hazardous on the manifest using EPA waste identification codes. Furthermore, contrary to legislative intent, the Agency engaged in the use of comparative risk assessment to determine whether wastes should be prohibited from land disposal.

The issues, when examined in conjunction with the stated desire to "cap off" excess treatment" with health-based standards, gives one pause. It appears that the primary concern was to ensure that generators and disposers would not have to undertake the slightest bit of additional treatment based on the health-based thresholds, rather than to ensure that the best, most protective treatment was used wherever possible.

Of particular significance is the EPA's use of the petition process. The Agency's definition of "no migration" is essentially, "no migration that will harm human health and the environment," as opposed to no migration of any constituent. This appears to be at direct variance with

234/Hazardous Waste Regulation: The New Era

the statutory requirements. Otherwise there would be little purpose in having two separate statutory decision mechanisms (the "substantially minimize" standard for pre-treatment, and the "no migration" standard for petitioners). The no-migration standard was intended to be a distinctly more difficult burden. It is anticipated that several of these issues will be debated during the comment period and are likely to be changed before the issuance of a final rule by late Fall, 1986.

NOTES

1. K. Stoddard, G. Davis, H. Freeman, "Alternatives to the Land Disposal of Hazardous Wastes," prepared by the Toxic Waste Assessment Group, Governor's Office of Appropriate Technology, Edmund G. Brown, Jr., 1981.

2. RCRA, Section 3004(d) (2).

3. "Management of Hazardous Industrial Wastes," Report of the Committee on Disposal of Hazardous Industrial Wastes, National Materials Advisory Board, National Research Council, National Academy Press (Publication NMAB-398), p. iii, Washington, D.C., 1983.

4. "Technologies and Management Strategies for Hazardous Waste Control," U.S. Congress, Office of Technology Assessment, pp. 8–17, Washington, D.C., March 1983.

5. Testimony of Peter Montague, Subcommittee on Commerce Transportation and Tourism, House Committee on Energy and Commerce, Hearings on RCRA Reauthorization, March 31, 1982, Serial No. 97-169, p. 59. Also see EPA's concurrence with this finding as reflected in early drafts of the land disposal regulations, 46 Fed. Reg. 11128 (February 5, 1981).

6. Case of Village of Wilsonville, Ill. v. SCA Inc. 16 ERC 1105. Testimony of George Kush, Vice-President for Environmental Affairs, SCA Chemical Services, before Subcommittee on Commerce Transportation and Tourism, House Committee on Energy and Commerce, Hearings on the Hazardous Waste Control and Enforcement Act of 1983, March 22, 1983, Serial No. 98-32, p. 130. Also see testimony of Leslie F. Nute, Director, Legislative and Regulatory Affairs, Dow Chemical Co., pp. 597–8.

7. "Surface Impoundment Assessment National Report," Office of Drinking Water, U.S. EPA (EPA 570/9-84-002), pp. 114–16, Washington, D.C., December 1983.

8. "Toxic Ponds: Antiquated Methods and Unacceptable Dangers," Assembly Office of Research, California State Assembly, prepared for the Speaker and Members of the Assembly, pp. 5–16, April 1984.

   Also see "Hazardous Waste Surface Impoundments: the Nation's Most Serious and Neglected Threat to Groundwater," a summary of major studies and evaluations prepared by Citizens for a Better Environment (Sacramento, Cal.), and the Natural Resources Defense Council (New York, N.Y.), pp. i–iii, September 15, 1983.

9. "National Survey of Hazardous Waste Generators and TSDFs Regulated Under RCRA in 1981," U.S. EPA, Office of Solid Waste (Contract No. 68-01-6861), performed under contract by Westat, Inc., Rockville, Md., April 1984. Frequently referred to as the "Westat Report."

10. U.S. Department of the Interior, Geological Survey, Water Resources Division, communication regarding the Presque Isle, Penn., injection site from David E. Click to Clifford L. Jones, Secretary, Pennsylvania Dept. of Environmental Resources,

March 17, 1980. Also see memorandum from Edward Shoener, Project Officer, Superfund/RCRA Compliance Section to Thomas C. Voltaggio, Chief, Compliance Branch, U.S. EPA Region III Office, May 4, 1982.

"Summary of Known Failures or Enforcement Actions at Class I Injection Wells," Hazardous Waste Treatment Council (Washington, D.C.) Freedom of Information Act Request, U.S. EPA Office of Drinking Water, January 1983.

"Deep Well Injection of Hazardous Waste," prepared for the Hazardous Waste Treatment Council (Washington, D.C.) by David C. Anderson, K.W. Brown and Associates, Inc., College Station, Tex., September 1984.

"Use of Injection Wells for Hazardous Waste Disposal," Staff Memorandum Prepared by the Office of Technology Assessment, July 13, 1983.

"An Assessment of Class I Hazardous Waste Injection Wells," prepared by Professor Patrick J. Sullivan, Ball State University, in conjunction with the AAAS/EPA Environmental Science and Engineering Fellows Program, 1983.

"What Goes Down the Deep Well," editorial, *Chemical Week*, p. 3, October 14, 1981.

"Environmental Assessment of Commercial Class I and Class II Sites of the State of Louisiana's Underground Injection Control Program," Final Report, prepared for Office of Conservation, DNR, State of Louisiana, by Mr. E.J. Senat, Institute for Environmental Studies, Louisiana State University, Baton Rouge, La.

"Pollution of the St. Clair River (Sarnia Area)," A Situation Report Prepared by Environment Canada and the Ontario Ministry of Environment (under the auspices of Canada-Ontario Agreement respecting Great Lakes water quality), November 18, 1985. Also see " 'St. Clair Situation Awesome,' Minister Says," *Globe and Mail*, November 20, 1985.

11. "Waste Management to Settle Charges Over Disposal Site," *Wall Street Journal*, May 3, 1984; "Waste Concern to Pay Ohio $10 Million in Fines," *New York Times*, May 3, 1984.

12. Statement of Con. Dennis E. Eckart, *Business Week*, July 4, 1983, p. 36. R. Fortuna, "Same Wastes, New Solutions," in *Beyond Dumping*, Greenwood Press, Hartfold, Conn., 1983. Also see testimony of Nelson Mossholder on behalf of Hazardous Waste Treatment Council, Senate Environment and Public Works Committee, June 8, 1983, S. Hrg. 98-342, p. 39.

13. D. Lennett and L. Greer, "State Regulation of Hazardous Waste," *Ecology Law Quarterly*, Vol. 12, No. 2, p. 183, 1985.

14. Letter from Ann M. Gorsuch to Congressman John J. LaFalce, July 28, 1981.

15. Testimony of Rita LaVelle, Assistant Administrator for Solid Waste and Emergency Response, before the House Committee on Science and Technology, Subcommittee on Natural Resources, Agriculture Research, and Environment, December 16, 1982.

16. RCRA, Section 1002(b); 1003(a), (b). P.L. 98-616, Section 101. Conference Report 98-1133, pp. 4–5, 80. Senate Report 98-284, p. 65

17. RCRA, Section 3004(c) (1). P.L. 98-616, Section 201(a). Conference Report 98-1133, pp. 7, 83–4. Senate Report 98-284, pp. 22–3. 40 CFR 264.314 (final permitted facilities). 40 CFR 265.314 (interim status facilities).

18. 50 *Fed. Reg.* 18370 (April 30, 1985), final rule regarding the use of Paint Filter Test, "Update II to SW-846," GPO Document Number 055-002-81001-2.

19. "Statutory Interpretive Guidance—Treatment for Bulk Hazardous Liquids," U.S. EPA Office of Solid Waste, from John Skinner, May 9, 1985, pp. 3–4.

20. See supra note 17. 50 *Fed. Reg.* 28704-5 (July 15, 1985) (Codification Rule). Senate Report 98-284, pp. 22–3. Also see "Guide to the Disposal of Chemically Stabilized and Solidified Wastes," GPO Document No. 055-000-00226-6.

21. 50 *Fed. Reg.* 28704-5 (July 15, 1985) (Codification Rule).

22. RCRA, Section 3004(c) (2). P.L. 98-616, Section 201(a). Conference Report 98-1133, pp. 7, 83–4.
23. RCRA, Section 3004(c) (3). P.L. 98-616, Section 201(a). Conference Report 98-1133, pp. 7, 83–4. 50 *Fed. Reg.* 28705 (July 15, 1985) (Codification Rule).
24. RCRA, Section 3004(k). P.L. 98-616, Section 201(k).
25. RCRA, Section 3004(j).
26. RCRA, Section 3004(d) (1). Conference Report 98-1133, pp. 6–8, 83–4.
27. House Report 98-198 Part 1, p. 32.
28. *Ibid.*, p. 33.
29. 40 CFR 264.272(a).
30. RCRA, Section 3004(g) (1)–(4).
31. 50 *Fed. Reg.* 23250 (May 31, 1985).
32. "Documentation for the Development of Toxicity and Volume Scores, for the Purposes of Scheduling Hazardous Wastes," U.S. EPA, Docket Clerk Office of Solid Waste, 202-382-300, 800-424-9346.
33. RCRA, Section 3004(e).
34. RCRA, Section 3004(d) (2).
35. RCRA, Section 3004(g) (5)–(6).
36. *Ibid.*
37. Record of deliberations of House and Senate Conferees on H.R. 2867. Also see Senate Report 98-284, p. 19.
38. P.L. 98-616, Section 701. Conference Report 98-1133, pp. 72–3. "Report to Congress on Injection of Hazardous Waste," U.S. EPA Office of Drinking Water (EPA 570/9-85-003), May 1985. Letter to Victor Kimm from Natural Resources Defense Council, Hazardous Waste Treatment Council, Legal Environmental Assistance Foundation, Underground Injection Coalition, National Wildlife Federation, and Environmental Policy Institute, May 14, 1985.
39. RCRA, Section 3004(d)(e)(f)(g)(m). Congressional Record, H8135, Oct. 6, 1983.
40. RCRA, Section 7010.
41. Senate Report 98-284, p. 21.
42. RCRA, Section 3004(d) (1), (e) (1), (g) (5).
43. Senate Report 98-284, p. 15.
44. RCRA, Section 3004(m).
45. Senate Report 98-284, pp. 16–17.
46. RCRA, Section 3004(h).
47. See note 42.
48. *Ibid.*
49. House Report, 98-198 Part 1, p. 37. The "hardship" waiver only affected the timing of the prohibitions, not the prohibitions themselves.
50. RCRA, Section 3004(g) (4). RCRA 3005(j) (11) (Storage and Treatment Impoundments); RCRA-3004(j) (Definition of storage of prohibited wastes).
51. P.L. 98-616, Section 215.
52. 51 *Fed. Reg.* 1602 (Jan. 14, 1986).
53. *Ibid.* See proposed 40 CFR 268.30.
54. *Ibid.* See proposed 40 CFR 268.31

CHAPTER TEN

Minimum Technology Requirements

EPA'S PRE-HSWA REQUIREMENTS

The July 26, 1982, land disposal permitting standards, particularly as they applied to landfills, surface impoundments, and waste piles, were based in large part on a "liquids management strategy." This strategy represented EPA's "first line of defense" and consisted of regulations intended to reduce the formation of leachate in the units, and to remove waste leachate from the disposal unit before it reached the groundwater.[1] If this first line of defense failed, a groundwater monitoring and cleanup program would serve as a backup to the liquids management strategy (see Chapter 11). EPA had considered relying solely upon the monitoring and cleanup requirements to protect groundwater resources underlying land disposal units. However, EPA believed attempts to minimize groundwater contamination by controlling the source of contamination was "sound public policy" because the technologies for detecting and remedying groundwater contamination were "subject to error," and remedying groundwater contamination was much more expensive, time-consuming, and difficult to perform than the minimization of leakage from the unit.[2]

Unfortunately, the permitting standards as issued were not consistent with this rationale. The design standards EPA issued were substantially weaker than state-of-the-art containment designs.

EPA's permitting standards for new landfills, surface impoundments, and waste piles required the installation of only one liner. A second liner that would contain any leakage through the first liner before it entered the groundwater was not required. In addition, for new surface impoundments, no leachate collection and removal system was required. Such systems enhance liner performance by removing the leachate and thus protecting the liner from the physical and chemical degradation effects associated with prolonged exposure to leachate. EPA had previously considered leachate collection and removal systems important components of bulk liquid waste containment systems in landfills. Since surface impoundments handle only bulk liquids, and can thus be considered "worst case" landfills, the absence of a leachate collection and removal system requirement for impoundments contrasted sharply with EPA's policy justifications for requiring a similar system at landfills handling bulk liquids.[3]

Existing units which had received hazardous waste did not need to be lined at all to obtain a permit, thus requiring no barrier at all between the waste and groundwater. The exemption for existing units applied regardless of the feasibility of retrofitting the unit or the environmental threat posed by the unit. EPA's dual justification for this "existing portion exemption" was that many facilities lacked the temporary storage space necessary for retrofitting land disposal units, and that there werê safety problems associated with waste removal prior to installing the liners, particularly at landfills.[4] However, EPA exempted *all* existing units rather than attempting to write a provision to account for these concerns, and never ascertained the true extent of the temporary storage problem. In its January 1981 regulations, EPA had required the retrofitting of existing waste piles and surface impoundments used for storage and treatment to meet dual-liner containment standards. The change of policy in just eighteen months was not adequately explained or justified.

Existing units, particularly surface impoundments, represent a serious threat to groundwater because many were designed to leak and are known as "seepage ponds." In 1983, as EPA accumulated additional information on land disposal units, it determined that 655 existing impoundments were totally unlined and 684 existing impoundments had one liner of unknown quality.[5] EPA also estimated that 95% of the existing impoundments were within one-quarter mile of a drinking water supply.[6] Therefore, for many existing units, EPA permitting standards did not ensure a first line of defense where one was clearly required.

EPA exacerbated the existing portion exemption by defining "existing portion" as the surface area on which waste was placed prior to permitting. Thus, even the replacement, expansion, or construction of new units at interim status facilities fell within the exemption and did not need to be lined. Clearly, EPA concerns about retrofitting did not apply in these instances.

Compounding the shortcomings in the design standards was the absence of location standards to protect important groundwater resources. New and existing units could be located at or below the water table, regardless of whether the unit was lined and regardless of the importance of the aquifer. In addition, there were still no location standards prohibiting or otherwise restricting the location of land disposal facilities from areas where groundwater was or would likely be relied upon for domestic and other uses.

Groundwater monitoring waivers were provided for units which met dual-liner design standards and which were located above the water table. To encourage state-of-the-art containment designs, EPA sacrificed its second line of defense.

Shortly after the July 1982 permitting standards were issued, EPA initiated a major study and review of design requirements, which resulted in a contractor report concluding that a dual-liner system consisting of one synthetic liner and one clay liner would provide significantly greater containment performance than a single liner of either type.[7] In addition, a significant number of states were requiring or had proposed to require two liners at new units, or at new and existing units, without waiving groundwater monitoring and response requirements.[8] Based on this information, and ongoing technical guidance from the Agency, Congress chose to strengthen EPA's permitting standards.

In addition, Congress reacted to a December 1982 EPA announcement of several additional "regulatory relief" measures EPA would be considering pursuant to Executive Order 12291. Among the provisions which were under review was the performance standard issued for new and existing permitted incinerators.[9] In particular, the review would focus on the 99.99% Destruction and Removal Efficiency (DRE) requirement for certain organic containments in the waste (see Chapter 8). EPA still believed the standard was feasible, but it questioned the standard's "cost effectiveness."[10] Congress disapproved of weakening this standard and enacted a provision which would prevent EPA from doing so.

THE HSWA AMENDMENTS

The National Policy Directive

In Section 101 of HSWA, Congress established a national policy which directs EPA to place greater emphasis on preventing waste migration into the environment. First, Congress made several findings relating to EPA's weak waste containment strategy:

> the placement of inadequate controls on hazardous waste management will result in substantial risks to human health and the environment; and

> if hazardous waste management is improperly performed in the first instance, corrective action is likely to be expensive, complex, and time consuming.

Second, Congress declared it to be national policy that "waste should be treated, stored, or disposed of so as to minimize the present and future threat to human health and the environment." This policy reflects amendments adding two new congressional objectives of RCRA:

> assuring that hazardous waste management practices are conducted in a manner which protects human health and the environment; and

> requiring that hazardous waste be properly managed in the first instance thereby reducing the need for corrective action at a future date.

Congress viewed these amendments as part of a comprehensive waste management strategy. In conjunction with amendments encouraging waste minimization and establishing land disposal restrictions, the strategy called for a massive reduction of land disposal, and where land disposal continues, that it be conducted only under the most stringent conditions.[11]

Landfill and Impoundment Permitting Standards

HSWA added a new RCRA Section 3004(o) which established design standards for permitting new units, replacement units, and lateral expansions of existing landfills and surface impoundments. Those design standards are two or more liners, a leachate collection system between the liners, and for landfills, a second leachate collection system above the top liner. The standards apply to all new, replacement, or expansion units receiving a permit after November 8, 1984, regardless of when the permit application was submitted. Congress also described an acceptable liner system which would satisfy these new requirements. This design includes a top synthetic liner capable of preventing waste migration into the liner during the unit's active life and the post-closure period, and a bottom liner made of at least 3 feet of clay or other natural material with a permeability of no more than 1×10^{-7} cm/sec. This design is considered acceptable until EPA issues regulations or guidance on the implementation of the new design standards, which Congress required no later than November 8, 1986.

Waivers from the design standards are provided in two instances. One instance is where the owner/operator can demonstrate that an alternative design, coupled with operating practices and site-specific conditions, such as climate and geology, will achieve equivalent containment to the minimum design standard. The burden of overcoming scientific uncertainties in such a waiver demonstration is on the owner/operator; in the event those uncertainties cannot be overcome, the statutory design standard is to be applied. Congress intended that few facilities would qualify for this waiver.[12]

The second waiver opportunity is limited to units containing only hazardous waste from foundry furnace emission controls or metal casting molding sands (the "monofill waiver"). To quality for the waiver, these wastes cannot contain constituents what *would* render the waste hazardous for any other reason than the EP Toxicity Characteristic, regardless of the actual regulatory status of the waste. Appendix VIII screening of the waste will be necessary to determine the presence of other hazardous constituents.[13] In addition, the units must either have one functioning liner which is not leaking, be located more than one-quarter mile from an underground source of drinking water (USDW), and achieve compliance with groundwater monitoring requirements; or be located, designed, and operated so that no hazardous waste constituents will migrate into groundwater or surface water at any future time.

A liner is defined as a synthetic liner which will prevent waste from migrating into it for the active life of the facility, or a clay or natural soil liner which will prevent waste migration beyond the liner during the active life of the facility. A USDW is defined in regulations under the Safe Drinking Water Act as a non-exempt aquifer which supplies a public water system, or an aquifer which contains sufficient groundwater to supply a public system and currently supplies drinking water or contains fewer than 10,000 mg/1 dissolved solids.

Expansions During Interim Status

New RCRA Section 3015 applies the minimum design standards (including the waivers) for permitted landfills and surface impoundments to each new unit, replacement of existing units, or lateral expansion of an existing unit during interim status. This requirement is effective beginning May 8, 1985, and applies to all units not in existence on November 8, 1984, the day HSWA became effective. In other words:

1. Interim status units "in existence" (see below) prior to November 8, 1984, need not meet the minimum design standards.
2. Owners/operators of interim status units not in compliance with the minimum design standards, which came into existence after November 8, 1984, could continue to receive hazardous waste in these units until May 8, 1985, at which time they had to stop receiving hazardous waste at those units. They were then required to upgrade the entire unit to comply with the minimum design standards, or use another unit which meets minimum design standards.
3. Interim status units not in existence before November 8, 1984, and continuing to receive hazardous waste after May 8, 1985, must be in compliance with the minimum design standards.

In order to implement this provision, EPA had to define several terms. It defined the term "unit" the way it has in the past, as a bounded area designed to contain waste with either natural or artificial boundaries. Evidence of berms, excavation, or other construction will be considered an indication of the boundaries of a unit.[14] In addition, the facility operating record and Part A permit application will also be considered.[15] The consequence of EPA's definition is that an owner/operator of a unit in existence after November 8, 1984, may continue to receive waste after May 8, 1985, by subdividing the unit with a berm to create two separate units, and constructing the unit which will continue to receive hazardous waste after May 8 to meet the minimum design standards.

EPA has interpreted the terms "existing" to mean having already received hazardous *or* solid waste and be operational prior to November 8, 1984. "Operational" means constructed to comply with *all* federal, state, and local requirements in effect prior to HSWA.[16] If only a portion of the unit was operational, only that portion can be considered an existing unit. As stated above, existing units need not comply with the minimum design standards. However, where an existing unit is taken out of service and emptied by removing all or substantially all of the waste, the unit will be considered a replacement unit and thus subject to the minimum design standards.[17] In addition, portions of existing surface impoundments and landfills not covered with waste at the time of permitting must still meet EPA's pre-HSWA design standards for new units (i.e., a single liner) as previously required by EPA.[18]

In summary, the combined effect of new RCRA Sections 3004(o) and 3015 requires any landfill or surface impoundment unit, including a replacement or expansion unit, which first received waste or is operational after November 8, 1984, to meet the minimum design standards on May 8, 1985, or at permitting, whichever occurs first.

Owners/operators who install the appropriate containment systems during interim status in good faith, and satisfy the applicable requirements and EPA guidance, will not be required to install a different containment system for those units at the time of permitting as long as there is no reason to believe the installed liners are leaking. This provision is intended to take into account the reduced supervision that the permitting authority exercises over an interim status facility. The owner/operator must, however, notify EPA (or an authorized state) at least 60 days prior to the unit receiving waste to enable an inspection of the installed liner system. EPA considers a submission of the facility's ID number; whether the unit is new, replacement, or expansion; the date the unit will receive hazardous waste; and a statement that the information is accurate as sufficient notification. In addition, the owner/operator must submit a Part B permit application for the facility within six months of filing such notice, if it has not done so already.

To ensure good faith compliance, EPA will issue guidance on the design standards and the information the owner/operator must develop and retain to demonstrate compliance.[19] Drafts of the guidance currently available to the authors will be discussed below.

New RCRA Section 3015 also requires new, replacement, or lateral expansions of existing waste pile units receiving waste after May 8, 1985, to meet EPA's design standards for new permitted waste piles, as codified at 40 CFR 264.251, or provide equivalent protection. EPA has interpreted the term "equivalent protection" to allow continued use of established waivers from the design standards for waste piles which are inside or under a structure (see 40 CFR 264.250(c)), or where the owner/operator can demonstrate that an alternative design, coupled with operating practices and location characteristics, will prevent the migration of any hazardous constituents into the groundwater or surface water at any future time (see 40 CFR 264.251(b)).

The extent to which owners/operators of TSDFs can expand during interim status is governed by 40 CFR 270.72. Increases in the design capacity of a TSDF may be made upon approval of the Regional Administrator (or an authorized state) because of a lack of available treatment, storage, or disposal capacity at other TSDFs. Additional processes or changes in the processes (i.e., building a landfill at a TSDF where none currently exists) also require prior approval, and such approval is authorized only where the expansion is necessary to alleviate an emergency situation or to comply with federal, state, or local law. Under no circumstances can an expansion amount to reconstruction of a facility, defined as more than 50% of the capital cost of constructing a comparable new TSDF. Significantly, this provision applies even when new units are proposed as part of a facility closure plan (see Chapter 11); thus if the proposed units amount to reconstruction, the owner/operator must obtain a permit prior to the construction of the new units.[20]

Existing Surface Impoundments

In addition to applying minimum design standards to new, replacement, and expansion impoundments, Congress also required existing impoundments to meet the minimum design standards by November 8, 1988. This responsibility is statutory, meaning it does not require the issuance of a regulation or a permit to be effective. Congress required the retrofitting of impoundments because the waste they handle is liquid, thereby increasing the potential for waste migration. Many existing impoundments are inadequately designed, and impoundments are a well-documented souce of groundwater contamination.[21]

New RCRA Section 3005(j) applies the minimum design standards to existing impoundments, and it provides three waivers from the basic requirement.

The first waiver (called the single-liner waiver) is for impoundments with one liner which is not leaking, that are located more than one-quarter mile from an underground source of drinking water, and are in compliance with groundwater monitoring requirements. A liner means either a synthetic liner capable of preventing waste migration into the liner during the active life of the facility, or a clay or natural material liner capable of preventing waste migration beyond the liner during the active life of the facility. When liners of the latter type are the basis for the waiver, all waste residues, all contaminated liner material, and all contaminated soil to the extent practicable must be removed or decontaminated at closure. If all contaminated soil is not removed or decontaminated, the owner/operator must comply with post-closure requirements, including groundwater monitoring and, potentially, corrective action.

The second waiver (called the wastewater treatment waiver), is for an impoundment:

1. containing treated wastewater during the "secondary or subsequent phases" of an "aggressive biological treatment facility" subject to a Section 402 Clean Water Act discharge permit or holding waste after such treatment and prior to discharge;
2. in compliance with groundwater monitoring requirements; and

3. which is part of a facility in compliance with Section 301(b)(2) of the Clean Water Act; or

4. where no Clean Water Act effluent guidelines have been issued and no permit under Section 402(a)(1) of the Clean Water Act implementing Section 301(b)(2) requirements has been issued, which is part of a facility in "compliance" with a Section 402 permit that is achieving "significant degradation" of toxic pollutants and hazardous constituents in the untreated waste stream, and about which the permitting authority has been informed of the toxic pollutants and "hazardous constituents" in the wastewater.

An "aggressive biological treatment facility" is defined in Section 3005(j)(12)(B) as a system of impoundments beginning with a secondary treatment aeration impoundment which has either a retention time of not more than 5 days on an annual average basis, or not more than 30 days as long as the sludge in the impoundment is not an EP toxic hazardous waste, or, regardless of the retention time, the system utilizes activated sludge treatment in the early stages of secondary treatment.

Several terms of this waiver were further explained during the Senate floor deliberations. Compliance with a Section 402 Clean Water Act (CWA) permit does not require "absolute" compliance but allows for a small percentage of instances where limits are exceeded.[22] "Significant degradation" is to be judged by analyzing the entire wastewater treatment system, not each impoundment's individual contribution or even the contribution of the impoundment system itself where treatment occurs prior to placement in the impoundments.[23] Finally, in notifying the permitting authority of hazardous constituents in the wastewater, the owner/operator need not perform an Appendix VIII analysis of the wastewater but may identify those constituents known to be in the wastewater.[24]

The third waiver (known as the no-migration waiver) is available if the owner/operator can demonstrate that the impoundment's design, together with operating practices and location characteristics, will prevent the migration of any hazardous constituent into the groundwater or surface water at any future time.

To quality for a waiver, an owner/operator must apply to EPA (or an authorized state) for a waiver by November 8, 1986. The failure to file a timely waiver application eliminates the availability of the waiver. EPA, or an authorized state, may also override the waivers where an impoundment is likely to release hazardous constituents into the groundwater, and may in such instances impose requirements necessary to protect human health and the environment, including the minimum design standards. A decision on the waiver application is required within twelve months after receipt of the application. However if EPA or an authorized state fails to meet this deadline, the waiver is not automatically granted. Thus, the retrofit requirement remains in effect.

For existing impoundments which first become subject to regulation after November 8, 1984, because of new waste listings for example, 4 years from the promulgation of the waste listing is provided to achieve minimum design standards. Two years from promulgation is provided to file waiver applications. The same is true for impoundments which had received a temporary exclusion but could not quality for a final delisting prior to expiration of the exclusion (see Chapter 2).

Impoundments qualifying for the single-liner waiver or the no-migration waiver that are subsequently determined to be leaking must meet the minimum design standards within 2 years of the discovery of the leakage. Impoundments qualifying for the wastewater treatment waiver but subsequently determined to be leaking are required to meet the minimum design standards unless such standards are not necessary to protect human health and the environment, and must do so within 3 years of the leakage discovery. Leakage can be detected by a significant increase in the presence of hazardous constituents in the groundwater over background, by visual evidence, or by sudden drops in the liquid level of the impoundments.[25]

Similarly, where the impoundments no longer satisfies any waiver condition due to a change in conditions that allowed the initial qualification, the owners/operators of impoundments with single-liner or no-migration waivers must meet minimum design standards within 2 years of the discovery of the change in condition. Impoundments with wastewater treatment waivers are allowed 3 years to meet the minimum design standards.

As with expansions during interim status, good faith compliance protection is provided for the installation of containment systems during interim status unless the liner is leaking. In addition, owners/operators of impoundments subject to consent orders or agreements entered into prior to October 1, 1984, that require the performance of corrective action providing equivalent protection of human health and the environment to the minimum design standards, may continue to abide by the terms of such order or agreement in lieu of meeting the minimum design standards.

Finally, several provisions of new RCRA Section 3005(j) concern the relationship between these retrofit requirements and the phased-in restrictions on land disposal described in Chapter 9. Surface impoundments are considered land disposal units and are thus subject to the land disposal prohibitions of HSWA. However, wastes otherwise prohibited from land disposal may be placed in a surface impoundment for treatment under certain conditions. One condition is that the treatment residues that are hazardous be removed from the impoundment (by dredging or pumping, for example) within one year of the entry of the waste into the impoundment. The second condition is that the impoundment meet the minimum design standards of new Section 3004(o) of RCRA unless the impoundment qualifies for either the single-liner or no-migration waiver from the general retrofit requirements. Significantly, there is no wastewater treatment waiver or special dispensation for impoundments subject to pre-October 1, 1984, corrective action consent decrees applicable to treatment impoundments receiving waste otherwise prohibited from land disposal. Therefore, owners/operators of treatment impoundments not required to retrofit under the generally applicable retrofit requirements may nevertheless need to retrofit if the impoundments receive waste otherwise prohibited from land disposal.

Furthermore, all treatment impoundments receiving waste otherwise prohibited from land disposal must meet the minimum design standards (or the appropriate waiver conditions) when the land disposal restrictions become effective. In some cases, this may require retrofitting at an earlier date than November 8, 1988. (See Chapter 9 for a detailed discussion of the land disposal restrictions and the schedule for their implementation.)

Groundwater Monitoring Variances

Congress strengthened EPA's second line of defense in case of liner failure by eliminating many of the variances from groundwater monitoring requirements in EPA's regulations. Specifically, in new RCRA section 3004 (p), Congress eliminated the variances for double-lined surface impoundments, waste piles and landfills, and the variance for single-lined waste piles where the wastes are periodically removed for liner inspection. These variances were eliminated because the risk of leakage at such facilities was sufficiently high for Congress to conclude that a regulatory approach consisting of total reliance on waste containment was insufficient to protect human health and the environment.[26]

Congress did, however, provide authority for a new variance for facilities presenting less of a risk of leakage. The variance applies to an "engineered structure" which will, with reasonable certainty, prevent waste constituent migration beyond the containment area during the active life and the post-closure care period. This structure cannot manage liquid waste and must utilize multiple-leak detection systems within the structure that are operated and maintained through the post-closure period. The structure must also be designed and operated to *exclude* liquid infiltration from precipitation and runoff.

The Senate floor discussion of this variance describes the engineered structure as something other than a conventional land disposal facility. For example, the precipitation and runoff design requirement could not be satisfied by a clay or synthetic cap.[27] Indeed, the sole example of an engineered structure provided by proponents of this provision was aboveground concrete vaults containing waste placed on liners with internal leak detection systems located above, between, and below the liners. EPA has developed a seven-part test for applying this variance.[28]

New RCRA Section 3004(p) does not affect other groundwater monitoring waivers provided by EPA in prior regulations. Thus owners/operators of permitted waste piles, surface impoundments, landfills, and land treatment facilities must now comply with the 40 CFR 264 Subpart F groundwater monitoring and response requirements unless:

1. the unit is an "engineered structure" as described above;
2. the unit is an enclosed waste pile meeting 40 CFR 264.250(c) requirements;
3. there is no potential for liquid migration from the regulated unit (now defined as a unit which received hazardous waste after July 26, 1982) into the uppermost aquifer during the active life of the unit and the post-closure period based on assumptions that maximize liquid migration; or
4. with respect to the post-closure period only, the owner/operator of a regulated land treatment unit demonstrates that the unit's treatment zone does not contain levels of hazardous constituents significantly above background, and unsaturated zone monitoring has not shown significant increases in the presence of those constituents below the treatment zone during the unit's active life.

Location Standards

New Section 3004(o) also requires EPA to revise the design standards from time to time using the dual-liner design requirement as a minimum standard, and in particular, to specify criteria for the acceptable location of new and existing TSDFs besides the existing fault zone and floodplain regulations. Examples of new criteria that Congress intended EPA to develop include proximity to drinking water supplies, wetlands, and population concentration.[29] In addition, EPA is required to publish guidance criteria identifying areas of vulnerable hydrogeology by May 8, 1986.

Air Emissions

Toxic air emissions from storage and disposal facilities, such as uncovered tanks, surface impoundments, and landfills, are not monitored or controlled under pre-HSWA federal regulations. Although there is considerable evidence that these air emissions can pose a significant risk to human health, EPA has not regulated the emissions because of inadequate data and experience in the area.[30] Congress has set a deadline of May 8, 1987, for EPA to issue regulations for the monitoring and control of these air emissions.

Leak Detection

Congress also requested EPA to develop leak detection regulations which require earlier warning of liner failure than the presence of waste constituents in the groundwater. The new regulations, requested by May 8, 1987, would require EPA to set standards for these new early warning systems. The regulations would apply only to units on which construction is commenced after the promulgation of the regulations. Although proponents of this provision cited 15 patents for new leak detection technologies, they did not describe any of these systems, so it is difficult to predict the consequences of this provision at the present time.[31]

Incinerator Standards

New RCRA Section 3004(o) enacts into law the present 99.99% DRE requirement for incinerators as the minimum performance standard for new and existing incinerators. The feasibility of achieving this standard coupled with the uncertainty of assessing the human health impacts of a lower performance standard justified the establishment of the minimum performance standard.[32] Congress also expects EPA to set a higher performance standard where necessary to protect human health and the environment, and to revise the regulations whenever control or measurement techologies are improved. EPA has required a 99.9999% DRE requirement for the incineration of certain dioxin wastes.[33]

Additional Permitting Requirements

An often overlooked but potentially very important provision is new RCRA Section 3005(c)(3). The last sentence of this section authorizes the Administrator (or the authorized state) to add additional terms to a permit above and beyond terms required by the regulations when necessary to protect human health and the environment. Examples of such instances are site-specific situations not addressed by particular regulations, and regulations which do not reflect recent improvements in technology.[34] Thus, additional location restrictions, and additional monitoring and control requirements for example, may be imposed on TSDFs under this new authority.

IMPLEMENTATION ISSUES

EPA has developed and will continue to develop guidance on many of the HSWA provisions concerning design and performance standards. In this section, the most important information currently available to the authors will be discussed. Readers are urged to contact EPA for additional information since most of the guidance available to the authors is in draft form and additional guidance is forthcoming. The implementation of HSWA will be an evolving process for both EPA and the regulated community.

Application of the Minimum Design Standards

EPA guidance considers the applicability of the minimum design standards of HSWA to a variety of waste management scenarios:

1. Existing units at which berms are constructed for higher waste placement over the same area after May 8, 1985, need not meet minimum design standards provided that the unit was granted the legal authority

for the vertical expansion prior to November 8, 1984, and the expansion results in no lateral placement of waste. If the unit was not legally allowed to expand vertically prior to November 8, 1984, the expansion does not meet the existing unit criteria of being operational on November 8, 1984.[35]

2. A unit receiving a final RCRA permit prior to November 8, 1984, is not required to meet the minimum design standards even if the unit has not yet been constructed. The owner/operator should note, however, that a review of the permit is required 5 years after issuance and must be modified to reflect current requirements.

3. The key issue for identifying replacement units is whether normal flow to the unit has ceased and the unit is taken out of service. Replacement units include units where the waste was totally or substantially removed to inspect the liner or base and subsequently reused, thus subjecting them to minimum design standards. Generally, the purpose for the removal is not relevant to the status of the unit, including removal for the purpose of recovering materials.

4. There are no closure requirements applicable at the time of replacement. However, owners/operators of units that stopped receiving hazardous waste on May 8, 1985, because the units do not meet minimum design standards, were required to initiate closure proceedings for those units.

5. The minimum technology requirements for liners and leachate collection systems extend to any area of the unit in contact with the waste, including the side walls of the unit.[36]

Demonstrating Good Faith Compliance

To satisfy the burden of demonstrating compliance, owners/operators must present evidence that all appropriate units were lined, and that the liner and leachate collection systems were designed and installed according to EPA guidance and regulations. This requires proper maintenance and submission of facility operating records, including differentiating between new and existing units. In addition, the owner/operator should prepare and follow a construction quality assurance (CQA) plan, which could be reviewed by EPA during the 60-day notification period and/or at the time of permitting. EPA has developed draft guidance on CQA plan preparation, some of which will be discussed below. The Agency is also preparing guidance on the equivalent alternate design and operating practices waiver, but it is not intending to prepare guidance on the monofill waiver.

Until the equivalency guidance is issued, waiver requests will be evaluated against the statutory double-liner standard. Three factors—design, operation, and location—will be considered and evaluated against the objective of maximizing leachate removal and minimizing the future escape of hazardous constituents. For example, EPA will examine the unit's liquids management strategy. The presence of bulk liquids which enhance waste migration will make it more difficult to qualify for the waiver, so surface impoundments will find it more difficult to qualify. Climatic conditions such as very low rainfall will also be relevant in estimating leachate formation within the unit.

However, notwithstanding the presence of liquids, the owner/operator may test the leachate to prove it does not contain hazardous constituents or that the constituents present in the waste will not leach due to prior treatment, climate, or both. Soil attenuation may also be considered, but it is not likely to be considered significant for most organic constituents.

Double-lined Landfills and Surface Impoundments

Recent EPA draft guidance describes two unit designs which would satisfy HSWA requirements.[37] Other designs may be used, but the burden is on the owner/operator to prove compliance with HSWA. These two designs are in addition to the design in revised Section 3004(o)(5)(B) of RCRA described above which Congress deemed acceptable on a temporary basis. However, as noted in available EPA guidance, EPA does not believe the statutory design of only a 3-foot bottom clay liner will sufficiently prevent waste migration out of the bottom liner in most cases. In fact, EPA has expressed strong reservations about clay bottom liners of any thickness as will be explained below. Both of the designs in EPA's draft guidance require that the entire liner system be located above the seasonal high water table.

The first and preferred design is called the FML/composite double-liner system. It consists of a top synthetic flexible membrane liner (FML), and a bottom liner system made up of two components: a second FML liner, on top of at least 3 feet of compacted natural soil with low permeability (see Figures 10-1, 10-2).

The performance standard for the top liner is that it must be designed, operated, and constructed to prevent waste migration into the liner during the unit's active life and the post-closure period. Thus the top liner should be at lease 30 mils thick, 45 mils thick if it is exposed to the weather or unprotected from waste placement practices. Furthermore, many liners will need to be thicker based on a variety of site-specific factors such as maintenance activities, climate, hydrostatic pressure, abrasion, and operating conditions. Surface impoundments are like to require thicknesses in the 60 to 100 mils range.

The FML should be chemically resistant to the waste, and test data will generally be required to make this demonstration. A liner in landfills will also need at least 30 centimeters of materials above and below it to protect it from physical damage from the waste load. Uncovered sidewalls should have gas venting capabilities in the bedding below them where the potential for gas generation exists.

The upper component of the composite bottom liner is also a FML liner, which must prevent waste migration into the liner during the unit's

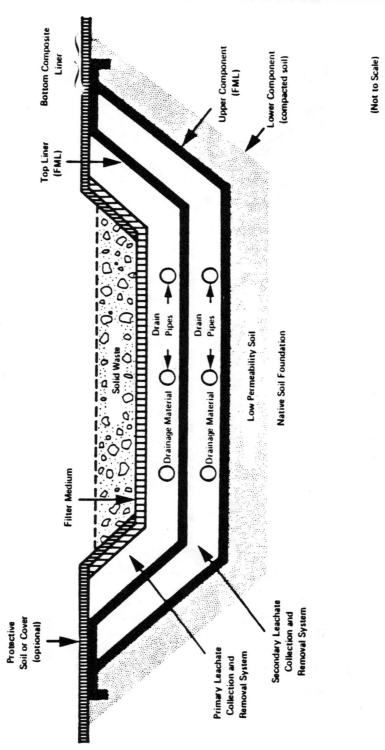

Figure 10-1   Schematic of an FML/composite double-liner system for a landfill

(Not to Scale)

Bottom Composite Liner

Upper Component (FML)

Lower Component (compacted soil)

Top Liner (FML)

Filter Medium

Solid Waste

Drain Pipes

Drain Pipes

Drainage Material

Drainage Material

Low Permeability Soil

Native Soil Foundation

Protective Soil or Cover (optional)

Primary Leachate Collection and Removal System

Secondary Leachate Collection and Removal System

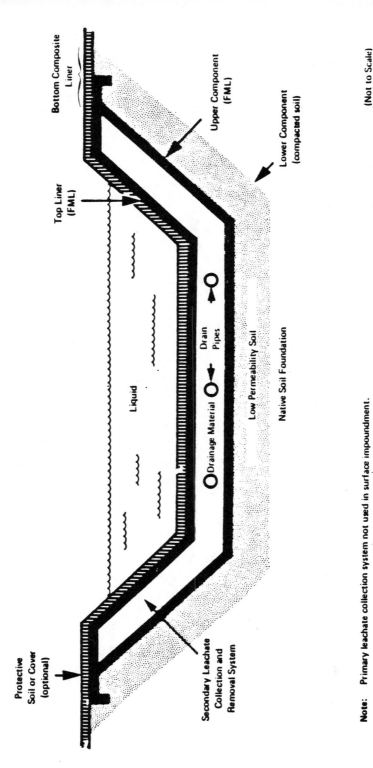

Figure 10-2 Schematic of an FML/composite double-liner system for a surface impoundment

Note: Primary leachate collection system not used in surface impoundment.

(Not to Scale)

active life and the post-closure period. It must be at least 30 mils thick; a thicker liner may be required depending upon site-specific conditions. The FML must also be chemically resistant to the waste, and must be in direct contact with the natural soil component of the composite bottom liner to form a "compression connection."

The performance standard for the natural soil component of the composite liner system is it must be designed, constructed, and operated to minimize the migration of any hazardous constituent through the FML component if a breach of the FML occurs during the active life of the unit or the post-closure period. The natural soil should also provide protective bedding for the FML component, serve as a structurally stable base, and attenuate constituents which leak through the FML component. The soil component should consist of at least 3 feet of compacted soil with permeability of 1×10^{-7} cm/sec or less.

EPA recommends the use of a test fill to verify the soil permeability rates because laboratory demonstrations have proven to be too optimistic. Laboratory liner tests typically use liners without defects normally associated with construction, and the laboratory liners are not subject to the climatic variables of the real world. The guidance recommends that the test fill be least four times wider than the widest construction equipment used, and be constructed using the same materials and equipment as the actual facility. Techniques such as capturing and measuring the under-drainage from the test fill are recommended to obtain quality permeability data.

The second acceptable unit design is called the FML/Low-Permeability Soil Double Liner System. It consists of a top FML liner designed, operated, and constructed to prevent waste migration into the liner during the unit's operation and the post-closure period; and a bottom liner designed, operated, and constructed to prevent waste migration through the liner during this period (see Figures 10-3, 10-4). This design has the same liner performance standards as revised RCRA Section 3004(o)(5)(B), but in the statute 3 feet of recompacted clay with a permeability of no more than 1×10^{-7} cm/sec is an acceptable bottom liner while EPA guidance requires *at least* 3 feet of clay with equally low permeability.

In fact, EPA has "strong reservations" about the use of this design at all because of the difficulties an owner/operator would have in meeting the standard for the bottom liner. These difficulties include:

1. the lack of field verified techniques available for breakthrough determinations; and
2. the economic feasibility of constructing a clay liner thick enough to prevent breakthrough over 40 years (the liner may need to be at least 10 feet thick).

In evaluating the efficiency of a proposed clay liner, the permit writer must assume that leakage in the top FML liner would begin during the

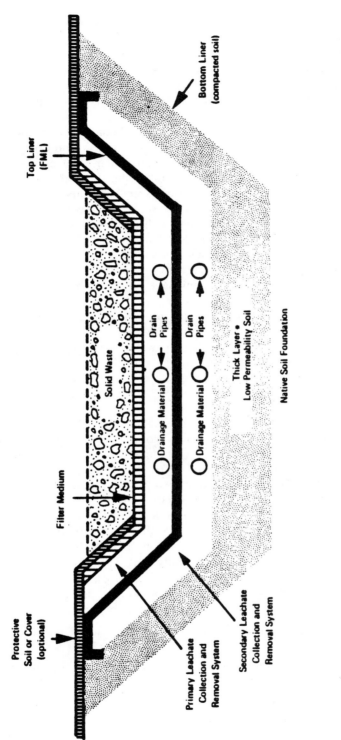

Figure 10-3   Schematic of an FML/compacted soil double-liner system for a landfill

* Thickness to be determined by break through time.

(Not to Scale)

254

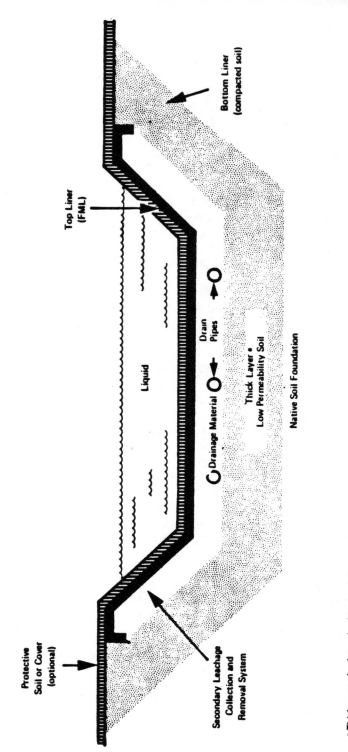

Protective
Soil or Cover
(optional)

Secondary Leachate
Collection and
Removal System

Top Liner
(FML)

Bottom Liner
(compacted soil)

Liquid

Drain
Pipes

Drainage Material

Thick Layer *
Low Permeability Soil

Native Soil Foundation

(Not to Scale)

* Thickness to be determined by breakthrough time.
Note: Primary leachate collection system not used
        in surface impoundment.

Figure 10-4   Schematic of an FML/compacted soil double-liner system for a surface impoundment

255

unit's first year due to faulty installation, and would continue during the operating period, thus contributing to the importance of the breakthrough determination for the clay liner.

The composite secondary liner outlined above is preferred by EPA because a synthetic liner located below the leachate collection system between the liners improves the performance of the collection system. The FML prevents waste migration into the bottom liner thereby making the liquid available for collection and removal. A clay liner would not perform this function as well because it may absorb the waste before it can be detected by the collection system. However, clay liners do not suffer from the installation problems associated with FMLs such as seam failure and puncture holes. Therefore, the natural soil component of a composite liner can minimize leakage should FML failure occur.

Regardless of the liner system employed, leachate collection and removal systems are required between the liners, and in the case of landfills, above the top liner as well. The system above the top liner, known as the primary system, must be designed so that the leachate depth above the top liner does not exceed one foot. It should consist of a drainage layer at least 12 inches thick with a permeability no less than 1×10^{-2} cm/sec and a minimum bottom slope of 2%. It should also be chemically resistant to the waste, designed and operated to function without clogging through the post-closure period, cover the bottom and sidewalls of the unit, and have a pump for each unit capable of automatic and continuous operation through the post-closure period.

The leachate collection and removal system between the liners, or the secondary system, must be designed to collect and remove liquid rapidly, resulting in the formation of little or no head on the bottom liners. It should also consist of a minimum slope of 2%, and a permeability of no less than 1×10^{-2} cm/sec. A pump is also required for each unit, separate from the sump for the primary system. A daily inspection of the sump for the presence of liquids is recommended, and if liquids are detected, the owner/operator should notify the Regional Administrator. On a case-by-case basis, the owner/operator may be required to respond to leaks through the top liner.

To ensure compliance with these requirements, the development and implementation of a CQA plan is required, and the plan should be kept on-site as part of the facility operating record. Draft guidance on the CQA plan is described below.

Single-lined Waste Piles, Landfills, and Surface Impoundments

This draft EPA guidance on acceptable designs applies to new, replacement, and expansion non-enclosed waste pile units; to portions of landfills in existence on November 8, 1984, which are not covered by waste at the time of permitting; and to portions of surface impoundments in existence on November 8, 1984, that qualify for a waiver from the general retrofitting requirement but must nevertheless be single-lined because the portion was not covered with waste at the time of permitting.[38] Thus, this guidance implements 40 CFR Sections 264.221(a), 264.251(a), and 264.301(a). The designs can be used only if the liner system is above the seasonal high water table; the burden is on the owner/operator to prove other designs above or below the seasonal high water table meet RCRA requirements.

The appropriate liner for waste piles and surface impoundments depends upon whether the waste and waste residues will be removed or decontaminated at closure. If they will be, a FML or a lower permeability soil liner is acceptable, as long as the liner is designed, constructed, and operated to contain the waste within the liner during the active life of the unit (see Figure 10-5). Landfills, and waste piles and surface impoundments where waste residues or contaminated soil will remain on-site after closure, require a FML designed and constructed to prevent waste migration into the liner during the active life of the unit.

The FML specifications are as described for the top liner of double-lined systems, including the consideration of site-specific factors to determine appropriate liner thickness. The soil liners for waste piles and impoundments, where authorized, must consist of at least 3 feet of compacted soil with permeability of no more than 1×10^{-7} cm/sec and must be thick enough to prevent waste migration through the liner during the unit's active life. Conservative assumptions should be utilized in estimating appropriate liner thickness when considering such factors as hydraulic head, leachate development, attenuation, and the duration of leachate infiltration into the liner. EPA also recommends a test fill be utilized for soil liners to verify permeability rates as decribed above for soil liners in double-lined systems.

A leachate collection and removal system is required above the liner for waste piles and landfills only. The system should be designed so that the leachate depth above the liner does not exceed one foot. It should consist of at least a 12-inch drainage layer chemically resistant to the waste with a permeability not less than 1×10^{-2} cm/sec and a minimum slope of 2%. It should be designed to function without clogging through the closure period, be constructed to withstand disturbances from overlying wastes and equipment operation, and be operated to collect and remove leachate through the scheduled closure of the unit. The system should cover the bottom and sidewalls of the unit, and should operate automatically whenever leachate is present in the sump.

A CQA plan is also required for the installation of these single-lined containment systems, containing similar components as the plan for double-lined systems.

Preparing and Implementing a CQA Plan

EPA has developed draft guidance on the preparation and implementation of construction quality assurance plans for land disposal facilities,[39] which

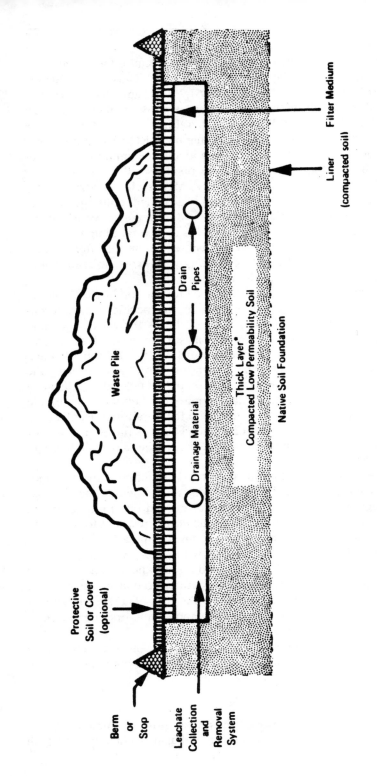

Figure 10-5 Schematic of a compacted soil single-liner system for a waste pile

*Thickness to be determined by break-through time.

(Not to Scale)

has been released to the public for review and comment.[40] Some of the important features of the draft guidance are described below. When the final guidance becomes available, interested readers should obtain a copy because EPA may make modifications to the draft in response to public comment.

The purpose of a CQA plan is to ensure that land disposal units meet or exceed design standards. This is accomplished by carefully supervising the construction of the facility and guarding against flaws in construction materials and/or installation procedures which can lead to containment failure. A CQA plan will be required for all permitted land disposal facilities. For owners/operators expanding during interim status and retrofitting surface impoundments, however, the CQA plan will be the chief means of demonstrating to the permit writer "good faith" compliance with the minimum technology requirements of HSWA, as described above. The failure to develop and implement an adequate CQA plan may have particularly severe consequences for these owners/operators. The permitting authority may require the installation of new liners and leachate collection systems at the time of permitting if good faith compliance cannot be demonstrated for the previously installed systems.

EPA's guidance describes five required elements of a CQA plan. They are responsibility and lines of authority, personnel qualifications, inspection activities, sampling requirements, and documentation.

The first element, responsibility and lines of authority, must identify those persons and organizations involved in designing and constructing the land disposal units. These persons should include a CQA officer and supporting inspection staff. The CQA plan should clearly delineate the specific responsibilities and authorities of each of the CQA staff.

Second, the CQA plan should include documentation regarding the education and experience of all CQA personnel. The CQA officer should be formally trained in engineering or closely associated disciplines. He or she should also be independent of the construction contractor(s) and report to the owner/operator.

The third element of the CQA plan, inspection activities, must address each facility component. The EPA guidance discusses six facility components: foundation, dikes, soil liners, synthetic liners (FMLs), leachate collection systems, and final cover systems. These program components are each further divided into areas of preconstruction, construction,and post-construction inspection activities.

In general, the objective of the inspection activities is to determine whether the construction materials and installed components meet design specifications. The draft guidance contains a list of particular methods that can be used to test land disposal facility components.

For soil liners, preconstruction activities include visual inspection and testing of the soil to determine if it meets design specifications. Soil properties of concern include permeability, soil density and moisture content relationships, particle size, water content, and susceptibility to frost damage.

As stated above, test fills are recommended for soil liners to verify that permeability values can be achieved in the full-scale facility using the materials and construction procedures proposed. The CQA plan should describe all the tests to be performed on the test fill, including a description of the sampling array. The plan should also relate the results of these tests to the full-scale facility by describing in detail how actual test-fill permeability and other results can be used to develop "indicator" or "surrogate" permeability tests for the full-scale facility. Since the test fill is intended to mimic the full-scale facility, the same materials and construction procedures should be used for the test fill as the full-scale facility. The test fill should be at least four times wider than the widest piece of construction equipment to be used on the full-scale facility, and long enough to allow equipment to reach normal operating speed within the test fill.

During construction of the full-scale facility, CQA inspection staff should continuously observe the compaction process and test the compacted liner at specified intervals. The testing program should be described in detail in the CQA plan. The objective of the testing is, in part, to detect and correct:

> Regions of higher than specified liner permeability caused by the use of improper materials, inadequate moisture control, insufficient soil compaction, and poor filling of test holes.
>
> Less than specified liner thickness due to failures in soil placement and compaction operations.
>
> Leaks around liner penetrations (piping) resulting from improper sealing and compaction.

After construction, the soil liner should be inspected for cracks, holes, or other defects which would increase permeability. Defective areas should be removed.

For synthetic liners, or FMLs, preconstruction inspection activities should include tests to determine if the liner as manufactured meets performance specifications. Tests may evaluate such properties as liner thickness, tear and puncture resistance, density, stability, chemical and ultraviolet resistance, and heat aging. All factory seams should be checked, and defective seams should be documented and repaired.

The FMLs should also be inspected upon delivery to the site to determine if it was damaged during packaging and transport. The objective of these inspections is to detect and correct nail and splinter punctures, tears or crumpling in the liner from inadequate packaging, and damage due to exposure to extreme temperatures. On-site storage of the FMLs should be brief and the liners should be protected from adverse weather conditions.

During construction, FML placement inspection activities should be designed to detect and correct:

Liner damage resulting from adverse weather conditions, inadequate anchoring, and rough handling.

Improper liner placement.

Poor quality seams and non-welded or non-seamed sections.

Seaming must be conducted under the proper climatic conditions (generally between 40 and 100 degrees Fahrenheit with relative humidity of less than 70%). The membrane surfaces should be free from dirt, dust, and moisture, and placed on a firm foundation. After the seams are installed, all field and factory seams should be evaluated visually or through tests. Some seams should be removed and evaluated in the laboratory.

Liner penetrations (e.g., piping) also require special scrutiny to ensure the seals around the penetrations are strong and impermeable to leachate. Finally, the entire liner surface should be visually inspected for tears, punctures, and thin spots.

After FML installation and seam testing, another thorough visual inspection should be conducted, and defective areas marked and repaired. In addition, to check for leaks, the owner/operator may fill the unit with water and measure seepage from the site. This testing method can be used to evaluate the leachate collection system as well.

Preconstruction activities for the leachate collection system(s) involve ensuring the construction materials conform to design specifications and examination of the foundation or bedding for the system. During construction, inspection activities associated with pipe network installation are required to detect and correct the clogging of the system from fine particle accumulation and piping malfunctions due to faulty pipe installations. In addition, particular attention must be devoted to drainage layer and filter layer placement, as well as the installation of pumps, collection equipment, and other ancillary equipment. After construction, all of the system components should be inspected, and the pumps tested at design capacity.

The fourth element of a CQA plan is the sampling program that will be utilized as part of the CQA activities for the facility. The sampling program should address, for each facility component, the criteria for dividing materials or work into units for sampling, the number of samples per unit, sample locations, the criteria for acceptance of the unit of work or materials, how individual test results deviating significantly from the norm will be handled, and test verification procedures for work or materials initially deemed unacceptable. The draft EPA guidance does not mandate a particular sampling strategy, except in certain instances where 100% sampling is required (i.e., all FML seams must be tested). Instead, the draft guidance describes "judgment sampling," where plans are based on the experience of CQA personnel, and "statistical sampling," where plans are based on the laws of probability. EPA clearly disfavors, however, judgment sampling because CQA personnel biases may misrepresent the material or work under assessment thereby devaluing the testing program.

The fifth and final element of the CQA plan is documentation. EPA's draft guidance recommends preparation of daily summary reports of inspections and other CQA activities; inspection data sheets for all observations; field and laboratory tests; problem identification and corrective measures reports for each unit of material or work not meeting design specifications; photographs; evaluation reports on each separable unit of materials or work to be observed or tested; a response to this information by the designer of the facility including all deviations from original specifications; and as-built drawings. During construction, the CQA officer is responsible for these records, which are kept at the facility. After construction, the originals should be stored by the owner/operator and a copy kept at the facility. A third copy should be kept by the permitting authority for public inspection.

NOTES

1. 47 *Fed. Reg.* 32284 (July 26, 1982).
2. Ibid., p. 32313.
3. See 45 *Fed. Reg.* 33213–4 (May 19, 1980).
4. 47 *Fed. Reg.* 32315 (July 26, 1982).
5. 129 *Cong. Rec.* H8137 (daily ed. Oct. 6, 1983) (Statement of Representative Breaux).
6. Letter from Lee Thomas, EPA Assistant Administrator, to Representative James Broyhill (Oct. 5, 1983), reprinted in 129 *Cong. Rec.* H8145 (daily ed. Oct. 6, 1983).
7. Lennett and Greer, "State Hazardous Waste Regulation," *Ecology Law Quarterly*, Vol. 12, No. 2, 1985, p. 245, fn. 519.
8. Ibid., pp. 244–55.
9. 47 *Fed. Reg.* 55880 (Dec. 12, 1982).
10. Ibid. See also 47 *Fed. Reg.* 27518 (June 24, 1982).
11. 130 *Cong. Rec.* H11141 (daily ed. Oct. 3, 1984) (Statement of Representative Florio).
12. See Senate HSWA Report, pp. 27–28.
13. 129 *Cong. Rec.* H9158 (daily ed. November 3, 1983) (Statement of Rep. Florio). The monofill waiver or the waiver based on equivalent containment are not available in the State of Alabama.
14. 50 *Fed. Reg.* 28706 (July 15, 1985).
15. Ibid.
16. 50 *Fed. Reg.* 28707 (July 15, 1985).
17. See Senate HSWA Report, p. 24.
18. 50 *Fed. Reg.* 28708 (July 15, 1985).
19. 50 *Fed. Reg.* 28709–10 (July 15, 1985).
20. See Memorandum from Bruce Weddle, Director of Permits and State Programs

Division, Office of Solid Waste, EPA to Hazardous Waste Division Directors and Branch Chiefs, Regions I-X, entitled Permitting Units Created for Facility Closure, dated September 11, 1985.

21. 130 *Cong. Rec.* S9182 (daily ed. July 25, 1984). EPA guidance on this provision is expected in the summer of 1986.
22. Ibid., p. S9183 (Statement by Sen. Bentsen).
23. Ibid.
24. Ibid. (Statement by Senator Chafee).
25. HSWA Conference Report, p. 99.
26. Senate HSWA Report, p. 64.
27. 130 *Cong. Rec.* S9179 (daily ed. July 25, 1984).
28. 50 *Fed. Reg.* 28716 (July 15, 1985).
29. Senate HSWA Report, p. 30.
30. Lennett, supra note 7, pp. 240–42.
31. See 129 *Cong. Rec.* H8150 (daily ed. of Oct. 6, 1983).
32. Senate HSWA Report, pp. 29–30.
33. See 50 *Fed. Reg.* 1978 (January 14, 1985).
34. Senate HSWA Report, p. 31.
35. Letter from John Skinner, Director, Office of Solid Waste, EPA to John Quarles, dated August 30, 1985.
36. 50 *Fed. Reg.* 28709 (July 15, 1985).
37. Minimum Technology Guidance on Double Liner Systems—Design, Construction, and Operation (Draft—Second Version), May 24, 1985. EPA has proposed to codify the essential elements of this guidance. See 51 *Fed. Reg.* 10707 (March 28, 1986).
38. Minimum Technology Guidance on Single Liner Systems for Landfills, Surface Impoundments, Waste Piles—Design, Construction and Operation (Draft—Second Version), May 24, 1985.
39. Construction Quality Assurance for Hazardous Waste Land Disposal Facilities: Public Comment Draft, October 1985.
40. 50 *Fed. Reg.* 48129 (November 21, 1985).

CHAPTER ELEVEN

Environmental Monitoring and Cleanup Requirements

In 1982, EPA had developed a two-pronged groundwater protection strategy for regulating permitted hazardous waste land disposal facilities: leachate minimization and control through design and operating requirements, and groundwater monitoring and response requirements should leachate nevertheless reach the groundwater. In a variety of ways, the EPA regulations concerning each prong contained substantial shortcomings prompting Congressional modification in HSWA. Chapter 10 contains the changes mandated by HSWA to the first prong of EPA's groundwater protection strategy. In this chapter, the HSWA-mandated changes to the groundwater monitoring and response requirements will be examined, as well as cleanup responsibilities imposed with respect to other environmental media.

THE PRE-HSWA GROUNDWATER MONITORING AND RESPONSE REQUIREMENTS

EPA established in its land disposal permitting standards applicable to permitted landfills, surface impoundments, waste piles, and land treatment facilities, a three-phased groundwater monitoring and response program. The importance of this groundwater monitoring and response program is evident considering EPA's acknowledgement that liners and other containment devices will leak at some future time.[1] When this leakage occurs, it is the subsequent determination of the rate and extent of leakage and the potential health and environmental effects of this leakage which enable states and EPA to satisfy their statutory mandate to protect human health and the environment. Only by requiring land disposal facility owners/operators to detect and clean up those releases into groundwater which jeopardize human health and the environment can EPA and the states protect human health despite the deficiencies of state-of-the-art containment methodologies.[2] EPA called the three phases of the program detection monitoring, compliance monitoring, and corrective action. These phases represent graduated levels of activity in response to detected contamination. The last part of this chapter contains detailed descriptions of these phases, as well as the groundwater monitoring requirements applicable during interim status.

Significantly, Congress did not modify the basic structure of EPA's groundwater monitoring and response regulations but instead focused on their scope, applicability, and exemptions. One set of exemptions Congress eliminated was that based on certain design features of the units, such as the exemptions for double-lined landfills, waste piles and surface impoundments, and single-lined waste piles where the waste in the piles is removed periodically to inspect the liners. The justification for eliminating these exemptions and a description of the specific HSWA provisions eliminating these exemptions are presented in Chapter 10, since the provisions are closely associated with minimum design standards as well.

Limitations of the Pre-HSWA Regulations

EPA's corrective action or cleanup requirements applied only to regulated units at the time of permitting. Regulated units were defined as units receiving waste after January 26, 1983. Since the regulations were issued on July 26, 1982, 6 months were provided for owners/operators to adjust their waste management practices so as to remove those units from potential corrective action. The adjustment could be made in one of two ways. The owner/operator could stop receiving hazardous waste either at his *entire* facility, or at selected land disposal units within the facility.

Information from EPA files revealed that owners/operators of approximately 50 land disposal facilities had stopped receiving hazardous waste at all land disposal units at their facilities between July 26, 1982, and January 26, 1983, to take advantage of this loophole.[3] Not suprisingly, some of these facilities had already contaminated groundwater.[4] EPA had no idea how many land disposal facility owners/operators stopped accepting waste at some but not all of their units to avoid cleanup responsibilities for the units no longer in use.

As already stated, the groundwater monitoring and response requirements applied only at the time of permitting. The interim status standards included groundwater monitoring and investigation of the extent of contamination, but did not require cleanup of the contamination detected. The lack of cleanup requirements during interim status was justified by EPA because of the need for interim status standards to be self-implementing and the temporary nature of the regulations.[5] However, delays in the permitting program are likely to result in at least 8 years of reliance on interim status standards for regulating some land disposal facilities. Furthermore, these standards apply to units which have been operating for many years before the interim status standards were issued. Substantial contamination may have already been caused by these units prior to permitting. Indeed, a recent Congressional report found that 40% of the interim status facilities monitoring groundwater correctly have caused varying degrees of groundwater contamination.[6] Allowing such contamination to continue and worsen over time increases risks to human health and the environment, and adds to the complexity and expense of future corrective action.

The groundwater monitoring and response requirements also did not apply to non-regulated units at the same facility which were contaminating groundwater. These non-regulated units could be hazardous waste units which stopped receiving hazardous waste prior to January 26, 1983, July 26, 1982, or even November 19, 1980, when the RCRA program became effective. Alternatively, they could be units which managed or continue to manage wastes not currently designated hazardous but which are nevertheless leaking and contaminating groundwater. In the latter category are often found unlined impoundments, unlined industrial solid waste landfills, and open dumps.[7]

Such distinctions based on when units stopped receiving hazardous waste or whether the waste in the units is currently designated hazardous can impede rather than assist the protection of groundwater resources. The detection and cleanup of groundwater, already a complex and expensive task, becomes even more complex and expensive if it is necessary to determine the precise source of groundwater contamination, particularly at facilities where so-called regulated units and non-regulated units are in close proximity. In addition, from an economic or environmental standpoint, it is not an efficient utilization of private or public resources to create such distinctions and implement a regulatory program accordingly. For example, it would not be an efficient resource expenditure to install a groundwater monitoring system aimed at assessing hazardous constituent migration from some pollution sources but not at others nearby impacting the same aquifer (assuming such a system was technically feasible to install). Nor is it efficient to design a corrective action program to address only the aquifer contamination traceable to the regulated units where other sources contribute to the degradation of the same aquifer and will continue to do so in the absense of some cleanup response.

In some cases, contamination from a non-regulated unit may actually impede the detection of contamination from regulated units. As explained below, the presence of groundwater contamination is determined by comparing well samples upgradient and downgradient from the RCRA unit. EPA's regulations, however, require the placement of the upgradient (background) well(s) at a location unaffected by leakage from a *regulated unit*. The regulations thus allow contamination from a non-regulated unit in the background well(s), which can camouflage leakage from a regulated unit by elevating background levels. Again, considering the environmental goal of protecting groundwater resources, the important information to obtain and assess is whether and to what extent groundwater has been impaired by any waste management activity at the facility, not just the marginal contribution from a regulated unit.

It is true that non-regulated units could be addressed by the Superfund program or in an enforcement action under Section 7003 of RCRA (see Chapter 13). However, these authorities involve different EPA programs and personnel, place more burdensome requirements on EPA to take appropriate action, and involve different criteria for decisionmaking and management priorities. In addition, these programs are already overburdened with sites requiring cleanup not associated with the RCRA program.[8] Consequently, while these authorities are theoretically available, as a practical matter they are *not,* and even when utilized would not be properly coordinated with the RCRA corrective action authorities. For these reasons, EPA has indicated a preference for utilizing RCRA regulatory and permitting authorities to address contamination at RCRA facilities where such authorities are available.[9]

Finally, EPA's corrective action requirements under the 1982 regulations applied only to contamination within the property boundary of the facility. Off-site contamination would not have to be addressed because EPA could not guarantee adjoining property owners would provide the necessary permission to the owner/operator to conduct correction action off-site.[10]

Since off-site contamination often results in the greatest human exposure and therefore presents the most substantial risk to human health and the environment, EPA's justification for this approach was extremely ill-advised. No examples were provided where owners/operators were denied permission, and no discussion of the likelihood of such a denial accompanied the regulation. EPA did not adopt the obvious solution—require an off-site corrective action response *unless* permission was denied, thereby addressing EPA's concerns. Instead, EPA explained that off-site contamination could be addressed under Superfund or other authorities; but as shown, these authorities are generally not satisfactory.

THE HSWA PROVISIONS

Definition of Regulated Unit

New Section 3005(i) of RCRA requires that groundwater monitoring and corrective action requirements established for new permitted land disposal units apply to interim status land disposal units accepting hazardous waste after July 26, 1982. One of the purposes of this provision is to close the loophole that allowed owners/operators of land disposal units to stop accepting hazardous waste between July 26, 1982, and January 26, 1983, to escape corrective action requirements. Accordingly, EPA has modified the definition of "regulated" unit so that Subpart F groundwater monitoring and response requirements apply to land disposal units receiving hazardous waste after July 26, 1982.[11]

This amendment may also expand EPA's ability to address groundwater contamination during the closure of interim status facilities, particularly at surface impoundments. The last part of this chapter will describe the interrelationship of this amendment, other HSWA provisions, and the interim status closure and post-closure process.

Interim Status Corrective Action Orders

Congress granted EPA additional authority under a new RCRA provision, Section 3008(h), to issue "corrective action orders" and require other action by owners/operators in response to releases of hazardous waste from interim status facilities. The purpose of the provision is to overcome problems caused by delays in the permitting process by allowing EPA to address environmental contamination prior to permitting if a response measure is necessary to protect human health and the environment.[12] An order can be issued to require an owner/operator to determine the nature and extent of contamination, perform temporary cleanup measures, submit a corrective action plan, and/or clean up the contamination.[13] Accordingly, a series of modifications to an order at different stages in the detection, evaluation, and cleanup response phases would be appropriate.

The scope of this provision has been interpreted broadly by EPA. It applies to releases into any environmental medium (i.e., air, soil, surface water, or groundwater) and includes releases from any hazardous or solid waste management unit at the facility.[14]

The definition of release is interpreted by EPA at least as broadly as the release definition of Superfund, 42 U.S.C. 9601, which includes any spilling, leaking, pumping, pouring, emitting, emptying, discharging, injecting, escaping, leaching, dumping, or disposing into the environment.[15] EPA does not believe actual sampling data is necessary to prove there is or has been a release. Rather, design and operating characteristics of the unit and the hydrogeology of the area may provide sufficient evidence a release has occurred. Exemptions applicable under the Superfund law for releases to the workplace would *not* apply under Section 3008(h).[16]

Furthermore, EPA has interpreted the term "hazardous waste" in Section 3008(h) broadly so as not to be limited to the current universe of waste designated hazardous by EPA regulations. According to EPA, Section 3008(h) may be used to require cleanup activities for releases of hazardous constituents (the approximately 375 substances listed in 40 CFR 261 Appendix VIII) from hazardous or solid waste.

A "solid waste management unit" includes any container, tank, surface impoundment, waste pile, land treatment unit, landfill, incinerator, and underground injection well containing solid or hazardous waste, whether or not the unit is a regulated unit. In addition, the term "solid waste management unit" also includes a unit granted an exemption by EPA from substantive standards (i.e., recycling units, wastewater treatment tanks), as well as a unit potentially subject to a RCRA permit-by-rule because of regulatory authorities available under other laws (i.e., underground injection wells, publicly owned treatment works). [17]

Significantly, the Section 3008(h) authority may not be limited to releases from solid waste management units, since the language of the provision refers to releases "from the facility" into the environment. A facility includes all contiguous property under the owner/operator's control. Thus, it may not be necessary for a release to originate from a discernible unit to trigger Section 3008(h). However, EPA does not believe Section 3008(h) can be relied upon to address releases from underground storage tanks regulated under Subtitle I of RCRA (see Chapter 12).[18]

Continuing Releases at Permitted Facilities

Section 206 of HSWA, RCRA Section 3004(u), imposes substantial new cleanup responsibilities on owners/operators of permitted TSDFs. The provision requires that such owners/operators perform corrective action for all releases of hazardous waste or constituents from any solid waste management unit at a TSDF receiving a RCRA permit. It applies regardless of when the waste was placed in the solid waste management unit. Because of the importance of this provision, it is reproduced here in full:

> Standards promulgated under this section shall require, and a permit issued after the date of enactment of the Hazardous and Solid Waste Amendments of 1984 by the Administrator or a State shall require, corrective action for all releases of hazardous waste or constituents from any solid waste management unit at a treatment, storage, or disposal facility seeking a permit under this subtitle, regardless of the time at which waste was placed in such unit. Permits issued under section 3005 shall contain schedules of compliance for such corrective action (where such corrective action cannot be completed prior to issuance of the permit) and assurances of financial responsibility for completing such corrective action.

EPA has interpreted various terms in this provision, thereby establishing the broad scope of the amendment based on Congressional intent:

release—broadly defined as under Section 3008(h) and includes all environmental media

hazardous constituents—the constituents listed in Appendix VIII of 40 CFR Part 261

solid waste management unit—broadly defined as under Section 3008(h)

permit—any operating permit or post-closure permit issued after November 8, 1984

facility—the entire site that is under the control of the owner/operator engaged in hazardous waste management[19]

corrective action—required where necessary to protect human health or the environment, which with respect to groundwater contamination, applies to releases which exceed 40 CFR 264 Subpart F groundwater protection standards (i.e., background levels, drinking water standards, or alternative concentration limits).

In summary, therefore, this provision requires an owner/operator seeking an operating permit or a post-closure permit to perform corrective action for all releases of Appendix VIII constituents into any environmental medium from a solid waste management unit located within the property boundary of the site as may be necessary to protect human health and the environment. The provision applies regardless of when the waste was placed in the unit. This remains true even if the unit was under control of a previous owner/operator when such waste placement occurred. The present owner/operator could take legal action seeking renumeration from prior owners/operators for corrective action costs, but is nonetheless responsible for compliance with Section 3004(u).[20]

In the event that corrective action is not completed at the time of permitting, which is likely to be the case with most facilities requiring corrective action, Section 3004(u) provides that the permit can be issued but must include corrective action compliance schedules and financial assurances for completing the corrective action. The compliance schedule can consist of a schedule for completing corrective action, or a schedule for gathering the information necessary to determine the appropriate corrective action. In the latter case, the schedule will include determining the cost of corrective action and demonstrating financial assurance when the cost has been determined.[21] When the permit is modified at a later date to incorporate more specific corrective action, the modification will be considered a major modification triggering public participation permitting procedures (see Chapter 6).

Regulated units, now defined as land disposal units which receive hazardous waste after July 26, 1982, are a subset of the universe of solid waste management units. However, EPA regulations require regulated units to be in compliance with 40 CFR 264 Subpart F at the time of permitting, and permit application requirements already require the gathering of information on releases into groundwater from such units. Therefore, compliance schedules are not appropriate for groundwater releases from regulated units.[22] In addition, financial assurances for corrective action must be presented at the time of permitting for regulated units.[23]

In available guidance on Section 3004(u), EPA has divided the implementation process into three phases: site assessment, remedial investigations and development of proposed corrective actions, and selecting and performing corrective action.

During the site assessment phase, solid waste management units (SWMUs) are identified; characterized by size, location, date of operation, and the type of waste placed in the unit; and release information is provided for each unit. The burden is on the owner/operator to provide this information and include it in the Part B permit application. At this stage, however, the burden is limited to information reasonably available, so new investigations are not required.

Based on the Part B information, the EPA Region and/or the state should perform a preliminary assessment/site investigation (PA/SI) to determine whether a release posing a risk to human health or the environment has occurred. The PA is a "desk top" review of available information including the Part B permit application, aerial photographs, citizen complaints, compliance history, and prior notifications under Section 103(c) of Superfund.[24] The SI is a site visit for gathering physical evidence on the occurrence of or likelihood of releases, such as the examination of waste management practices resulting in air emissions, unlined disposal units or other design characteristics, damaged vegetation, discolored soils, and indications of surface water runoff. The SI may also include environmental sampling. The depth and extent of the SI will depend on the size, complexity, and compliance history of the facility. In some cases, particularly where there is already evidence of releases at the site, EPA may use its enforcement authorities under Section 3008(h) or 3013 of RCRA to order the owner/operator to perform the SI (see Chapter 13).

If the permit writer determines, after performance of the PA/SI, that it is not likely that a release at the facility has occurred which poses a risk to human health and the environment, Section 3004(u) poses no additional burden on the owner/operator. If the permit writer has determined a release has occurred, or is likely to have occurred, a permit may be issued, but it must include a schedule of compliance for the subsequent phases of Section 3004(u) implementation.

Little guidance is available at press time on the subsequent phases of the Section 3004(u) implementation process. Remedial investigations should be conducted pursuant to available guidance for the Superfund program until RCRA guidance is prepared. Additional guidance is also expected regarding corrective action for underground injections wells, the use of schedules of compliance and enforcement authorities, and the demonstration of financial assurances.

EPA has determined that Federal facilities are subject to Section 3004(u) to the same extent as private parties, including the property-wide definition of facility. However, the owner of the facility is the individual Federal agency, not the Federal government itself; thus Federal lands owned by the United States but administered by different Federal agencies, or major subdivisions of agencies, are considered separate facilities for the purposes of compliance with Section 3004(u). EPA also intends to propose additional rules regarding the implementation of 3004(u) at Federal facilities.[25]

Cleanup Beyond the Property Boundary

Section 207 of HSWA, new RCRA Section 3004(v), requires EPA to modify its regulations so that corrective action addresses off-site releases unless the owner/operator cannot obtain the necessary permission despite his "best efforts." The statute specifies that the regulations will apply to all regulated units. EPA interprets the off-site release authority to extend to releases from SWMUs addressed pursuant to 3008(h) and 3004(u).[26] Pending modification of the regulations, corrective action orders addressing off-site contamination are to be issued on a case-by-case basis.

Exposure Information and Health Assessments

Beginning August 8, 1985, Section 247 of HSWA or new RCRA Section 3019 requires that Part B permit applications for landfills and surface impoundments must be accompanied by information on the potential for human exposure to releases of hazardous constituents from such units. Owners/operators with Part B applications submitted prior to August 8 are required to submit the exposure information by August 8; applications submitted after August 8 must be accompanied by the exposure information when submitted. The information required must address:

1. reasonably foreseeable potential releases from normal operations and accidents of the unit, including transportation to or from the unit;
2. the potential pathways of human exposure to such releases; and
3. the potential magnitude and nature of the exposure resulting from such releases.

The provision does not require the performance of new release investigations; only the information "reasonably ascertainable" by the owner/operator is required. On the other hand, if sophisticated risk analyses have already been performed, or more detailed information gathered for whatever reason (i.e., audit by insurance company), that information must also be provided. The provision applies to both operating and post-closure permits, and EPA interprets the term "release" as broadly as it has for Sections 3008(h) and 3004(u).[27]

EPA has also interpreted the Congressional directive that the information "accompany" the permit to mean the information is *not* part of the Part B permit application. Thus, a permit may be processed and issued for a facility not in compliance with this requirement, although noncompliance is still enforceable as a violation of RCRA.

The exposure assessment information can be utilized in a variety of ways. Based on the information provided by the owner/operator, Section 3019 of RCRA authorizes EPA or an authorized state to request the Agency for Toxic Substances and Disease Registry (ATSDR), a branch of the U.S. Public Health Service, to perform a health assessment and other appropriate investigations. A health assessment includes assessments of the risk posed by the landfill or surface impoundment based on a variety of factors such as the size and susceptibility of the community within the likely pathways of exposure. The assessment also must include a risk evaluation of other sources of hazardous constituents in the community. Based on this preliminary assessment and other information, ATSDR can then determine whether more substantial health studies and medical evaluations of the community should be performed. Section 3019(c) allows members of the public to submit exposure information to EPA, ATSDR, or authorized states.

EPA also intends to utilize the exposure information to assist the RCRA program in other ways, such as determining whether immediate threats exist at the site, establishing permit conditions beyond those required by the regulations (see Chapter 10 discussion of new Section 3005 (c)(3) of RCRA), taking appropriate action under Sections 3004(u) and 3008(h) of RCRA, and evaluating waivers from the impoundment retrofit requirement.[28] If the information is to have any value for these purposes, EPA will need it at the time of permitting or before.

The information must be sent to the appropriate EPA Region until the State is authorized to implement Section 3019 (see Chapter 14). Copies should be sent to the State as well because some states may be authorized to implement Section 3019 in the not too distant future.

Generally speaking, a substantial amount of the required exposure information should already be in the Part B permit application. To assist the owner/operator in preparing the Exposure Information Report (EIR), EPA has prepared a checklist which the owner/operator can use to cross-reference information contained in the Part B or in other information submitted to EPA.

Besides the information contained in the Part B, the owner/operator must provide additional information, including analyses of at least the 10 largest waste streams by volume handled at the facility, as well as landfill leachate and the wastes contained in impoundments. EPA recommends that the analyses determine the presence and concentrations of about 120 hazardous constituents, plus the 10 organic compounds not listed that are detected at the highest concentrations by gas chromatographic methods.[29] In lieu of this analysis, the owner/operator may submit a discussion of why analyses already submitted are adequate based on the uniformity of the process generating the waste and the waste management practices at the facility.

The owner/operator must also describe the nature and magnitude of known releases if the information has not already been provided (such as pursuant to Section 3004(u)). Releases requiring a description include: air releases, overtopping of impoundments, uncontrolled run off, and washout or flooding. Evidence of releases may include monitoring well data, complaints from the public, fish kills, and soil discoloration.

Finally, for each site, the owner/operator must prepare a narrative discussion of the potential exposure to the public to hazardous constituents from releases at the unit by each potential pathway. The narrative should discuss the potential exposure from both normal operations and accidents near the units, and should discuss direct human exposure and contamination of food chain crops. Location, design, and operating factors reducing the potential for exposure (i.e., liners, leachate collection systems, treatment processes, venting systems), as well as factors increasing exposure potential (i.e., rapid groundwater flow, downgradient wells in use, shallow aquifer, porous soils, frequent air inversions) should be included in the discussion. EPA believes a narrative of 2 to 3 pages for each pathway will generally be sufficient.[30]

GROUNDWATER MONITORING AND RESPONSE REQUIREMENTS

This section will provide a detailed analysis of the groundwater monitoring and response regulations currently in effect for both interim status and permitted facilities. Particular attention will be devoted to developing an adequate interim status groundwater monitoring system because of the importance of these requirements in the RCRA program, the difficulty owners/operators have had in achieving compliance, and the prospect of additional facilities becoming RCRA TSDFs as additional wastes are designated hazardous. In addition, since many interim status facilities will close rather than seek an operating permit, this section will contain an analysis of potential interim status closure issues and the interaction of various EPA regulations and HSWA provisions affecting such closures. Finally, during the next several years, some of the interim status land disposal facilities which are closing will need a post-closure permit, and other facilities will seek an operating permit, thereby triggering the groundwater monitoring and response requirements applicable to permitted facilities. The successful transition of these facilities from interim status to permitted status will require an understanding of both the differences between the interim status and permitting standards, and certain permit application requirements; thus, additional information in these areas is also provided.

Who Must Comply

Interim status groundwater monitoring requirements apply to owners/operators of interim status landfills, surface impoundments, and land treatment facilities under federal law. While permitted waste piles are subject to groundwater monitoring and response requirements, waste piles are not subject to the interim status standards for groundwater monitoring. In the near future, some existing tanks may also be subject to interim status groundwater monitoring requirements (see Chapter 12).

Two exemptions are available from the interim status groundwater monitoring requirements. One requires the owner/operator to demonstrate that "there is a low potential for migration of hazardous waste or hazardous waste constituents from the facility via the uppermost aquifer to water supply wells (domestic, agricultural, or industrial) or to surface water." EPA (or the authorized state) need not be notified of the owner/operator's decision to claim this waiver. The demonstration is kept at the facility, and is evaluated by EPA (or an authorized state) generally upon inspection of the facility. The demonstration must be certified by a qualified geologist or geotechnical engineer and include information specified in 40 CFR 265.90(c)(1) and (2).

The second exemption applies to owners/operators of surface impoundments handling waste that is designated hazardous only because of it corrosivity (either through listing or the characteristic), and requires a demonstration "that there is no potential for migration of hazardous wastes from the impoundment." This demonstration must be certified by a "qualified professional," and is evaluated by the regulatory authority in the same manner as the other exemption.

The groundwater monitoring and response regulations for permitted facilities apply to regulated units, now defined as landfills, surface impoundments, waste piles, and land treatment facilities receiving hazardous waste after July 26, 1982. In the near future, some existing tanks may be subject to some or all of these regulations (see Chapter 12). These regulations, codified at 40 CFR 264 Subpart F, apply to facilities receiving both operating permits or post-closure permits. Post-closure permits are required for interim status units closing in a manner requiring post-closure care after January 26, 1983.[31]

Four exemptions are currently available from the 40 CFR 264 Subpart F requirements reflecting modifications mandated by HSWA:

1. certain engineered structures (see Chapter 10);
2. enclosed waste piles designed and operated in compliance with 40 CFR 264.250(c);
3. where the Regional Administrator (or an authorized state) determines that there is no potential for migration of liquid from a regulated unit to the uppermost aquifer during the active life of the unit and the post-closure care period using assumptions which maximize the rate of liquid migration; and
4. during the post-closure care period only, where the Regional Administrator (or an authorized state) finds the treatment zone of a land treatment regulated unit does not contain hazardous constituents at levels significantly above background, and unsaturated zone monitoring has not shown a significant increase in hazardous constituents below the treatment zone during the unit's active life.

Installing a Detection Monitoring Well System

The installation of a detection monitoring well system in compliance with interim status monitoring requirements (or the permitting standards of 40 CFR 264 Subpart F) requires proper well placement. Only through the performance of detailed, site-specific hydrogeological studies can the owner/operator provide a sufficient scientific basis to support decisions regarding well placement. The studies are needed to develop reliable information on the character of subsurface geology below the TSDF, the groundwater flow paths below the TSDF, the hydraulic conductivity of the uppermost aquifer, and the vertical extent of the uppermost aquifer down to the first confining layer. Techniques to obtain this data are provided in Table 11-1; the checked techniques are considered mandatory

Table 11-1 Hydrogeologic Investigatory Techniques

Investigatory Tasks	Investigatory Techniques	Data Presentation Formats/ Assessment Outputs
Definition of Subsurface Materials [geology]	✓ Soil borings and rock corings ✓ Survey of existing geologic information ✓ Material tests (grain-size analyses, standard penetration tests, etc.) • Geophysical well logs (resistivity and/or electromagnetic conductance, gamma ray, gamma density) • Surface geophysical surveys (D.C. resistivity, E.M., seismic) • Hydraulic conductivity measurements of cores (unsaturated zone) • Aerial photography (fracture trace analysis)	✓ Narrative description of geology ✓ Geologic cross sections ✓ Geologic or soil map (l″ = 200′) ✓ Boring logs or coring logs • Structure contour maps of aquifer and aquitards (plan view) • Raw data and interpretive analysis of geophysical studies ✓ Raw data and interpretive analysis of material tests
Identification of Groundwater Flowpaths [hydrology] Groundwater flow directions (including vertical and horizontal components of flow) Hydraulic conductivities	✓ Installation of piezometers; water-level measurements at different depths ✓ Slug tests and/or pump tests • Tracer studies	✓ Narrative description of groundwater with flow patterns ✓ Water table or potentiometric maps (plan view) with flow lines (1″ = 200′) ✓ Hydrologic cross-sections • Raw data and interpretive analysis of slug tests, pump tests, and tracer studies

✓ Minimum techniques and corresponding outputs that should be used to define site hydrogeological conditions.

by EPA in the draft guidance on groundwater monitoring available to the authors prior to publication.[32]

The characterization of the site subsurface will require information on the strata below the site, as well as bedrock characteristcs and depth. The texture, uniformity, grain size, and mineral composition of each strata layer should be determined and zones of significant fracturing identified. According to EPA's draft guidance, use of bore holes to obtain this data is required. The appropriate distance between bore holes used for taking strata samples will depend on a variety of factors including the complexity of the subsurface geology, but the initial perferred distance is approximately 300 feet. An increase or decrease in the appropriate distance between bore holes from 300 feet will depend on a variety of factors (see Table 11-2). Boring log data should include the types of information listed in Table 11-3, and should characterize site geology to a depth of 10 feet of bedrock or the first confining layer below the uppermost saturated zone.

The identification of groundwater flow paths requires the use of piezometers to measure groundwater depth accurate to the nearest tenth of a foot. Groundwater depth must be monitored frequently enough and over a long enough period of time to account for both intermittent and continuous pumping of groundwater into nearby wells, seasonal variations of precipitation and evaporation, and other factors affecting groundwater depth. Identifying flowpaths requires determining the direction of groundwater flow (horizontal and vertical directions); establishing variations based on season, withdrawals, and other factors; and determining the hydraulic conductivity of portions of the site.

Table 11-2   Factors Influencing Boring Well Spacing

Factors That May Substantiate Wider Boring Spacing:	Factors That May Substantiate Closer Spacing:
• Simple geology (i.e., horizontal, thick, homogeneous geologic strata that are continuous across site that are unfractured and are substantiated by regional geologic information). • Use of geophysical data to correlate well log data. Preferred methods: DC resistivity, seismic reflection or seismic refraction, geophysical well logging. • Relatively constant hydraulic conductivity values between wells and no indication of proximal off-site influences on groundwater (tidal effects, industrial, agricultural, domestic groundwater use, etc.)	• Fracture zones encountered during drilling. • Suspected pinchout zones (i.e., discontinuous units across the site). • Geologic formations that are tilted or folded. • High zones of permeability that have not been defined by drilling at 300-foot intervals. • Laterally transitional geologic units with irregular permeability (e.g., sedimentary facies changes). • Groundwater features that are unexplained by 300-foot spacing (e.g., irregular or nonlinear flow). • Indication of proximal off-site influences on groundwater. • Nonuniform hydraulic conductivity values exist below the site.

Table 11-3   Field Boring Log Information

General

- Project name
- *● Hole name/number
- *● Date started and finished
- *● Geologist's name
- *● Driller's name

- Sheet number
- *● Hole location; map and elevation
- *● Rig type
  bit size/auger size

Information Columns

- *● Depth
- *● Sample location/number
- Blow counts and advance rate

- *● Percent sample recovery
- *● Narrative description

Narrative Description

- Geologic observations:

  *—rock type
  *—color
  *—gross mineralogy
  *—gross petrography
  —friability
  *—moisture content

  *—crystalinity
  *—presence of
   carbonate (HCL)
  *—fractures
  *—solution cavities
  *—bedding

  *—depositional
   structures
  *—organic content
  *—odor
  *—suspected
   contaminant

- Drilling Observations:

  —loss of circulation
  *—advance rates
  —rig chatter
  *—water levels
  —amount of air used

  *—drilling difficulties
  *—changes in drilling
   method or
   equipment

  *—amounts and type of
   any liquids used
  *—running sands
  *—caving/hold stability

- Other Remarks:

  —equipment failures
  *—possible sources of contamination
  *—deviations from drilling plan
  *—weather

*Indicates the owner/operator should record, at a minimum.

Hydraulic conductivity tests must be conducted to identify areas of high and low conductivity within each formation. The areas of highest hydraulic conductivity have the greatest potential for contaminant flow. Field tests, as opposed to laboratory tests, are required to measure *in situ* hydraulic conductivity.

Finally, the owner/operator must identify the uppermost aquifer, from which groundwater samples will eventually be taken to determine the facility's impact on groundwater. The uppermost aquifer extends from the water table to the first confining geologic formation; there should be no interconnection with lower aquifers. Significantly, the uppermost aquifer was chosen by EPA as the focus of concern because of its importance as a pathway for contaminant flow. Thus, whether or not a geological formation is the uppermost aquifer will depend primarily on its potential as a pathway. Factors such as poor quality or low yield are generally not determinative.[33] Aquifers connected to the uppermost aquifer must also be identified and eventually monitored. The owner/operator bears the burden of properly defining the uppermost aquifer, including the absence of hydraulic connections between aquifers.

Once these hydrogeologic studies have been adequately performed, decisions must be made regarding the placement of monitoring wells. A detection monitoring well system must be capable of determining a facility's impact on the groundwater quality in the uppermost aquifer underlying the facility. The number, depth, and locations of upgradient (background) wells must be selected to produce representative samples of groundwater unaffected by the facility. The number, depths, and location of downgradient wells must be selected to immediately detect statistically significant increases in contaminants migrating from the facility into the uppermost aquifer. Data from upgradient and downgradient wells will be statistically compared to determine if such increases have occurred.

The important concerns in placement of the background wells are whether the wells are unaffected by the facility, if the number of wells is sufficient to account for spatial variations in background quality, and whether there are enough wells to allow for depth discrete comparisons with downgradient wells. The regulations specify the minimum number of upgradient wells is one, but very rarely will one well adequately account for spatial variability. In most cases, at least four is the more appropriate minimum number of background wells.[34]

The chief concerns in the placement of downgradient wells are the number of wells necessary to ensure immediate detection of leakage, the appropriate distance between the wells so contamination does not move between monitoring wells undetected, the distance of the wells from the waste management units, and appropriate depths for sampling.

The regulations specify that the minimum number of downgradient wells is three, but almost always more are required. The greater the variability in the subsurface, the more wells and the smaller the distance required between wells. Generally, 150 feet is the baseline point for evaluating proper well spacing, from which site-specific factors can increase or decrease the appropriate distance between wells (see Table 11-4).[35] The wells should be located as close to the units as possible.

The well system should be designed to yield samples from all aquifers hydraulically connected to the uppermost aquifers, requiring an assessment of appropriate sampling depths. Care should be taken in well design to avoid the dilution of samples by mixing groundwater samples of different depths, particularly in areas of high hydraulic conductivity. Multiple wells may be required at a sampling location in a thick, complex, saturated zone, expecially where the waste consists of light- and heavy-phase immiscibles. Decisions regarding well placement and depth may need to be made concurrently.

A monitoring system which meets the detection monitoring interim status standards for design and location as described above should generally meet permitting standards for detection monitoring as well. Although the interim status standards require placement of the downgradient wells "at the limit of the waste management area" and permitting standards

Table 11-4 Factors Used to Adjust Horizontal Spacing of Monitoring Wells

WELLS MAY BE LESS THAN 150 FEET APART IF THE SITE:		WELLS MAY BE SPACED MORE THAN 150 FEET APART IF THE SITE:
• Manages or has managed liquid waste		• Has never managed liquid waste
• Is very small (i.e., the down gradient perimeter of the site is less than 150 feet)		
• Has a double liner (and may leak over a relatively small area)		
• Has waste incompatible with liner materials		
• Is an old facility, with less certainty on design features and past waste disposal practices		• Is new, with more certainty on facility design features and planned/current waste disposal practices
• Has fill material near the waste management units (where preferential flow might occur)		• Uses appropriate and proven geophysical techniques to supplement monitoring wells in the detection monitoring program
• Has buried pipes, utility trenches, etc., where a point-source leak might occur		
• Has complicated geology —closely spaced fractures —faults —tight folds —solution channels —discontinuous structures		• Has simple geology —no fractures —no faults —no folds —no solution channels —continuous structures
• Has heterogenous conditions —variable hydraulic conductivity —variable lithology		• Has homogeneous conditions —uniform hydraulic conductivity —uniform lithology
• Is located in or near a recharge zone		
• Has a high (steep) or variable hydraulic gradient		• Has a low (flat) and constant hydraulic gradient

LESS THAN

150 FEET

GREATER THAN

require well placement at the "point of compliance," the definitions of these two terms mean essentially the same thing.

Detection Monitoring and Responding to Contamination

Under the interim status standards, the owner/operator is required to sample for parameters specified in the regulations quarterly for one year to determine background water quality. After determining background quality, some parameters must be sampled at least annually and others at least semi-annually at both the background and downgradient wells. Groundwater elevation must also be measured annually. EPA's draft guidance discusses appropriate sampling and analysis procedures.

The existence of groundwater contamination is determined by a statistical comparison of indicator parameter concentrations from background and downgradient wells. Indicator parameters, such as total organic carbon or pH, are broad measures of changes in groundwater quality that can result from a variety of sources. Analyzing groundwater samples for them is a less expensive but less reliable measure of the presence of contamination than analyzing for particular contaminants. The interim status regulations do not specify the use of a particular statistical test, but do require that a student's t-test be used. EPA has indicated that Cochrans Approximation to the Behrens-Fisher t-test or the average replicate t-test are acceptable. If a statistically significant increase is revealed and subsequently confirmed after additional sampling, the owner/operator must submit to EPA (or an authorized state) an assessment monitoring plan and implement a groundwater assessment program. This program should be capable of determining the rate and extent of the horizontal and vertical migration of certain contaminants in the groundwater and the concentration of those constituents. Once an initial determination has been made by the owner/operator, a written report assessing groundwater quality must be submitted to EPA (or an authorized state). Assessment monitoring continues until closure or permit issuance, unless the owner/operator successfully demonstrates the previous indications of contamination were "false positives" (see Figure 11-1).[36] No cleanup of the contamination detected is required by the interim status regulations.

Under the permitting standards, there are three phases in the groundwater monitoring and response requirements: detection monitoring, compliance monitoring, and corrective action. The obligations of the owner/operator expand from one phase to the next in response to detected contamination. Detection monitoring is the first phase, implemented at facilities where contamination has not yet been detected. In detection monitoring, the specific chemicals or parameters to be monitored are determined for each TSDF by the Regional Administrator (or the authorized state) and are part of the permit, thus allowing for greater specificity than the interim status standards based on the wastes managed at the site. Quarterly sampling is required to determine groundwater quality.

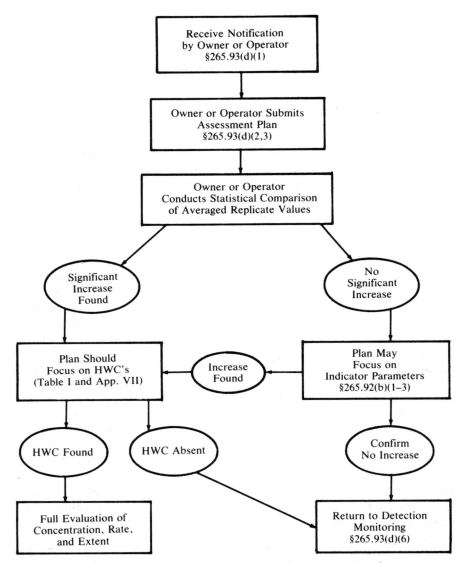

Figure 11-1   Recommended procedure for reviewing assessment plans

Downgradient samples to determine the concentrations of the chemicals or parameters in the groundwater must be taken at least twice a year thereafter; flow rate and direction must be determined at least annually.

Using specified statistical procedures, the owner/operator must determine whether there has been a statistically significant increase over background for each parameter or chemical tested. If a significant increase has been detected, the owner/operator must:

1. notify the Regional Administrator (or an authorized state) within seven days;

2. sample all wells for all "hazardous constituents," specifically the list of constituents in Appendix VIII of 40 CFR Part 261;[37]

3. establish a background value for each hazardous constituent;

4. within 90 days submit to the Regional Administrator (or an authorized state) a permit modification application for a compliance monitoring plan; and

5. within 180 days submit an engineering feasibility study for a corrective action program.

The second phase of these monitoring regulations is compliance monitoring. The purpose of the compliance monitoring program is to determine if the groundwater contamination detected exceeds acceptable levels.

At this phase of the monitoring and response program (unless it was established at the time of permitting), the groundwater protection standard is established in the permit. The standard includes concentration limits for all hazardous constituents detected in the groundwater reasonably derived from waste in the unit, unless constituents have been excluded from consideration because they are not capable of posing a substantial present or potential hazard at the site at any time. The violation of this standard will determine if cleanup of the groundwater is to be required. The baseline protection standard is the background level of the constituent, or the maximum contaminant limits established in the National Interim Primary Drinking Water Regulations (NIPDWR) under the Safe Drinking Water Act (see Table 11-5), whichever is higher. There are only 14 constituents covered by NIPDWR, mostly heavy metals, therefore the background level would apply for most constituents. However, within 180 days of the discovery of a significant increase under detection monitoring (or at the time of permitting), the owner/operator could request an alternate concentration limit (ACL) for each and every constituent by demonstrating that the constituent would not pose a "substantial present or potential hazard" to human health and the environment at the site as long as the ACL is not exceeded. At press time, EPA was developing guidance on the issuance of ACLs.

If the owner/operator requests an ACL for every constituent in the groundwater, he can postpone the submission of the engineering feasibility study. The owner/operator is also given the option of attempting to demonstrate that errors in sampling or analysis caused the increase in contamination, or the source of contamination is not the regulated unit. In the absence of such a demonstration, EPA would assume the contamination came from the regulated unit. To make the demonstration, the owner/operator must notify the Regional Administrator of his intent to do so within 7 days of the discovery of the statistically significant increase, and present evidence in support of the demonstration and a permit mod-

Table 11-5   Maximum Concentration of Constituents for Groundwater Protection

Constituent	Maximum Concentration*
Arsenic	0.05
Barium	1.0
Cadmium	0.01
Chromium	0.05
Lead	0.05
Mercury	0.002
Selenium	0.01
Silver	0.05
Endrin (1,2,3,4,10,10-hexachloro-1,7-epoxy-1,4,4a,5,6,7,8,9a-octahydro-1, 4-endo, endo-5,8-dimethano naphthalene)	0.0002
Lindane (1,2,3,4,5,6-hexachlorocyclohexane, gamma isomer)	0.004
Methoxychlor (1,1,1-Trichloro-2,2-bis (p-methoxyphenylethane)	0.1
Toxaphene ($C_{10}H_{10}Cl_6$, Technical chlorinated camphene, 67–69 percent chlorine)	0.005
2,4-D (2,4-Dichlorophenoxyacetic acid)	0.1
2,4,5-TP Silvex (2,4,5-Trichlorophenoxypropionic acid)	0.01

*Milligrams per liter.

ification application to change the detection monitoring program within 90 days. The owner/operator is not relieved of the responsibility to submit a compliance monitoring permit modification by opting to make this demonstration until or unless the demonstration is successful. Even if successful, the owner/operator now can be required to clean up the contamination under Section 3004(u) of RCRA.

Compliance monitoring continues throughout the "compliance period" as specified in the permit. "Compliance period," a term of art, is defined as "the number of years equal to the active life of the waste management area," including the time prior to permitting and during closure. It begins when a compliance monitoring program has begun. If the compliance period ends before the end of the post-closure care period, the owner/operator must return to detection monitoring for the remainder of the post-closure period. If the post-closure care period ends first, the Regional Administrator (or authorized state) has the discretion to extend it.

In this phase, owners/operators may or may not be required to install new wells or make physical alterations to the monitoring system in place. Often, this will depend on whether the plume of contamination is narrow; a narrow plume may necessitate installing additional wells to find the center of the plume. However, operating procedures will always be modified to provide for more comprehensive sampling and analysis. For example, at least quarterly sampling is required during the compliance period, and Appendix VIII sampling is required at least annually.

During compliance monitoring, the owner/operator must determine if groundwater samples exhibit a statistically significant increase in the levels of hazardous constituents over the levels specified as the ground-water protection standard in the permit. If such an increase has occurred, the owner/operator must:

1. notify the Regional Administrator (or an authorized state) within 7 days; and
2. submit within 180 days a permit modification to establish a corrective action program (within 90 days if an engineering feasibility study has already been submitted).

Here again the owner/operator is provided another opportunity to demonstrate the increase was due to sampling or analysis errors, or the contamination was not from a regulated unit, but just as before, attempting to make this determination does not relieve the owner/operator of the obligation to submit the corrective action permit modification until and unless he is successful. In addition, the owner/operator can now be required to clean up contamination caused by non-regulated units under Section 3004(u) of RCRA.

Corrective action, the third and last phase of the Subpart F regulations, requires the owner/operator to employ remedial technologies to prevent hazardous constituents from exceeding the groundwater protection standard by removing the constituents or treating them in place. In addition, a monitoring program must be implemented to determine if the corrective action program is working, which may include the installation of new wells. Corrective action cannot be terminated until the owner/operator can demonstrate that the groundwater protection standard has not been exceeded for three consecutive years, irrespective of whether this time frame extends beyond the compliance period.

Table 11-6 contains a capsulized summary of the interim status and permitting groundwater monitoring and response requirements. Adjustments from detection monitoring to compliance monitoring to corrective action are considered major permit modifications subject to public participation requirements (see Chapter 6).

Transition from Interim Status to Permitted Status

To complete a successful transition from interim status to permitted status, detailed knowledge of the two sets of requirements and the significant differences between them is desirable. In addition, awareness of certain permit application requirements is important.

In particular, 40 CFR 270.14(c)(4) requires the permit applicant to describe any plume which has entered the groundwater from a regulated unit, including defining the extent of the plume and identifying the concentration of hazardous constituents in the plume. Significantly, this requirement can apply to facilities where plumes have been detected during interim status, facilities where EPA (or an authorized state) has little confidence in the interim status groundwater monitoring system installed at

Table 11-6 Summary of Federal Groundwater Monitoring and Response Requirements

	Purpose of Monitoring or Response Requirement	Installation of Wells Required	Parameters Monitored	Sampling Frequency	Statistical Analysis	Cleanup Required
Interim Status Detection Monitoring Requirements 40 CFR 265 Subpart F	To determine whether units have leaked hazardous waste into uppermost aquifer in quantities sufficient to cause a change in groundwater quality.	Yes; minimum of 1 upgradient and 3 downgradient (see text for additional guidance).	Three sets of parameters; 20 parameters listed in Appendix III of 40 CFR Part 265, ground water quality parameters (chloride, iron, manganese, phenols, sodium and sulfate) listed in §265.92(b)(2) of 40 CFR, and groundwater contamination indicators (pH, specific conductance, total organic carbon, total organic halogen) listed in §265.92(b)(3) of 40 CFR.	All wells sampled quarterly for each parameter for one year. Background mean values and variances determined for upgradient well samples after first year. In second year and beyond, 265.92(b)(2) parameters at least annually sampled and 265.92(b)(3) parameters sampled at least twice a year.	Each 265.92(b)(3) parameter sampling requires statistical comparison with background mean values using unspecified type of student's t-test to .01 level of significance. If analysis reveals significant increase over background, a second sampling must be performed to confirm the results. If results confirmed, groundwater assessment must be initiatied.	No
Interim Status Groundwater Assessment Requirements 40 CFR 265 Subpart F	Initial purpose is confirm the presence of hazardous waste constituents in groundwater. If presence confirmed, further monitoring is conducted to determine rate, extent, and nature of contamination.	Yes if necessary to determine the horizontal and vertical extent of contamination.	"Hazardous waste constituents" defined as Appendix VII of 40 CFR Part 261 for listed wastes, the substance listed in 40 CFR 261.33 (e) or (f) if discarded, or constituents with MCLs under the NIPDWS.	Quarterly once contamination is confirmed until closure or permit issuance.	Same as interim status detection monitoring to confirm presence of hazardous waste constituents in groundwater.	No

Detection Monitoring Permitting Requirements 40 CFR 264 Subpart F	Same as Interim Status Detection Monitoring.	New units/TSDFs yes; interim status units no unless interim status groundwater monitoring system is not adequate or units were not required to monitor during interim status.	Specified in permit based on wastes managed in regulated units.	Quarterly sampling to establish background values, and semi-annual sampling thereafter.	The Cochran's Approximation to the Behren's Fisher Student's t-test to .05 level of significance or an equivalent technique. If contamination detected, application for compliance monitoring permit modification required.	No
Compliance Monitoring Permitting Requirements 40 CFR 264 Subpart F	To establish a groundwater protection standard for facility and determine if leakage of 40 CFR Part 261 Appendix VIII constituents has exceeded the standard. The standard will consist of 1. MCLs established by NIPDWR. 2. background level of constituents, or	Perhaps if more wells necessary to characterize plume such as if plume is narrow or localized.	All constituents listed in Appendix VIII to 40 CFR Part 261 unless owner/operator demonstrates constituents could not originate from regulated unit or constituent is not capable of posing a substantial present or potential risk to human health and the environment.	At least quarterly, and for all Appendix VIII constituents (regardless of demonstrations made by owner/operator) at least annually until end of compliance period. This period begins when compliance monitoring is initiated and lasts for a period of time equal to the active life of the waste management area.	No statistical procedure or level of significance specified in regulations. Background values may be determined by pooling available data at time of permitting, or establishing new values after each upgradient well sampling where there is high temporal correlation between background and downgradient levels of	No

Table 11-6 Continued

Requirement	Groundwater Protection Standard	Detection Monitoring	Compliance Monitoring	Corrective Action Monitoring
	3. ACLs if owner/operator can demonstrate ACLs will not pose a substantial present or potential hazard to human health and the environment if not exceeded. constituents in groundwater. If groundwater protection standard exceeded. application for corrective action permit modification required.	May be same as compliance monitoring.	May be same as compliance monitoring. May be same as compliance monitoring but may be more frequent where plume is concentrated.	Yes until facility is in compliance with groundwater cleanup protection standard for 3 consecutive years.
Corrective Action Monitoring and Response Requirements 40 CFR 264 Subpart F	To bring regulated units back into compliance with groundwater protection standard by removing or treating in place the constituents in violation of the standard and to monitor the effectiveness of the cleanup measures.	Yes, if necessary to determine the effectiveness at, near, or beyond waste management area.		

288

the facility, or facilities with no groundwater monitoring data available at all. In other words, it applies to any facility that has *not* demonstrated the absence of contamination through compliance with interim status standards.

The major differences in the groundwater monitoring regulations affecting the facility moving from interim status to permitted status are the units covered by the regulations, and the parameters monitored to determine if groundwater contamination has occurred. For example, waste piles are not subject to the interim status requirements but are subject to the permit application requirements and the permitting standards. The same situation may apply to owners/operators of facilities who correctly or incorrectly claimed a waiver from the interim status requirements but who cannot qualify for one of the different waivers available for permitted units.

With respect to the monitoring parameters, the interim status standards focus on a potential increase of certain indicator parameters and "hazardous waste constituents," while the permitting standards *and* applications requirements focus on a potential increase of "hazardous constituents." As defined by the regulations, hazardous waste constituents are an extremely small subset of "hazardous constituents," the latter term applying to Appendix VIII of 40 CFR Part 261 and including approximately 375 substances. Thus, contamination as defined under the permitting standards can go undetected under interim status monitoring because the owner/operator is not required to analyze samples for a broad range of contaminants.

The interim status indicator parameters used in detection monitoring are also not capable of revealing contamination as defined in the permitting standards. These parameters are subject to large natural variations which can obscure the presence of contamination. In addition, they are not sufficiently sensitive to register some changes in water chemistry indicating leakage, and their responsiveness is generally inferior to monitoring waste-specific indicator parameters.[38] The statistical procedures employed during interim status are also not as sensitive to the presence of contamination as the procedures for permitted units.

For a variety of reasons, therefore, the transition from interim status to permitted status, including the permit application process, is an opportune time to learn more about a facility's impact on groundwater so that the appropriate monitoring phase for the facility can be selected for the initial permit. For example, a facility may be contaminating groundwater to a much greater extent than determined under interim status assessment monitoring, when applying for a permit. In addition, facilities not in compliance with interim status requirements may be submitting monitoring data of little value for determining the presence of contamination due to improper well placement. Finally, facilities with no groundwater data may also be contaminating groundwater. Using available enforcement authorities, however, EPA (or an authorized state) can require the owner/operator to provide additional information and make significant modifications to the facility's monitoring system, so that the permit writer can determine both the nature and extent of contamination at the site, and whether detection monitoring, compliance monitoring and/or corrective action requirements belong in the initial permit. Table 11-7 contains a list of potential violations of interim status groundwater monitoring and relevant permit application requirements.

As an example of how this enforcement process might work, if an inadequate interim status groundwater monitoring system is in place when the permit application is filed, and monitoring data nevertheless indicates contamination or the regulatory authority reasonably suspects contamination has occurred, enforcement of the interim status standards and the permit application requirements can require the owner/operator to perform the following tasks while *still* in interim status:

1. Upgrade the detection monitoring system by conducting a hydrogeological investigation of the facility and installing an appropriate well system.

2. Sample the wells on an expedited basis for an expanded list of indicator parameters based on the chemical compositon of waste in the regulated units.

3. If the presence of contamination is confirmed, test for some or all Appendix VIII constituents in all additional well samples.

4. If the downgradient levels of Appendix VIII constituents are significantly higher than background, develop a corrective action plan and apply for a corrective action permit.

5. If the Appendix VIII constituents are present at levels not significantly higher than background, apply for a compliance monitoring permit and submit a corrective action feasibility study pursuant to 40 CFR 270.14(c)(7).

The time EPA (or an authorized state) allows for performing these tasks may be quite short (see Figure 11-2). Similar tasks may also be requested of owners/operators of waste piles, facilities wrongly claiming an interim status waiver, and facilities in compliance with the interim status standards where monitoring data does not indicate contamination but the regulatory authority reasonably suspects contamination has occurred. A reasonable suspicion may result from the design of the regulated units (i.e., unlined), operating practices (i.e., past or present handling of liquid wastes), or the characteristics of the site (i.e., shallow water table).

Where contamination has not been detected upon achieving compliance with interim status standards and 40 CFR 270.14(c)(4), the interim status facility owner/operator will comply with 40 CFR 270.14(c)(6) and provide information to establish a detection monitoring program under 40 CFR 264 Subpart F.

	2 to 4 MONTHS*	2 MONTHS	4 to 6 MONTHS
FACILITIES THAT HAVE NOT FORMALLY TRIGGERED ASSESSMENT MONITORING	Fill in gaps in hydrogeologic assessment Upgrade existing well network to meet Part 265 standards Develop list of expanded indicator parameters that includes constituents expected to be derived from waste found at the facility	Determine whether contamination has occurred based on a comparison of data from up- and downgradient wells collected on an accelerated schedule over a short period of time. NOTE: Determination is no longer based on comparison of current values to "background" values established over 1 year.	If contamination is confirmed, begin assessing plume based on monitoring of Appendix VIII constituents. Sample to establish background for all Appendix VIII constituents detected in groundwater for possible inclusion in groundwater protection standard. Develop compliance monitoring and/or corrective action program for incorporation in permit.
FACILITIES THAT HAVE MANAGED TO TRIGGER ASSESSMENT MONITORING DESPITE INADEQUATE DETECTION SYSTEM			*IMMEDIATELY* begin installation of assessment wells downgradient from "hot" well(s). *SIMULTANEOUSLY* fill in gaps in hydrogeologic assessment and upgrade detection network. Proceed as above

*Time frames will vary depending on site-specific factors

Figure 11-2 New groundwater compliance strategy based on condensed monitoring sequence

Table 11-7   Relationship of Technical Inadequacies to Groundwater Performance Standards

Examples of Basic Elements Required by Performance Standards	Examples of Technical Inadequacies that may Constitute Violations	Regulatory Citations
1. Uppermost Aquifer must be correctly identified	• failure to consider aquifers hydraulically interconnected to the uppermost aquifer	§265.90(a) §265.91(a)(1) (a)(2) §270.14(c)(2)
	• incorrect identification of certain formations as confining layers or aquitards	§265.90(a) §265.91(a)(1) (a)(2) §270.14(c)(2)
	• failure to use test drilling and/or soil borings to characterize subsurface hydrogeology	§265.90(a) §265.91(a)(1) (a)(2) §270.14(c)(2)
2. Groundwater flow directions and rates must be properly determined	• failure to use piezometers or wells to determine groundwater flow rates and directions (or failure to use a sufficient number of them)	§265.90(a) §265.91(a)(1) (a)(2) §270.14(c)(2)
	• failure to consider temporal variations in water levels when establishing flow directions (e.g., seasonal variations, short-term fluctuations due to pumping)	§290.90(a) §295.91(a)(1) (a)(2) §270.14(c)(2)
	• failure to assess significance of vertical gradients when evaluating flow rates and directions.	§265.90(a) §295.91(a)(1) (a)(2) §270.14(c)(2)
	• failure to use standard/consistent benchmarks when establishing water level elevations	§265.90(a) §265.91(a)(1) (a)(2) §270.14(c)(2)
	• failure of the O/O to consider the effect of local withdrawal wells on groundwater flow direction	§265.90(a) §265.91(a)(1)
	• failure of the O/O to obtain sufficient water level measurements	§265.90(a) §265.91(a)(1)
3. Background wells must be located so as to yield samples that are not affected by the facility	• failure of the O/O to consider the effect of local withdrawal wells on groundwater flow direction	§265.90(a) §265.91(a)(1)
	• failure of the O/O to obtain sufficient water level measurements	§265.90(a) §265.91(a)(1)
	• failure of the O/O to consider flow path of dense immiscibles in establishing upgradient well locations	§265.90(a) §265.91(a)(1)
	• failure of the O/O to consider seasonal fluctuations in groundwater flow direction	§265.90(a) §265.91(a)(1)

Table 11-7 **Continued**

Examples of Basic Elements Required by Performance Standards	Examples of Technical Inadequacies that may Constitute Violations	Regulatory Citations
	• failure to install wells hydraulically upgradient, except in cases where upgradient water quality is affected by the facility (e.g., migration of dense immiscibles in the upgradient direction, mounding of water beneath the facility)	§265.90(a) §265.91(a)(1)
	• failure of the O/O to adequately characterize subsurface hydrogeology	§265.90(a) §265.91(a)(1)
	• wells intersect only groundwater that flows around facility	§265.90(a) §265.91(a)(1)
4. Background wells must be constructed so as to yield samples that are representative of *in situ* groundwater quality	• wells constructed of materials that may release constituents of concern	§265.90(a) §265.91(a)
	• wells improperly sealed— contamination of sample is a concern	§265.90(a) §265.91(a) §265.91(c)
	• nested or multiple screen wells are used and it cannot be demonstrated that there has been no movement of groundwater between strata	§265.90(a) §265.91(a)(1) §265.91(a)(2)
	• improper drilling methods were used, possibly contaminating the formation	§265.90(a) §265.91(a)
	• well intake packed with materials that may contaminate sample	§265.90(a) §265.91(a) §265.91(c)
	• well screens used are of an inappropriate length	§265.90(a) §265.91(a)(1) §265.91(a)(2)
	• wells developed using water other than formation water	§265.90(a) §265.91(a)
	• improper well development yielding samples with suspended sediments that may bias chemical analysis	§265.90(a) §265.91(a)
	• use of drilling muds or nonformation water during well construction that can bias results of samples collected from wells	§265.90(a) §265.91(a)
5. Downgradient monitoring wells must be located so as to ensure the immediate detection of any contamination migrating from the facility	• wells not placed immediately adjacent to waste management area	§265.90(a) §265.91(a)(2)
	• failure of O/O to consider potential pathways for dense immiscibles	§265.90(a) §265.91(a)(2)

Continued

Table 11-7   **Continued**

Examples of Basic Elements Required by Performance Standards	Examples of Technical Inadequacies that may Constitute Violations	Regulatory Citations
	• inadequate vertical distribution of wells in thick or heavily stratified aquifer	§265.90(a) §265.91(a)(2)
	• inadequate horizontal distribution of wells in aquifers of varying hydraulic conductivity	§265.90(a) §265.91(a)(2)
	• likely pathways of contamination (e.g., buried stream channels, fractures, areas of high permeability) are not intersected by wells	§265.90(a) §265.91(a)(2)
	• well network covers uppermost but not interconnected aquifers	§265.90(a) §265.91(a)(2)
6. Downgradient monitoring wells must be constructed so as to yield samples that are representative of *in situ* groundwater quality	See #4	
7. Samples from background and downgradient wells must be properly collected and analyzed	• failure to evacuate stagnant water from the well before sampling	§265.90(a) §265.92(a) §265.93(d)(4) §270.14(c)(4)
	• failure to sample wells within a reasonable amount of time after well evacuation	§265.90(a) §265.92(a) §265.93(d)(4) §270.14(c)(4)
	• improper decisions regarding filtering or non-filtering of samples prior to analysis (e.g., use of filtration on samples to be analyzed for volatile organics)	§265.90(a) §265.92(a) §265.93(d)(4) §270.14(c)(4)
	• use of an inappropriate sampling device	§265.90(a) §265.92(a) §265.93(d)(4) §270.14(c)(4)
	• use of improper sample preservation techniques	§265.90(a) §265.92(a) §265.93(d)(4) §270.14(c)(4)
	• samples collected with a device that is constructed of materials that interfere with sample integrity	§265.90(a) §265.92(a) §265.93(d)(4) §270.14(c)(4)
	• samples collected with a non-dedicated sampling device that is not cleaned between sampling events	§265.90(a) §265.92(a) §265.93(d)(4) §270.14(c)(4)

Table 11-7 **Continued**

Examples of Basic Elements Required by Performance Standards	Examples of Technical Inadequacies that may Constitute Violations	Regulatory Citations
	• improper use of a sampling device such that sample quality is affected (e.g., degassing of sample caused by agitation of bailer)	§265.90(a) §265.92(a) §265.93(d)(4) §270.14(c)(4)
	• improper handling of samples (e.g., failure to eliminate headspace from containers of samples to be analzyed for volatiles)	§265.90(a) §265.92(a) §265.93(d)(4) §270.14(c)(4)
	• failure of the sampling plan to establish procedures for sampling immiscibles (i.e., "floaters" and "sinkers")	§265.90(a) §265.92(a) §265.93(d)(4) §270.14(c)(4)
	• failure to follow appropriate QA/QC procedures	§265.90(a) §265.92(a) §265.93(d)(4) §270.14(c)(4)
	• failure to ensure sample integrity through the use of proper chain-of-custody procedures	§265.90(a) §265.92(a) §265.93(d)(4) §270.14(c)(4)
	• failure to demonstrate suitability of methods used for sample analysis (other than those specified in SW-846)	§265.90(a) §265.92(a) §265.93(d)(4) §270.14(c)(4)
	• failure to perform analysis in the field on unstable parameters or constituents (e.g., pH, Eh, specific conductance, alkalinity, dissolved oxygen)	§265.90(a) §265.92(a) §265.93(d)(4) §270.14(c)(4)
	• use of sample containers that may interfere with sample quality (e.g., synthetic containers used with volatile samples)	§265.90(a) §265.92(a) §265.93(d)(4) §270.14(c)(4)
	• failure to make proper use of sample blanks	§265.90(a) §265.92(a) §265.93(d)(4) §270.14(c)(4)
8. In Part 265 assesssment monitoring the O/O must sample for the correct substances	• failure of the O/O's list of sampling parameters to include certain wastes that are listed in §261.24 or §261.33, unless adequate justification is provided	§265.93(d)(4)
	• failure of the O/O's list of sampling parameters to include Appendix VII constituents of all wastes listed under §§261.31 and 261.32, unless adequate justification is provided.	§265.93(d)(4)

Continued

Table 11-7 **Continued**

Examples of Basic Elements Required by Performance Standards	Examples of Technical Inadequacies that may Constitute Violations	Regulatory Citations
9. In defining the Appendix VIII makeup of a plume the O/O must sample for the correct substances	• failure of the O/O's list of sampling parameters to include all Appendix VIII constituents, unless adequate justification is provided	§270.14(c)(4)
10. In Part 265 assessment monitoring and in defining the Appendix VIII makeup of a plume the O/O must use appropriate sampling methodologies	• failure of sampling effort to identify areas outside the plume	§265.93(d)(4) §270.14(c)(4)
	• number of wells was insufficient to determine vertical and horizontal gradients in contaminant concentrations	§265.93(d)(4) §270.14(c)(4)
	• total reliance on indirect methods to characterize plume (e.g., electrical resistivity, borehole geophysics)	§265.93(d)(4) §270.14(c)(4)
11. Part B applicants who have either detected contamination or failed to implement an adequate Part 265 GWM program must determine with confidence whether a plume exists and must characterize any plume	• failure of O/O to implement a monitoring program that is capable of detecting the existence of any plume that might emanate from the facility	§270.14(c)(4)
	• failure of O/O to sample both upgradient and downgradient wells for all Appendix VIII constituents See also items #1, #2	§270.14(c)(4)

Although 40 CFR 270.14(c)(4) requires the owner/operator to monitor for *each* Appendix VIII constituent if a regulated unit has caused groundwater contamination at the time of permit application, recently issued EPA guidance substantially reduces this requirement in many cases. Relying on 40 CFR 270.14(a), the guidance authorizes federal and state permit writers to waive the monitoring requirement for a substantial portion of the Appendix VIII constituents. EPA believes that waivers are justified in many cases because analytical methods for the omitted chemicals are either not available, or not possible to perform in a timely manner. This guidance also recommends, however, that permit writers require monitoring for an additional 25 constituents which appear on the Superfund's list of hazardous substances but do not yet appear on Appendix VIII. Authority to require the monitoring of chemicals not yet on Appendix VIII is derived from new RCRA Section 3005(c)(3) as described in Chapter 10. Appendix E is the list of the 25 new constituents to be monitored, and Appendix F is the list of Appendix VIII constituents which EPA be-

lieves, as of February 1986, can and should be analyzed for in compliance with 40 CFR 270.14(c)(4). Permit writers still retain the discretion to require monitoring for the hazardous constituents not listed in Appendix F, particularly if the chemical is produced at the facility as a product or a waste. In those instances where a waiver of some of the Appendix VIII testing is granted by the permit writer, permits subsequently issued should include conditions that will "reopen" the permit and require monitoring should EPA fail to omit the particular substances from Appendix VIII in an upcoming rulemaking. Interested readers are urged to obtain EPA's "Guidance on Issuing Permits to Facilities Required to Analyze Ground Water for Appendix VIII Constituents," released in February 1986, and to contact EPA for the status of the rulemaking to modify Appendix VIII. The guidance does not apply to listing and delisting procedures, as described in Chapter 2.

Corrective Action and the Closure of Interim Status Land Disposal Facilities

Many experts believe that the vast majority of interim status land disposal facilities in this country will voluntarily close rather than seek an operating permit. The percentage of closures may be even higher for surface impoundments because of the provision requiring the retrofitting of many of these impoundments by November 8, 1988 (see Chapter 10). Still others closed involuntarily due to a HSWA provision which terminates interim status if owners/ operators cannot certify compliance with several of the interim status standards by November 8, 1985, thereby requiring closure (see Chaper 13).

The closure process for these facilities raises difficult environmental and regulatory issues. For example, a significant percentage of these facilities are probably leaking, since many of the units are unlined and have been operating for many years. Addressing the contamination caused by closing units will be a major challenge for owners/operators, regulatory authorities, and concerned citizens in the next several years.

In addition, the groundwater monitoring systems installed prior to closure may not be able to determine satisfactorily the presence of cantamination, or may not have been installed long enough to yield sufficient data on the integrity of the closing units by the time of closure. In such cases, regulatory authorities will not be able to determine whether the closing units have caused contamination at the time of closure. This raises issues regarding the monitoring and cleanup responsibilities of the owner/ operator during and after closure of the units, particularly where the owner/ operator of a surface impoundment or waste pile is closing under sections of the regulations which free the owner/operator from post-closure responsibility for the units.

This section of Chapter 11 will describe the interplay of HSWA and the EPA regulations in the closure process, thereby providing the reader with the regulatory framework involved. In addition, this section will identify the grey areas where EPA has not yet formalized RCRA guidance or policy.

EPA's interim status closure regulations are in two parts. One part is 40 CFR 265 Subpart G, the general closure regulations applicable to all TSDFs. Briefly, these regulations include the general performance standard for closure, and the regulations requiring the owner/operator to develop a closure plan, submit it to EPA (or an authorized state) for approval before closure of the unit begins, and public participation requirements.[39]

The closure performance standard, 40 CFR 265.111, requires that all TSDFs close in a manner that:

1. minimizes the need for further maintenance; and
2. controls, minimizes or eliminates, to the extent necessary to protect human health and the environment, post-closure escape of hazardous waste, hazardous waste constituents, leachate, contaminated rainfall or waste decomposition products to the ground or surface waters or to the atmosphere.

By May 1981, the owner/operator of interim status facilities were required to have a written closure plan which included a description of how and when each RCRA unit will be closed. The owner/operator must submit the plan to EPA (or an authorized state) at least 180 days prior to the date the owner/operator expects the unit to receive the last volume of waste.

The plan is subject to approval by EPA (or an authorized state) before closure can begin. Public notice and opportunity for comment, and a public hearing if necessary to clarify issues regarding the plan, are required. Within 90 days of the completed plan's receipt, the regulatory authority must either approve, modify, or reject the plan. If the plan is rejected, the owner/operator is provided another 30 days to submit a second plan for approval. The second plan is then either approved or modified by the regulatory authority within 60 days.

Closure activities must be performed in accordance with the plan. When closure is completed, the owner/operator and an independent registered professional are required to certify to the regulating authority that closure has been performed and completed in accordance with the plan.

The second part of the interim status closure regulations is found under the various interim status standards applicable to individual types of TSDFs. For land disposal facilities, these are 40 CFR 265 Subparts K (impoundments), L (waste piles), M (land treatment units), and N (landfills).[40] These regulations include more specific design and performance standards for closure activities, the design aspects of which are discussed in Chapter 8.

For waste piles and surface impoundments, owners/operators may close with waste materials in place thereby requiring compliance with post-closure care regulations, or may close by removing or treating those waste materials at closure to obviate the need for post-closure care. This latter regulatory option can be very significant for some owners/operators with regulated or other solid waste management units causing significant groundwater contamination. Post-closure care, which includes groundwater monitoring of the units, will require a permit for all units which have not been *certified* closed by January 26, 1983.[41] For units which received hazardous waste after July 26, 1982, this permit requirement will trigger compliance with the 40 CFR 264 Subpart F permitting standards for groundwater monitoring applicable to regulated units, which mandate the performance of corrective action where the groundwater protection standard is exceeded. In addition, the necessity of a permit will trigger compliance with Section 3004(u), which can require the performance of corrective action for releases from RCRA units which stopped receiving waste prior to July 26, 1982, and from any other solid waste management unit at the facility. Compliance with these provisions is a mandatory obligation on the part of permitees, and requires the demonstration of financial assurances to discharge these responsibilities.

On the other hand, owners/operators of waste piles and surface impoundments closing in a manner not requiring post-closure care are under no regulatory obligation to address contamination from any solid waste managements units which are not the subject of the closure proceeding. In addition, under certain circumstances, it is unclear whether the owners/operators of surface impoundments have a regulatory obligation to address the contamination caused by the units closing. This grey area will be described in detail below.

In cases where no permits are involved, EPA's interim status corrective action order (Section 3008(h)) authority is the principal authority available to EPA for addressing groundwater and other environmental contamination. While Section 3008(h) is theoretically similar to Section 3004(u) authority, practical considerations may result in significant differences in the way the two provisions are actually applied. First, the use of the 3008(h) authority is discretionary while compliance with Section 3004(u) is mandatory. In addition, the informational burden on the regulatory authority to trigger 3008(h) orders is greater; authorized states may not possess 3008(h) or similar authority, thereby placing much of the resource burden on EPA in this area; and there are no public participation procedures in place for the issuance of 3008(h) orders. Finally, it is not clear whether 3008(h) authority is available when the facility has been certified closed and is no longer in interim status, although EPA considers it available regardless of the closure status of the facility.[42]

The application of this regulatory framework is especially complicated for surface impoundments. Under 40 CFR 265.228, the owner/operator is provided three options for closing an impoundment:

a. removing the liquids, wastes, waste residues, the liner (if any), and contaminated soil which includes the groundwater in the saturated soils;

b. removing only those materials in paragraph (a) which are hazardous wastes by definition; or

c. closing the impoundment as if it were a landfill (see description below) and providing post-closure care.

Under the first two options, the owner/operator is not required to perform post-closure care, thereby obviating the need for a post-closure permit for the impoundment. Section 3004(u) would not apply to the facility unless another RCRA unit at the facility requires an operating or post-closure permit.

The lack of post-closure care requirements may be an appropriate result with respect to contamination caused by the unit closing under the 225.228(a) option, since the owner/operator is required to address the contamination as a condition of closure. However, under the 40 CFR 265.228(b) option, only the materials considered *hazardous waste* must be removed as a condition of closure. For impoundments handling only characteristic wastes, this option may not require the removal of most of the contamination which may have occurred at the site. This result is a function of the mixture rule and the limited nature of the current waste characteristics.

As explained in Chapter 2, a characteristic waste is no longer considered a hazardous waste when it stops exhibiting the characteristic, even if mixing the waste with non-hazardous waste or dilution is the only reason the waste no longer exhibits the characteristic.[43] Thus, characteristic waste leaking from an impoundment may no longer be hazardous because of dispersal or other reactions which occur as it contaminates soil and groundwater. Contrast this result with a listed waste which remains hazardous until it is delisted by EPA regardless of subsequent mixing or dilution.[44]

In addition to the mixture rule, most of the contamination would remain unaddressed because of the regulatory focus on the presence of hazardous "waste" as opposed to hazardous "constituents." With respect to toxicity concerns, the only applicable waste characteristic definition is EP toxicity which assesses the presence of 14 substances. Compare these 14 with approximately 375 hazardous "constituents," the presence of which is considered evidence of groundwater contamination under the permitting standards.[45] In addition, for the 14 substances covered by the EP toxicity characteristic, the level of contamination necessary to trigger the "waste" definition is at least 100 times federal drinking water standards, while cleanup may be triggered for violation of the drinking water standards under the permitting regulations.[46]

On its face, the 265.228(b) option appears in conflict with the general closure performance standard, which includes references to the post-closure escape of leachate and waste decomposition products. In addition, it conflicts with the underlying policy behind the general performance standard to require TSDFs to remove all hazardous constituents at closure unless they are closing as a landfill and are performing post-closure care.[47]

The 265.228(b) option is also in apparent conflict with new RCRA Section 3005(i), which requires that the same standards for groundwater monitoring and corrective action for permitted facilities apply to interim status facilities receiving waste after July 26, 1982. Permitted impoundments have no 265.228(b) closure option; post-closure groundwater monitoring, and corrective action where appropriate, is required unless all contaminated waste residues and contaminated soils are removed or decontaminated at closure.[48] Under 265.228(b), however, no post-closure groundwater monitoring or corrective action is required as long as the impoundment did not contain listed wastes and the contaminated soils or groundwater do not exhibit a hazardous waste characteristic.

Despite these apparent contradictions, EPA has not yet taken action to limit the use of 40 CFR 265.228(b). Therefore, until such action is taken, Section 3008(h) authority is the principal RCRA authority EPA will rely upon to address contamination from impoundments closing under the 265.228(b) option, contamination from other solid waste management units at facilities with impoundments closing under the 265.288(a) or (b) option, and contamination from any solid waste management units at facilities with impoundments certified closed prior to January 26, 1983.[49] The owner/operator of an impoundment closing pursuant to 265.228(c) after January 26, 1983, must obtain a post-closure permit and must comply with 40 CFR 264 Subpart F (if the impoundment is a regulated unit) and Section 3004(u). As stated above, Secton 3004(u) is also available if other units at a facility require a RCRA permit.

Owners/operators of interim status waste piles must make all "reasonable efforts" to remove or decontaminate all waste residues, contaminated liners, and subsoils. If the owner/operator finds that all the contaminated soils cannot be practically removed, the waste pile must be closed as a landfill and post-closure monitoring and maintenance are required.[50] Therefore, owners/operators of waste piles leaving contaminated materials on-site will require a post-closure permit it they are not certified closed prior to January 26, 1983. Section 3008(h) authorities will be relied upon to address contamination from waste piles certified closed prior to January 26, 1983, and from other solid waste management units at a facility with waste piles not requiring a permit.[51]

Another set of issues arise with respect to surface impoundments and waste piles which close by removing or decontaminating all contaminated material pursuant to 265.228(a) or 265.258(a). In some cases, it may not be possible to rely upon existing groundwater monitoring data to determine the extent of contamination caused by the closing units. The existing data may not be sufficient because the monitoring system in place is inadequate, the system has not been in place long enough, or no monitoring wells were ever installed. The lack of monitoring wells could be the result of non-compliance, a waiver rightfully or incorrectly claimed from groundwater monitoring requirements, or in the case of waste piles, no applicable groundwater monitoring requirement. Without adequate monitoring data, it may not be possible to determine that all contaminated soils and waste residues will be removed or decontaminated at closure.

There is no EPA guidance available yet which directly addresses how to approach this problem, although EPA has indicated it will not allow owners/operators to "walk away" from units with inadequate monitoring systems and groundwater contamination at closure.[52] One option is to require the installation and implementation of an adequate post-closure monitoring program for a specified period of time as a condition of approving the closure plan. This option may be particularly appropriate if non-compliance is the reason for insufficient data at the time of closure. Where the owner/operator was not legally required to provide groundwater monitoring at closure, it may be appropriate to require a phased site investigation of the owner/operator where there exists a reasonable likelihood a release took place. First, the owner/operator may be required to perform an analysis of the soil underlying the unit for Appendix VIII constituents to determine if a release took place. If the presence of contamination is confirmed, the installation of a groundwater monitoring system may also be required to determine if groundwater quality has been impaired. These tasks may be required pursuant to the closure regulations, Section 3005(i), and Section 3008(h) authorities.

Another grey area is the appropriate concentration level of hazardous constituents present in the soil at which compliance with the closure requirements would be considered discharged, or the methodology for determining when enough soil has been removed or treated. There is no definitive EPA RCRA guidance available before publication in this area either.[53]

Owners/operators of land treatment units and landfills necessarily leave waste on-site after closure, therefore they are required to perform post-closure groundwater monitoring and other activities. Those units not certified closed prior to Janury 26, 1983, will require a post-closure permit, thereby triggering Section 3004(u) requirements. Regulated units will also be subject to 40 CFR 264 Subpart F. Units certified closed prior to January 26, 1983, and other solid waste management units at the same facility will be subject to Section 3008(h) authority.[54]

Table 11-8 is a summary of these various closure provisions, and permitting and cleanup requirements.

Table 11-8 Regulatory Framework for Closing Interim Status Facilities

	Performance Standard	Subject to 3008(h) Orders	Post-Closure Permits Required	Compliance with Groundwater Monitoring and Corrective Action Provisions of 40 CFR 264 Subpart F Required	Subject to Section 3004(u) of RCRA
1. *Container Storage Units* (March 19, 1985, proposal—50 *Fed. Reg.* 11091. Note: Final regulation may be different.)	All contaminated equipment, structures and soils must be disposed of or decontaminated	Yes	No	No	No unless other units at facility require a RCRA operating or post-closure permit.
2. *Tank Storage Units* (June 26, 1985 proposal—40 CFR 265.197—50 *Fed. Reg.* 26503. Note: Final regulation may be different.	a) All hazardous waste residues; and contaminated liners, soils, and equipment must be removed or decontaminated; or	Yes	No	No	No unless other units at facility require a RCRA operating or post-closure permit.
	b) Close as a landfill if all contaminated soils cannot be practically removed or decontaminated.	Yes	Yes, if tank not certified closed by January 26, 1983.	Proposal requires compliance with detection monitoring provisions of 40 CFR 264 Subpart F; cleanup would be addressed under Section 3004(u) authorities.	Yes if post-closure permit required or if other units at facility require a RCRA operating or post-closure permit.
3. *Surface Impoundments* (40 CFR 265.228)	a) Remove standing liquids, waste and waste residues, liner(s) (if any), and contaminated soil; or	Yes	*No	*No	*No unless other units at facility require a RCRA operating or post-closure permit.
	b) Remove all materials in paragarph (a) which are hazardous waste, or	Yes	*No	*No	*Same as above.
	c) Close as a landfill by covering the impoundment and	Yes	Yes, if impoundment not certified closed by 1/26/83.	Yes, if impoundment received hazardous waste after 7/26/82.	Yes, if post-closure permit required or other units at facility

Continued

303

Table 11-8 Continued

	Performance Standard	Subject to 3008(h) Orders	Post-Closure Permits Required	Compliance with Groundwater Monitoring and Corrective Action Provisions of 40 CFR 264 Subpart F Required	Subject to Section 3004(u) of RCRA
	providing post-closure care.				require a RCRA operating or post-closure permit.
4. Waste Piles (40 CFR 265.258)	a) Remove or decon-taminate all waste liners, soils and equipment; or	Yes	*No	*No	*No, unless other units at facility require a RCRA operating or post-closure permit.
	b) Close as a landfill if all contaminated soils cannot be practically removed or decontaminated.	Yes	Yes, if waste pile not certified closed by 1/26/83.	Yes, if waste pile received hazardous waste after 7/26/82.	Yes, if post-closure permit required or if other units at facility require a RCRA operating or post-closure permit.
5. Land Treatment Units (40 CFR 265.280)	Control migration of hazardous waste and hazardous waste constituents into groundwater, releases of contaminated run-off into surface water, releases of particulate contaminants into the air, and ensure compliance with certain food-chain crop growth restrictions.	Yes	Yes, if unit not certified closed prior to 1/26/83.	Yes, if unit received hazardous waste after 7/26/82.	Yes, if post-closure permit required or if other units at facility require a RCRA operating or post-closure permit.
6. Landfills (40 CFR 265.310)	Landfill must be covered, pollutant migration and surface water infiltration must be controlled, and erosion prevented.	Yes	Yes, if landfill not certified closed prior to 1/26/83.	Yes, if landfill received hazardous waste after 7/26/82.	Yes, if post-closure permit required or if other units at facility require a RCRA operating or post-closure permit.
7. Incinerators and Thermal Treatment Units (40 CFR 265.351, 381)	All hazardous waste and hazardous waste residues (including ash, and scrubber water and sludges) must be removed.	Yes	No	No	No, unless other units at facility require a RCRA operating or post-closure permit.

Note: Off-site releases are subject to Section 3004(v) of RCRA.

NOTES

1. 47 *Fed. Reg.* 32285 (July 26, 1982).
2. Ibid.
3. Environment Reporter Current Developments, BNA, June 10, 1983, p. 239.
4. Ibid.
5. HSWA Conference Report at 110.
6. Groundwater Monitoring Survey, Subcommittee on Oversight and Investigations of the Energy and Commerce Committee, U.S. House of Representatives, 99th Congress, 1st Session, April 1985 at 4.
7. *Superfund Strategy,* Office of Technology Assessment, U.S. Congress, April 1985, pp. 126–137. As of November 1984, 37 sites considered for EPA's National Priority list for Superfund cleanup were facilities granted interim status to continue operating under RCRA.
8. Ibid.
9. 50 *Fed. Reg.* 14115 (April 10, 1985).
10. 47 *Fed. Reg.* 32311 (July 26, 1982).
11. 50 *Fed.Reg.* 28711 (July 15, 1985).
12. HSWA Conference Report, pp. 111–12.
13. Ibid.
14. 50 *Fed. Reg.* 28716 (July 15, 1985).
15. 50 *Fed. Reg.* 28713 (July 15, 1985). See also "RCRA Section 3008(h)—The Interim Status Corrective Action Authority," EPA, Dec. 16, 1985, pp. 4–5.
16. 50 *Fed. Reg.* 28713 (July 15, 1985).
17. 50 *Fed. Reg.* 28715 (July 15, 1985).
18. EPA Guidance, note 15, p.7.
19. 50 *Fed. Reg.* 28712 (July 15, 1985).
20. 50 *Fed. Reg.* 28714 (July 15, 1985). See also "Point and Counterpoint," *The Environmental Forum,* Environmental Law Institute, Oct. 1985, pp. 22–30.
21. Ibid. The owner/operator can generally demonstrate financial assurances using the mechanisms currently authorized under 40 CFR 264 Subpart H, but EPA will need to modify Subpart H for corrective action and may restrict the use of some mechanisms under certain circumstances. For example, an owner/operator using the financial test for multiple assurances must demonstrate qualification for the entire cost of all the assurances and not rely on other mechanisms for portions of the assurances. See Memorandum from Jack McGraw, Acting Assistant Administrator, EPA, to Addressees, entitled "Guidance on Corrective Action for Continuing Releases," dated January 30, 1985. Financial assurances must be provided until corrective action is no longer required to protect human health and the environment. In the case of groundwater contamination, corrective action can be terminated when the groundwater protection standard has not been exceeded for at least three years. Section 208 of HSWA authorizes EPA to issue regulations governing financial responsibility for corrective action.
22. 50 *Fed. Reg.* 28715 (July 15, 1985).
23. Ibid.
24. Memorandum from Jack McGraw, Acting Assistant Administrator, to Addressees regarding Guidance on Corrective Action for Continuing Releases (Draft), January 30, 1985, p. 9. See also draft RCRA PA/SI guidance, Office of Solid Waste, EPA, Aug. 5, 1985. EPA recently proposed to require owners/opertors to perform PA/SI sampling and analyses. See 51 *Fed. Reg.* 10713 (March 28, 1986).

25. 51 *Fed. Reg.* 7722, 7723 (Mar. 5, 1986).

26. 50 *Fed. Reg.* 28716 (July 15, 1985).

27. 50 *Fed. Reg.* 28726 (July 15, 1985).

28. Permit Applicant's Guidance Manual for Exposure Information Requirements Under RCRA Section 3019, Office of Solid Waste, EPA, July 3, 1985, p. 1-5.

29. Ibid., p. 2-4, and Appendix D to the Guidance.

30. Ibid., p. 3-1.

31. 40 CFR 270.1(c). EPA recently proposed to require post-closure permits for certain regulated units, regardless of when they closed. See 51 *Fed. Reg.* 10715 (March 28, 1986) and note 48.

32. RCRA Groundwater Technical Enforcement Guidance Document (Draft), Office of Solid Waste and Emergency Response, August 1985, p. 1-2. This draft guidance contains valuable checklists which can be used to evaluate the adequacy of hydrogeological studies, the placement of detection monitoring wells, monitoring-well design and construction, groundwater sampling and analyses, and an assessment monitoring program.

33. Yield becomes a factor, however, when it is so low that the formation is no longer an aquifer. Aquifer is defined as a formation capable of yielding a "significant" amount of water to wells or springs. See 40 CFR 260.10.

34. Draft Enforcement Guidance, supra note 32, p. 2-27.

35. Ibid., p. 2-5.

36. EPA Headquarters has developed guidance on the demonstration of false positives. See Memorandum from John Skinner, Director, Office of Solid Waste, EPA to EPA Regional Directors, Air and Hazardous Materials Division entitled Guidance on Implementation of Subpart F Requirements for Statistically Significant Increases in Indicator Parameter Values, November 30, 1983.

37. EPA has proposed to eliminate some Appendix VIII constituents from testing requirements and has proposed a screening procedure for testing others. See 49 *Fed. Reg.* 38786 (Oct. 1, 1984). EPA is expected to propose in 1986 a second and more far reaching cutback of Appendix VIII testing requirements rather than finalize the 1984 proposal. At the same time, however, EPA may also add additional constituents to the Appendix VIII list, particularly chemicals that appear on Superfund's list of hazardous substances but do not appear in Appendix VIII. Appendix E is a list of 25 substances which EPA may add to Appendix VIII of 40 CFR 261, and which EPA may require owners/operators to monitor for as of February 1986 under authority of new Section 3005(c)(3) of RCRA as described in Chapter 10. See "Guidance on Issuing Permits to Facilities Required to Analyze Ground Water for Appendix VIII Constituents," issued in February 1986 by EPA's Office of Solid Waste and Emergency Response.

38. Groundwater Compliance Order Guidance, Office of Solid Waste and Emergency Response, August 1985, pp. 5-11, 5-12.

39. EPA recently finalized changes to Subpart G of 40 CFR 265. which become effective October 29, 1986. See 51 *Fed. Reg.* 16422 (May 2, 1986).

40. There are no specific RCRA interim status closure standards applicable to underground injection wells. See 40 CFR 265 Subpart R.

41. 40 CFR 270.1(c). See also notes 31 and 48.

42. The regulations do not specify when interim status terminates for facilities not seeking a permit. See 40 CFR 270.73. Section 3005(e)(1) of RCRA suggests that a formal administrative action is necessary to terminate interim status, even at a closed facility. EPA considers Section 3008(h) applicable to owners/operators of closed facilities even where interim status has been formally terminated under 40

CFR Part 124 or Sections 3005(c) and 3005(e)(2) of RCRA. See EPA Guidance, note 15, p.11. Significantly, an owner/operator cannot avoid Section 3008(h) merely by withdrawing its Part A permit application if the owner/operator has been engaged in hazardous waste management since Nov. 19, 1980.

43. 40 CFR 261.3(d)(1).
44. 40 CFR 261.3(d)(2)
45. Compare 40 CFR 261.24 Table 1 to Appendix VIII of 40 CFR 261.
46. Compare 40 CFR 261.24 Table I to 40 CFR 264.94 Table 1.
47. See 50 *Fed. Reg.* 11074 (March 19, 1985).
48. See 40 CFR 264.228(a), (b). Relying upon Section 3005 (i) of RCRA, EPA recently proposed to require post-closure permits for all regulated units that were closed in a manner which would not meet the applicable closure standards for permitted units. If the proposal is finalized, owners/operators of regulated units closed under 40 CFR 265.228 (b) may need to perform additional cleanup activities to meet 40 CFR 264.228. In addition, the post-closure permitting requirement will trigger compliance with Section 3004(u). See 51 *Fed. Reg.* 10715 (March 28, 1986.)
49. Section 7003 of RCRA may also be utilized if the site may be presenting an imminent and substantial endangerment to human health or the environment.
50. 40 CFR 265.258.
51. Section 7003 is also available in some cases. See notes 31 and 48.
52. Memorandum from J. Winston Porter, Assistant Administrator, Office of Solid Waste and Emergency Response, EPA, to Regional Administrators, entitled RCRA Policies on Ground-Water Quality at Closure, dated August 27, 1985.
53. By analogy, however, preamble guidance on the removal option for permitted facilities strongly indicates the provision requires total removal of all hazardous constituents. See 48 *Fed. Reg.* 32320 (July 26, 1982). EPA has indicated the removal option for interim status and permitted impoundments are very similar. See 47 *Fed. Reg.* 32385 (July 26, 1982). In addition, soils contaminated due to releases of listed wastes are also considered hazardous wastes until and unless they are delisted by virtue of the "derived from" rule. See 40 CFR 261.3(c)(2) and Chapter 2. In the absence of a delisting, the removal option would require total removal of all soils considered hazardous waste under the regulations. HSWA now requires that EPA consider the presence of all Appendix VIII constituents in evaluating delisting petitions (see Chapter 2).
54. Section 7003 is also available in some cases.

CHAPTER TWELVE

Tank Standards

Prior to the passage of HSWA, EPA's regulatory authority under RCRA with respect to tanks was limited to those tanks used for the storage or treatment of hazardous waste. EPA issued regulations governing such tanks in 1980 and 1981, and on June 26, 1985, proposed major revisions to these regulations.

With the passage of HSWA, however, EPA's regulatory authority now extends to underground storage tanks that contain petroleum and a wide range of chemical products. HSWA included a new Subtitle I to RCRA, which phases in a regulatory program for product storage tanks over the next few years.

This chapter will describe the requirements that apply to waste storage tanks, the proposed modifications to these requirements, and the regulatory framework Congress established for underground product storage tanks.

EPA'S INITIAL HAZARDOUS WASTE TANK STANDARDS

EPA has issued tank standards under Subtitle C of RCRA applicable to owners/operators of interim status facilities, permitted facilities, and generators temporarily accumulating hazardous waste in tanks on-site. Significantly, "wastewater treatment tanks" subject to regulation under the Clean Water Act, and "elementary neutralization tanks" handling corrosive only wastes are exempt from these requirements (see Chapter 6). Similarly, tanks used only to recycle certain hazardous wastes (i.e., they are not used for storage) are exempt from most regulations. Under 40 CFR 261.6(c)(2), owners/operators of such tanks need only notify EPA of the recycling activity and comply with selected manifest requirements.

Interim Status Standards

The interim status standards require compliance with the generic interim status requirements applicable to all facilities, including: waste analysis, security, emergency preparedness and prevention, manifest tracking, closure and financial responsibility requirements (see Chapter 7). They also include specific requirements applicable to tanks. For example, EPA requires that waste which would cause premature tank failure not be placed in a tank. In addition, a 2-foot freeboard for uncovered tanks has to be provided unless another system or containment structure could catch overflow volumes equal to the top 2 feet of the tank. If waste is continuously fed into the tank, a means to stop the inflow is required. Additional waste analyses are required if new and substantially different wastes are treated or stored in the tank or a different treatment process is used in the tank. Daily inspections of discharge control systems, monitoring equipment, and waste levels in the tank and weekly inspections of tank structure integrity and the area surrounding the tank for evidence of leakage are also required. Special requirements are imposed for ignitable, reactive, and imcompatible waste. At closure, all hazardous waste and waste residues must be removed from the tanks. These requirements have been codified at 40 CFR 265 Subpart J.

Permitting Standards

The tank permitting standards include generic requirements applicable to all permitted facilities, including location, waste analysis, emergency preparedness and prevention, manifest tracking, closure, and financial responsibility requirements (see Chapter 7). In addition, there are requirements specifically applicable to tanks. They include provisions similar to the interim status standards for closure and handling ignitable, reactive, and incompatible wastes. The permitting standards also impose design standards, operating requirements, and additional inspection requirements. To be permitted, the tank must have sufficient shell strength to prevent collapse or rupture. A minimum shell thickness is established for each tank by the Regional Administrator (or an authorized state) based upon a variety of factors. Protection from "accelerated corrosion" is required if materials incompatible with the tank are placed in the tank. Closed tanks require pressure controls, and controls such as waste feed cutoff systems and the maintenance of freeboard are needed for uncovered tanks to prevent overfilling. Tanks storing or treating certain dioxin wastes must have systems which "detect and adequately contain" spills and leaks. Inspection regulations require daily inspections of overfilling control systems, monitoring equipment (i.e., pressure gauge), and the level of waste in uncovered tanks; weekly inspections of the tank and the surrounding area to look for evidence of corrosion and leakage; and the development of a schedule for assessing the integrity of the tank, including shell thickness. The hazardous waste tank permitting standards are codified at 40 CFR 264 Subpart J. Significantly, these regulations do not apply to underground tanks which cannot be entered for inspection. EPA considered a complete ban on underground tanks because of serious damage incidents associated with these tanks, but no permitting standards were issued, so underground tanks with interim status could continue to receive hazardous waste indefinitely.[1]

Generators storing hazardous waste temporarily in tanks may do so without a permit or interim status for up to 90 days (longer for small quantity generators), as long as the generator complies with requirements found in 40 CFR 262.34. These requirements are listed in Table 4-1.

THE JUNE 1985 HAZARDOUS WASTE TANK PROPOSAL

EPA proposed modifications to the hazardous waste tank standards for a variety of reasons. First, EPA believed aspects of the initial regulations were "unworkable," particularly the provisions concerning the establishment and maintenance of a minimum shell thickness. In addition, the initial regulations did not adequately ensure containment of hazardous waste for as long as the waste remains in storage. Corrosion protection for steel tanks was not required even though corrosion is the major cause of failure in metal tank systems. Nor was secondary containment required to prevent releases into the environment in the event the tank leaked. Examples of secondary containment include the construction of a vault around the tank or double-walled tanks with a leak detection system between the walls. Finally, permitting standards had to be issued for underground tanks that cannot be entered for inspection. The principal features of the June 1985 proposal will follow.

For existing interim status tanks, EPA proposed that within one year of the effective date of the revised regulation, owners/operators must either install full secondary containment for the tank and ancillary equipment (i.e., piping), or implement an interim status groundwater monitoring program (see Chapter 11) and install partial secondary containment for aboveground portions of the tank system. Tanks containing wastes with EPA ID Nos. F020–23, F026, and F027 (see Chapter 2) must have complete secondary containment.

In addition, owners/operators of tanks without full secondary containment must submit a tank assessment to the Regional Administrator (or an authorized state) within six months of the effective date of the regulations. The assessment must include a leak test for underground tanks and piping, and an assessment of cracks, leaks, erosion, and corrosion. Similar leak tests must be performed on underground tank systems without full secondary containment at least every six months thereafter. Owners/operators of tanks found susceptible to corrosion must provide corrosion protection to ensure tank integrity for its intended life. Tanks found leaking must be removed from service, and either repaired or replaced. Replacement tanks must have full secondary containment. The leakage must be reported to the Regional Administrator (or an authorized state) and may be subject to an interim status corrective action order for cleanup of contaminated soils and/or groundwater (see Chapter 11). At closure, the owner/operator must make all reasonable efforts to remove or decontaminate all hazardous waste residues and contaminated soil. If he cannot accomplish such removal or decontamination after making all reasonable efforts, he must comply with the post-closure care requirements for landfills, including obtaining a post-closure permit thereby subjecting him to Section 3004(u) requirements for corrective action (see Chapter 11).

The proposed permitting standards also allow owners/operators of existing tanks (including underground tanks) the choice between complete secondary containment or partial secondary containment and groundwater monitoring. New tanks and tanks containing F020-F023, F026, and F027 wastes must have complete secondary containment.

The proposed permitting standards also require a corrosion assessment for all metal tanks in contact with the soil, and corrosion protection must be provided to ensure tank system integrity for its intended life. Design standards for new tanks, including leak detection systems, are provided, and quality control procedures during installation are specified. The closure requirements are similar to the interim status standards. Significantly, no restrictions are placed on installing new underground tank systems, including installation directly in the water table.

Under EPA's proposal, generators engaged in temporary storage (i.e., less than 90 days for large generators) in tanks must install secondary containment within one year of the effective date of the revised regulations. Generators who choose not to install secondary containment must close the tank by that date or change the designation of the tank to interim status and comply with the interim status standards, including groundwater monitoring. Generators choosing to close their tanks must comply with interim status closure standards, but need not obtain EPA or state approval of the closure procedures they will follow, so presumably they decide for themselves whether they have complied or not. Generators also need not determine if their tanks had been leaking prior to closure or the installation of secondary containment. Indeed, one of the principal shortcomings in the EPA proposal is the complete absence of cleanup requirements with respect to these prior releases. Regulatory authority is imperative in this instance because generators engaged in no other waste management activity are not interim status facility owner/operators nor must they obtain a permit, therefore they are not subject to the corrective action authorities of Section 3008(h) or Section 3004(u) of RCRA. According to EPA, 1537 of the 2100 generators storing waste in tanks on a temporary basis would not be subject to Section 3008(h) or 3004(u) authorities.[2]

EPA expects to finalize this proposal by June 1986. HSWA required the permitting standards for underground tanks that cannot be entered for inspection by March 1, 1985.

NEW PROGRAM TO REGULATE UNDERGROUND TANKS OF PETROLEUM AND CHEMICALS

Growing concern over industry- and government-sponsored surveys, and documented damage incidents of underground storage tanks leaking gasoline and toxic chemicals that were not hazardous wastes, prompted the enactment of Subtitle I of RCRA. The available information at the time of passage indicated that between 2.8 and 5 million underground tanks storing petroleum and chemicals exist in the United States,[3] and a large percentage of these are leaking. Perhaps as many as 350,000 gasoline tanks alone are now leaking, and as many as 75% of the existing tanks will leak in the next 10 years.[4] Incidences of contamination have been reported in all 50 states,[5] and the state of Michigan has concluded that storage tanks are the leading cause of groundwater contamination in that state.[6] At least 11 other states have experienced "severe groundwater contamination" from leaking underground storage tanks.[7]

Scope of Subtitle I

The new RCRA requirements apply to "underground storage tanks." These are tanks (and connecting pipes) which contain 10% or more of a "regulated substance" beneath the ground. A regulated substance includes petroleum (including crude oil or any liquid fraction of crude oil), or any of a long list of "hazardous substances" (but not hazardous waste) identified under Superfund. The list of hazardous substances was published in the *Federal Register* of April 4, 1985, page 13546. Readers who are not sure if a particular chemical is considered a hazardous substance should call EPA's RCRA/Superfund hotline at 800-424-9346.

Congress has exempted certain tanks from coverage even if they contain regulated substances. Exempted tanks include:

1. farm or residential tanks of up to 1100-gallon capacity containing motor fuel for noncommercial purposes
2. tanks used for storing heating oil for consumptive use on-site
3. septic tanks·
4. surface impoundments
5. storm water or wastewater collection systems
6. flow-through process tanks
7. certain energy-related pipeline facilities and liquid trap or associated gathering lines directly related to oil or gas production and gathering operations
8. storage tanks underground but above the surface of the floor such as a basement, cellar, shaft, or tunnel.

Notification Requirements

Section 9002 of RCRA imposes three sets of notification requirements. One is for owners of tanks in use on or after November 8, 1984, the second is for owners of tanks who begin using a tank after May 8, 1986, and the third is for owners of tanks taken out of service after January 1, 1974, where the tanks remain in the ground. In each instance, these owners must fill out a form developed by EPA, or a form prepared by their state if the state chooses to use its own form, and send it to the state agency designated in Appendix A. Readers should consult this table and contact their state to determine which form to use. Notification is not required for tanks taken out of the ground prior to May 8, 1986, or taken out of operation on or before Janaury 1, 1974. It is also not required if notice regarding the tank was already provided under Section 103(c) of Superfund.

Owners of tanks in use on or after November 8, 1984, or tanks taken out of operation after January 1, 1974 (but still in the ground) must submit the appropriate form to the designated state agency by May 8, 1986. Owners who bring tanks into use after May 8, 1986, must submit the form within thirty days of bringing the tank into use.

Significantly, the responsibility for notification is placed on the tank owner, not the operator. An operator is generally the person with daily responsibility for the operation of the tank, but may not be the tank owner. Where tanks have had multiple owners, EPA has indicated in some circumstances which owners are responsible. If a tank was taken out of operation between January 1, 1974, and November 8, 1984, RCRA requires that the person who last owned the tank before it was taken out of use bears the notification responsibility. In some cases, however, a prior tank owner who has taken the tank out of operation may not know if a subsequent tank owner returned the tank to service. This return to service would relieve the prior tank owner of compliance responsibilities. EPA believes if the prior owner "knows or has reason to know" the tank was *permanently* taken out of service (i.e., tank is filled with solid material, intakes and vents are paved over, or access piping is disconnected or removed), that owner should notify. In addition, EPA has provided a box on the form marked "ownership uncertain," which can be checked where there is confusion about who should notify. Persons are encouraged to notify when in doubt even where double reporting may result, because of the need to develop a complete inventory of underground tanks. Notification of tanks in use on or after November 8, 1984, must be provided by the tank's owner on November 8, 1985, regardless of whether or when it was taken out of service.

The EPA form was published in the *Federal Register* of November 8, 1985, at pages 46614–5. Copies of the EPA form, or the state form where the state has substituted its own, should be obtained from the state agencies in Appendix A. The EPA form is provided as Figure 12-1.

Civil penalties of up to $10,000 can be assessed for each tank for which notification is not provided or for which false information is submitted.

To assist EPA and the states in educating tank owners about these requirements, persons who "deposit" regulated substances in an underground storage tank must "reasonably notify" tank owners of their obligation. According to EPA, persons who "deposit" these substances are those selling the regulating substances to the tank owner, not the person physically delivering the material. Therefore, this responsibility to notify tank owners will primarily fall upon suppliers like refiners or marketers

Notification for Underground Storage Tanks

FORM APPROVED
OMB NO 2050-0049
APPROVAL EXPIRES 6-30-88

	STATE USE ONLY
I.D. Number	
Date Received	

GENERAL INFORMATION

Notification is required by Federal law for all underground tanks that have been used to store regulated substances since January 1, 1974, that are in the ground as of May 8, 1986, or that are brought into use after May 8, 1986. The information requested is required by Section 9002 of the Resource Conservation and Recovery Act, (RCRA), as amended.

The primary purpose of this notification program is to locate and evaluate underground tanks that store or have stored petroleum or hazardous substances. It is expected that the information you provide will be based on reasonably available records, or, in the absence of such records, your knowledge, belief, or recollection.

Who Must Notify? Section 9002 of RCRA, as amended, requires that, unless exempted, owners of underground tanks that store regulated substances must notify designated State or local agencies of the existence of their tanks. Owner means—

(a) in the case of an underground storage tank in use on November 8, 1984, or brought into use after that date, any person who owns an underground storage tank used for the storage, use, or dispensing of regulated substances, and

(b) in the case of any underground storage tank in use before November 8, 1984, but no longer in use on that date, any person who owned such tank immediately before the discontinuation of its use.

What Tanks Are Included? Underground storage tank is defined as any one or combination of tanks that (1) is used to contain an accumulation of "regulated substances," and (2) whose volume (including connected underground piping) is 10% or more beneath the ground. Some examples are underground tanks storing: **1.** gasoline, used oil, or diesel fuel, and **2.** industrial solvents, pesticides, herbicides or fumigants.

What Tanks Are Excluded? Tanks removed from the ground are not subject to notification. Other tanks excluded from notification are:
1. farm or residential tanks of 1,100 gallons or less capacity used for storing motor fuel for noncommercial purposes;
2. tanks used for storing heating oil for consumptive use on the premises where stored;
3. septic tanks;

4. pipeline facilities (including gathering lines) regulated under the Natural Gas Pipeline Safety Act of 1968, or the Hazardous Liquid Pipeline Safety Act of 1979, or which is an intrastate pipeline facility regulated under State laws;
5. surface impoundments, pits, ponds, or lagoons;
6. storm water or waste water collection systems;
7. flow-through process tanks;
8. liquid traps or associated gathering lines directly related to oil or gas production and gathering operations;
9. storage tanks situated in an underground area (such as a basement, cellar, mineworking, drift, shaft, or tunnel) if the storage tank is situated upon or above the surface of the floor.

What Substances Are Covered? The notification requirements apply to underground storage tanks that contain regulated substances. This includes any substance defined as hazardous in section 101 (14) of the Comprehensive Environmental Response, Compensation and Liability Act of 1980 (CERCLA), with the exception of those substances regulated as hazardous waste under Subtitle C of RCRA. It also includes petroleum, e.g., crude oil or any fraction thereof which is liquid at standard conditions of temperature and pressure (60 degrees Fahrenheit and 14.7 pounds per square inch absolute).

Where To Notify? Completed notification forms should be sent to the address given at the top of this page.

When To Notify? **1.** Owners of underground storage tanks in use or that have been taken out of operation after January 1, 1974, but still in the ground, must notify by May 8, 1986. **2.** Owners who bring underground storage tanks into use after May 8, 1986, must notify within 30 days of bringing the tanks into use.

Penalties: Any owner who knowingly fails to notify or submits false information shall be subject to a civil penalty not to exceed $10,000 for each tank for which notification is not given or for which false information is submitted.

INSTRUCTIONS

Please type or print in ink all items except "signature" in Section V. **This form must be completed for each location containing underground storage tanks.** If more than 5 tanks are owned at this location, photocopy the reverse side, and staple continuation sheets to this form.

Indicate number of continuation sheets attached [   ]

I. OWNERSHIP OF TANK(S)	II. LOCATION OF TANK(S)
Owner Name (Corporation, Individual, Public Agency, or Other Entity)	(If same as Section 1, mark box here ☐)
	Facility Name or Company Site Identifier, as applicable
Street Address	
	Street Address or State Road, as applicable
County	
	County
City State ZIP Code	
	City (nearest) State ZIP Code
Area Code Phone Number	

Type of Owner (Mark all that apply ☒)

☐ Current ☐ State or Local Gov't ☐ Private or Corporate
☐ Former ☐ Federal Gov't (GSA facility I.D. no. _____) ☐ Ownership uncertain

Indicate number of tanks at this location [   ]

Mark box here if tank(s) are located on land within an Indian reservation or on other Indian trust lands ☐

III. CONTACT PERSON AT TANK LOCATION

Name (If same as Section I, mark box here ☐)   Job Title   Area Code   Phone Number

IV. TYPE OF NOTIFICATION

☐ Mark box here only if this is an amended or subsequent notification for this location.

V. CERTIFICATION (Read and sign after completing Section VI.)

I certify under penalty of law that I have personally examined and am familiar with the information submitted in this and all attached documents, and that based on my inquiry of those individuals immediately responsible for obtaining the information, I believe that the submitted information is true, accurate, and complete.

Name and official title of owner or owner's authorized representative	Signature	Date Signed

CONTINUE ON REVERSE SIDE

EPA Form 7530-1 (11-85)

Page 1

Figure 12-1a

VI. DESCRIPTION OF UNDERGROUND STORAGE TANKS *(Complete for each tank at this location.)*					
Tank Identification No. (e.g., ABC-123), or Arbitrarily Assigned Sequential Number (e.g., 1,2,3...)	Tank No.	Tank No.	Tank No.	Tank No.	Tank No.
1. Status of Tank *(Mark all that apply ☒)* Currently in Use Temporarily Out of Use Permanently Out of Use Brought into Use after 5/8/86	▭▭▭▭	▭▭▭▭	▭▭▭▭	▭▭▭▭	▭▭▭▭
2. Estimated Age (Years)					
3. Estimated Total Capacity (Gallons)					
4. Material of Construction *(Mark one ☒)* Steel Concrete Fiberglass Reinforced Plastic Unknown Other, Please Specify	▭▭▭▭ ___	▭▭▭▭ ___	▭▭▭▭ ___	▭▭▭▭ ___	▭▭▭▭ ___
5. Internal Protection *(Mark all that apply ☒)* Cathodic Protection Interior Lining (e.g., epoxy resins) None Unknown Other, Please Specify	▭▭▭▭ ___	▭▭▭▭ ___	▭▭▭▭ ___	▭▭▭▭ ___	▭▭▭▭ ___
6. External Protection *(Mark all that apply ☒)* Cathodic Protection Painted (e.g., asphaltic) Fiberglass Reinforced Plastic Coated None Unknown Other, Please Specify	▭▭▭▭▭ ___	▭▭▭▭▭ ___	▭▭▭▭▭ ___	▭▭▭▭▭ ___	▭▭▭▭▭ ___
7. Piping *(Mark all that apply ☒)* Bare Steel Galvanized Steel Fiberglass Reinforced Plastic Cathodically Protected Unknown Other, Please Specify	▭▭▭▭▭ ___	▭▭▭▭▭ ___	▭▭▭▭▭ ___	▭▭▭▭▭ ___	▭▭▭▭▭ ___
8. Substance Currently or Last Stored in Greatest Quantity by Volume *(Mark all that apply ☒)* **a. Empty** **b. Petroleum** Diesel Kerosene Gasoline (including alcohol blends) Used Oil Other, Please Specify **c. Hazardous Substance** Please Indicate Name of Principal CERCLA Substance OR Chemical Abstract Service (CAS) No. Mark box ☒ if tank stores a mixture of substances **d. Unknown**	▭ ▭▭▭▭ ___ ▭ ___ ___ ▭ ▭	▭ ▭▭▭▭ ___ ▭ ___ ___ ▭ ▭	▭ ▭▭▭▭ ___ ▭ ___ ___ ▭ ▭	▭ ▭▭▭▭ ___ ▭ ___ ___ ▭ ▭	▭ ▭▭▭▭ ___ ▭ ___ ___ ▭ ▭
9. Additional Information (for tanks permanently taken out of service) **a.** Estimated date last used (mo/yr) **b.** Estimated quantity of substance remaining (gal.) **c.** Mark box ☒ if tank was filled with inert material (e.g., sand, concrete)	/ ___ ▭	/ ___ ▭	/ ___ ▭	/ ___ ▭	/ ___ ▭

EPA Form 7530-1 (11-85) Reverse

Figure 12-1b

rather than transportation firms. This notification requirement is effective 30 days after EPA issues the notification form and lasts for 18 months thereafter, or from December 8, 1985, to June 8, 1987.

EPA has indicated there are a variety of acceptable methods that depositors could use to satisfy their notification responsibilities. They include a one-time certified letter to tank owners or operators, or a warning statement on shipping tickets and invoices. EPA has suggested language for one-time notification letters and for shipping tickets and invoices, which are reprinted in the November 8, 1985, *Federal Register* on page 46619.

Tank sellers assume a similar education responsibility beginning 30 days after performance standards are issued for new tanks, as described below. These standards are anticipated by February 8, 1987, for tanks storing petroleum and its fractions, and by August 8, 1987, for tanks storing other regulated substances.

Regulating Underground Storage Tanks

Sections 9003(a) and (b) of RCRA contain the schedule for promulgating regulations governing underground storage tanks:

> Regulations governing all tanks storing petroleum or their fractions—due February 8, 1987.
>
> Regulations governing new tanks storing non-petroleum regulated substances—due August 8, 1987.
>
> Regulations governing existing tanks storing non-petroleum regulated substances, and financial responsibility requirements for all tanks (if EPA decides these are necessary and desirable)—due August 8, 1988.

The regulations become effective three months after promulgation. All the regulations must include, at a minimum:

1. requirements for a leak detection system or a comparable system or method designed to identify releases from the tank
2. recordkeeping of release identification data
3. reporting of releases and response actions
4. cleanup requirements
5. closure standards to prevent future releases.

New tanks standards must also include design, construction, installation, release detection, and compatibility standards. To the extent deemed "necessary and desirable" by EPA, regulations must also require evidence of financial responsibility for corrective action and liability to third parties for bodily injury and property damage.

By November 8, 1988, EPA is required to modify its permitting standards for underground tanks containing hazardous waste which cannot be entered for inspection to include the requirements issued for product storage tanks, if necessary to protect human health and the environment.

Congress included this requirement to encourage consistency in the regulation of tanks storing regulated substances and hazardous waste.

Interim Prohibition on Installation of New Underground Storage Tanks

Until standards governing new non-petroleum storage tanks are effective (November 8, 1987), the installation of certain underground tanks for storing regulated substances (i.e., steel tanks without corrosion protection) is prohibited effective May 7, 1985. Specifically, Congress prohibited the installation of underground tanks of substandard design or construction. These are tanks which:

1. will not prevent releases due to corrosion for the tank's operational life;
2. will not prevent releases due to structural failure for the tank's operational life; or
3. are incompatible (including the lining of such tanks) with the stored regulated substance.

A limited exception to the corrosion protection requirements is provided where the soil resistivity is sufficiently high (12,000 ohm/cm) to discourage corrosion.

To implement this prohibition, EPA has issued draft guidance on the causes of corrosion and techniques available to prevent corrosion, causes of structural failure besides corrosion, secondary containment systems which can prevent releases into the environment, and tank and liner compatibility considerations.[8] The guidance essentially describes a series of options available to properly install a new underground storage tank without recommending a particular course of action.

CORROSION PROTECTION Three types of corrosion protection methodologies are described in EPA's guidance: cathodic protection, the use of corrosion resistant materials, and the use of corrosion-resistant coatings. Two types of cathodic protection are described: the use of sacrificial anodes and impressed current. Sacrificial anodes are generally metal rods with little corrosion resistance (i.e., magnesium, zinc) attached to the tank. They are designed to attract the flow of electric current between the tank and the surrounding soils, which causes corrosion, thereby "sacrificing" themselves to save the tank. Impressed current involves supplying sufficient electric current to the tank system to reverse the direction of the tank-to-soil, corrosion-causing current flow. Both systems require careful and periodic monitoring.

In lieu of installing a cathodically protected steel tank, tank and ancillary piping may be constructed of noncorrosive materials, such as fiberglass-reinforced plastic. Significantly, these tanks require very careful installation, since they are lighter and less flexible than steel, and may rely on backfill for most of their structural support.

Finally, a tank system may be coated with electrically resistant materials, such as coal tar epoxy or fiberglass-reinforced plastic. The effectiveness of the coating depends on the quality and completeness of its coverage, the durability of the coating, and the compatibility of the coating with the stored regulated substance. If there is a flaw in the coating, corrosion-producing electric currents will concentrate at the flaw, thereby causing corrosion at an accelerated pace.

As stated above, Congress did not require corrosion protection where tanks are installed in soils with a resistivity of 12,000 ohm/cm or higher. Soil resistivity should be measured using ASTM Method G57-78 (the "Wenner Method").

Significantly, EPA does not believe this soil resistivity measurement is sufficient to warrant the installation of a nonprotected tank. EPA believes additional factors contribute to corrosion such as stray currents (i.e., currents from underground power systems); nitrate, sulfide and chloride levels in the soils; acidity of the soil; and the dissolved oxygen content of the soil. In addition, the particular ASTM method recommended has two significant limitations since it yields an average soil resistivity measurement over a significant area on a given day. First, a lack of soil uniformity over a given area may mask strips of low soil resistivity where the tank may actually be installed. Second, the moisture content of the soil can substantially affect soil resistivity, thus a measurement on a dry day may not account for periods of high rainfall or seasonal variations. For these reasons, readers may wish to assume all soils are corrosive and employ appropriate corrosion protection techniques, even though it is not legally required.

The use of secondary containment systems can also prevent releases of regulated substances into the environment, particularly when accompanied by a leak detection system which notifies the tank operator when a tank is leaking. Three secondary containment systems are described by EPA: double-walled tanks, pit lining systems, and vaults. Double-walled tanks consist of a tank within a shell, with the space between used for leak detection. Pit lining systems consist of a tank installed over a depression covered with a liner of low permeability (i.e., clay, synthetic liner), which should be sloped leading to a sump pump for leak detection and removal purposes. Vaults consist of a concrete floor upon which a tank is supported, four concrete walls, and a roof. The concrete may be lined to prevent leakage through it. (See Figure 12-2).

STRUCTURAL FAILURE   EPA has concluded that most structural tank failures are due to faulty installation rather than faulty design or construction. The most common installation mistakes are:

inadequate pit design
improper handling of the tank

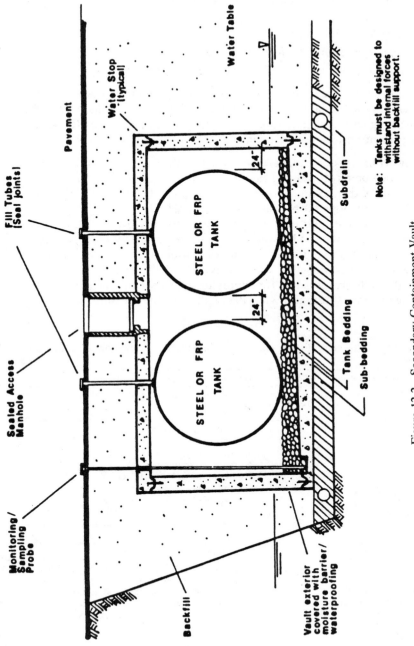

Figure 12-2   Secondary Containment Vault

319

improper tank bedding and replacement
inadequate backfilling procedures
incorrect tank depth
inadequate tank anchoring
improper installment of ancillary equipment

EPA guidance recommends a series of installation practices, drawing heavily upon available industry guides.[9] The guidance also recommends consulting with Underwriters' Laboratories, Inc., guides on the structural integrity of various tank designs.[10]

COMPATIBILITY CONSIDERATIONS   Incompatibility between the regulated substance being stored and the tank or its lining can result in accelerated corrosion and cracking, and increased seepage through the tank structure. EPA has developed a partial list of chemicals that are incompatible with certain tank liner and construction materials (see Table 12-1). EPA recommends consultation between tank owners and suppliers regarding compatibility, and the performance of compatibility tests where information is not otherwise available. Accordingly, EPA believes a tank owner should hold the seller responsible for supplying a tank which meets his particular storage needs. If a tank owner desires to change the substance stored in

Table 12-1   Compatibility of Hazardous Substances with Storage Tank and Liner

Construction Material	Generally Incompatible with
Steel	Mineral acids; nitric, hydrochloric, dilute sulfuric acids
Aluminum	Alkalies; potassium hydroxide, sodium hydroxide, mineral acids
Magnesium	Mineral acids
Lead	Acetic acid, nitric acid
Copper	Nitric acid, ammonia
Zinc	Hydrochloric acid, nitric acid
Tin	Organic acids, alkalies
Titanium	Sulfuric acid, hydrochloric acid
Fiberglass-reinforced plastics	Sulfuric acid 95%, nitric acid 50%, hydrofluoric acid 40%, aromatic solvents, ketone solvents, chlorinated solvents

Lining Material	Generally Incompatible with
Alkyds	Strong mineral acids, strong alkalies, alcohol, ketones, esters, aromatic hydrocarbons
Vinyls (polyvinylchloride—PVC)	Ketones, esters, aromatic hydrocarbons
Chlorinated rubbers	Organic solvents
Epoxy (aminecured, polyamide cured, or esters)	Oxidizing acids (nitric acid), ketones
Coal tar epoxy	Strong organic solvents
Polyesters	Oxidizing acids, strong alkalies, mineral acids, ketones, aromatic hydrocarbons
Silicones	Strong mineral acids, strong alkalies, alcohols, ketones, aromatic hydrocarbons

a tank, a test should be performed to determine if the new substance is compatible with the tank (and its lining), piping, *and* any residue in the tank.

Miscellaneous Provisions

A study by EPA on underground petroleum storage tanks was required by Congress no later than November 1985. A study on non-petroleum storage tanks is due November 1987. The studies are intended to provide information on tank failure rates and the reasons for failure, assessing potential factors such as age, construction material, installation methods, hydrogeology of tank locations, and soil conditions. The studies should also examine the effectiveness and cost of leak detection systems, tank testing, and inventory control. A third study of farm and heating oil tanks is also required, designed to estimate their number and locations, and to analyze the likelihood of releases from such tanks.

Separate inspection and enforcement authorities have been included in Subtitle I in lieu of Sections 3007 and 3008 of RCRA. However, the Section 7002 citizen suit provisions and the Section 7003 imminent hazard provisions remain applicable to underground storage tanks (see Chapter 13).

Finally, states may be authorized to administer the Subtitle I regulatory program instead of EPA. The authorization may apply to petroleum tanks, non-petroleum tanks, or both. To obtain authorization, states must demonstrate to EPA their programs are no less stringent (they can be more stringent) than the federal program and that they provide for adequate enforcement. The states may begin applying in May 1987 and have a grace period of 1 to 3 years after the issuance of new federal regulations during which the programs can be less stringent and still be authorized.

NOTES

1. Several states have prohibited or restricted the installation or use of underground hazardous waste tanks. See Lennett and Greer, State Regulation of Hazardous Waste, *Ecology Law Quarterly*, Vol. 12, No. 2 (1985), pp. 242–4.
2. EPA Data Request M850548, dated August 17, 1985. On Dec. 16, 1985, EPA proposed to exempt from regulation tanks used for storage in a closed-loop reclamation process where the hazardous wastes are re-used in the original manufacturing process within a year of being reclaimed. See 50 *Fed. Reg.* 51264.
3. 130 *Cong. Rec.* S9164 (daily ed. July 25, 1984) (statement of Sen. Durenberger).
4. *Ibid.*
5. *Ibid.*
6. HSWA Conference Report, p. 128.
7. *Ibid.*
8. *The Interim Prohibition: Guidance for Design and Installation of New Underground Storage Tanks* (Draft), Office of Solid Waste, EPA, June 1985.
9. *Ibid.* p. 2-2.
10. *Ibid.* p. 2-8.

CHAPTER THIRTEEN

Inspection and Enforcement Authorities

This chapter will describe the Resource Conservation and Recovery Act provisions authorizing federal enforcement activity to ensure compliance with RCRA. These provisions can be used by EPA to enforce federal law in states where EPA is administering some or all of the RCRA program, and to enforce authorized state requirements in programs approved by EPA to operate in lieu of the federal program (see Chapter 14). In addition, each state has its own enforcement authorities and policies with which the reader should become familiar.

Prior weaknesses in the federal enforcement effort spawned a series of strengthening amendments to federal law as part of HSWA. These amendments will be described below.

INSPECTION AUTHORITY

Section 3007 of RCRA authorizes EPA employees, their representatives (including EPA contractors), or employees of authorized state programs or their representatives, to enter at reasonable times the establishment of any person where hazardous wastes *are* or *have been* generated; transported from; or treated, stored, or disposed. This authorization includes the ability to inspect the facility, obtain samples, and obtain and copy records and information related to the hazardous wastes. Significantly, the term hazardous wastes in Section 3007 is not limited to those wastes *currently* listed or identified as hazardous. Therefore, the inspection authority applies to facilities where any wastes which *would* meet the statutory definition of hazardous (see Chapter 2) are or were generated or managed.[1] The inspections can be performed to gather information for either enforcement or regulation development purposes.

The information obtained in these inspections will be made available to the public unless a claim of confidentiality is asserted and granted under EPA's Freedom of Information Act procedures.[2] All information, including confidential information, must be made available to the Congress upon written request.

Prior to the passage of HSWA, RCRA did not specify how often facilities should be inspected or the appropriate depth of the inspections. These decisions were left to the discretion of EPA and authorized states. The result was an inspection program of uneven quality, because too few inspections were performed and the scope of the inspections varied widely.[3] Congress was particularly concerned that Reagan Administration efforts to trim EPA's budget and state grant funds was the cause for the shortfall in EPA and state inspection capabilities.[4]

Consequently, HSWA now requires EPA and the authorized states to "thoroughly inspect" every interim status or permitted TSDF *at least* once every two years, beginning November 8, 1985. The actual frequency, and the scope of the inspections, is to be decided by EPA after a rule-making proceeding which has not yet begun (in early 1986). At a minimum, storage facilities will be inspected more frequently due to this provision, since prior to HSWA they were typically inspected once every four years.[5]

HSWA requires more frequent inspections of TSDFs owned or operated by a federal agency, or operated by a state or local government. These provisions require thorough inspections at least annually, and the inspections must be performed by EPA or its representatives.

EPA also has the authority under Section 3013 of RCRA to order the owner/operator of a facility where hazardous waste *is* or *has been* treated, stored, or disposed, to perform monitoring, testing, or analyses necessary to determine the nature and extent of a potential hazard to human health and the environment existing at the site. A prior owner/operator may be ordered to perform these activities if the present owner/operator cannot reasonably be expected to know about the presence of the waste or its potential for release. These orders are enforceable in federal district court if the owner/operator refuses to comply. EPA may perform these activities where an owner/operator is not available or unwilling to discharge the responsibilities adequately, and obtain reimbursement from present or prior owner/operators for the costs of such activity.

EPA ENFORCEMENT AUTHORITIES

To address RCRA violations, Section 3008(a) of RCRA authorizes EPA to issue an administrative order or file suit in federal district court against the non-complier. The choice of enforcement action is at the discretion of the government. In authorized states, however, EPA must first notify the state before initiating either kind of enforcement action. Among remedies typically sought by EPA in such actions are compliance with RCRA, and penalties for past and current violations.

In practice, most federal RCRA enforcement activity is administrative rather than judicial. If an administrative order is issued, the alleged violator can contest the order but must do so within thirty days. Typical grounds for contesting an order issued by EPA are: the violations did not occur as alleged, or the penalties assessed are excessive. The procedures for contesting an administrative order can be found at 40 CFR Part 22.

Penalties imposed by EPA administratively can include the suspension or revocation of a permit and/or fines of up to $25,000 per day for each violation. Permit revocation proceedings are governed by 40 CFR Part 124.[6]

EPA has established a RCRA Civil Penalty Policy for assessing administrative penalties and as guidance for seeking fines in judicial cases.[7]

Table 13-1

		Extent of Deviation from Requirement		
		Major	Moderate	Minor
	Major	$25,000 to 20,000	$19,999 to 15,000	$14,999 to 11,000
Potential for Harm	Moderate	$10,999 to 8,000	$7,999 to 5,000	$4,999 to 3,000
	Minor	$2,999 to 1,500	$1,499 to 500	$499 to 100

The policy consists of several phases of penalty calculation. First, a "gravity-based penalty" for a particular violation is determined based on the potential harm posed by the violation and the extent of deviation from the applicable law or regulation. The greater the potential for harm and the greater the deviation from compliance, the larger the penalty, as indicated in Table 13-1.

EPA has grouped RCRA violations into two classes, with Class I violations considered the most serious.[8] Examples of RCRA violations and how they are classified are provided in Appendix G.

A separate penalty can be assessed for each independent violation (i.e., the violation is a result of a separate act, or the same violation exists in different locations). Continuing violations may also be subject to separate per day assessments, particularly for "egregious" violations, until the non-compliance is corrected. In such cases, the total gravity-based penalty for each violation is the product of multiplying the per-day penalty by the number of days of violation.

The remaining phases of penalty calculation involves adjustments to the gravity-based penalty. The gravity-based penalty is increased when a violation results in significant economic benefit to the violator. EPA will generally adjust the penalty upward to an amount equal to or greater than the economic benefit of non-compliance. EPA calculates the economic benefit of non-compliance by combining savings estimates from compliance delay and compliance avoidance.

EPA will also adjust the gravity-based penalty upward or downward based on five other factors generally related to the owner/operator's behavior and financial status, those adjustments generally not exceeding 25% for each factor. The five factors are: the presence or lack of presence of good faith on the part of the owner/operator, degree of willfulness or negligence exhibited by the violation, the history of non-compliance at all the owner/operator's sites (upward adjustment only), the owner/operator's ability to pay (downward adjustment—amount determined case-by-case), and "other unique circumstances." A sample penalty computation worksheet is provided as Figure 13-1.

Company Name: _____

Regulation Violated: _____

Assessments for each violation should be determined on separate worksheets and totalled.

(If more space is needed, attach separate sheet.)

Part I— Seriousness of Violation Penalty

1. Potential for Harm: _____

2. Extent of Deviation: _____

3. Matrix Cell Range: _____

   Penalty Amount Chosen: _____

   Justification for Penalty Amount
     Chosen: _____

4. Per-Day Assessment: _____

Part II—Penalty Adjustments

	Percentage Change*	Dollar Amount
1. Good Faith Efforts to Comply/Lack of Good Faith:	_____	_____
2. Degree of Willfulness and/or Negligence:	_____	_____
3. History of Noncompliance:	_____	_____
4. Other Unique Factors:	_____	_____
5. Justification for Adjustments:	_____	
6. Adjusted Per-day Penalty (line 4, part I + lines 1–4, part II):	_____	
7. Number of Days of Violation:	_____	
8. Multi-day Penalty (number of days × line 6, part II):	_____	
9. Economic Benefit of Noncompliance:	_____	
Justification:	_____	
10. Total (lines 8 + 9, part II):	_____	
11. Ability to Pay Adjustment:	_____	
Justification for Adjustment:	_____	
12. Total Penalty Amount (must not exceed $25,000 per day of violation):	_____	

*Percentage adjustments are applied to the dollar amount calculated on line 4, part I.

Figure 13-1   PENALTY COMPUTATION WORK SHEET

Section 3008(d) of RCRA imposes criminal liability upon a person who "knowingly" violates EPA regulations by: 1) transporting or causing the transportation of hazardous wastes to an unlicensed TSDF; 2) managing hazardous wastes without a permit or in violation of a permit or interim status standards; 3) failing to comply with recordkeeping and reporting requirements, or destroying, falsifying, or altering such records; 4) disobeying manifest tracking requirements; or 5) exporting hazardous waste without the consent of the receiving country or in violation of an international agreement governing such export. Significantly, the term "person" includes employees of a company, as well as the company itself, if the employees knew or should have known of the non-compliance.[9] Penalties can range up to $50,000 per day for each violation and/or imprisonment of up to 5 years for the first two types of violations, and up to 2 years for the remaining violations. For second convictions, the maximum punishment is doubled.

Under Section 3008(e) of RCRA, a person who knowingly violates Section 3008(d) and knew at the time of the violation that he had placed another person in imminent danger of death or serious bodily injury is subject to fines of up to $250,000 and/or imprisonment of up to 15 years. An organization in violation can be fined up to $1,000,000. Under Section 3008(e), the term "knowing" means the defendant must be actually aware that his conduct placed another person in jeopardy. Knowledge possessed by someone else cannot be attributed to the defendant. Section 3008(f) of RCRA elaborates on the state of mind necessary for criminal liability under Section 3008(e).

To enforce the criminal provisions of RCRA, the U.S. Justice Department has established an Environmental Crimes Unit and EPA has hired criminal investigators. A number of states have established criminal task forces as well to prosecute violations of state law.

Section 3008(h) of RCRA authorizes EPA to issue administrative orders seeking corrective action or any other response measure necessary to protect human health and the environment at an interim status facility where a release of hazardous waste into the environment has occurred. EPA is also authorized to assess a civil penalty of up to $25,000 per day for non-compliance with these orders. EPA is expected to rely substantially upon Section 3008(h), among a variety of regulatory and enforcement provisions, to address contamination of soils and groundwater at interim status facilities. A more detailed discussion of this provision, and its relationship to other cleanup authorities, can be found in Chapter 11.

Finally, under Section 7003 of RCRA, EPA may file suit or issue an administrative order regarding sites which "may present an imminent and substantial endangerment to health or the environment," seeking cleanup and other appropriate injunctive relief. EPA is authorized to take such action against any past *or* present waste generator, transporter, or owner/operator of a TSDF who *has* contributed or *is* contributing to the endangerment.[10] The provision applies to management activities for both solid and hazardous waste, and therefore it is not limited to wastes currently identified as hazardous.

The Section 7003 authority has been utilized generally to address sites not otherwise regulated under RCRA (i.e., no hazardous waste management occurred after November 19, 1980). It was particularly important prior to the passage of the Superfund law in 1980 because it was the principal enforcement provision available to EPA to obtain cleanup of those sites.[11] Now, Superfund contains similar enforcement authorities, as well as a fund to finance cleanup responses where responsible parties are unwilling or unavailable. Thus, Superfund and Section 7003 of RCRA are the principal authorities presently available for addressing these so-called uncontrolled sites.

EPA had also planned to use Section 7003 of RCRA and Superfund authorities to address off-site contamination from RCRA regulated units and releases from non-regulated units at RCRA permitted facilities, but various HSWA provisions now require EPA to address such releases as part of the RCRA permitting process (see Chapter 11). Therefore, as a result of these HSWA provisions, the principal use of Section 7003 of RCRA will continue to be the cleanup of uncontrolled sites.

OTHER ENFORCEMENT AUTHORITIES

A variety of HSWA provisions are intended to improve federal and state enforcement efforts by encouraging the participation of concerned citizens in the RCRA enforcement process. These provisions are intended to both increase the availability of information to the public about RCRA violations, and authorize law suits by concerned citizens where federal and state agencies have not taken appropriate action.

These provisions were deemed necessary because of the failure of EPA and the states, from the outset, to establish a credible RCRA enforcement program. The effects of this failure are still visible today. As recently as April 1985, EPA admitted in testimony before Congress that there was still "a serious lack of compliance" with interim status groundwater monitoring requirements.[12] This lack of compliance was particularly significant because these requirements had been in effect since November 19, 1981, and were first announced in May 1980 so that the regulated community would have eighteen months to achieve compliance when the regulations became effective.[13] In addition, the groundwater monitoring requirements are among the most important RCRA requirements currently in effect.

These violations were still occurring in 1985 because they were not corrected in 1982 and 1983. EPA was simply not referring cases to the Justice Department for prosecution at that time. As a House Subcommittee report stated, "EPA's enforcement effort during the first fourteen months of the Reagan Administration came to a virtual halt and created a widespread perception that the agency lacked a strong enforcement arm."[14]

Enforcement activity to address uncontrolled sites was also conspicuously absent in the first several years of the Reagan Administration. Between fiscal years 1980 and 1981, EPA referrals to the Justice Department for civil action under RCRA and Superfund declined from 46 to 8.[15] In terms of cases actually filed, 12 RCRA Section 7003 cases had been filed in 1979, and another 43 cases had been filed in 1980.[16] However, under the Reagan Administration, only 7 cases were filed in 1981, 3 cases in 1982, and 2 cases through April of 1983.[17] Even less activity had occurred using Superfund enforcement authorities.[18]

EPA's failure to devote adequate resources to RCRA enforcement was a principal cause of continued non-compliance by the regulated community. In 1983, EPA had 85 full-time technical positions devoted to RCRA enforcement in Headquarters and the 10 Regional offices. In contrast, the water program had 365 positions.[19] EPA lawyers fared no better, complaining of a resource shortfall of "crisis" proportions.[20]

Compliance with Interim Status Standards

As a first step toward improving RCRA compliance, Congress enacted new RCRA Sections 3005(e)(2) and (3), which required an owner/operator of a land disposal facility granted interim status before November 8, 1984, to certify compliance with "all applicable groundwater monitoring and financial responsibility requirements" by November 8, 1985, or lose interim status. In addition, the owner/operator had to submit a Part B permit application for the land disposal units by November 8, 1985, or lose interim status. Similarly, the owner/operator of a land disposal facility granted interim status after November 8, 1984, must certify compliance with the same requirements within 12 months of the date the land disposal unit becomes subject to those requirements and submit a Part B permit application for those units by then as well.

This "loss of interim status provision" applies to all interim status landfills, land treatment units, surface impoundments (used for storage, treatment, or disposal), waste piles, and Class I underground injection wells. It also applies to owners/operators for these facilities without interim status but who are nevertheless allowed to operate as "late notifiers." These persons were not granted interim status because they did not comply with Section 3010 notification requirements in a timely manner, but EPA, exercising enforcement discretion, chose not to shut them down. The provision also applies to owners/operators granted temporary exclusions from hazardous waste regulation via the filing of a delisting petition (see Chapter 2). However, if the land disposal units are receiving only waste which has been temporarily excluded from regulation, the unit is subject to the provision but is not subject to any applicable interim status groundwater monitoring, financial responsibility, or permit application requirements, thereby providing temporary relief from the potential loss of interim status. Nevertheless, the interim status and permit application requirements will become applicable again when the temporary exclusion is revoked (required by HSWA no later than November 8, 1986) unless a final delisting is granted. When the exclusion is revoked, the unit will have one year to achieve compliance or lose interim status.

The applicable groundwater monitoring requirements (except for underground injection wells) can be found at 40 CFR 265 Subpart F (or the state analog in authorized states) and are described in Chapter 11. Financial responsibility' requirements (except for UIC wells) can be found at 40 CFR 265 Subpart H (or the state analog in authorized states) and are described in Chapter 7.[21] In the case of UIC wells, applicable groundwater monitoring and financial responsibility requirements are found at 40 CFR 144.28(g)(1)(iii) (where applicable), 144.28(d), and 40 CFR 144 Subpart F (or their state analogs in states with approved UIC programs). In many cases, the state analogs will govern, because of the large number of states authorized.

Compliance is considered actual or "physical compliance." Thus, owners/operators who have admitted in an enforcement action that their units are not in physical compliance must have achieved compliance by November 8, 1985, regardless of the terms of an existing compliance schedule. False certification is subject to civil and criminal enforcement action pursuant to Section 3008(a) and 3008(d) of RCRA. An *original* certification should have been sent to the EPA Region and to authorized states. It should have included the information specified in the September 25, 1985 issue of the *Federal Register,* and should have been signed by appropriate corporate officers or persons in accordance with 40 CFR 270.11(a).

In cases where a facility has more than one hazardous waste management unit, EPA has interpreted HSWA to require the loss of interim status for only those units not certified in compliance or for which a Part B permit application has not been submitted. The remainder of the facility which is certified in compliance or to which Sections 3005(e)(2) and (3) do not apply can continue operating.

The owner/operator with units or facilities losing interim status must stop receiving waste at those units when interim status has terminated (i.e., November 8, 1985) and comply with closure and post-closure requirements for those units. The closure regulations require the owner/operator to submit a closure plan for approval within 15 days of the loss of interim status (i.e., November 23, 1985), according to 40 CFR 265.118(c). An owner/operator with units requiring post-closure care will be required to submit a post-closure permit application for those units. Although these units have lost interim status, the owner/operator is still subject to enforcement action for non-compliance with closure and post-closure requirements, interim status correction action orders (see Chapter 11), and Section 3004(u) of RCRA if a post-closure permit is required (see Chapter 11).

EPA provided its interpretation of these HSWA provisions in the *Federal Register* of September 25, 1985, beginning at page 38946. According to EPA data as of January 3, 1986, the owners/operators of 884 facilities failed to certify compliance with the applicable groundwater monitoring and financial responsibility requirements by November 8, 1985. An additional 107 did not submit the mandated Part B permit application.

Availability of Information

HSWA also requires that authorized states make available to the public information obtained by the state regarding TSDFs "in substantially the same manner and to the same degree" as if EPA were administering the RCRA program in the state. Prior to the passage of HSWA, authorized states were not required to release important information to the public, such as inspection reports or groundwater monitoring data. Since most states are expected to administer the RCRA program in lieu of EPA, the public could have been barred from effective participation in permitting and enforcement proceedings in those states if they were not allowed to examine information needed to evaluate the facilities of concern. In non-authorized states, where EPA possesses the relevant information regarding TSDFs, EPA is required to comply with the Freedom of Information Act[22] and 40 CFR Part 2, which generally provides for the release of this information. Therefore, prior to HSWA, public access to information was dependent upon whether a state was authorized and a state's public access policies. Now as a result of HSWA, the public is ensured access to information on TSDFs as provided under federal law, irrespective of whether a state is authorized.

This provision of HSWA was codified by EPA as a requirement for state authorization on July 15, 1985.[23] States which received final authorization for the pre-HSWA RCRA program without a state analog to 40 CFR Part 2 must revise their programs to retain pre-HSWA authorization.[24] EPA is expected to issue guidance explaining what states must do to comply with this new requirement in the spring of 1986.

Inventory of Federal Facilities

HSWA also imposes upon each federal agency a continuing obligation to compile and submit to EPA and to authorized states information on each hazardous waste TSDF the federal government owns or operates, or has owned or operated at any time in the past. The required information includes the location of the site and the site hydrogeology; the amount, nature, and toxicity of the waste managed at the site; information known on the extent of environmental contamination at the site; and the reasons for a lack of monitoring data where none is available. This inventory must be submitted every two years, beginning January 31, 1986.

If a federal agency fails to compile this inventory EPA must notify the head of that agency of the violations and perform the inventory if it is not completed within 90 days of such notification. These responsibilities are mandatory, and can be enforced by citizen suits (see discussion below).[25]

This provision was aimed solely at federal facilities because it had been difficult for the public to obtain information regarding these facilities, particularly on uncontrolled sites. Since EPA's enforcement authority against other federal agencies is limited, because it is the government's position that one executive branch agency cannot sue another, the states and the public play a critical role in enforcing RCRA requirements at federal facilities.[26] Thus, this provision of HSWA was intended to reaffirm federal agency compliance responsibilities and "shine a light" on agency performance by ensuring public availability of critical information.[27]

Citizen Suits

The 1976 RCRA contained the standard citizen suit provision in environmental laws which authorizes citizens to sue federal agencies and other generators, transporters, and TSDF owners/operators in violation of a permit, regulation, or RCRA requirement. This authority, in Section 7002 of RCRA, is contingent upon the notification of the violator, EPA, and the state of the alleged violation in advance of filing the suit; and it is contingent upon EPA or the state not initiating and "diligently prosecuting" their own law suit before the citizen suit is filed. Section 7002 also authorizes suits against EPA for a failure to perform a non-discretionary duty such as issuing regulations mandated by Congress.

HSWA expands this citizen suit authority in two very significant ways. First, in law suits against a member of the regulated community for non-compliance with a RCRA permit, regulations, etc., citizens can now seek the imposition of penalties for past and present violations, as well as court orders mandating future compliance and other appropriate injunctive relief.[28] This authority to seek penalties in the same manner as EPA may encourage defendants to negotiate compliance schedules with citizen plaintiffs shortly after the case is filed, since penalties can be imposed on a per-day basis, thereby increasing the potential economic impact of protracted litigation. The fines and penalties which are imposed in citizen suits are paid to the U.S. Treasury; however, defendants can be required to pay plaintiff's attorneys' fees and expenses if the plaintiff prevails or substantially prevails.

Second, Congress expanded RCRA's citizen suit authority to include suits to abate an imminent and substantial endangerment in the same manner and against the same persons as EPA could initiate under Section 7003 of RCRA. This expansion of authority was unprecedented but deemed appropriate for several reasons. One reason is there are too many uncontrolled sites potentially requiring enforcement activity for EPA and the states to address them in a timely manner. Estimates vary, but the number of uncontrolled sites which will require some type of response activity ranges from 1,500 to 10,000, and much of this response activity will be enforcement related.[29] Considering EPA's track record from 1981 to 1983, even if federal and state authorities were theoretically capable of meeting this challenge, EPA did not appear ready, willing, and able to do so. Consequently, this new citizen suit authority was intended to supplement federal and state enforcement efforts.[30]

In addition, it seemed incongruous that citizen suit authority was available to rectify permit violations irrespective of the immediacy of the risk to public health posed by the violation, but the authority to sue for abatement was not available where a site was posing an imminent and substantial endangerment to public health. In effect, citizen suits were not authorized for the situations posing the greatest immediate risk.[31] In providing this citizen suit authority, Congress imposed substantial limitations on its use consistent with the intent that the provision supplement rather than hinder ongoing federal and state cleanup efforts. No citizen suit alleging an endangerment can be brought unless 90-day advance notice has been given to EPA, the state, and the persons alleged to contribute to the endangerment. In this manner, government agencies are given time to determine whether they wish to proceed with their own litigation or take other appropriate action. In addition, these suits may not be brought where the government is actively responding to the endangerment at the site. Thus citizen suits are not authorized if EPA is diligently prosecuting its own suit under Section 7003 of RCRA or similar authorities under Section 106 of Superfund, or if EPA is actively engaged in fund-financed cleanup activities at the site under Section 104 of Superfund. Similarly, the suits are not authorized if EPA enforcement efforts have forced responsible parties to determine the extent of contamination and evaluate cleanup options for the site, or perform cleanup activities at the site or if the state is engaged in similar cleanup or enforcement activities. Finally, these suits cannot be brought to challenge the siting of a TSDF or the issuance of a permit, thereby ensuring that the citizen suit authority would not be used as a vehicle for collateral attacks on RCRA permitting decisions.

Where the government takes enforcement action, HSWA provides for some additional public participation in the process, but the precise extent of the new provisions is not clear. The Senate bill clearly provided that, in Section 7003 cases brought by EPA, persons living near the site posing the endangerment may intervene in the case as a matter of right unless the government can demonstrate it is adequately representing their interests. The intent of the Senate bill was to make participation in these suits easier for persons at risk so they may participate in the development of a cleanup program for the site.[32] While the legislative history of HSWA contains no evidence that the final law as adopted would alter this intent in any way, the Justice Department has seized upon a drafting error in the final law to argue there is no statutory right of intervention in Section 7003 cases.[33] The issue will require a judicial or Congressional resolution.

One undisputed change occurs where the government does not file suit under Section 7003 of RCRA but issues an administrative order or otherwise enters into a contract settling claims with persons who contributed to the endangerment posed by a site. In those instances, EPA must provide the public with both an opportunity for a meeting near the site and a chance to comment on the proposed settlement before the settlement is finalized.

NOTES

1. 40 CFR 261.1(b). Civil and criminal penalties may be imposed upon a person who fails to respond to a reasonable request for information. *United States* v. *Liviola*, 605 F. Supp. 96 (N.D. Ohio 1985).

2. See 40 CFR Part 2.

3. HSWA Conference Report, p. 110.

4. Senate HSWA Report, p. 42.

5. *Ibid.*

6. 40 CFR 270.43.

7. RCRA Civil Penalty Policy, May 8, 1984.

8. Enforcement Response Policy, December 1984.

9. *United States* v. *Johnson and Towers, Inc.*, 741 F.2d 662 (3rd Cir. 1984).

10. The liability of railroads may be limited where due care was exercised in the management of the waste by the railroads and the endangerment resulted from actions taken by others after the waste left the control of the railroad (see Section 7003 of RCRA). Technical amendments clarified that non-negligent generators who shipped wastes off-site are liable for contributing to the endangerment at the site (see HSWA Conference Report at 119).

11. 42 U.S.C. 9601 *et seq.*

12. Statement of Jack McGraw, Acting Assistant Administrator, EPA, before the Subcommittee on Oversight and Investigations, Committee on Energy and Commerce, U.S. House of Representatives, April 29, 1985.

13. 40 CFR 265.90.

14. Hazardous Waste Enforcement, Report of the Subcommittee on Oversight and Investigations, Committee on Energy and Commerce, U.S. House of Representatives, 97th Cong., 2nd Session, December 1982, p. 31.

15. *Ibid.*

16. *Ibid.*, p. 32.

17. Hazardous Waste Control and Enforcement Act of 1983, Hearings before the Subcommittee on Commerce. Transportation and Tourism of the Committee on Energy and Commerce, U.S. House of Representatives, 98th Congress, 1st Session, Ser. No. 98-32, p. 384.

18. Hazardous Waste Enforcement, supra note 14, p. 30.

19. Hearings supra note 17, p. 364.

20. See Chapter 1.

21. Some states with interim authorization do not have analogs for the financial responsibility requirements, in which case there are no applicable financial responsibility requirements in those states.

22. 5 U.S.C. 552.

23. 50 *Fed. Reg.* 28730 (July 15, 1985).

24. *Ibid.* In the *Federal Register* of January 6, 1986, EPA proposed to delay the deadline for states to make the necessary revisions to July 1, 1986, or July 1, 1987, if a statutory change was required. See 51 *Fed. Reg.* 499, 500.

25. Senate HSWA Report, p. 44.
26. See e.g. *LEAF* v. *Hodel*, 586 F. Supp. 1163 (E.D. Tenn. 1984).
27. Senate HSWA Report, p. 45.
28. The Clean Water Act contains similar authority. See 33 U.S.C. 1365(a).
29. *Superfund Strategy*, Office of Technology Assessment, U.S. Congress, April 1985, pp. 11–13.
30. House HSWA Report, p. 53.
31. 130 *Cong. Rec.* S9151 (daily ed. July 25, 1984) (statement of Senator Mitchell).
32. Senate HSWA Report, p. 56.
33. See Brief for the United States and the State of California in *United States* v. *Stringfellow,* No. 84-5682 (9th Cir. filed December 1984); *U.S.* v. *Stringfellow,* 24 ERC 1089, 1094 fn. 7 (9th Cir. 1986).

CHAPTER FOURTEEN

The Relationship Between EPA and State Regulatory Agencies

Until the passage of HSWA, states which obtained authorization from EPA to administer a RCRA program did so *in lieu of* EPA. Authorized states issued the RCRA permits, and received the reports and monitoring data that the regulated community submitted in compliance with the state equivalent of the federal RCRA regulations. Compliance with state regulations in authorized states was sufficient to satisfy federal law. In contrast, EPA issued the RCRA permits in non-authorized states and compliance with state law was not considered sufficient to satisfy federal requirements.

Because only state regulations had legal force and effect in authorized states, newly issued EPA regulations and federal self-implementing statutory provisions did not become effective immediately in authorized states. The federal requirements did not become effective in those states until the states modified their own regulations to reflect the federal changes. Federal regulations governing the time for making these modifications allowed states up to 30 months in some cases to make the necessary changes. This lag time posed substantial problems for the drafters of HSWA. If HSWA did not alter this federal/state relationship, the profound policy shifts reflected in HSWA would not be realized in the short-term, and in some cases could have deleterious environmental consequences. For example, land disposal restrictions effective only in non-authorized states could encourage the increased disposal of otherwise prohibited wastes into landfills in authorized states where the HSWA regulations were not yet effective. Since hazardous waste is often shipped interstate, states not yet reflecting HSWA policies could become dumping grounds, thereby concentrating the disposal of wastes of greatest concern. This result is contrary to the policy behind a federal law designed to establish uniform minimum national standards.

Consequently, Congress modified the structure established in the 1976 law by making the HSWA requirements (including the self-implementing provisions and regulations mandated by HSWA) effective in all states at the same time regardless of whether the state had been authorized for the non-HSWA RCRA program. EPA was given the responsibility to implement the HSWA provisions in authorized states until the states are authorized to implement the HSWA provisions. Meanwhile, states could continue to administer the non-HSWA components of the RCRA program. Therefore, the federal/state relationship for the HSWA requirements differs significantly from the relationship for non-HSWA requirements, particularly in authorized states.

In this chapter, the authorization process prior to HSWA will be described because the majority of states have been authorized or are seeking authorization to implement the non-HSWA RCRA requirements. In addition, the HSWA modification to this process will be examined, as will the effect of these modifications on authorized states and the regulated community in these states.

NON-HSWA AUTHORIZATION

Sections 3006 and 3009 of RCRA establish the basic federal/state relationship in the RCRA program. Section 3006 empowers the Administrator to evaluate and authorize state programs to administer the RCRA program in lieu of EPA and provides that a permit issued by an authorized state has the same legal status as a permit issued by EPA. The provision also includes procedural and substantive requirements for approving state programs, which will be described below.

Section 3009 requires an authorized state program to be no less stringent than federal regulations, but does not prohibit state programs from imposing more stringent state requirements. In practice, many states have imposed more stringent requirements in one or more areas.[1] Readers are thus encouraged to investigate whether and to what extent state requirements differ from the requirements described in this book. Generally, the regulated community must comply with the more stringent of the federal and state requirements. To obtain copies of the state regulations, contact the state agency administering the hazardous waste regulatory program. In some cases, states have prepared summary sheets highlighting those state regulations more stringent than the federal requirements.

There are actually two forms of authorization potentially available to states: interim authorization and final authorization. The former is temporary, intended to encourage states to develop RCRA programs over time and eventually achieve final authorization. Final authorization is permanent unless it is withdrawn by EPA upon request of the state, or because the state is not properly implementing the program. It is not necessary for a state to obtain interim authorization before applying for final authorization.

Interim Authorization

Section 3006(c) of RCRA enabled a state to seek interim authorization for hazardous waste programs that were "substantially equivalent" to the non-HSWA federal program. Because of EPA delays in issuing the federal regulations, the pre-HSWA interim authorization process was divided into phases and components. Phase I covered the regulations defining terms and how wastes were designated hazardous (40 CFR Parts 260 and 261), the generator and transporter standards (40 CFR Parts 262 and 263), and the interim status standards (40 CFR Part 265). Phase II was divided into three components. Generally, Phase II A consisted of the permitting standards for containers and tanks. Phase II B consisted of the incinerator permitting standards, and Phase II C consisted of the July 1982 land disposal regulations.

States could be authorized for Phase I only, or Phase I and Phase II A, or Phase I and all the components in Phase II. EPA would administer those portions of Phase II for which a state was not authorized. State permits were considered RCRA permits only for the portion of the program authorized. States could apply for interim authorization until July 26, 1983, but by July 26, 1983, states without interim authorization for any or all of the Phase II components had to apply for interim authorization for all of the RCRA program or lose the partial interim authorization previously granted.[2] After July 26, 1983, states could only apply for final authorization. These deadlines could be extended for "good cause."

The minimum content of the interim authorization application and the minimum substantive requirements in the state regulations necessary to obtain interim authorization were established in federal regulations, and codified at 40 CFR 271.124–129. The application content requirements included: a program description with an accounting of resources available to administer and enforce the program; an opinion from the state Attorney General that state law met federal requirements accompanied by copies of the relevant state statutes and regulations; a Memorandum of Agreement between the state and the EPA Region providing for the sharing of information both to enable EPA to conduct oversight and enforcement activities, and to help coordinate state and federal RCRA activities; and an authorization plan describing efforts the state will take to obtain final authorization. Within 30 days of receiving a complete application, the EPA Regional Administrator had to issue a notice in the *Federal Register* soliciting public comment and announcing a public hearing. Within 90 days of the *Federal Register* notice, EPA had to make a final decision on the application and publish the final decision in the *Federal Register*.

Under the 1976 law, interim authorization was intended to last only 24 months. However, since the interim authorization process actually occurred in phases, the last phase beginning with the January 26, 1983, effective date of the July 1982 land disposal regulations, interim authorization was extended administratively by EPA from November 1980 through January 1985. In addition, Section 227 of HSWA extended interim authorization for the non-HSWA RCRA requirements for one additional year, until January 31, 1986. On February 1, 1986, the authority to administer RCRA programs in states which did not have final authorization automatically reverted to EPA.[3] When the reversion occurred, state regulations remained in effect but only with respect to satisfying the mandate of state law. Compliance with RCRA required adherence to federal regulations, thus the regulated community had to begin complying with two sets of requirements.

Final Authorization

Section 3006(b) provides states with the option of obtaining final authorization to administer and enforce the RCRA program. To obtain final authorization, the state program must be "equivalent" to the federal program, "consistent" with the federal program and other state programs, and provide for adequate enforcement.

The regulations specifying what EPA considers equivalent are codified at 40 CFR 271.9–14, and generally require that the same universe of wastes be regulated in the same manner as under the federal regulations. Again, state requirements may be more stringent.

With respect to inconsistency, EPA has interpreted the term to mean a program which unreasonably restricts the interstate movement of hazardous waste, imposes prohibitions on hazardous waste management which have no basis in human health or environmental protection, or does not require the use of the Uniform Hazardous Waste Manifest as specified in federal regulations.[4] Adequate enforcement means having: sufficient resources to meet inspection and enforcement goals; acceptable procedures for receiving, collecting, and evaluating compliance data (40 CFR 271.15); and sufficient enforcement authority, including the ability to seek fines and penalties from, and the imprisonment of, non-compliers (40 CFR 271.16).

The application for final authorization must include a program description, an Attorney General opinion, a Memorandum of Agreement, and copies of all relevant state statues and regulations, as specified in 40 CFR 271.5–8. Before submitting the application to EPA for approval, the state must provide an opportunity for the public to comment on the proposed application, including a public hearing if sufficient interest is expressed. The state's authorization application must include copies of all the comments received on the state application and a responsiveness summary addressing these comments.

Within 90 days of receiving a complete application, the EPA Administrator must make a tentative decision to approve or deny the application, and publish the decision in the *Federal Register*. Accompanying the publication must be a request for public comment and the announcement of a public hearing. Within 90 days of the *Federal Register* notice, the Administrator must reach a final decision on the authorization application and publish that decision in the *Federal Register* as well.

Once a state is authorized, the state regulations have the force and effect of federal law. As stated above, new non-HSWA federal requirements do not become immediately effective in that state until the state modifies its own regulations. In addition, state applications for final authorization need only reflect the federal regulations issued and the statutory provisions in effect 12 months (or in some cases 18 months) prior to the submission of the application.[5] Thus, to retain equivalency with the federal program, authorized states must continue to modify their programs after they receive final authorization to reflect changes in the federal requirements.

The deadline for making these modifications is one year from the date of promulgation of the RCRA regulation or the effective date of the self-implementing federal statutory provision, unless a statutory amendment to state law is required to make the necessary modifications, in which case two years is provided.[6] Significantly, in the case of a state's authorization application not reflecting newly issued federal regulations or statutory provisions, a state may be required to make modifications very soon after receiving final authorization to meet this deadline. The deadline may be extended by up to 6 months if the state has made a good faith effort to meet the deadline but could not do so. The modifications must be submitted to EPA for approval as to their equivalency, and are subject to public comment.[7]

As stated above, final authorization is permanent unless the authorization is withdrawn. A state may voluntarily request withdrawal, or EPA or a third party may initiate withdrawal because the state program is no longer satisfying the minimum federal statutory and regulatory requirements. Examples of the latter cause for withdrawal include poor enforcement efforts and the failure to adhere to public participation requirements.[8] In such a case, EPA or a third party may initiate a withdrawal proceeding, the requirements for which are codified at 40 CFR 271.23. The proceeding is supervised by a Presiding Officer who makes a recommendation to the Administrator at the conclusion of the proceeding. If the Aministrator determines the state program is deficient, the state will be provided additional time to correct those deficiencies before authorization is actually withdrawn.

Non-authorized Programs

Some states will not seek or will not obtain final authorization to administer the RCRA program by January 31, 1986. In non-authorized states, permits must be issued by EPA to have the force and effect of federal law, and compliance with federal regulations is required. This is not to say that the regulated community can ignore state law. Rather, both federal and state law must be obeyed, so two permits may be required and separate recordkeeping and reporting requirements may be imposed. These dual requirements apply even if a state requirement is equivalent to or more stringent than the corresponding federal requirement.

Techniques may be employed by EPA in non-authorized states to avoid duplication of effort. Through cooperative agreements or contracts, EPA may employ states to undertake such efforts as information collection activities and inspections. EPA may also employ other mechanisms for efficient management of the program such as joint (shared) permit proceedings with the state. However, EPA must assume primary responsibility for approving or denying the RCRA permit. EPA will also assume primary responsibility for enforcing RCRA requirements. Therein lies a critical difference between authorized and non-authorized states. In authorized states, EPA retains authority to enforce authorized portions of state programs but often will not take action until the state requests assistance.[9] In non-authorized states, EPA will utilize its enforcement authorities as the lead enforcement agency.

HSWA AUTHORIZATION

General Description

Section 228 of HSWA, new RCRA Section 3006(g), provides that any "requirement or prohibition" imposed by HSWA is effective in all states at the same time regardless of whether a state is authorized to implement the non-HSWA requirements. EPA is to implement the HSWA provisions in each state until the state is authorized (in interim or final form) to admimister the HSWA provisions. Section 227 of HSWA clarifies EPA's authority to issue or deny RCRA permits in authorized states based on the HSWA provision until the authorized programs are amended to reflect the HSWA provisions.

EPA has interpreted the phrase "requirement or prohibition" broadly to include all of the self-implementing provisions and EPA regulations mandated by HSWA.[10] Consequently, until states become authorized for the HSWA provisions, there will be dual requirements in effect in all states, and EPA will assume significant lead agency regulatory responsibilities in all states. This is true even if state regulations are equivalent or more stringent than the HSWA provisions. As a practical matter, the regulated community must comply with both federal and state requirements, and the more stringent of the HSWA provisions and state rules will govern industry practices in a given state. EPA will assume primary responsibility for those HSWA provisions for which the state has not received authorization, and the state will administer all of its requirements.

As stated above, states applying for non-HSWA authorization must generally submit applications reflecting federal statutory requirements and regulations issued 12 months prior to submittal of the application. This requirement also applies to the HSWA provisions. Thus, state applications for final authorization filed prior to November 8, 1985, need not reflect HSWA provisions, but applications filed after November 8, 1985, must reflect the HSWA provisions and rules in effect for 12 months or more.

Under existing regulations, states with programs already authorized for the non-HSWA requirements must maintain equivalency to the federal program and seek authorization to implement the HSWA provisions as they become effective. As described above, one year is generally allowed for regulatory changes, and two years is allowed for statutory changes. However, EPA may suspend the modification deadlines for the HSWA provisions, so states with non-HSWA authorization may be able to wait for many of the HSWA rules to be promulgated and then apply for authorization for the HSWA requirements.[11]

States may apply for either interim or final authorization to administer the HSWA provisions in lieu of EPA. Section 228 of HSWA, new RCRA Section 3006(g)(2), empowers states with interim or final authorization for the non-HSWA RCRA program to obtain interim authorization upon demonstrating "substantial equivalency" to the federal program. The expiration date for interim authorization for the HSWA requirements will be established by EPA in a regulation yet to be issued. To determine whether a state is authorized for the non-HSWA components of the RCRA program, or some or all of the HSWA requirements, contact the state or the EPA Regional Office for that state.

Permitting Under HSWA

Because many states may not obtain authorization to administer the HSWA provisions for some time, many owners/ operators of TSDFs will need to obtain state *and* federal permits. In most cases, EPA and the state will participate in a joint permit proceeding, resulting in either the issuance of one permit signed by federal and state officials or two permits individually signed and issued simultaneously. However, where authorized states issued draft permits (thereby initiating formal public review of the permit application) prior to April 8, 1985, the state will be allowed to proceed with its permit proceeding, and EPA will attempt to accelerate its own permitting process. In such circumstances, terms of the state permit may conflict with the federal permit when the latter is subsequently issued. States will be urged to modify or reopen their permits to make the permits consistent, or the federal permit will clearly indicate where it supersedes less stringent state requirements.[12]

A state not authorized to administer the HSWA provisions may assume an active assistance role in reviewing the permit application, preparation of the draft and final permits, and responding to public comments, but the EPA Region makes the final decisions with respect to the HSWA requirements. Each state will define its own working relationship with the EPA Region as to the level of involvement it will have in a particular permit proceeding.

For the TSDF owner/operator, the joint permitting process means each agency must receive a copy of the permit application. Determinations with respect to the completeness of applications may be issued jointly, or may come from either agency depending on the nature of the deficiency. The draft permit (or intent to deny) must await a completeness determination by both the state and the EPA Region.

Public participation activities, including public hearings, will be conducted jointly. EPA will generally adhere to the state procedures, although EPA may choose not to participate in procedures not mandated by RCRA, such as hearings before state siting boards. A federal official will serve as the hearing officer for the HSWA permit provisions.

The final decision on the permit application will be issued simultaneously. Appeals, however, will be handled separately. Appeals of the federal HSWA provisions are directed to the EPA Administrator pursuant to 40 CFR 124.19. State law will govern the appeal of non-HSWA permit provisions.

NOTES

1. See Lennett and Greer, "State Regulation of Hazardous Waste," *Ecology Law Quarterly*, Vol. 12, (1985), pp. 183–269.
2. 40 CFR 271.122(c), 271.137.
3. 50 *Fed. Reg.* 28731 (July 15, 1985).
4. 40 CFR 271.4. See also 50 *Fed. Reg.* 46437–40 (November 8, 1985) describing the application of this regulation to a South Carolina disposal fee which sets a higher rate for wastes generated out of state.
5. 40 CFR 271.21(e)(1). Instead of regulations *issued* 12 months prior to the application submission, EPA recently proposed that the requirement be changed to regulations *in effect* 12 months prior to the application submission. Since in most cases, there is a 6-month lag between the issuance of a regulation and its effective date, the proposed change will make it easier for states to file complete applications. See 51 *Fed. Reg.* 496 (January 6, 1986).
6. 40 CFR 271.21(e), but see note 11 below describing a recent EPA proposal on state program modifications.
7. 51 *Fed. Reg.* 7540 (Mar. 4, 1986).
8. 40 CFR 271.22(a)
9. 40 CFR 271.18(e).
10. 50 *Fed. Reg.* 28729 (July 15, 1985). The list of the HSWA requirements and prohibitions will be published by EPA as Table 1 to 40 CFR 271.1(j) as they become effective.
11. 50 *Fed. Reg.* 28732 (July 15, 1985). On January 6, 1986, EPA proposed to cluster the HSWA rules that are issued or take effect between November 8, 1984, and June 30, 1987. States would be required to adopt state analogs to these rules by July 1, 1988, if only state regulatory changes are needed, or by July 1, 1989, if statutory changes are required. In addition, for non-HSWA rules and for HSWA rules issued after June 30, 1987, states would be required to modify their programs by July 1 for all changes made by EPA between the July two years before and the June of the previous year. An additional year may be provided if statutory changes are required. All these deadlines can be extended for an additional 6 months by the Regional Administrator. See 51 *Fed. Reg.* 496.
12. RCRA Reauthorization Statutory Interpretation #5, Jack McGraw, Acting Assistant Administrator, EPA Office of Solid Waste and Emergency Response, July 1, 1985, pp. 3–5.

APPENDIX A

STATE AGENCIES TO CALL ABOUT LAWS WHERE YOU LIVE

State and Territorial Hazardous Waste Management Agencies

*ALABAMA
Alabama Department of
Environmental Management
1751 Federal Drive
Montgomery, Alabama 36130
(205) 271-7737

*ALASKA
Department of Environmental
Conservation
Pouch O
Juneau, Alaska 99811
(907) 465-2666

*ARIZONA
Arizona Department of Health
Services
2005 North Central, Room 301
Phoenix, Arizona 85004
(602) 257-0022

*ARKANSAS
Solid and Hazardous Waste
Division
Arkansas Department of
Pollution Control and Ecology
P.O. Box 9583
Little Rock, Arkansas 72219
(501) 562-7444

CALIFORNIA
Department of Health Services
714 P Street
Sacramento, California 95814
(916) 324-1781

**CALIFORNIA
Ed Anton
California Water Resources
Control Board
P.O. Box 100
Sacramento, California 95801
(916) 445-9552

*COLORADO
Waste Management Division
Colorado Department of Health
4210 East 11th Avenue
Denver, Colorado 80220
(303) 320-8333, Ext. 4364

CONNECTICUT
Hazardous Materials Management
Unit
Connecticut Department of
Environmental Protection
165 Capitol Avenue
Hartford, Connecticut 06106
(203) 566-5712

---

* Uses EPA Form for Underground Tank Notification (see Chapter 12).
** Underground Tank Notification forms are sent here.

DELAWARE
William Razor, Supervisor Solid
and Hazardous Waste
Management Branch
Delaware Department of Natural
Resources and Environmental
Control
89 Kings Highway
P.O. Box 1401
Dover, Delaware 19901
(302) 736-4781

*DISTRICT OF COLUMBIA
Department of Consumer and
Regulatory Affairs
Pesticides and Hazardous Waste
Branch
5010 Overlook Avenue, S.W.
Room 114
Washington, D.C. 20032
(202) 767-8414

FLORIDA
Solid and Hazardous Waste
Florida Department of
Environmental Regulation
2600 Blair Stone Road
Tallahassee, Florida 32301
(904) 488-0300

*GEORGIA
Georgia Department of National
Resources
Land Protection Branch
270 Washington Street, S.W.
Room 723
Atlanta, Georgia 30334
(404) 656-2833

**GEORGIA
Georgia Department of Natural
Resources
Environmental Protection
Division
Underground Storage Tank
Program
3240 Norman Berry Drive
Hapeville, Georgia 30354

GUAM
Jim Branch, Administrator
Guam EPA
P.O. Box 2999
Agana, Guam 96910
(Overseas Operator) 646-8863

*HAWAII
Hawaii Department of Health
Environmental Protection and
Health Services Division
Noise and Radiation Branch
P.O. Box 3378
Honolulu, Hawaii 96810
(808) 548-3075

*IDAHO
Department of Health and
Welfare
450 West State Street
Boise, Idaho 83720
(208) 334-4060

*ILLINOIS
Division of Land Pollution
Control
Illinois Environmental Protection
Agency
2200 Churchill Road
Springfield, Illinois 62706
(217) 782-6761

* Uses EPA Form for Underground Tank Notification (see Chapter 12).
** Underground Tank Notification forms are sent here.

**ILLINOIS
  Underground Storage Tank
  Coordinator
  Division of Fire Prevention
  Office of State Fire Marshal
  3150 Executive Park Drive
  Springfield, Illinois 62703-4599

*INDIANA
  Hazardous Waste Management
  Branch
  Division of Land Pollution
  Control
  Indiana State Board of Health
  1330 West Michigan Street
  Indianapolis, Indiana 46206
  (317) 243-5021

**INDIANA
  Division of Land Pollution
  Control
  UST Program
  Indiana State Board of Health
  P.O. Box 7015
  Indianapolis, Indiana 46207
  (317) 243-5060

IOWA
U.S. EPA, Region 7
726 Minnesota Avenue
Kansas City, Kansas 66101
(816) 374-6534

**IOWA
  Iowa Department of Water, Air
  and Waste Management
900 East Grand
Des Moines, Iowa 50319
(515) 281-8692

*KANSAS
  Kansas Department of Health
  and Environment
  Forbes Field
  Topeka, Kansas 66620
  (913) 862-9360 Ext. 297

KENTUCKY
Department of Environmental
Protection
18 Reilly Road
Frankfort, Kentucky 40601
(502) 564-6716, Ext. 151

LOUISIANA
Office of Solid and Hazardous
Waste
Louisiana Department of
Environmental Quality
P.O. Box 94307
Baton Rouge, Louisiana 70804
(504) 342-1227

**LOUISIANA
  Patricia Norton
  Louisiana Department of
  Environmental Qualtiy
  P.O. Box 44066
  Baton Rouge, Louisiana 70804
  (504) 342-1265

MAINE
Bureau of Oil and Hazardous
Materials Control
Maine Department of
Environmental Protection
State House - Station 17
Augusta, Maine 04333
(207) 289-2651

---

 * Uses EPA Form for Underground Tank Notification (see Chapter 12).
** Underground Tank Notification forms are sent here.

*MARYLAND
Office of Environmental
  Programs
201 West Preston Street
Baltimore, Maryland 21201
(301) 383-5734

*MASSACHUSETTS
Division of Solid and Hazardous
  Waste
Department of Environmental
  Quality Engineering
One Winter Street, 5th Floor
Boston, Massachusetts 02108
(617) 292-5851

**MASSACHUSETTS
  UST Registry, Department of
  Public Safety
1010 Commonwealth Avenue
Boston, Massachusetts 02215
(617) 566-4500

*MICHIGAN
Hazardous Waste Division
Department of Natural
  Resources
P.O. Box 30038
Lansing, Michigan 48909
(517) 373-2730

**MICHIGAN
Ground Water Quality Division
Department Natural Resources
Box 30157
Lansing, Michigan 48909

MINNESOTA
Minnesota Pollution Control
  Agency
1935 West Country Road B2
Roseville, Minnesota 55113
(612) 296-7340

*MISSISSIPPI
Department of Natural
  Resources
Bureau of Pollution Control
Division of Solid Waste
  Management
P.O. Box 10385
Jackson, Mississippi 39209
(601) 961-5171

*MISSOURI
Missouri Department of Natural
  Resources
Division of Environmental
  Quality
P.O. Box 1368
Jefferson City, Missouri 65102
(314) 751-3241

**MISSOURI
Gordon Ackley, UST
  Coordinator
Missouri Department of Natural
  Resources
P.O. Box 176
Jefferson City, Missouri 65102

*MONTANA
Department of Health and
  Environmental Sciences
Solid and Hazardous Waste
  Management Bureau
Cogswell Building, Room B-201
Helena, Montana 59620
(406) 444-2821

* Uses EPA Form for Underground Tank Notification (see Chapter 12).
** Underground Tank Notification forms are sent here.

*NEBRASKA
Department of Environmental
Control
Hazardous Waste Management
Section
P.O. Box 94877
Statehouse Station
301 Centennial Mall South
Lincoln, Nebraska 68509
(402) 471-2186

**NEBRASKA
Nebraska State Fire Marshall
P.O. Box 94677
Lincoln, Nebraska 68509-4677

*NEVADA
Department of Conservation and
Natural Resources
Division of Environmental
Protection
Capitol Complex
Carson City, Nevada 89710
(702) 885-4670

*NEW HAMPSHIRE
Division of Public health
Services
Office of Waste Management
Health and Welfare Building
Hazen Drive
Concord, New Hampshire 03301
(603) 271-4609

**NEW HAMPSHIRE
Water Supply and Pollution
Control Commission
Hazen Drive
P.O. Box 95
Concord, New Hampshire
03301

NEW JERSEY
Division of Waste Management
Department of Environmental
Protection
P.O. Box CN028
32 East Hanover Street
Trenton, New Jersey 08625
(609) 292-8341

**NEW JERSEY
Underground Storage Tank
Coordinator
Department of Environmental
Protection
Division of Water Resources
(CN-029)
Trenton, New Jersey 08625
(609) 292-0424

*NEW MEXICO
Hazardous Waste Section
New Mexico Environmental
Enforcement Division
P.O. Box 968
Sante Fe, New Mexico 87504-
0968

*NEW YORK
Division of Solid and Hazardous
Waste
Department of Environmental
Conservation
50 Wolf Road
Albany, New York 12233
(518) 457-0530

* Uses EPA Form for Underground Tank Notification (see Chapter 12).
** Underground Tank Notification forms are sent here.

**NEW YORK
Bulk Storage Section
Division of Water
Department of Environmental
Conservation
50 Wolf Road, Room 326
Albany, New York 12233
(518) 457-4351

OHIO
Division of Solid and Hazardous
Waste Management
Ohio Environmental Protection
Agency
361 Broad Street
Columbus, Ohio 43215-1049
(614) 466-7220

**OHIO
State Fire Marshal's Office
Department of Commerce
8895 E. Main Street
Reynoldsburg, Ohio 43068
(800) 282-1927

*NORTH CAROLINA
Department of Human Resources
Solid and Hazardous Waste
Management Branch
P.O. Box 2091
Raleigh, North Carolina 27602
(919) 733-2178

*OKLAHOMA
Waste Management Section
Oklahoma State Department of
Health
P.O. Box 53531
Oklahoma City, Oklahoma
73152
(405) 271-5338

**NORTH CAROLINA
Ground Water Section
Department of Natural
Resources & Community
Development
P.O. Box 27687
Raleigh, North Carolina 27611
(919) 733-5083

**OKLAHOMA
Underground Storage Tank
Program
Oklahoma Corporation
Commission
Jim Thorpe Building
Oklahoma City, Oklahoma 73105

NORTH DAKOTA
Division of Hazardous Waste
Management and Special
Studies
North Dakota State Department
of Health
1200 Missouri Avenue,
Room 302
Bismark, North Dakota 58501
(701) 224-2366

OREGON
Department of Environmental
Qualtiy
Hazardous and Solid Waste
Division
522 S.W. 5th Avenue
Portland, Oregon, 97207
(503) 229-5913

* Uses EPA Form for Underground Tank Notification (see Chapter 12).
** Underground Tank Notification forms are sent here.

*PENNSYLVANIA
Department of Environmental
  Resources
P.O. Box 2063
Harrisburg, Pennsylvania 17120
(717) 787-6239

*PUERTO RICO
Environmental Quality Board
P.O. Box 11488
Santurce, Puerto Rico 00910-
  1488
(809) 722-0439

*RHODE ISLAND
Department of Environmental
  Management
204 Cannon Building
75 Davis Street
Providence, Rhode Island 02908
(401) 277-2797

SOUTH CAROLINA
Department of Health and
  Environmental Control
J. Marion Sims Building
2600 Bull Street
Columbia, South Carolina 29201
(803) 758-5681

*SOUTH DAKOTA
Department of Water and
  Natural Resources
Foss Building
523 E. Capitol
Pierre, South Dakota 57501

*TENNESSEE
Division of Solid Waste
  Management
Customs House, 4th Floor
701 Broadway
Nashville, Tennessee 37219-5403
(615) 741-3424

**TENNESSEE
Division of Ground Water
  Protection
Tennessee Department of
  Health and Environment
150 Ninth Avenue, North
Nashville, Tennessee 37219-
  5404
(615) 741-7206

*TEXAS
Industrial and Industrial Service
  Facilities:
Industrial Solid Waste Section
Texas Department of Water
  Resources
P.O. Box 13987, Capitol Station
Austin, Texas 78711
(512) 475-2041

TEXAS
Commercial Service, Municipal,
  State and Federal Facilities:
Texas Department of Health
Bureau of Solid Waste
  Management
1100 West 49th Street
Austin, Texas 78756
(512) 458-7271

---

* Uses EPA Form for Underground Tank Notification (see Chapter 12).
** Underground Tank Notification forms are sent here.

**TEXAS
Underground Storage Tank
  Program
Texas Water Commission
P.O. Box 13087
Austin, Texas 78711

*UTAH
Division of Environmental
  Health
P.O. Box 45500
State Office building, Room 4321
Salt Lake City, Utah 84145
(801) 533-4145

VERMONT
Agency of Environmental
Conservation
Air and Solid Waste Division
State Office Building
Montpelier, Vermont 05602
(802) 828-3395

*VIRGINIA
Department of Health
Division of Solid and Hazardous
  Waste Management
Monroe Building, 11th Floor
101 North 14th Street
Richmond, Virginia 23219
(804) 225-2667

**VIRGINIA
Virginia Water Control Board
P.O. Box 11143
Richmond, Virginia 23230-1143
(804) 257-6685

*VIRGIN ISLANDS
Hazardous Waste Program
Division of Natural Resources
  Management
Department of Conservation and
  Cultural Affairs
P.O. Box 4340
Charlotte Amalie
St. Thomas, Virgin Islands 00801
(809) 774-3320

**VIRGIN ISLANDS
205(J) Coordinator
Division of Natural Resources
  Management
14 F Building 111, Watergut
  Homes
Christianstead, St. Croix,
  Virgin Islands 00820

WASHINGTON
Department of Ecology
Office of Hazardous Substances
Mail Stop PV-11
Olympia, Washington 98504
(206) 459-6299

*WEST VIRGINIA
Solid and Hazardous Waste/
  Ground Water Branch
Department of Natural
  Resources
Division of Water Resources
1201 Greenbriar Street
Charleston, West Virginia 25311
(304) 348-5935

---

* Uses EPA Form for Underground Tank Notification (see Chapter 12).
** Underground Tank Notification forms are sent here.

WISCONSIN
Department of Natural Resources
Bureau of Solid Waste
 Management
P.O. Box 7921
Madison, Wisconsin 53707
(608) 266-1327

*WYOMING
EPA Region 8
Waste Management Division
Hazardous Waste Branch
 (8HWM-ON)
1860 Lincoln Street
Denver, Colorado 80295
(303) 293-1502

**WYOMING
 Water Quality Division
 Department of Environmental
  Quality
 Herschler Building, 4th Floor
  West
 122 West 25th Street
 Cheyenne, Wyoming 82002
 (307) 777-7781

**WISCONSIN
 Bureau of Petroleum Inspection
 P.O. Box 7969
 Madison, Wisconsin 53707
 (608) 266-7605

* Uses EPA Form for Underground Tank Notification (see Chapter 12).
** Underground Tank Notification forms are sent here.

APPENDIX B   SMALL BUSINESS LIKELY TO PRODUCE HAZARDOUS WASTES

Motor vehicle repair and maintenance firms
Electroplaters and other metal manufacturers
Printers
Dry cleaners and launderers
Laboratories
Construction firms
Residential and commercial exterminators
Textile manufacturers, dyers, and finishers
Pesticide manufacturers and formulaters
Furniture manufacturers and finishers
Cosmetics and cleaning agent manufacturers
Wood preservers
Lawn and garden chemical treaters

Vehicle Maintenance

IF YOU REPAIR OR MAINTAIN

- cars
- vans
- trucks
- heavy equipment
- farm equipment

or if you

- remove oil or grease
- remove rust, dirt or paint
- repair or rebuild
- refinish or restore
- paint
- replace lead-acid batteries

the products you use on the vehicles, and on your equipment, tools, hands, or floor may contain hazardous materials, and the wastes generated by using these products may be hazardous wastes.

PRODUCTS CONTAINING HAZARDOUS MATERIALS

Everyday mechanics, bodymen and others use products containing hazardous materials. Products like:

- Rust removers, which contain strong acid or alkaline solutions
- Carburetor cleaners, which contain flammable or combustible liquids
- Used rags containing combustible or flammable solvents
- Paints with flammable or combustible thinners or reducers
- Auto and truck batteries

contain chemicals or materials which are hazardous to human health and the environment. **Table 1** lists typical operations/ processes which use products that may contain hazardous materials and which probably generate hazardous wastes. **If you generate 220 pounds (about half of a 55-gallon drum) or more of hazardous waste per month, you must fill out a Uniform Hazardous Waste Manifest when you ship this waste off your property.**

UNIFORM HAZARDOUS WASTE MANIFEST

Item 11 of the Uniform Hazardous Waste Manifest requires the proper Department of Transportation (DOT) shipping description, which includes:

- the proper DOT shipping name for each waste. To help you complete this item, **Table 2** provides this information for some of the hazardous wastes you are most likely to generate. To obtain the DOT shipping name, hazard class and UN/NA identification number: **Select** the typical process/operation from column 1 of Table 1. **Match** the ingredients from column 3 and the waste type generated from column 4 of Table 1 with the waste type and ingredient in column 1 of Table 2.

Not all vehicle maintenance operations generate hazardous wastes. If you don't see a particular chemical that you use, or if you generate a waste not listed, or if you need any type of help, call your state hazardous waste management agency.

NOTE: Under current federal law, you do not have to use a Manifest when you ship:

- used/dead lead acid batteries that are destined for recycling
- used motor oil. Be aware, however, that the regulations for used oil may change. You should still use environmentally sound methods for the collection, storage and recycling of used motor oil.

Remember—your state may have its own requirements for lead acid batteries or used oil. Be sure to check with your state hazardous waste management agency.

Table 1
TYPICAL OPERATIONS USING MATERIALS WHICH MAY GENERATE HAZARDOUS WASTES

TYPICAL PROCESS/ OPERATION	TYPICAL MATERIALS USED	TYPICAL MATERIAL INGREDIENTS ON LABEL	GENERAL TYPES OF WASTES GENERATED
Oil and grease removal	degreasers—(gunk), carburetor cleaners, engine cleaners, varsol, solvents, acids/alkalies	petroleum distillates, aromatic hydrocarbons, mineral spirits	ignitable wastes, spent solvents, combustible solids, waste acid/ alkaline solutions
Engine, parts and equipment cleaning	degreasers—(gunk), carburetor cleaners, engine cleaners, solvents, acids/alkalies, cleaning fluids	petroleum distillates, aromatic hydrocarbons, mineral spirits, benzene, toluene, petroleum naphtha	ignitable wastes, spent solvents, combustible solids, waste acid/ alkaline solutions
Rust removal	naval jelly, strong acids, strong alkalies	phosphoric acid, hydrochloric acid, hydrofluoric acid, sodium hydroxide	waste acids, waste alkalies
Paint preparation	paint thinners, enamel reducers, white spirits	alcohols, petroleum distillates, oxygenated solvents, mineral spirits, ketones	spent solvents, ignitable wastes, ignitable paint wastes, paint wastes with heavy metals
Painting	enamels, lacquers, epoxys, alkyds, acrylics, primers	acetone, toluene, petroleum distillates, epoxy ester resins, methylene chloride, xylene, VM&P naphtha, aromatic hydrocarbons, methyl isobutyl, ketones	ignitable paint wastes, spent solvents, paint wastes with heavy metals, ignitable wastes
Spray booth, spray guns, and brush cleaning	paint thinners, enamel reducers, solvents, white spirits	ketones, alcohols, toluene, acetone, isopropyl alcohol, petroleum distillates, mineral spirits	ignitable paint wastes, heavy metal paint wastes, spent solvents
Paint removal	solvents, paint thinners, enamel reducers, white spirits	acetone, toluene, petroleum distillates, methanol, methylene chloride, isopropyl alcohol, mineral spirits, alcohols, ketones, other oxygenated solvents	ignitable paint wastes, heavy metal paint wastes, spent solvents
Used lead acid batteries	car, truck, boat, motorcycle, and other vehicle batteries	lead dross, less than 3% free acids	used lead acid batteries, strong acid/alkaline solutions

Table 2
WASTE DESCRIPTIONS[1]

WASTE TYPE	DESIGNATIONS/ TRADE NAMES	DOT SHIPPING NAME	HAZARD CLASS	UN/NA ID NUMBER
STRONG ACID/ALKALINE WASTES				
Ammonium Hydroxide	Ammonium Hydroxide, NH4OH, Spirit of Hartshorn, Aqua Ammonia	Waste Ammonium Hydroxide (containing not less than 12% but not more than 44% ammonia)	Corrosive Material	NA2672
		(containing less than 12% ammonia)	ORM-A	NA2672
Hydrobromic Acid	Hydrobromic Acid, HBr	Waste Hydrobromic Acid (not more than 49% strength)	Corrosive Material	UN1788
Hydrochloric Acid	Hydrochloric Acid, HCl, Muriatic Acid	Waste Hydrochloric Acid	Corrosive Material	NA1789
Hydrofluoric Acid	Hydrofluoric Acid, HF, Fluorohydric Acid	Waste Hydrofluoric Acid	Corrosive Material	UN1790
Nitric Acid	Nitric Acid, HNO2, Aquafortis	Waste Nitric Acid (over 40%)	Oxidizer	UN2031
		(40% or less)	Corrosive Material	NA1760
Phosphoric Acid	Phosphoric Acid, H3PO4, Orthophosphoric acid	Waste Phosphoric Acid	Corrosive Material	UN1805
Potassium Hydroxide	Potassium Hydroxide, KOH, Potassium Hydrate, Caustic Potash, Potassa	Waste Potassium Hydroxide Solution	Corrosive Material	UN1814
		Dry Solid, Flake, Bead, or Granular	Corrosive Material	UN1813
Sodium Hydroxide	Sodium Hydroxide, NaOH, Caustic Soda, Soda Lye, Sodium Hydrate	Waste Sodium Hydroxide Solution	Corrosive Material	UN1824
		Dry Solid, Flake, Bead, or Granular	Corrosive Material	UN1823
Sulfuric Acid	Sulfuric Acid, H2SO4, Oil of Vitriol	Waste Sulfuric Acid	Corrosive Material	UN1830
Chromic Acid	Chromic Acid	Waste Chromic Acid Solution	Corrosive Material	UN1755
IGNITABLE WASTES				
Ignitable Wastes NOS[2] Aromatic Hydrocarbons Petroleum Distillates	Carburetor Cleaners, Ignitable Wastes NOS	Waste Flammable Liquid NOS	Flammable Liquid[3]	UN1993
		Waste Combustible Liquid NOS	Combustible Liquid[4]	NA1993
		Waste Flammable Solid NOS	Flammable Solid	UN1325
IGNITABLE PAINT WASTES				
Ethylene Dichloride	Ethylene Dichloride, 1,2-Dichloroethane	Waste Ethylene Dichloride	Flammable Liquid	UN1184
Benzene	Benzene	Waste Benzene (benzol)	Flammable Liquid	UN1114
Toluene	Toluene	Waste Toluene (toluol)	Flammable Liquid	UN1294
Ethyl benzene	Ethyl benzene	Waste Ethyl benzene	Flammable Liquid	UN1175
Chlorobenzene	Chlorobenzene, Monochlorobenzene, Phenylchloride	Waste Chlorobenzene	Flammable Liquid	UN1134
Methyl Ethyl Ketone	Methyl Ethyl Ketone, MEK, Methyl Acetone, Meetco, Butanone, Ethyl Methyl Ketone	Waste Methyl Ethyl Ketone	Flammable Liquid	UN1193
SPENT SOLVENTS				
White Spirits, Varsol	White Spirits, Mineral Spirits, Naphtha	Waste Naphtha	Flammable Liquid Combustible Liquid	UN2553 UN2553
1,1,1-Trichloroethane	Aeothane TT, Chlorlen, Chloroethene, Methyl-Chloroform, Alpha. T, Chlorotene	Waste 1,1,1-Trichloroethane	ORM-A	UN2831
Petroleum distillates	Petroleum Distillates	Petroleum Distillate	Flammable Liquid Combustible Liquid	UN1268 UN1268
PAINT WASTES WITH HEAVY METALS				
Paints with heavy metals Lead Nickel Chromium	Heavy Metals Paint	Hazardous Waste, Liquid or Solid, NOS	ORM-E	NA9189

[1] These descriptions may change given variations in waste characteristics or conditions.

[2] NOS—Not otherwise specified.

[3] A flammable liquid has a flash point below 100°F.

[4] A combustible liquid has a flash point between 100°F and 200°F.

B2

Printing and Allied Industries

Your firm is included in Printing and Allied Industries if it is involved in:

Preparation

▶ Typesetting
▶ Lithography
▶ Letterpress
▶ Gravure
▶ Engraving (stationery)
▶ Photoengraving

Printing

▶ Heatset Lithography
▶ Non Heatset Lithography
   ▶ Thermography
   ▶ Business Form Printing
   ▶ Sheetfed Lithography
▶ Letterpress Printing (including flexography)
▶ Gravure Printing
▶ Screen Press Printing

Finishing Operations

▶ Looseleaf Binder Manufacturers
▶ Trade Binding Operations
▶ Book Binding Operations
▶ In House Binding Operations
▶ Magazine and Catalog Binding Operations

Not all printing or allied industry operations produce hazardous waste. However, if you use ignitable (flash point ≤ 140°F) solvents, strong acid/alkaline solutions, paint or ink containing solvents or heavy metals (in concentrations greater than the EP Toxicity levels) or both, the wastes you generate may be hazardous. If so, you may be subject to new Resource Conservation and Recovery Act (RCRA) provisions concerning the generation and transportation of hazardous wastes. Table 1 lists typical processes/operations in the printing and allied industries which could produce hazardous wastes.

HAZARDOUS WASTES FROM PRINTING AND ALLIED INDUSTRIES

Printing generates waste ink and ink sludges that may contain solvents and sometimes heavy metals. The composition of inks used in printing and allied industries varies greatly depending on whether an ink is to be used for lithography, letterpress, gravure, flexography, or screen printing. Oil-based or paste inks are generally composed of colorant or pigments (carbon black, inorganic, and organic), varnish (drying oils, alkyd, resin-phenolic, resin-ester), drier (cobalt, manganese, or zirconium fatty acid compounds), sometimes an extender, solvents and modifiers (waxes, petroleum solvents, and magnesia). Fluid inks contain a vehicle comprised of resin and solvent or oil, and additives such as waxes, drier and wetting agents. While not all waste inks and ink sludges will be hazardous, those containing solvents or heavy metals generally are.

Photographic processes are used in all of the major printing operations for image conversion and plate-making. Photographic wastes, therefore, comprise a large portion of the hazardous waste generated in these industries. Photographic processing solutions, developers, hardeners, plating chemicals, fountain solutions, or fixing baths that are sent to publicly-owned treatment works (POTWS) for disposal, however, are exempt from new (RCRA) requirements. Silver-containing solutions that pass through electrolytic, chemical replacement, or ion exchange silver recovery units located on your premises are similarly exempt. However, if you send your wastes off-site for recycling (i.e., silver recovery or solvent recovery) the wastes must be accompanied by a Manifest.

If your business produces 220 pounds or more of hazardous waste per month, you are required to use a Uniform Hazardous Waste Manifest when you ship such wastes off your premises. Item 11 on the Manifest requires the Department of Transportation (DOT) shipping description: the proper DOT shipping name, hazard class, and UN/NA identification number. This information is provided in Table 2. If you do not find your waste listed here, but suspect it may be hazardous, please contact your state hazardous waste management agency for additional assistance.

Table 1

HAZARDOUS WASTES GENERATED BY VARIOUS PRINTING OPERATIONS

TYPICAL PROCESS/ OPERATION	TYPICAL MATERIALS USED	TYPICAL MATERIAL INGREDIENTS	GENERAL WASTE TYPES
PLATE PREPARATION			
*Counter-etch to remove oxide	Phosphoric acid	Phosphoric acid	Acid/alkaline waste
*Deep-etch coating of plates	Deep etch bath	Ammonium dichromate, ammonium hydroxide	Acid/alkaline waste, heavy metals, waste etch bath
*Etch baths	Multimetal plate and plate coating	Ferric chloride (copper), aluminum/zinc chloride/ hydrochloric acid (chromium), nitric acid (zinc, magnesium), gum arabic	Waste etch bath, acid/ alkaline waste, heavy metal wastes
Apply light sensitive coating	Resins, binders, emulsion, photosensitizers, gelatin, photoinitiators	PVA/ammonium dichromate, polyvinyl cinnamate, fish glue/albumin, silver halide/gelatin emulsion, gum arabic/ ammonium dichromate	Photographic waste
Develop plates	Developer	Lactic acid, zinc chloride, magnesium chloride, hydroquinone	Photographic waste
Wash/clean plates, type, die, press blankets and rollers	Alcohols, solvents	Ethyl alcohol, benzene, toluene, xylene, isopropyl alcohol, methyl ethyl ketone, trichloroethylene, perchloroethylene, carbon tetrachloride, gasoline, naphtha, kerosene	Spent solvents
*Apply lacquer	Resins, solvents, vinyl lacquer, lacquer developers	PVC, PVA, maleic acid, methyl ethyl ketone, cyclohexanone, isophorone	Spent solvents
Using Ink (lithography, letterpress, screen printing, flexography)	Pigments, dyes, varnish, drier, extender, modifier, fountain solutions	Titanium oxide, iron blues, molybdated chrome orange, phthalocyanine pigments, oils, hydrocarbon solvents, waxes, cobalt/zinc/manganese oleates, plasticizers, barium-based pigments	Waste ink with solvents/ chromium/lead/barium, ink sludges with chromium/lead/barium
Making gravure cylinders	Acid plating bath	Copper, chromic acid, chrome	Spent plating waste
STENCIL PREPARATION FOR SCREEN PRINTING			
Lacquer stencil film	Solvents, polyester film, vinyl film, dyes	Aliphatic acetates, cellulose-based lacquer, plasticizers	Spent solvents
Photographic stencil film	Organic acids, gelatin (pigmented), polyester film base	Acids, alkalis, peroxide-forming compounds, plasticizers, surfactants	Hydrogen peroxide
Photoemulsion	Resins, binders, photosensitizers, dyes	PVA, PVAC, ammonium or potassium bichromate, diazonium compounds	Photographic waste
Blockout (screen filler)	Pigmented polymers, solvents, acetates	Methylene chloride, methanol, methyl cellulose acetates	Spent solvents

*Older technologies

Table 2 notes:

[1] These descriptions may change given variations in waste characteristics and conditions.
[2] Trade names will differ among manufacturers. Check Material Safety Data Sheets for the presence of the following chemicals.
[3] The difference between the combustible and flammable liquid hazard class designations is based on the flash point of the material (flammable 0-100°F; combustible 100-200°F). The flash point will depend in large part on the solvents in the waste.
[4] Not Otherwise Specified.

L2

Table 2

WASTE DESCRIPTIONS[1]

WASTE TYPE	DESIGNATION/ TRADE NAMES[2]	DOT SHIPPING NAME	HAZARD CLASS	UN/NA ID NUMBER
PHOTOGRAPHIC WASTES				
Heavy Metal Solutions	Photographic processing waste containing heavy metals	Hazardous Waste Solution containing Cadmium, Chromium, Lead, and/or Cyanide	ORM-E	NA9189
Trichloroethylene	Trichloroethylene, Trichloroethene, Ethinyl trichloride, Tri-Clene, Trielene, Tri	Waste Trichloroethylene	ORM-A	UN1710
SPENT SOLVENTS				
Carbon Tetrachloride	Carbon tetrachloride, Perchloromethane, Necatorina, Benzinoform, CCl4	Waste Carbon Tetrachloride	ORM-A	UN1846
Ethanol	Ethanol, Ethyl alcohol	Waste Ethyl Alcohol	Flammable Liquid	UN1170
Isopropanol	Isopropanol, Isopropyl alcohol	Waste Isopropanol	Flammable Liquid	UN1219
Ethyl Benzene	Ethyl benzene	Waste Ethyl Benzene	Flammable Liquid	UN1175
1,1,1-Trichloroethane	1,1,1-Trichloroethane, Aerothene TT, Chlorten, Inhibisol, Trichloroethane, Chlorothen NU, NCI-C04626, Methylchloroform, Chlorothene VG, Chlorothane NU, Chlorotene	Waste 1,1,1-Trichloroethane	ORM-A	UN2831
Methylene Chloride	Dichloromethane, Methane dichloride, Methylene bichloride, NCI-CS0102, Methylene dichloride, Solaesthin, Aerothene NM, Narkotil, Solmethine	Waste Dichloromethane or Methylene Chloride	ORM-A	UN1593
WASTE INK WITH SOLVENTS OR HEAVY METALS				
Waste Ink	Various Constituent Solvents: Carbon tetrachloride, Chloroform, Methylene chloride, 1,1,1-Trichloroethane, 1,2-Dichloroethane, Benzene, Toluene, Ethyl benzene, Tetrachloroethylene, Trichloroethylene Various Constituents from Pigments: Chromium, Copper, Lead, Zinc, Cyanide, Aluminum, Cadmium, Nickel, Cobalt	Waste Ink	Combustible Liquid[3] Flammable Liquid	UN2867 UN1210
STRONG ACID/ALKALINE WASTES				
Ammonium hydroxide	Ammonium hydroxide, Aqua Ammonia, Spirit of Hartshorn, NH4OH	Waste Ammonium Hydroxide (containing not less than 12%, but not more than 44% ammonia)	Corrosive Material	NA2672
		(containing less than 12% ammonia)	ORM-A	NA2672
Hydrochloric Acid	Hydrochloric acid, Muriatic acid, HCl	Waste Hydrochloric Acid Mixture	Corrosive Material	NA1789
Nitric Acid	Nitric acid, Aquafortis, HNO3	Waste Nitric Acid (over 40%)	Oxidizer	UN2031
		(40% or less)	Corrosive Material	NA1760
Phosphoric Acid	Phosphoric acid, Orthophosphoric acid, H3PO4	Waste Phosphoric Acid	Corrosive Material	UN1805
Sodium Hydroxide	Sodium hydroxide, Caustic Soda, Soda Lye, Sodium hydrate, NaOH	Waste Sodium Hydroxide Solution	Corrosive Material	UN1824
		Dry Solid, Flake, Bead, or Granular	Corrosive Material	UN1823
Sulfuric Acid	Sulfuric acid, Oil of Vitriol, H2SO4	Waste Sulfuric Acid, Spent	Corrosive Material	UN1832
Chromic Acid	Chromic acid	Waste Chromic Acid Solution	Corrosive Material	UN1755
SPENT PLATING WASTES				
Spent Plating Wastes	Spent etch baths, spent plating solutions and sludges, stripping and cleaning baths	Hazardous Waste, Liquid or Solid, NOS[4]	ORM-E	NA9189
INK SLUDGE WITH CHROMIUM OR LEAD				
Ink sludge with Chromium or Lead	Ink sludge containing heavy metals	Hazardous Waste, Liquid or Solid, NOS	ORM-E	NA9189
IGNITABLE WASTES NOS				
Ignitable Wastes NOS	Ignitable Wastes NOS	Waste Flammable Liquid, NOS Waste Combustible Liquid, NOS	Flammable Liquid Combustible Liquid	UN1993 UN1993
		Waste Flammable Solid, NOS	Flammable Solid	UN1325

L3

Drycleaning and Laundry Plants

INDUSTRY OVERVIEW

The establishments covered under Drycleaning and Laundry Plants include:

▶ Retail drycleaning stores

▶ Industrial and linen supply plants with drycleaning operations

▶ Leather and fur cleaning plants

▶ Self-service laundromats with drycleaning equipment

▶ Other establishments with drycleaning operations.

While not all of these facilities will produce hazardous waste, those facilities using hazardous solvents may be subject to new Resource Conservation and Recovery Act (RCRA) provisions regarding the treatment, storage, disposal, and transportation of small quantities of hazardous waste. These solvents include:

▶ **Perchloroethylene**, otherwise known as perc, PCE, or tetrachloroethylene

▶ **Valclene***, also known as fluorocarbon 113 or trichlorotrifluoroethane

▶ **Petroleum solvents,** such as Stoddard, quick-dry, low-odor and other solvents with a flash point less than 140°F. ("140-F solvent" and other solvents with a flash point equal to or greater than 140°F are not considered hazardous under EPA RCRA designation. If you are unsure of the flash point, check with the distributor of the solvent.)

Table 1

TYPICAL QUANTITIES OF HAZARDOUS WASTE FROM DRYCLEANING

(Pounds of waste per 1,000 pounds of clothes cleaned)

WASTE TYPE	CLEANING METHOD		
	PERC	VALCLENE	PETROLEUM SOLVENTS
	Average Quantity of Hazardous Waste (pounds)		
Still Residues	25	10	20
Spent Cartridge Filters:			
Standard (carbon core)	20	15	*
Adsorptive (split)	30	20	*
Cooked Powder Residue	40	NA	NA
Drained Filter Muck	NA	NA	*

*Well-drained filter cartridges or drained filter muck are solids and do not meet the criteria for classification as an ignitable solid; therefore, they are not hazardous wastes.

Table 2

WASTE DESCRIPTIONS*

Information for Item 11 of the Manifest

WASTE	DOT SHIPPING NAME	HAZARD CLASS	UN/NA ID NUMBER
Perc	Waste Perchloroethylene or Waste Tetrachloroethylene	ORM-A	UN 1897
Valclene	Hazardous Waste, NOS	ORM-E	UN 9189
Petroleum Solvents	Waste Petroleum Distillate	Combustible Liquid**	UN 1268
	Waste Petroleum Naphtha	Combustible Liquid**	UN 1255

*In certain situations, other DOT descriptions may be applicable to the wastes listed.

**If the flash point of the solvent or residue *as disposed of* is less than 100°F, the hazard class would be "flammable liquid." Although the flash point of petroleum drycleaning solvents is above 100°F, the presence of contaminants (such as printing inks) could lower the overall flash point to below 100°F.

HAZARDOUS WASTES FROM DRYCLEANING OPERATIONS

Perchloroethylene plants potentially produce three types of hazardous wastes:

▶ Still residues from solvent distillation (the entire weight)

▶ Spent filter cartridges (total weight of the cartridge and remaining solvent after draining)

▶ Cooked powder residue (the total weight of drained powder residues from diatomaceous or other powder filter systems after heating to remove excess solvent).

Valclene plants potentially produce two types of hazardous wastes:

▶ Still residues from solvent distillation (the entire weight)

▶ Spent filter cartridges (total weight of the cartridge and remaining solvent after draining).

Petroleum solvent plants potentially produce only one type of hazardous waste:

▶ Still residues from solvent distillation (the entire weight). However, if 140-F solvent is used, the still residue will *not* normally be a hazardous waste.

Well-drained filter cartridges or drained filter muck (powder residues from diatomaceous filter systems) are solids and do not meet the criteria for classification as an ignitable solid; therefore, they are not hazardous wastes.

WASTE QUANTITIES AND DESCRIPTIONS

If your plant produces 220 pounds or more of hazardous waste per month, you are subject to certain requirements, including the use of a Uniform Hazardous Waste Manifest when shipping hazardous waste off your premises.

To determine whether your plant qualifies as a regulated small quantity generator and to complete the Manifest, you will have to weigh the hazardous waste your plant generates. Table 1 lists common types and average quantities of hazardous waste produced per 1,000 pounds of clothes cleaned.

Item 11 on the Manifest is the Department of Transportation (DOT) description of the waste, which includes the proper shipping name, hazard class, and UN/NA identification number. This information is provided in Table 2 to aid in preparing the Manifest; other DOT descriptions and identification codes, however, may be applicable in some circumstances.

WASTE DISPOSAL METHODS

Generally there are three methods for proper disposal of hazardous wastes that are currently considered acceptable by both EPA and most state hazardous waste management agencies:

▶ Disposal in an authorized hazardous waste landfill

▶ Disposal at an authorized high-temperature incineration facility

▶ Disposal through an authorized recycler of hazardous wastes.

From an environmental perspective, recycling or incineration is generally preferable to land disposal.

BAN ON LAND DISPOSAL OF PERC AND VALCLENE WASTES

Under the new RCRA, EPA is required to issue, by November 8, 1986, new regulations that will ban the disposal on or into the land of hazardous waste containing certain solvents, including perchloroethylene and Valclene. In the near future, therefore, hazardous waste disposal options will be further restricted.

C1

APPENDIX D   DEPARTMENT OF TRANSPORTATION HAZARD CLASSES

Flammable Liquid	Any liquid having a flash point below 100° F as determined by tests listed in 49 CFR 173.115(d). Exceptions are listed in 49 CFR 173.115(a).
Combustible Liquid	Any liquid having a flash point above 100° F and below 200° F as determined by tests listed in 49 CFR 173.115(d). Exceptions are listed in 49 CFR 173.115(b).
Flammable Solid	Any solid material, other than an explosive, liable to cause fires through friction or retained heat from manufacturing or processing, or which can be ignited readily creating a serious transportation hazard because it burns vigorously and persistently. (49 CFR 173.150)
Oxidizer	A substance such as chlorate, permanganate, inorganic peroxide, or a nitrate, that yields oxygen readily to stimulate the combustion of organic matter. (49 CFR 173.151)
Organic Peroxide	An organic compound containing the bivalent -O-O- structure and which may be considered a derivative of hydrogen peroxide where one or more of the hydrogen atoms have been replaced by organic radicals. Exceptions are listed in 49 CFR 173.151(a).
Corrosive	Liquid or solid that causes visible destruction or irreversible alterations in human skin tissue at the site of contact. Liquids that severely corrode steel are included. (49 CFR 173.240(a))

Flammable Gas	A compressed gas, as defined in 49 CFR 173.300(a), that meets certain flammability requirements. (49 CFR 173.300(b))
Non-flammable Gas	A compressed gas other than a flammable gas.
Irritating Material	A liquid or solid substance which upon contact with fire or when exposed to air gives off dangerous or intensely irritating fumes. Poison A materials are excluded. (49 CFR 173.381)
Poison A	Extremely dangerous poison gases or liquids belong to this class. Very small amounts of these gases or vapors of these liquids, mixed with air, are dangerous to life. (49 CFR 173.326)
Poison B	Substances, liquids, or solids (including pastes and semi-solids), other than Poison A or Irritating Materials, that are known to be toxic to humans. In the absence of adequate data on human toxicity, materials are presumed to be toxic to humans if they are toxic to laboratory animals exposed under specified conditions. (49 CFR 173.343)
Etiologic Agent	A viable microorganism, or its toxin, which causes or may cause human disease. These materials are limited to agents listed by the Department of Health and Human Services. (49 CFR 173.386)
Radioactive Material	A material that spontaneously emits ionizing radiation. Further classifications are made within this category according to levels of

	radioactivity. (49 CFR 173, subpart I)
Explosive	Any chemical compound, mixture, or device, the primary or common purpose of which is to function by explosion, unless such compound, mixture, or device is otherwise classified. (49 CFR 173.50)
	Explosives are divided into three subclasses:
	Class A Explosives are detonating explosives. (49 CFR 173.53)
	Class B Explosives generally function by rapid combustion rather than detonation. (49 CFR 173.88)
	Class C Explosives are manufactured articles, such as small arms ammunition, that contain restricted quantities of Class A and/or Class B explosives, and certain types of fireworks. (49 CFR 173.100)
Blasting Agent	A material designed for blasting, but so insensitive that there is very little probability of ignition during transport. (49 CFR173.114(a))
ORM (Other Regulated Materials)	Any material that does not meet the definition of the other hazard classes. ORMs are divided into five subclasses: **ORM-A** is a material which has an anesthetic, irritating, noxious, toxic, or other similar property and can cause extreme annoyance or discomfort to passengers and crew in the event of leakage during transportation. (49 CFR 173.500(a)(1))

ORM-B is a material capable of causing significant damage to a transport vehicle or vessel if leaked. This class includes materials that may be corrosive to aluminum. (49 CFR 173.500(a)(2))

ORM-C is a material listed in the Hazardous Materials Table, which has other inherent characteristics not described as an ORM-A or ORM-B, but which make it unsuitable for shipment unless properly identified and prepared for transportation. (49 CFR 173.500(a)(3))

ORM-D is a material such as a consumer commodity which, although otherwise subject to regulation, presents a limited hazard during transportation due to its form, quantity, and packaging. (49 CFR 173.500(a)(4))

ORM-E is a material that is not included in any other hazard class, but is subject to the requirements of this subchapter. Materials in this class include hazardous wastes and hazardous substances not otherwise classified. (49 CFR 173.500(a)(5))

APPENDIX E   SUPERFUND CONSTITUENTS RECOMMENDED FOR ANALYSIS

Benzoic acid
Acetone
Isophorone
2-Nitroaniline
2-Nitrophenol
2-Methylnaphthalene
3-Nitroaniline
Ethyl benzene
Styrene
Benzyl alcohol
Vinyl acetate
4-Methyl-2-pentanone
Dibenzofuran
2-Hexanone
Xylene (total)
4-Chlorophenyl phenyl ether
Aluminum
Iron
Magnesium
Manganese
Potassium
Sodium
Tin
Cobalt
Calcium

APPENDIX F   CONSTITUENTS RECOMMENDED FOR ANALYSIS

Acetonitrile
Acetophenone
2-Acetylaminofluorene
Acrolein
Acrylonitrile
Aldrin
Allyl alcohol
4-Aminobiphenyl
Aniline
Antimony (total)
Aramite
Arsenic (total)
Barium (total)
Benz[a]anthracene
Benzene
Benzenethiol
Benzidine
Benzo[b]fluoranthene
Benzo[a]pyrene
p-Benzoquinone
Beryllium (total)
Bis(2-chloroethoxy) methane
Bis(2-chloroethyl) ether
Bis(2-ethylhexyl) phthalate
Bis(2-chloroisopropyl) ether
Bromomethane
4-Bromophenyl phenyl ether
Butyl benzyl phthalate
2-sec-Butyl-4,6-dinitrophenol
Cadmium (total)
Carbon disulfide
Chlordane
Chloroethane
p-Chloroaniline
Chlorobenzene
Chlorobenzilate
2-Chloro-1,3-butadiene
p-Chloro-m-cresol
2-Chloroethyl vinyl ether
Chloroform
Chloromethane
2-Chloronaphthalene
2-Chlorophenol
3-Chloropropene
3-Chloropropionitrile
Chromium (total)
Chrysene

Copper (total)
Acenaphthene
Acenaphthalene
Anthracene
Benzo[ghi]perylene
Benzo[k]fluoranthene
Fluorene
Phenanthrene
Pyrene
ortho-Cresol
para-Cresol
Cyanide
DDD
DDE
DDT
Dibenz[a,h]anthracene
Dibenzo[a,e]pyrene
Dibenzo[a,h]pyrene
Dibenzo[a,i]pyrene
1,2-Dibromo-3-chloropropane
1,2-Dibromoethane
Dibromomethane
Di-n-butyl phthalate
o-Dichlorobenzene
m-Dichlorobenzene
p-Dichlorobenzene
3,3'-Dichlorobenzidine
trans-1,4-Dichloro-2-butene
Dichlorodifluoromethane
1,1-Dichloroethane
1,2-Dichloroethane
trans-1,2-Dichloroethene
1,1,-Dichloroethylene
Dichloromethane
2,4-Dichlorophenol
2,6-Dichlorophenol
2,4-Dichlorophenoxyacetic acid
1,2-Dichloropropane
cis-1,3-Dichloropropene
trans-1,3-Dichloropropene
Dieldrin
Diethyl phthalate
0,0-Diethyl 0-2-pyrazinyl phosphorothioate
3,3'-Dimethoxybenzidine
p-Dimethylaminoazobenzene
7,12-Dimethylbenz[a]anthracene

3,3'-Dimethylbenzidine
alpha, alpha-Dimethylphenethylamine
2,4-Dimethylphenol
Dimethyl phthalate
meta-Dinitrobenzene
4,6-Dinitro-o-cresol
2,4-Dinitrophenol
2,4-Dinitrotoluene
2,6-Dinitrotoluene
Di-n-octyl phthalate
1,4-Dioxane
Diphenylamine
1,2-Diphenylhydrazine
Di-n-propylnitrosamine
Disulfoton
Endosulfan I
Endosulfan II
Endrin
Endrin aldehyde
Ethyl cyanide
Ethylene oxide
Ethyl methacrylate
Fluoranthene
Chlorodibromomethane
Bromodichloromethane
Heptachlor
Heptachlor epoxide
Hexachlorobenzene
Hexachlorobutadiene
alpha-BHC
beta-BHC
delta-BHC
gamma-BHC
Hexachlorocyclopentadiene
Hexachlorodibenzo-p-dioxins
Hexachlorodibenzofurans
Hexachloroethane
Isodrin
Hexachlorophene
Hexachloropropene
Fluoride
Sulfide
Indeno(1,2,3-cd)pyrene
Iodomethane
Isobutyl alcohol
Isosafrole
Kepone
Lead (total)
Malononitrile

Mercury (total)
Methacrylonitrile
Methapyrilene
Methoxychlor
3-Methylcholanthrene
4,4'-Methylenebis(2-chloroaniline)
Methyl ethyl ketone
Methyl methacrylate
Methyl methanesulfonate
Methyl parathion
Naphthalene
1,4-Naphthoquinone
1-Naphthylamine
2-Naphthylamine
Nickel (total)
p-Nitroaniline
Nitrobenzene
4-Nitrophenol
N-Nitrosodiphenylamine
N-Nitrosodi-n-butylamine
N-Nitrosodiethylamine
N-Nitrosodimethylamine
N-Nitrosomethylethylamine
N-Nitrosomorpholine
N-Nitrosopiperidine
N-Nitrosopyrrolidine
5-Nitro-o-toluidine
Osmium (total)
Parathion
Pentachlorobenzene
Pentachlorodibenzo-p-dioxins
Pentachlorodibenzofurans
Pentachloroethane
Pentachloronitrobenzene
Pentachlorophenol
Phehacetin
Phenol
Phorate
Famphur
2-Picoline
Aroclor 1016
Aroclor 1221
Aroclor 1232
Aroclor 1242
Aroclor 1248
Aroclor 1254
Aroclor 1260
Pronamide
2-Propyn-1-ol

Pyridine
Resorcinol
Safrole
Selenium (total)
Silver (total)
1,2,4,5-Tetrachlorobenzene
2,3,7,8-Tetrachlorodibenzo-p-dioxin
Tetrachlorodibenzo-p-dioxins
Tetrachlorodibenzofurans
1,1,1,2-Tetrachloroethane
1,1,2,2-Tetrachloroethane
Tetrachloroethene
Carbon tetrachloride
2,3,4,6-Tetrachlorophenol
Tetraethyldithiopyrophosphate
Thallium (total)
Toluene

Toxaphene
Tribromomethane
1,2,4-Trichlorobenzene
1,1,1-Trichloroethane
1,1,2-Trichloroethane
Trichoroethene
Trichloromethanethiol
Trichloromonofluoromethane
2,4,5-Trichlorophenol
2,4,6-Trichlorophenol
2,4,5-T
Silvex
1,2,3-Trichloropropane
Tris(2,3-dibromopropyl) phosphate
Vanadium (total)
Vinyl chloride
Zinc (total)

APPENDIX G   EXAMPLES OF VIOLATION CLASSIFICATION

Violation	Classification
Failure of a handler to meet a compliance schedule in an order, decree, agreement or permit	I
Construction of a new facility without a permit	I
Failure of the generator to comply with requirements relating to the manifest system	I
Failure of a generator to meet the packaging, labeling, marking, or placarding requirements	I
Failure to comply with the "small quantity generator requirements"	I
Failure of a transporter to comply with the requirements for immediate action and clean up of discharges	I
Failure of the transporter to comply with requirements relating to the manifest system	I
Failure of a facility owner/operator to comply with manifest requirements	I
Failure of an owner/operator to conduct required waste analyses	I
Failure of an owner/operator to properly handle ignitable, reactive, or incompatible wastes	I
Failure to install, operate, and maintain an adequate groundwater monitoring system, including failure to begin assessment monitoring when required under the interim status regulations	I
Self-granting, by an owner or operator, of an unjustifiable waiver from groundwater monitoring requirements	I
Failure to meet the closure performance standard	I
Failure to develop a complete and adequate closure plan	I
Failure to meet specified standards for post-closure care	I
Failure to develop a complete and adequate post-closure plan	I
Failure to develop an adequate estimate of closure and post-closure costs	I
Failure to establish and maintain a financial assurance mechanism for closure and post-closure costs	I
Discrepancies in wording such that the financial instrument is ineffective	I
Improper cancellation of a bond by the surety	I
Cancellation or reduction of value, without Regional Administrator's consent, of surety bond or insurance policy	I

Violation	Classification
Failure to include information regarding all facilities that are covered by the same instrument	I
Failure to obtain or maintain coverage for sudden accidental occurrences	I
Failure to obtain or maintain coverage for nonsudden accidental occurrences	I
Failure of owner/operator to submit a timely and complete Part B application	I
Storage of wastes in containers that are not in good condition or have begun to leak	I
Failure of an owner/operator to meet the requirements regarding storage of ignitable, reactive, or incompatible wastes	I
Failure to provide for proper containment of leachate or runoff from a waste pile	I
Failure of an owner/operator to meet applicable general operating requirements	I
Failure of a land treatment owner/operator to meet the requirements regarding food chain crops	I
Failure of a land treatment owner/operator to prepare and plan for monitoring of the unsaturated zone or failure to monitor the unsaturated zone	I
Failure of a thermal treatment facility to meet the requirements regarding open burning and waste explosives	I
Failure to submit the biennial report	II
Failure of an owner/operator to provide notice regarding international shipments of hazardous wastes	II
Failure to provide required notices regarding transfers of ownership or foreign shipments of waste	II
Failure to make emergency arrangements with local authorities	II
Failure to maintain copy of closure plan at the facility	II
Failure to meet the timeframes set out for facility closure	II

HSWA Implementation Schedule

November 8, 1984

Delisting decisions made by EPA must be based on original listing criteria and other factors which could cause waste to be hazardous. Ban on EPA delistings of hazardous waste without prior notice and comment. (3001(f)(1))

Ban imposed on use of hazardous waste; or hazardous waste mixed with waste oil, used oil, or other material used as dust suppressant. (3004(l))

TSDF permitting standards for new, replacement, or expansion landfills and surface impoundments require in most cases double liners and groundwater monitoring. Incinerator permitting standards require a minimum 99.99% destruction and removal efficiency. Limited waivers from dual-liner requirements available to those that can demonstrate equivalency of natural settings and for monofills of certain foundry wastes (except in Alabama). (3004(o))

TSDF permits shall require corrective action for all releases of hazardous constituents from any solid waste management unit which threatens human health and the environment. Regulations to be issued as soon as possible post-enactment. (3004(u))

Corrective action required beyond the property boundary unless TSDF owner/operator unable to obtain necessary permission to undertake such action. (3004(v))

Ban on burning of most hazardous waste in cement kilns located in city of more than 500,000 people unless cement kilns comply with standards applicable to incinerators. (3004(g)(2)(C))

40 CFR 264, Subpart F, groundwater monitoring and corrective action requirements apply to permitted land disposal units receiving hazardous waste after July 26, 1982. (3005(i))

Groundwater monitoring required for non-enclosed waste piles obtaining permits. (3004(p))

Permits shall contain terms and conditions in addition to those mandated by regulations where necessary to protect human health and the environment. Maximum permit duration is 10 years; land disposal permits must be reviewed every 5 years and modified to comply with currently applicable requirements. (3005(c)(3))

TSDFs operated by state or local governments shall be inspected at least annually by EPA. (3007(d))

Generally, the placement of any hazardous waste in a salt dome or bed, or an underground mine or cave, is prohibited until EPA issues standards for such activities and permits for the facilities concerned. (3004(b))

February 6, 1985

Warning label required on hazardous waste derived fuels. (3004(r)) (Superceded by manifesting and invoice requirements—see Chapter 3.)

March 1, 1985

EPA required to issue permitting standards for underground tanks storing and/or treating hazardous wastes which cannot be entered for inspection (already late—expected mid-1986). (3004(w))

First annual report must be filed with EPA by persons exporting hazardous waste summarizing types, quantities, frequency, and destination of waste during previous calendar year. (3017(g))

April 1, 1985

EPA study on number and type of small quantity generators and the wastes they produce must be submitted to Congress. (HSWA, Section 221(c))

May 8, 1985

EPA must determine whether to list wastes containing chlorinated dioxins or chlorinated-dibenzofurans as hazardous waste. (3001(e))

Ban imposed on the placement of bulk or non-containerized liquids in landfills (whether or not absorbants have been added). (3004(c))

New, replacement, or expansion interim status landfills, surface impoundments, and waste piles operational after November 8, 1984, must meet permitting design standards if units continue to receive hazardous waste. (3004(o); 3015)

EPA must submit a report to Congress on the feasibility of using private inspectors for hazardous waste facilities. (3007(e)(2))

Federal procurement guidelines for recycled paper due. (6002(e))

Ban imposed on most uses of Class IV injection wells. (7010(a))

EPA national inventory of Class I and Class IV underground injection wells must be submitted to Congress. (HSWA, Section 701)

Ban imposed on the installation of underground tanks storing petroleum or toxic chemicals which are inadequately designed to prevent structural failure or corrosion. (9003(g))

Governors must designate appropriate state agencies to receive facility notification for underground storage tank program. (9002(b))

August 5, 1985

Previously exempted generators producing between 100 and 1000 kg/mo of non-acutely hazardous waste must comply with partial manifest requirements. (3001(d))

August 8, 1985

Permit applications for surface impoundments and landfills must be accompanied by information regarding potential human exposure due to accidental and intended releases from the unit. (3019)

September 1, 1985

Large quantity generators must certify on each manifest that they have a program in place to reduce waste volume or quantity and toxicity, and the proposed management method for the waste minimizes present and future threats to human health and the environment. (3002(b))

Permits for TSDFs where waste is generated on-site shall require annual certification similar to manifest certification. (3005(h))

October 1, 1985

Federal procurement guidelines for tires and other recycled materials due. (6002(e))

November 8, 1985

EPA must determine whether to list remaining halogenated dioxins and halogenated dibenzofurans as hazardous waste (already late—expected mid-1986). EPA must also propose whether to list used automobile and truck crankcase oil as a hazardous waste. (3001(e))

Restrictions imposed on the placement of non-hazardous liquids in landfills. (3004(c)(3))

Owner/operator of interim status land disposal facility must certify compliance with groundwater monitoring and financial responsibility requirements or stop receiving hazardous waste at uncertified units. Closure plans for uncertified units due November 23, 1985. (3005(e)(2))

Part B application must be submitted for each land disposal unit or unit loses interim status and cannot continue to receive hazardous waste. Closure plans for units lacking application due November 23, 1985. (3005(e)(2)

EPA must inspect all federal TSDFs at least annually, and EPA or authorized states shall inspect other TSDFs at least once every 2 years. (3007(c))

EPA must propose whether to list or identify used automobile and truck crankcase oil as hazardous wastes under 3001. (3014(b))

EPA shall promulgate regulations tightening controls on hazardous waste exports (already late—expected mid-1986). (3017(b))

New notification requirements imposed on persons intending to export hazardous waste. (3017(c))

EPA issues notification forms for present owners, and prior owners of underground tanks holding petroleum and toxic chemicals taken out of operation since January 1, 1974. (9002(b)(2))

EPA study on underground tanks storing petroleum submitted to Congress. (9009(a))

December 8, 1985

Persons depositing petroleum or certain toxic chemicals into underground tanks must inform tank owner of notification requirements. Responsibility lasts until June 9, 1987. (9002(a)(5))

January 31, 1986

State interim authorization for non-HSWA regulatory program expires. (3006 (c))

First biannual federal agency inventory of RCRA and pre-RCRA TSDFs due for submission to EPA. (3016(a))

February 8, 1986

EPA must determine whether to list the following wastes as hazardous: chlorinated aliphatics, chlorinated dioxins (completed), dimethyl hydrazine, toluene, diisocyanate (TDI), carbamates, bromacil, linuron, organobromines, solvents, refining wastes, chlorinated aromatics, dyes and pigments, inorganic chemical industry wastes, lithium batteries, coke byproducts, paint production wastes, and coal slurry pipeline effluent. (3001(e)(2))

EPA must issue regulations minimizing the disposal of containerized liquid waste including prohibition on use of biodegradable and compressible absorbents. (3004(c)) (Expected in 1987.)

Notification and recordkeeping requirements imposed on producers, burners, distributors, and marketers of hazardous waste derived fuels. (3004(s), 3010(a))

EPA report due to Congress on the types and quantities of hazardous waste disposed via the sewer system and whether or not such disposal is adequately regulated. (3018(a))

March 31, 1986

EPA regulations due for generators producing between 100 and 1000 kg/month or non-acutely hazardous waste. (3001(d))

May 8, 1986

EPA shall publish guidance criteria identifying areas of vulnerable hydrogeology. (3004(o)(7))

Owners of underground tanks presently storing petroleum or toxic chemicals or taken out of operations since January 1, 1974, required to notify states. (9002(a)(2))

October 1, 1986

EPA report to Congress on waste minimization and to what extent regulations can specify performance standards for quantity or toxicity reduction due. (8002(r))

November 8, 1986

Delistings granted by EPA without notice and comment prior to November 8, 1984, expire. (3001(f)(2)(B))

EPA required to develop new waste characteristics including toxicity characteristics (3001(h)), and to make final decision on listing of used automobile and truck crankcase oil and other used oil. (3014(b))

EPA standards for transporters, producers, burners, and distributors or hazardous waste derived fuels required due. (3004(q))

EPA schedule for future land disposal restriction determinations due, and a decision on solvents (F001–F005) and dioxins required (except for underground injection). (3004(e),(g))

New EPA design standards or guidance documents implementing HSWA minimum technology requirements and specifying additional location standards for new and existing TSDFs required. (3004(o)(1),(5)(A))

EPA standards governing generators and transporters of used oil that is recycled due. (3014(c))

Ban imposed on exports of hazardous waste without prior consent of receiving country. (3017(a))

Part B permit applications for interim status incinerators must be submitted to EPA or authorized state by owner/operator. (3005(c)(2)(C)(i))

To qualify for waiver from surface impoundment retrofit requirements, applications must be submitted to EPA or authorized state from owner/operator by this date. (3005(j)(5))

Study to extend useful life of sanitary landfills must be submitted to Congress. (8002(s))

February 8, 1987

EPA standards for new and existing underground storage tanks containing petroleum due. The regulations become effective May 8, 1987. (9003(a),(c),(f)(1))

March 8, 1987

EPA required to revise existing extraction procedure toxicity characteristic. (3001(g))

Underground tank sellers must notify tank purchasers storing petroleum of notification requirements. (9002(a)(6))

April 1, 1987

EPA studies to be submitted to Congress regarding small quantity generators and the manifest regulations, the feasibility of licensing waste transporters to assume small quantity generator manifest responsibilities, and hazardous wastes generated by high schools and universities. (HSWA, Section 221 (d),(e),(f) P.L. 98-616)

May 8, 1987

EPA standards due for leak detection systems in new landfills, surface impoundments, waste piles, underground tanks, and land treatment units. (3004(o)(4))

EPA regulations for the monitoring and control of air emissions from land disposal facilities and uncovered tanks due. (3004(n))

July 8, 1987

Land disposal prohibition determinations (except for underground injection wells) by EPA for "California" wastes required. (3004(d))

August 8, 1987

EPA regulations under RCRA or Clean Water Act required to address hazardous wastes inadequately controlled when disposed via the sewer system. (3019(b))

EPA standards for new underground tanks storing toxic chemicals due. These standards become effective November 8, 1987. (9003(a),(c),(f)(2))

September 8, 1987

Sellers of new underground tanks storing toxic chemicals must notify purchasers of notification requirements. (9002(a)(6))

November 8, 1987

Decisions on applications for waivers from surface impoundments retrofit requirements by EPA or authorized states due. (3005(j)(5))

EPA report to Congress due regarding location and likelihood of releases from non-petroleum underground storage tanks and farm and heating oil tanks.(9009(b)–(e))

EPA report to Congress due regarding the use of wastewater lagoons at POTWs and their effects on groundwater quality. (3018(c))

EPA report to Congress on extent to which design and technology requirements for hazardous waste landfills and lagoons should be applied to solid waste landfills. (4010(a),(b))

March 31, 1988

EPA required to revise criteria for solid waste facilities that may receive household hazardous waste or hazardous waste from small quantity generators. (4010(c))

August 8, 1988

Prohibition determinations by EPA due for the underground injection of solvents, dioxins, and the California wastes; and prohibition determinations due regarding first third of scheduled wastes for all methods of land disposal. (3004(f); 3004(g)(4), (5), (6)(A))

EPA standards for existing underground tanks storing toxic chemicals required. (9003(a),(c),(f)(3))

November 8, 1988

Temporary exemption from land disposal prohibitions for soil contaminated with solvents, dioxins, or California wastes expires. (3004(d)(3),(e)(3))

EPA required to modify standards for underground tanks storing or treating hazardous waste to cover all requirements applicable to underground tanks storing toxic chemicals as may be necessary to protect human health and the environment. (3004(w))

Existing surface impoundments for which waivers will not be granted must be retrofitted or closed by this date. (3005))(j)(l))

Final permits issued by EPA or authorized states for land disposal facilities by this date. Permit applications from owners/operators of a interim status storage facility owners/operators are due. (3005(c)(2)(A)(i))

May 8, 1989

States adopt and implement a solid waste facility permit program based on revised criteria for facilities that may receive household hazardous waste or waste from generators producing less than 100 kg/mo. (4010(c)(1)(A),(B))

June 8, 1989

EPA land disposal prohibition determinations due for second third of scheduled wastes. (3004(g)(4),(5),(6)(B))

November 8, 1989

Final permits should be issued for incinerators by EPA or authorized states by this date. (3005(c)(2)(ii))

May 8, 1990

EPA land disposal prohibition determinations due for final third of scheduled wastes and remaining characteristic wastes. (3004(g)(4), (5),(6)(C))

November 8, 1992

Final permits should be issued by EPA or authorized states for interim status storage facilities by this date. (3005(c)(2)(B))

Rolling or Shifting Deadlines

To the maximum extent practicable the Administrator shall publish a proposal to grant or deny a new delisting petition within 12 months after receiving a complete application, and issue a final determination within 24 months of such a submission. (3001(f)(2)(A))

EPA must make land disposal prohibition determinations within 6 months of new waste listing or characteristics. (3004(g)(4))

Delay of general land disposal deadlines for those wastes where the Agency finds that insufficient alternative treatment capacity exists. (3004(h)(2)). Case-by-case extensions are available for up to one year where binding contractual commitments exist to construct or provide such capacity. (3004(h)(3))

Owner/operator of newly regulated interim status land disposal facility has 12 months from date facility first becomes subject to regulation to certify compliance with groundwater monitoring and financial responsibility requirements, and file a Part B permit application or interim status will terminate. (3005(e)(3))

Permits for research, demonstration, and development treatment facilities can be issued for up to 365 operating days and renewed up to 3 times. (3005(g))

Owners/operators of newly regulated interim status impoundments are provided 2 years from date impoundment first becomes subject to regulation to apply for a waiver from the retrofit requirement. EPA or an authorized state must decide on the application within 12 months of the receipt of the application. If no waiver is granted, the owner/

operator must retrofit the impoundment within 4 years of when the impoundment first becomes subject to regulation. (3005(j)(6)(B))

Annual inspections of federally owned or operated facilities beginning November 8, 1985. (3007(c)

State RCRA facilities subject to annual inspection beginning November 8, 1984. (3007(d))

Directives to EPA without Deadlines

EPA is required to submit to Congress a report regarding dioxin emissions from resource recovery facilities burning municipal solid waste and publish advisories and guidelines regarding the control of dioxin emissions "as promptly as practicable." (1006(b))

EPA must establish an office of the Ombudsman to assist citizens in understanding the RCRA program. (2008)

EPA shall identify wastes as hazardous solely because of the presence of certain constituents, such as carcinogens or mutagens, at levels higher than those which endanger human health. (3001(b)(1))

Storage of wastes prohibited from land disposal allowed only in volumes to facilitate proper treatment, recovery, or disposal. (3004(j))

HSWA requirements and prohibitions take effect in authorized state on the same dates as such requirements take effect in other states. (3006(g))

EPA may issue orders under interim status requiring corrective action to protect public health and the environment from hazardous waste releases at interim status facilities. (3008(h))

Citizens are granted the authority to bring suits for imminent and substantial endangerments, except where EPA or a state is taking timely and appropriate action. (7002(a)(1)(B),7003(a))

Public participation in settlement must be assured through opportunity for public hearing in the affected area, and a reasonable opportunity to comment on the proposed settlement prior to finalization. (7003(d))

Index

About the Authors:

Richard C. Fortuna is currently executive director of the Hazardous Waste Treatment Council, a D.C.-based trade group dedicated to the use of treatment technology in the management of hazardous waste. Prior to 1983, Fortuna was a principal architect of the 1984 RCRA amendments while serving as staff toxicologist to Congressman James J. Florio and the House Energy and Commerce Committee. From 1979 to 1981, he served as legislative assistant to Congressman John D. Dingell during the original enactment of Superfund. Mr. Fortuna holds a master's in Public Health degree in toxicology and health policy from the University of Michigan, and currently resides in Washington, D.C.

David J. Lennett was the principal spokesperson for the environmental community during the drafting of the 1984 amendments. Since 1980, he has participated in most of the significant litigation and administrative proceedings relating to the RCRA program. Mr. Lennett has been the principal attorney for hazardous waste issues at the Environmental Defense Fund since 1979, is a frequent speaker at seminars and conferences, and participated as an advisor to the Congressional Office of Technology Assessment for its 1983 report on hazardous waste. Mr. Lennett received his J.D. from George Washington University National Law Center in 1979, and currently resides in Washington, DC.